The Sacred Anointing

Throughout his extraordinary ministry Martyn Lloyd-Jones did much thinking about the goals, methods, and spirituality of preaching in the Church, and his thoughts fully merited the large-scale, sympathetic, exact analysis that Sargent provides. Anyone who ever felt the power of God in a Lloyd-Jones sermon, in the flesh, on tape, or in print, will find this book fascinating and enriching. Preachers will gain from these pages a searching health check, and perhaps a needed course correction. Sargent's book is a landmark study.

J. I. Packer

The Sacred Anointing

The Preaching of Dr. Martyn Lloyd-Jones

Tony Sargent

The sermon itself is the main thing . . . the sacred anointing upon the preacher, and the divine power applying the truth to the hearer . . . these are infinitely more important than any details of manner.

C. H. Spurgeon[1]

CROSSWAY BOOKS • WHEATON, ILLINOIS
A DIVISION OF GOOD NEWS PUBLISHERS

Library of Congress Cataloging-in-Publication Data
Sargent, J. A., 1941–
    The sacred anointing : The preaching of Dr. Martyn Lloyd-Jones /
J. A. Sargent.
       p.   cm.
    Includes bibliographical references and indexes.
    1. Preaching—Great Britain—History—20th century. 2. Lloyd Jones, David Martyn. 3. Holy Spirit—History of doctrines—20th century. I. Title.
BV4208.G7S32 1994   251'.0092—dc20   94-15556
ISBN 0-89107-811-8

02	01	00	99	98	97	96	95	94
15	14	13	12	11	10	9	8	7	6	5	4	3	2	1

This book is affectionately dedicated with grateful thanks to the memory of the late

Tom Macbeth Paterson

constant encourager, teacher, adviser, pastor and one who, during the time I was his assistant, ensured that we regularly went to the Doctor!

CONTENTS

FOREWORD

by the Rev. Dr. Hywel R. Jones

It is indeed a privilege to have been invited to write a foreword to this important study, which represents not only a scholarly work, but a labour of love on the part of the author. Tony Sargent has read and listened to the written and spoken records of Doctor Lloyd-Jones's ministry and, in his overall evaluation, he has also added personal recollections and the reminiscences of others. The immense value of this book, however, lies in its main theme. This was central to the ministry of the Doctor and is so crucial for the Church at the end of the second millennium.

Like the author, I owe much to Doctor Lloyd-Jones personally and to his ministry. The sermon *Not in Word Only* set a benchmark for true preaching in my mind and spirit. It 'happened' to be preached on the eve of my ordination at the Association meetings of the Presbyterian Church of Wales in Abergavenny in September 1963. In addition, the Doctor was the guiding influence in the emergence of the London Theological Seminary, where I serve. This seminary exists to emphasise the primacy of preaching and the necessity of 'the sacred anointing' in connection with it.

A sharp distinction has been made by some between *logos* and *rhema* with regard to God's word. These two Greek nouns, both used in the New Testament, are closely related in meaning but the latter can mean 'speech' and not only 'word'. Related to God's word, *logos* stands for Scripture, while *rhema* is used for Prophecy. Rhema-word is 'God's now word' while, by inference and certainly by treatment, logos-word becomes a word for yesterday.

Though this differentiation was not expressed in the Doctor's own day, it is interesting to consider what his reaction would have been to it. I believe that he would strongly have repudiated it in one sense and yet responded to it positively in another, *but in that order*.

His repudiation would have been made because he believed that
Holy Scripture was both logos *and* rhema and part of an evangelical
doctrine of Holy Scripture and the Doctor would not, as Dr. Sargent
makes clear, allow any diminution of that. God, the Spirit of truth, who
caused the texts to be written (logos), continues to speak through them
(rhema). Though Scripture was completed, it is neither dead nor decaying. It is living and abiding in that it is alive in and relevant to every age.
As each Sunday approached, he would not have been asking, 'Is there
any word from the Lord?' He had a Bible. It had to be read and studied.

But he would have had some sympathy with the distinction, not
because of an uncritical view of contemporary prophecy, but because of
his belief about the nature of true preaching. This, like Scripture, must
be logos and rhema, that is the message of God *in His own voice*, albeit
through the words of His servants. Just as it is the Spirit, who infallibly
effected the union between the divine and the human in Scripture so He
can effect a union between frail and sometimes fallible preaching and
the utterance of God. That is what this book is about. Not to believe in
such a possibility, to desire it prayerfully and make room for it in one's
preaching, is to make living and abiding Scripture seem dull and bor-
ing—even to be decaying or dead. *The Sacred Anointing* on the glorious message of Scripture is vital. May this book promote such
preaching, all over the world.

London Theological Seminary

INTRODUCTION

Dr. Lloyd-Jones once remarked that ten years should pass before a book was written on a preacher and his ministry. Well, more than a decade has elapsed since his homecall in 1981. In this volume, I am attempting to assess his preaching method in the light of the influence which he exerted unconsciously on the author. I have endeavoured to absorb as much of his procedure as appropriate into my own ministry. Faced with a verse or passage of Scripture it has been helpful to ask, 'How would Lloyd-Jones have tackled this text? How would he have analysed and applied it?' In this book I seek to share my findings with a readership which probably includes a good percentage of preachers.

Would Dr. Lloyd-Jones have approved of such a project? Inasmuch as he gave lectures on preaching years ago in what has become a best-selling book[1] we feel his answer would have been positive. However, he would have urged that, in the final analysis, the preacher must be his own man.

Why a book on his method of preaching if he revealed all in his volume? My defence is that I have attempted an evaluation of his method by constant referral to his own addresses, whether released in print or tape form. I have tried thus to show how his principles are illustrated in his preaching and how his methodology can be adapted and usefully applied by men in the ministry. To do this, I have read virtually all the published sermons thus far available as well as ensuring that plenty of tapes were my companions in many journeyings.

Researching this book has been a fascinating project. The goal was to follow the evidence rather than be influenced by previous assumptions. Early on, a major adjustment had to be made to my skeleton outline. It became obvious that no book on Lloyd-Jones's homiletics could be offered without due consideration being given to his doctrine of the

Holy Spirit. And, without treading on ground so thoroughly gone over by his biographer, some personal references had to be incorporated into this thesis. You cannot grasp the measure of Lloyd-Jones's preaching without considering, in some fashion, the man. Also, in a manner which is unusual if not unique in contemporary preaching, it became clear that Lloyd-Jones's homiletics and hermeneutics are both contingent on his pneumatology. If the former is the fruit, the latter is the root. In the natural order of things, roots come first. Thus it became increasingly clear that I had to explore his convictions on the doctrine of the Spirit which he developed and crystallised over the years in relation to the act of preaching.

His plea was not that the pulpit should be graced by a more erudite standard of ministry but rather that the ministry should be Spirit-filled. Preachers are to be borne along by the Holy Ghost. Unction is the key. It held the pivotal place in his convictions. This is reflected in the amount of treatment I have given to this subject which, I claim, is justified by his emphasis. My purpose has not been to defend Lloyd-Jones but to define, declare, and illustrate the position that he took. Neither have I attempted a eulogy, though I recognise the danger because I owe him a great deal.

I am not suggesting that Dr. Lloyd-Jones was a faultless preacher or an infallible theologian. In some areas his theology is frayed and not systematic. Slavishly to follow his method would be counter-productive for those whose natural gifts are not equivalent to his and whose pulpit is not in a down-town, historic church. However, if our critiques of Dr. Lloyd-Jones and his method are not as sharp and our reservations are not as great as some might desire, my apologia follows that of Arnold Dallimore when researching the life of George Whitefield, which gave birth to his two-volume, magisterial biography:

> I have endeavoured to give my portrait of Whitefield both reality and depth. I make known not only his accomplishments and abilities, but also his foibles and his mistakes. I must confess, however, that I had almost wished his faults had been more pronounced, lest by reason of their fewness and feebleness, I should be charged with favouritism.[2]

As we concede, not everyone will be convinced by Dr. Lloyd-Jones's position on the doctrine of the Spirit. But surely no biblical preacher will oppose him in his contention that the supreme thing needed in the pulpit at the point of delivery of the sermon is unction. The extraordinary, ever-increasing output of his books, amply illustrates his conviction. A sensitive reading of the printed page reveals that he did have an unusually powerful experience of the Holy Spirit's anointing. Though he personally was not happy about tape ministries[3] (yet he did allow his sermons to be recorded), after his passing, a tape-library was established with the goal of making his preaching ministry widely available. Some of these give classic illustrations of a man in the act of preaching being borne along by the Holy Ghost.

In the US edition of this book some comment is perhaps needed about its relationship to another with a similar title. I refer to *The Anointing* by Benny Hinn (Thomas Nelson, 1992) which I had not read at the point of writing. Those who consider both volumes will soon conclude that they are authored from contrasting perspectives and that the similarity of titles is accidental rather than intentional. My contention is that Hinn's book justifies this one even though it was not intended as a riposte. The modern Charismatic movement has thrown up some colourful, not to say, controversial celebrities. Some of their practices have little in common with the pages of the Acts despite the repeated claims to have tapped into Early Church dynamics. No warrant is found in the New Testament to justify the show-biz style of healing crusade or glitzy celebration. When Christian leaders seemingly have more in common with Beverly Hills than Mars Hill, we are right to be wary.

Hinn gives little evidence of the expository and hermeneutical disciplines revealed by Lloyd-Jones. There are helpful comments, and some excellent application. But often these are blurred by a racy, anecdotal style, heaped up with personal references. The nonsense of slaying a congregation in the Spirit by the breath of one's mouth and the sweep of one's coat may have something to do with crowd psychology but little with New Testament unction. Appeals to Jonathan Edwards and George Whitefield for substantiation are laughable were the matter not so serious. Consistently presented in the apostolic records is the self-effacement of the various personalities which cross its pages. Where phenomena attended or preceded the proclamation of the Word it was unscripted: pre-publicity was totally absent. What was witnessed was the sovereign, surprising and spontaneous activity of the Holy Ghost.

However, though we submit, there is in Hinn's thesis a mixture of truth, strained exegesis and self-serving stories the danger actually lies not so much with the curious amalgam in its contents but the possibility of over-reaction by conservative evangelicals; an unnecessary knee-jerk which dismisses every aspect of the author's assertions.

Dr. Lloyd-Jones would consider Benny Hinn to be right in his view that there is an anointing for which the Christian, and especially the preacher should seek. But he is seriously off course in his definition of what this anointing is and his description of its manifestation. Lloyd-Jones knew he, himself, risked being misunderstood in the stance that he took. But I believe we are indebted to him for his brave and painstaking scriptural expositions and his excursions into Church History in order to illustrate what I later call experimental Calvinism. He believed that revivals might well be accompanied by spiritual phenomena traceable not to powerful psychological influences, or the mesmerism of a naturally forceful and charismatic personality but to the dynamic of the Spirit. Though pragmatically Hinn and Lloyd-Jones are poles apart at least they have in common the claim that there is an unction available for all Christians. This book in an attempt to biblically define this sacred anointing and to analyze how it affected Martyn Lloyd-Jones's philosophy of preaching.

In researching this book I have kept the needs of preachers in mind as well as those of the average member of any congregation mature enough to wish to study what the preaching ministry entails. Thus, when referring to sermons on tape, I have deliberately selected those which not only secure the point being made about Dr. Lloyd-Jones's theology and preaching but serve as an example, at a wider level, of high quality preaching. The Lloyd-Jones' Recording Trust was once asked if it stocked C. H. Spurgeon's ministry! The enquirer had obviously profited a great deal from the famous Baptist preacher's sermons. The request was not just to read what he had to say but hear how he said it. Alas, that tape recorders were not in those days available to eavesdrop on such an eloquent ministry. Students of Lloyd-Jones are much more favoured. It is my hope that many ministers and those in training will obtain some of the tapes referred to in order to hear Dr. Lloyd-Jones for themselves.

The nature of the book demands extensive quotation from DML-J's published material. I express heartfelt thanks to his daughter, Lady Elizabeth Catherwood, for giving free access to the tapes and graciously allowing ample quotation from her father's works. It is my intention to publish a glossary of quotations on a variety of topics from Dr. Lloyd-Jones's ministry. To have added this to the present volume would have made it too thick a book and rendered it unmanageable.

It was at Westminster Theological Seminary (Philadelphia) that Dr. Lloyd-Jones delivered his lectures which gave birth to his book on preaching. Westminster have now, in their Californian campus, a doctoral research programme dedicated to the exploration of homiletics and hermeneutics. This volume was part of the work that I attempted under their auspices particularly encouraged by Professor David Schuringa. It is released to a wider audience in the hope that the contents may benefit an increasing generation of preachers.

Much of my material has been written up between sessions of conferences at which I have preached in a variety of countries. I owe a great debt to ministers, pastors and church leaders who—from the borders of Afghanistan to the islands of Japan, from Tanzania to what was the Soviet Union—have invited me to conduct pastors' conferences. To Operation Mobilization and the Africa Inland Mission with whom I have been associated for more than fifteen years I am also indebted. They, and especially George Verwer, stimulated the more international aspects of a ministry which two decades ago never trespassed beyond the borders of the coastal resort of Worthing in the South of England.

I am grateful to my congregations into the pastorate of which I was inducted by Dr. Lloyd-Jones twenty-three years ago for their forbearance, patience and encouragement. Special thanks are also due to Kenneth Jowett and Joan Hall who spent hours helping me in my researches; to members of our pastoral team and particularly my gifted colleague Pastor Tim Saunders who, along with Dr. R.T. Kendall and Dr. H.R. Hywel-Jones, Principal of the London Theological Seminary, critiqued my efforts but have no responsibility at all for the finished product.

My appreciation too to Tony Chapman, Jenny Crutchfield, Gill Smith Boyes and to my one-time Sunday school teacher turned religious editorial consultant, Edward England, who seemed to take pleasure in the notion that one of his lads from our native city of Sheffield eventually appeared to have made good!

I would also like to express my thanks to Bob and Ramona Adams of Escondido, who opened their home to me and made me very much part of their family while engaging in my doctoral research programme; and to their church, the famous Emmanuel Faith Community Church, the pastors of which not only provided transport but entrusted their pulpit to me during my visits to California.

I express thanks to my loyal personal secretary for many years, Joyce Dyer, who typed my summations of Lloyd-Jones's works and to Gina Trimm who brilliantly corrected and upgraded my word-processing, giving it a professional standard of typesetting which never ceased to amaze me!

And to my wife, Rowena, whose theological eloquence is the statement of her life and far in advance of anything that I can manage either within or without the pulpit.

1

The Smile of God

To me there is nothing more terrible for a preacher, than to be in the pulpit alone, without the conscious smile of God.

Martyn Lloyd-Jones[1]

Our midnight is thy smile withdrawn.

Oliver Wendell Holmes

Dr. Lloyd-Jones, by his own statement, did not have a high estimation of himself as a preacher. Indeed, he declared that he would not cross the road to hear himself preach. It would have come as a complete surprise to those who for years benefited from his authoritative ministry to have realised the frustration he often felt. He found solace in the words of an American preacher, James Thornwell, who in an earlier century lamented:

> Depend upon it that there is but little preaching in the world, and it is a mystery of grace and of divine power that God's cause is not ruined in the world when we consider the qualifications of many of its professed ministers to preach it. My own performances in this way fill me with disgust. I have never made, much less preached, a sermon in my life, and I am beginning to despair of ever being able to do it. May the Lord give you more knowledge and grace and singleness of purpose.[2]

Reflecting on these words, DML-J found himself in utter agreement and commented:

> There is nothing to add to that. Any man who has had some glimpse of what it is to preach will inevitably feel that he has never preached. But he will go on trying, hoping that by the grace of God one day he may truly preach.[3]

He was to say a similar thing in a personal letter to his friend Philip Hughes:

> . . . Oh! How I long to know exactly what Paul meant in 1 Corinthians 2:1-5 and to experience it in my ministry. I have become tired of all else and when I read of Whitefield I feel that I have never really preached in my life.[4]

Lloyd-Jones's frustration with his performance as a preacher was to accompany him throughout the whole of his ministry. He challenged both himself and would-be preachers to an incredibly high view of preaching, the attainment of which is impossible at the human level. The remarkable heights of his eloquence and the quality of much of his exposition failed to make a mark on him. If they had, possibly it would have ruined his ministry. The man who feels he has arrived generally has not.

Frustration has its benefits if it deals with the pride which, according to Spurgeon, is the greatest danger in the pulpit and has felled many an occupant. Listen to Lloyd-Jones once again, at a different time in his life, bemoaning the feebleness of his preaching. He believes he has preached only two decent sermons, in circumstances not likely to encourage another attempt!

> I have a feeling that I have only really preached twice in my life, and on both occasions I was dreaming. I still remember the awful feeling of disappointment, on both occasions, when I found I was only dreaming. If only I could preach like that in the pulpit when I was awake.[5]

He used almost the same words in 1961 when addressing the Puritan Conference. He warned preachers against pride. In so doing, he revealed what was probably his own practice after feeling he had had a good day. Preachers should have a cup of tea or a light meal and then 'to keep themselves in order' on a Sunday night, they should pick up a volume of Whitefield's or Edwards's sermons. This would bring them back to earth! 'Indeed you will soon begin to feel that you have never preached in your life.' And then Lloyd-Jones proceeds to ask in language reminiscent of the above, 'Have we, I wonder, have we ever really preached? How many times?'[6]

It is a comforting thought to those who feel so distant from the pulpit giants and expository gifts of men like Lloyd-Jones that he had been preaching for over thirty years when he made this confession. And this when he had been judged by Emil Brunner as the greatest preacher of Reformed Theology in the twentieth century![7]

Martyn Lloyd-Jones might well be lined up alongside such predecessors as Charles Spurgeon and Charles Simeon. Our enquiry seeks to discover what it was about DML-J's ministry which made it so successful. It also seeks to examine his preaching methods. For what was he looking? And why did he often feel so frustrated despite the accolades which came his way? What are the lessons both negative and positive (a phrase Lloyd-Jones would have appreciated!) we can learn from him?

PROSPECTUS

To gain some background we take an excursion into the pages of the Old and New Testaments. Our enquiry will furnish us with a biblical perspective, enabling us to uncover the constituents of unction without which we will be hard pressed to understand Lloyd-Jones's concept of preaching. This will lead us to consider the role of the Holy Spirit not just in the act of preaching, but in the preparation of the address and in the life of the preacher. We will also appraise what is often forgotten in books on preaching but which was vital to DML-J: the Holy Spirit and the congregation. There is more to a sermon than just preaching. And there is more to preaching than preparation. Inextricably bound together are the preacher and the ones to whom the proclamation is made. The preacher is dependent on the Holy Spirit resting on them as well as on him in order to produce unction. We look at two men who particularly influenced Dr. Lloyd-Jones. But we are well ahead of ourselves!

We pause to locate our biblical moorings. We do so by highlighting the anointing and the call to ministry in both Testaments. As occasion demands we also draw attention to DML-J's application of the truths exposed.

ANOINTING IN THE OLD TESTAMENT

The term 'unction' does not occur in the Old Testament. The closest word is 'anoint'. Its usage does not immediately fit into the context of the proclamation of a message. A man may be anointed with oil or an unguent for medical purposes. More specifically, this is used in religious rites. The oil, or unguent, was applied to a person or a material object. A derivative from unguent is unctuous. Classically this term conveys the idea of being full of unction. In contemporary times, it suggests someone who flaunts an effected piety in an ostentatious and singularly unattractive fashion. But modern usage has departed from its etymological root. Literally, unctuous means to be overwhelmingly blessed. The unctuous person possesses depths of spirituality. Like the elderly Hebrews, Anna and Simeon (Luke 2:25-38), he waits before the Lord in such a manner that he reveals a discernment and godliness which is unusual.

In the Old Testament the high priest was anointed. The Hebrew word rendered 'anoint' (*masah*) is used some sixty-nine times. Sacred objects likewise were set apart and consecrated before they could be used in the service of the Tabernacle or the Temple (Exod. 30:32-33). Anointing indicates the favour of God (Ps. 23:5). Anointing conveys the idea of setting aside and authorising for God's service.[8]

Though an intermediary was used in the ritual it was believed that he was acting on behalf of God. When David was anointed king, significantly the historian records, 'from that day on the Spirit of the Lord came upon David in power' (1 Sam. 16:13, cf. 1 Sam. 10:6-8).

When anointing was applied to a person it was similar to baptism in the New Testament. It was understood as 'an outward sign indicative of an inward grace'. The copious pouring of the unguent on the priest had little value if there was not an inner anointing which marked the man out as the religious leader of the Israelite Community.[9] An effusion of oil meant nothing without an infusion of grace. The same might be said of the prophetic office.[10] Though no oil was applied, a man needed to give more proof of legitimacy for entry into the office than merely a verbal claim. Isaiah spoke personally as well as predictively when he declared: The Spirit of the Sovereign Lord is on me, because the Lord has anointed me to preach good news to the poor (Isa. 61:1).

It was the false prophets who shouted the loudest. Lacking anointing and unction, they rested their claims to office on personal assumption and connivance. Israel sank to no lower point in its history than when its threefold, foundational ministries—prophet, priest and king—were held by men whose only claim to rank was vocal and political.

A man who was both appointed to office by the Lord and anointed for service was vital for the nurturing of the redeemed community in the Old Testament. His anointing gave him an authority and a boldness which are the necessary ingredients of a ministry noted for its unction.

ANOINTING IN THE NEW TESTAMENT

Three words are translated as anoint: *chrio*, *aleipho* and *chrisma*. The common denominator is the concept of rubbing or spreading ointment.

• *chrio* is used five times. It is always employed figuratively and had to do with appointment or commissioning. Thus the declaration of the Lord in the synagogue at Nazareth when in preaching his first sermon he commenced with the words already quoted previously from the prophecy of Isaiah, 'The Spirit of the Lord is on me, because he has anointed me to preach good news to the poor' (Luke 4:18).

• *aleipho* is used literally[11] in the context of applying ointment or perfume to the body (e.g. Luke 7:38—where a woman anoints Jesus' feet).

• *chrisma* focuses not on the act of rubbing or spreading but rather on that with which one has been anointed.[12] We shall see the importance of this in the understanding of Lloyd-Jones when we later consider his interpretation of 1 John 2, vv. 20 and 27[13] (the Authorised Version rendering of these verses supplies the translation 'unction' v. 20 and 'anointing' v. 27).

The link between the Old and New Testaments is illustrated when in the former anointing is identified with the outpouring of God's Spirit. Thus, after Saul's anointing as the future King of Israel he is later depicted prophesying in the company of some prophets (1 Sam. 10:1, 10). In the Acts, our Lord is described as the man who has been anointed by the Holy Spirit. This indicates that God is with him and he is enabled to perform healings and demonstrate his superior power over that of the devil (Acts 10:38).

THE CALL IN THE OLD TESTAMENT

Moses and Jeremiah both had difficulty in responding positively to the divine summons. Amos ran up against considerable opposition and his credentials were questioned. Dr. Lloyd-Jones cites all three.[14]

Moses' immediate rejection of God's call upon him is not to be attributed to his meekness. His objections bordered on unbelief. The

sense of his reaction was 'Here I am Lord, but send someone else'!
(Exod. 4:13).

It is a serious matter when a man receives the call to lead and to minister and fails to realise that the Lord will equip those he chooses. At
least Moses can be exonerated from the charge of having a cavalier
approach to the ministry!

Lloyd-Jones gave special attention to the re-confirmation of the call
of Moses as the Hebrew entered into what might be called the second
stage of his ministry, leading his people to the borders of the Promised
Land. Of DML-J's twenty-four published sermons on revival, which
were preached during the centenary year of the 1859 Revival, eight are
based on Exodus 33. Here, reference is found not only to the plight of
the Hebrews, but also an account is given of the amazing exchange
between Moses and God concerning the Hebrews' future service. As his
call was reinforced, Moses responded in a manner which pleased the
Lord. No longer did he argue from the perspective of human weakness,
but he placed alongside this the omnipotence of God. His condition was,
'If you come with me I will do what you say, but without this guarantee I will not' (Exod. 33:12-23). The Lord warmed to Moses' pleading.

Lloyd-Jones cross-referenced this incident to Paul's confession of
weakness (1 Cor. 2:3-5) and added:

> I never tire of quoting the cases of certain Ministers used of God in
> the past who would not dare to go into the pulpit to preach until they
> had an absolute assurance that the Holy Spirit was going to accom-
> pany them there, and was going to empower them.[15] That is what
> Moses had come to. He realised his need of this exceptional power,
> so he prayed to God for it.[16]

A further parallel is found in Jeremiah's reaction to the divine call. He
too proclaimed his inability, '"Ah, Sovereign Lord," I said, "I do not
know how to speak; I am only a child"' (Jer. 1:6). The hand of God was
placed on him and he was dramatically ordained to be the Lord's herald. 'Then the Lord reached out his hand and touched my mouth and
said to me, "Now, I have put my words in your mouth"' (Jer. 1:9). This
gave the prophet the ability to go to those to whom the Lord sent him
and relay all that was in the Lord's mind. The anointing brought with
it an endowment for service which was needed continually. Moses and
Jeremiah were right: responding to the call would bring incredible personal strain and seemingly intractable problems. However, it was the
sense of call which kept them in their office.

Jeremiah obediently took up his ministry in Jerusalem despite his preference for a quieter life among the priests at the school at Anathoth. Pressures mounted. Far from being healthy, wealthy and happy, he knew what it was to be weary, worn and sad. He was tempted to give up. What stopped him, however, was his sense of call and the innermost longing to proclaim the word of the Lord. Sensitive man that he was, he found an enforced period in the stocks became more than he could bear. So he decided to resign! But it was not that easy. The reason is directly related to the anointing. Graphically and in what have become well-known words he confessed: 'But if I say, "I will not mention him or speak any more in his name," his word is in my heart like a burning fire, shut up in my bones. I am weary of holding it in; indeed I cannot (Jer. 20:9). The force with which a man is called to the ministry is not easy to withstand. If retirement is difficult, resignation is almost impossible.

Lloyd-Jones found it hard to understand how a man, called to the preaching ministry, could leave. One minister who had been remarkably used by God in the Midlands of England joined my congregation having returned, after many successful years as a preacher, to his earlier profession. He was most grieved that Dr. Lloyd-Jones could not sympathise with his action.

Why does the sense of call need to be so powerful? Because, sooner or later, the preacher will have to cope with depression and a temptation to despair. Only a deep conviction of the call to the ministry will keep him through what the Puritans, following St. John of the Cross termed 'the dark night of the soul'[17]—when all hell seems to be let loose and despondency threatens to stifle the preacher. Yet the call and the anointing sustain the ministry. Clearly, it was this that took Jeremiah through his time of crisis.

Similar lessons are discovered when considering the case of Amos. His credentials were questioned by the appointed leaders of Judaism. He had not gone through a process which merited their approval. From their perspective, he lacked the qualifications for the office that he assumed and he was trespassing on their parish! Instead of meeting their objections on their own terms, he boldly agreed that he did not come from recognised religious stock of either priestly or prophetic categories, 'I was neither a prophet nor a prophet's son . . . But the Lord took me from tending the flock and said to me, "Go, prophesy to my people Israel"' (Amos 7:14, 15). The untrained herdsman and gatherer of sycamore figs had, however, received the divine call and enabling. 'The lion has roared—who will not fear?' He put up a rhetorical question to silence those who doubted his authority—'The Sovereign Lord has spoken—who can but prophesy?' (Amos 3:8). No one should resist the divine imperative.

Dr. Lloyd-Jones gave less treatment to Jeremiah and Amos than he did to Moses, but the importance that he placed on their experiences warrants the time we have taken in examining their call and response. He referred to the power and authority that they received as 'foreshadowings' of New Testament unction. The success of their ministries he attributed to a 'divine afflatus' which not only filled them with knowledge but 'an ability to speak which astonished them themselves'.[18]

THE CALL IN THE NEW TESTAMENT

Lloyd-Jones argued that there is a call to which all believers respond as they commit themselves to the Lord as his followers. This is a dynamic call from God. Salvation is entirely of the Lord: 'a Christian is the result of the operation of God, nothing less, nothing else. No man can make himself a Christian. God alone makes Christians'.[19]

Beyond this DML-J was convinced that there is a special call to the preaching ministry. Our Lord selected twelve men and tutored them for three years, giving them preaching experience. Similarly men are called into the ministry today. The pattern followed is invariably the one found in the New Testament. This breaks open into at least three aspects.

The need is not the call [20]

This goes against the grain of much modern thinking. But in our Lord's day none of the twelve volunteered to follow Christ. They made no application, they completed no forms. On the contrary, it was the magnetic authority of the Lord which compelled them. Peter and James stopped mending their nets. In favour of fishing for fish they would become 'fishers of men' (Mark 1:16-18). Matthew left his remunerative employment as a tax collector (Mark 2:14-15). The vitality of the call could not be resisted. It was strong, powerful and, with the exception of Judas, it was lifelong.

We are struck by the force of the call especially when reading through the Acts of the Apostles. Though the Lord was no longer physically present with his followers, the sense of call did not wane. The Apostles were prepared to defy the authorities. If the alternatives were the command of God or the prohibition of men there really was no choice, as is apparent in their response, 'Judge for yourselves whether it is right in God's sight to obey you rather than God' (Acts 4:19) and, later in Paul's affirmation, 'necessity is laid upon me, yea, woe is unto me, if

I preach not the Gospel!' (1 Cor. 9:16 AV). Time and again it was the strength of the call which helped the leaders of the Church maintain their courage and confidence. Lloyd-Jones is surely right in using the word 'obsession'[21] to describe their response to it. Listen to him as he addressed the subject from a personal perspective:

> God knows, I do not enter the pulpit because I choose to do so. If it were not for the call of the Lord I would not be doing it. All I did was to resist that call. It is His way. He calls men, He separates them, He gives them the message, and the Spirit is present to give illumination. All this is a part of our Lord's way of nourishing the Church.[22]

In New Testament times men were apprehended by the Lord and directed into the preaching ministry. Lloyd-Jones felt that if the need was the call then everyone would have responded to that need and that 'is patently ridiculous'.[23] On another occasion he declared, 'we are not all meant to preach. But there is a teaching today which almost seems to say that we are'.[24]

The Church does not issue the call[25]

For the disciples, the call was the verbal command of the Lord. When he ascended to his Father he maintained the prerogative to direct men into the ministry and issue the call. The classic case, of course, is that of Saul of Tarsus. Opponent and persecutor of Christians, his whole life's course was changed radically when the risen Lord stopped and unhorsed him on the Damascus Road. Paul constantly bore testimony to God as the prime mover in his call to the ministry of preaching. He never lost the sense of amazement that he should be called, bearing in mind the terrible wrongs he had committed, especially as an accomplice to the murder of Stephen, the first Christian martyr.

Lloyd-Jones established his conclusion by citing verses from an epistle and a gospel. He took his hearers to Ephesians 4 and the passage which deals with the Lord's equipping his Church. He gives apostles, prophets, evangelists, pastors and teachers (v. 11). DML-J then turned to the statements about the fields being 'white unto harvest' (John 4:35 AV) and the need for labourers (Matt 9:37-38 AV). In both instances, the initiative is definitely with the Lord and not the Church. The Lord issues the call and summons men. He grants charismatically-endowed personnel to service the Church, bringing it to maturity and health. It is the Lord to whom the Church is to pray in order that labourers can be sent into the harvest fields. A local church is not to draw up a short list and by a process of elimination determine who to set in particular ministries. Lloyd-Jones presses the point home and hits a warning note:

> We do not thrust forth labourers, He does so; and all we do is to pray to Him to send them forth. In our carnal zeal and enthusiasm we often deem it to be our business to call people to tasks in the Church, and we do so in different ways. We suggest to our men that they should enter the ministry, or preach or teach. How scandalous this is![26]

The Church's function is to check the validity of the call[27]

DML-J takes us to Romans, to Paul's quotation from the Old Testament of the stated impossibility of hearing the Word of God without a preacher. But in order for him to be heard, he has to be sent (Rom. 10:13-15). The relevant question is, who does the sending? In other words, who affirms the call in order to ensure that the person who thinks he is set apart is not deluding himself? Lloyd-Jones answers:

> This is where the Church comes in. This is the teaching of the New Testament not only with regard to preaching and teaching but also with regard to the various offices in the Church . . . So before you can be quite sure that a man is called to be a preacher, his personal call must be confirmed by the Church, it must be attested by the Church.[28]

This brief excursion into both sections of the Bible warrants the conclusion that anointing and appointing are linked. A man should not seek to inveigle himself into office. Even if an unworthy candidate is successful in grasping the title nonetheless he cannot grasp the anointing. His claim is merely titular. It has no credibility. Phoney claims to a call when measured against the yardstick of performance and life reveal their hollowness. False prophets, dud priests and bad kings were a curse to Israel.

Similarly, in the New Testament, a genuine call is attested by a consecration. Both originate from the Lord. The Lord emboldens those he commissions. Pivotal to the success of all ministries is the maxim 'Not by might, nor by power, but by my spirit, saith the Lord' (Zech. 4:6 AV).

The above reasoning finds a choice, summary statement in the words of Lloyd-Jones:

> Ministers are given to the Church by God, and every gift and help in the Church is given by God. We are helpless in and of ourselves. No man can truly preach the Gospel in his own strength and power. He

can talk and perhaps talk eloquently; but talk is not preaching and it will lead to nothing. Whenever there is an effectual ministry it is because of this 'working', this 'energetic working' of the power of God through the Holy Spirit.[29]

LLOYD-JONES'S STANDARDS

Dr. Lloyd-Jones made high demands on himself in an endeavour to ful-fill the responsibilities which come with the call. He believed that 'the perfecting of the saints' is contingent on a valid and vital ministry.[30] As far as unction and empowering are concerned, he was aware that a 'way with words' and the Welsh *hwyl* could easily be considered by the spir-itually inept to be unction.[31] However, such are no substitute for the anointing that should attend a man called by God to be a preacher.

DML-J's natural eloquence would have qualified him to achieve prominence in several professions. His contemporary and fellow medi-cal doctor, Douglas Johnson, reckoned that his gift would have paved the way for him to become a first-class barrister presenting his case with razor-sharp logic couched in Welsh eloquence. Or he could have graced the Mother of Parliaments following the trail blazed by his fellow coun-tryman, whom he admired, Lloyd-George.[32] However, he teaches us that there is more than eloquence to preaching and that good preaching can occur even when natural giftedness is low and homiletical construction lacking.

Words are the preacher's tools. But woe to the man who has confi-dence in them alone. They could get in the way of the message—an obstacle to its free flow. The congregation then could be more fittingly described as an audience. They would have assembled not to experience theophany—the awareness of God—but rather to be spectators at an event, at best a rhetorician using his art, at worst, a man drawing atten-tion to himself. That, for DML-J, would be an abomination as great as that of Antiochus Epiphanes when he desecrated the Temple.

The goal of true preaching is to leave a congregation with a sense of God. Agility with words, exactness of expression, tidiness of com-position, are not its necessary components. Lloyd-Jones will remind us frequently that Paul broke the rules of grammar and syntax.[33] Indeed DML-J went on to argue that such niceties could be entirely lacking but the preaching itself still successful.

I can forgive the preacher almost anything if he gives me a sense of God, if he gives me something for my soul, if he gives me the sense that, though he is inadequate himself, he is handling something which is very great and very glorious, if he gives me some dim glimpse of the majesty and the glory of God, the love of Christ my Saviour, and the magnificence of the Gospel.[34]

This leads us to ask what it was that he looked for more than anything else in the act of preaching. What is it that gives a preacher authority and enables him to capture the attention of his congregation?

CHARISMATIC PREACHING

Long before new terms were being used to describe modern movements in the twentieth century Church, in the centre of London was a man who was defining and demonstrating what preaching is 'at the point of delivery'.[35] It is the often misunderstood, but biblical term, 'charismatic'. The word devolves from the Greek *charisma* which refers to the gifts of grace distributed to the Church by the Holy Spirit. Our salvation is described as the *charisma* of God (Rom. 5:15). The expression occurs seventeen times in the New Testament. There are three passages in particular where reference is found to charismatic gifts (Romans 12 and 1 Corinthians 12 and 14). There is a watershed of opinion as to whether all of these *charismata* are available today. Many preachers of Calvinistic persuasion, though by no means all, believe that some gifts were withdrawn at the end of the Apostolic era having fulfilled their function in the period before the Church received the full canon of Scripture.

In our view, to describe Lloyd-Jones as a charismatic preacher is not only accurate, but it is the key to understanding his philosophy of preaching. His belief in the empowering of the Spirit both in the preparation and delivery of sermons shaped his ministry. It deepened his dependence on God and his esteem for his congregation. It accounted for the relative brevity of the notes carried in his waistcoat pocket, his pulpit prayers and his choice of hymns. This is why he seemed dismissive of homiletics per se. To approach preaching as a science or a craft and to risk distancing oneself from the *charisma* , romance and total dependence on the Spirit of God was anathema. The absence of such ingredients explained the low quality to which he believed preaching had generally sunk. In turn, this is the reason why congregations were so sparse.

To preach in 'word only' and remain satisfied was impossible for him. This should be the case for any preacher. The one thing needed above all else is the accompanying power of the Spirit. This is what Charles Spurgeon dubbed 'the sacred anointing'. It is the afflatus of the Spirit resting on the speaker. It is 'power from on high'. It is the preacher gliding on eagles' wings, soaring high, swooping low, carrying and being carried along by a dynamic other than his own. His consciousness of what is happening is not obliterated. He is not in a trance. He is being worked on but is aware that he is still working. He is being spoken through but he knows he is still speaking. The words are his but the facility with which they come compels him to realise that the source is beyond himself. The man is overwhelmed. He is on fire. 'If preaching the word of God is the word of God'[36] then this is the only context befitting such a daring assertion. Such was Lloyd-Jones's understanding of unction.

Listen to him arguing the point. He has pleaded that preachers must know freedom in the pulpit—freedom from the restraints of time, freedom from being tied to notes prepared in the study, freedom to go where the Holy Spirit is directing them. He returns to a deeply felt and often repeated conviction. In the act of preaching there must be the unknown, dangerous, vulnerable element which leaves the preacher at the mercy of the Spirit. The Holy Ghost then takes over and the result is that:

> The preacher is a man who is possessed and he is aware of this. I do not hesitate to make this assertion. I would say that I only begin to know something about preaching on those occasions when, as it were, I am looking on. I am speaking, but I am really a spectator. I am amazed at what is happening. I am listening, I am looking on in utter astonishment, for I am not doing it. It is true preaching when I am conscious that I am being used; in a sense, I am as much a spectator as the people who are listening to me. There is this consciousness that it is outside me, and yet I am involved in it; I am merely the instrument and the vehicle and the channel of all this.[37]

Preaching with *charisma* makes a special impact on the hearer. Basil Howlett describes an invitation given for him to hear Lloyd-Jones, 'In my ignorance I replied, "Who is he?"' Howlett continues:

> As long as I live I shall never forget that night. There was a spiritual power in the meeting and I sat gripping the seat as the Doctor preached on 1 Corinthians 2 with such unction and authority. In the first half of the sermon all the doubts and delusions of modernism were smashed to the ground and so was I! In the second half of the

sermon I was lifted up and set on my feet by the glory of the Gospel. Almost twenty-seven years later the memory of it is still vivid.'[38]

Murray also described the effects of the Doctor's preaching. This was at a time of national election:

> As Paul's message to Felix was preached all else suddenly seemed trivial. The silent and packed congregation, whose feet rested on ancient flagstones covering the dead of other centuries, were not being addressed as voters but as immortals whose chief interests belonged to another world. The truth that all is transitory save the Word of God swept aside every thought and seemed to hold all captive to its power.[39]

Dr. Edmund Clowney prevailed on DML-J to speak about his method of sermon preparation and delivery. The lectures, given at Westminster Theological Seminary, were to find a much larger audience. His resulting book *Preaching and Preachers* became a bestseller (despite his publisher's brave but unproductive attempts to get him to revise them and put them more in essay form!). It was to Clowney that DML-J expressed his view about unction in a provocative way. When asked what it was, he responded that if a man had it, he would not know it![40] Doubtless he intended this to be taken hyperbolically. When he wrote a final, pastoral letter to his London congregation he remarked:

> What things we have experienced! To a preacher there is nothing so wonderful as to feel the unction of the Holy Spirit while preaching, and to hear of souls being brought under conviction of sin, and then experiencing the new birth.[41]

In his view, one could possess both natural ability and understanding of the truth necessary to follow the expository method, and yet still never be a preacher at all. The Holy Spirit must be active in preaching, not only in owning the truth as it is heard but in anointing the preacher himself. Only then is his heart as well as his mind engaged. The result will be speech attended by liveliness, unction and the extemporaneous element already mentioned.

Preachers know when the 'Dove' is resting on the head of one of their fellows and anointing his ministry. Such would gather to hear Lloyd-Jones in anticipation of it. Let Peter Lewis, a fellow Welshman (and no mean orator) highlight the issue:

Consequently the one thing that he prayed for, the one thing he relied on, the one thing he waited for and the one thing above all else and beyond most other preachers of his generation which thousands felt under his preaching was the unction, or anointing of the Holy Spirit; that scarcely definable accompaniment of solemn, sacred, searching truth as proceeding from the eternal presence of God, that breath of the still small voice which somehow goes beyond words, even God-words, so that the form of truth yields up its divine power. There was nothing formal about this, nothing automatic, nothing inevitable. It might come early or late in the sermon—it might not come at all; usually it came well on into the discourse, after the ground had been cleared of many prejudices, fears and errors and a foundation in great truth laid.[42]

UNCTION

What then is this 'sacred anointing'? We take an initial look at the concept and return to it for fuller treatment later.[43] Lloyd-Jones refers to it as a 'divine afflatus'[44] which drives the preacher to the point where he has so surrendered himself to the dynamic of God's power that he is driven along as he proclaims the message.

DML-J further lifted the veil and gave a glimpse of his understanding at both doctrinal and experiential levels. He did this in the course of his early addresses preached in 1955 as he commenced his studies on Paul's Epistle to the Romans. He was preaching on the text 'For God is my witness, whom I serve with my spirit in the Gospel of his Son' (Rom. 1:9). He prefaced his remarks by distinguishing between a profession and a calling. The Christian ministry demands the latter. A profession is something you take up. It is external to you. In one sense you control it. He illustrates the point, 'You take up your bag, and you put it down when you have done with it. Not so with this! This is something within a man.' The Apostle Paul, in the service he offered the Lord, never became perfunctory. Alas, this is the case with many a preacher. He preaches because he has to. He is like an actor. He writes the script. He plays the part. But the message is external to him. The delivery is not from the inner part of his being. There is, therefore, no fire. Dr. Lloyd-Jones , in an unusual autobiographical comment, warns preachers:

The greatest danger for me, the greatest temptation to me, is that I should walk into this pulpit twice next Sunday because it was announced last Sunday that I would be doing so. Of course, it is right that a man should not break his contract. It is right that a man should not break his word . . . Yes! But that I am simply doing it because, well, another Sunday has come and I am announced to preach twice, and I must preach two sermons, that is external service. I am not doing it 'in my spirit'. Oh! when a man does it in his spirit, it is because there is something in the very depths of his being that calls it out.[45]

Now the preacher cannot summon this unction down. It is all within the control of the Holy Spirit. But there are some safeguards he can take to ensure he presents no obstacle preventing the Spirit empowering him. He will try to keep himself out of sight. By this, Lloyd-Jones is warning against a conscious use and projection of one's own personality. For the pulpit is not the stage. The preacher is like the Baptist who prepares the way for Jesus, identifies the Lord and turns his congregation over to him—as Oswald Sanders succinctly put it, 'he prepares the way, clears the way, and gets out of the way'.[46] So DML-J appeals to Paul's memorable phrase, 'we preach not ourselves, but Christ Jesus the Lord' (2 Cor. 4:5 AV).

Dr. Lloyd-Jones argues that a man, particularly if he is gifted with words, should not deliberately fall back on this natural talent. Any eloquence will come unconsciously. He was personally aware of the temptation. This was one of his greatest fears. It had been faced by others. He approvingly cites the deliberate policy of Thomas Goodwin who 'would do something which I think is perhaps the most remarkable thing a preacher can ever do'. He was referring to Goodwin's practice of deliberately scratching out the purple passages in the script of his prepared sermon. He realised the congregation might be so taken up with them that they would forget Christ.[47]

He might well have called up also the example of Jonathan Edwards. He too was a naturally gifted man—probably the greatest theologian and philosopher that America has produced. But he deliberately hid his great learning in order to speak plainly to ordinary people.[48] Why did Lloyd-Jones emphasise this? Because of the yearning for himself and fellow preachers to minister as Paul testified 'with my spirit in the Gospel of His Son'.

EIGHTEENTH CENTURY INFLUENCE

Dr. Lloyd-Jones's longings for unction would often take him to the writings of preachers who ministered two hundred years ago. He sometimes referred to himself as an eighteenth-century man. By this he meant he drew great inspiration from preachers of this period. Among British preachers he particularly benefited from George Whitefield and Howell Harris. He acknowledged Whitefield to be the greatest English preacher. Harris, his compatriot, was also a great source of stimulus to Lloyd-Jones. He gave lectures on their ministries at two Puritan Conferences.[49]

George Whitefield (1714-70)

In his lecture Lloyd-Jones was deliberately provocative, remarking that 'John Calvin always needs George Whitefield'. He felt that Whitefield presents an excellent example which sustained his contention that correct doctrine in preaching is not enough. An academic Calvinism leaves one with what Lloyd-Jones called 'an ossified orthodoxy'.

No one was more correct in his doctrinal preaching than the boy who was brought up at the Bell Inn in Gloucester. George Whitefield's ministry was so empowered that many were felled under its influence as the Holy Spirit used it to bring sinners to repentance and faith.

How should Whitefield's preaching be described? 'Apostolic and seraphic' was DML-J's assessment.[50] On one occasion Whitefield identified what he called the 'thunder and lightning' in his sermons. By this he was referring to the felt power of God which came upon him, equipping him with an unusual authority and dynamism. Whitefield's diaries record the blessing which accompanied his ministry when he was at Cheltenham. He reported how 'God the Lord came down among us'. DML-J notes:

> That is what I am talking about. George Whitefield was a man who rarely preached without being aware of the unction and the power of the Holy Spirit . . . in Cheltenham, something quite exceptional happened, so exceptional that he makes a note of it. God came down. Oh yes, they had been enjoying the presence and the blessing of God before, but not like this, something wonderful had happened, God was in the very midst, God came down.[51]

It was Whitefield especially who caused him to see the distinction between what is preached and the act of preaching. Lloyd-Jones says, 'there is nothing that has so often discouraged me, if I may make a personal reference as a preacher, as the failure of people to differentiate between the message and the preaching'.

Whitefield believed in the direct leadings of the Spirit and that the Holy Spirit would place impressions on the mind. He had great powers of description, causing one nobleman in his congregation to lean forward, apparently attempting to stop a blind man, whom Whitefield had been describing, falling over a precipice![52]

Despite his eloquence Whitefield was not pedantic in his style and delivery. Often in a hurry, he sometimes did not have time to prepare his addresses thoroughly. Wesley reckoned that he had heard Whitefield actually preaching Matthew Henry! There was what one American preacher called 'a noble negligence' which ran through some of Whitefield's sermons. By that he meant the preacher was not over-concerned about tidiness of composition. 'Whitefield did not sit down and write wonderful literary masterpieces of sermons with every sentence perfectly balanced . . . he broke the rules of grammar, now and again he did not remember to finish his sentences always, but to those who know anything about preaching that is nothing. 'Noble negligence!' continued Lloyd-Jones, 'Oh that we had a little more of it . . .'[53]

Toward the end of his lecture on Whitefield, Dr. Lloyd-Jones recorded a story which is not without a tinge of humour. It also summarised his feelings about the anointed preaching represented by the ministries of both Whitefield and Harris.

Benjamin Franklin published a number of Whitefield's sermons. He had often contributed toward the orphanage in Georgia for which Whitefield had great and burdensome responsibilities. The English preacher's habit was to take offerings at his meetings to finance the project. On one occasion, Franklin was in the congregation. Beforehand, he determined not to make a further donation. He reported his reactions, 'as the preacher proceeded I began to soften, and concluded to give the copper. Another stroke of his oratory determined me to give the silver. And he finished so admirably that I emptied my pockets into the collector's dish—gold and all.'

Lloyd-Jones remarked—'that is preaching, oratory inspired by the Holy Ghost conveying the message of the Word of God and its glorious Gospel'.[54]

Howell Harris (1714-73)

Lloyd-Jones reminds us that Harris lived in the realm of the Spirit. He, too, believed in direct leadings. There is an abundance of information about him in the diaries which he kept meticulously.

He was a modest man. Often it would be thought by those who gathered to hear him that he was actually reading from a book as he kept his head down in the process of preaching. This was not the case. He was being borne along by the Holy Spirit. He failed to understand the mechanics of the experience but he knew when he was being endowed. He made disjointed notes in his ledger.

> I took no particular texts but discoursed freely as the Lord gave me utterance. As to the subject of my discourse, it was all given unto me in an extraordinary manner without the least premeditation, it was not the fruit of my memory, it was the effect of the immediate strong impulse felt in my soul.[55]

Harris's ministry knew a combination of two things. First there was his own attempt to expound the context of the particular passage. And then 'as the power came' words poured out from him. His preaching was heightened. He began in an ordinary fashion and then he was taken up and borne along. He received unction.[56]

Lloyd-Jones was engrossed by Harris's reflections on what happened in the meetings when he and his colleagues preached. His interest was fanned by such expressions as 'the great gale came down when I shewed the greatness of salvation' and, 'the Lord came down in power'. Other diary jottings referred to 'the authority' and 'arrived at such and such a place; preached. Felt the old authority.'[57]

Notice the similarity between these comments and Whitefield's assertion that the Lord came down. This dual testimony impressed Lloyd-Jones. It helped to shape further his view on preaching. He noted that Harris, if he was not conscious of 'the authority' when he preached was troubled. When it came, all was well. For such authority, Harris craved. He believed it was absolutely essential in order to preach 'the Gospel'.[58]

This 'authority' came in the process of expounding a biblical passage. '(When) I attempted to speak without the divine commission I was humbled'. In his lecture Lloyd-Jones asked, 'Do we know anything about that?' He was endorsing something that he believed since his earliest times as a preacher; there is a plus which is almost indefinable. For this preachers must constantly plead. He felt encouraged and vindicated as he read how both Whitefield and Harris testified to it.

A CORRECTIVE

Dr. Lloyd-Jones's convictions took him into a minority position when compared with many homileticians. Most books on preaching stress the need for preparation, for programmes and working to a clearly defined timetable. A random reading of modern contributions confirms the point. If reference is made to unction and dependence on the Spirit in the act of preaching, it tends to be incidental, a secondary feature for consideration. Lloyd-Jones would criticise such a grave omission. This is the reason many of the books on preaching fail to help preachers. They do not deal with this vital phenomenon. To consign unction to the side-lines and put the spotlight on planning and preaching schemes is culpable. In order to receive unction the preacher must be open and expectant as he moves into the pulpit. Any text books which fail to stimulate him to expect the afflatus of the Spirit to empower his ministry in an unusual way are of little value.

The preacher is to be a free man, not bound by study and his script. The curriculum has to be left in the hands of the Holy Spirit. This does not mean the preacher should stint his preparation or be slovenly. Lloyd-Jones's familiarity with so many books—theological, sociological, classical and medical—proves the point. He endeavoured to bring balance to modern views on preaching. He felt that evangelicals had become too academic in their attempts to match the liberals on their own ground. He was in favour of biblical scholarship. But the pulpit is no place for the presentation of carefully researched essays. Nor, he was to argue when interest had been raised again in the preaching of the Puritans and their reformed works, was the modern occupant of the pulpit to try and imitate his worthy predecessors. He lamented that some men were emptying the churches because of an attempt slavishly to copy the Puritans. 'A preacher should be his own man',[59] was advice which Lloyd-Jones frequently gave. Dependent on the Holy Spirit, he should enter the pulpit and open the Word of God. He should endeavour to unfurl the sails of his mind to the wind of the Spirit and proceed along the course which the Holy Spirit directs.

LENGTH OF SERMON

This should affect even the length of an address. The Holy Spirit will indicate when the preacher is to stop. This is one of the reasons DML-J, when engaged in itinerant ministry during the week and especially when preaching from the pulpits of men who belonged to the Westminster Fraternal, would plead with the congregations to 'give their preachers time'.[60]

He made his views clear right at the beginning of his monumental expositions on the Epistle to the Romans:

Furthermore, I do not announce a programme; and for this reason, that when you are studying the Word of God you never know exactly when you are going to end. At least, I have a very profound feeling that such should be the case, believing, as we do, in the presence and power of the Holy Spirit. We know from experience that He suddenly comes upon us—He illumines the mind and moves the heart—and I believe that any man who expounds the Scriptures should always be open to the influences of the Holy Ghost.[61]

Some might think he took this to an extreme. He would not allow his Sunday ministry ever to be broadcast. He felt that the Religious Broadcasting department of the BBC would not recognise the unction of the Spirit when such occurred! On one occasion, he personally made the point to an official.

'What would happen to your programmes if the Holy Spirit suddenly descended upon the preacher and possessed him; what would happen to your programmes?' He could not answer me. The answer would be, of course, that the preacher would be turned off. But what a terrible thing to do.[62]

REVIEW

We conclude this chapter by taking an overall view of what DML-J is saying. The call to the ministry is something which comes from the Lord himself. Moreover, men need a divine empowering to rise to the challenge of their commission. If Lloyd-Jones is right that churches are emptied in proportion to the failure of pulpit occupants to discover the anointing of the Spirit, preachers cannot remain untouched by the plea. But this should not leave them despairing. Far from it: Dr. Lloyd-Jones's perceptions should fill preachers with a sense of hope. He has conceded that scholarship and academic prowess are not the essential ingredients for pulpit 'success'. Though he does not eschew them neither does he consider them to be absolutely necessary. He argued encouragingly that good preaching can flow from a very mediocre preacher or an inadequately prepared sermon. Successful preaching rests on the 'plus factor'. It depends upon the descent of the Spirit to lift the preacher and carry him along. One cannot assume it, coerce it or imitate it. But the preacher can be committed to a theology espousing the immediacy of the Spirit and plead for unction.

R. C. Sproul speaks of an occasion when he was preaching in a black, urban church. The following day a student asked the bishop who had presided at the church service how Sproul had done. The response was 'Well, the prof got to preaching and the folks got to shouting and then the Ghost came by'![63] Lloyd-Jones would have appreciated the sentiments, though hardly endorsing the order or the choice of words. He always yearned for 'the Ghost to come by'. It was only then that he could preach—to use Whitefield's more acceptable description—'a felt Christ'.[64]

Elizabeth Catherwood recalls one of her father's favourite stories. It was of an old Welsh preacher who was late coming to the church. Thinking he had forgotten the appointment, one of the congregation was delegated to fetch him. He could be heard behind the door of his house speaking to someone, 'I will not go and preach to those people unless you come with me.' The language is reminiscent of Moses' protestations when asked to enter into a further phase of his ministry in guiding the Hebrews through Sinai. The Welsh minister had a biblical precedent in pleading for the divine accompaniment. So have we.[65]

No preacher should settle in his mind for anything less than unction as he enters the pulpit. To know the anointing of the Spirit in the act of expounding the Word should be one of the most sought-after phenomena. Above all a preacher wishes God 'to lift up the light of his countenance upon him'; in a word he wants the smile of God. This is the reason why DML-J considered the ministry of preaching to be such a high office and constantly reminded himself and his colleagues of this conviction.

We now consider the historical context surrounding Dr. Lloyd-Jones's ministry and enquire into his own experience of the Holy Spirit.

2

Background

I have never heard such preaching and was electrified. All that I know about preaching I can honestly say I learned from 'the Doctor'. I have never heard such another preacher with so much of God about him.

J. I. Packer[1]

Pneumatology is the term theologians give to the study of the Holy Spirit. The word comes from the Greek *pneuma* which means 'wind', 'breath', or 'spirit'. In the early part of this century, the doctrine of the Spirit did not command the interest that it did in later decades. This caused some to liken it to the Cinderella of Theology. In Britain, these were days when Puritan works were little read or known. What copies there were collected dust on the shelves of university libraries.

However, before proceeding, we need to qualify the use of the word 'background' as our chapter title. The explanation is that, while not seeking to give a cameo of the life of Dr. Lloyd-Jones, a great deal of the content pivots around him personally. We seek to set his beliefs in the recent, historical context. This demands that we come up close to some of the issues which surfaced and examine how he reacted to them; the interest, qualification or dismissal that he showed.

Then we take a step back and look to past generations of preachers and consider especially how Dr. Lloyd-Jones reacted to their ministry. We do this fairly uncritically. Finally, we consider his own experience of the Holy Spirit and the effect this had both on his ministry and his view of the ministry. This means that we are concentrating on DML-J and his reactions, all of which we sum up under our chapter title—Background. If a student of his ministry appreciates some of what is narrated in this chapter he will have a better context from which to interpret and learn from the preaching of Lloyd-Jones.

CHANGING TIMES

The rise and phenomenal growth of Pentecostalism followed later by the Charismatic Movement brought a lot of changes. Early Pentecostalists produced little in the way of scholarship but a lot of zeal for evangelism. Few of their pioneers knew of Reformation theology. Calvinism, where it was considered, was dismissed as anti-Evangelical. Talk of an elect and limited atonement was considered incompatible with the love of God and the global commission to preach the Gospel.

One young Pentecostal pastor, who had been influenced by listening to Lloyd-Jones, was sternly advised by an older minister to be cautious before he swallowed 'the pill of Calvinism'. Essentially, Pentecostalism is Arminian, though there have been exceptions. Pentecostalists claimed that they had received the power and dynamic of the Spirit in a fashion comparable to the events recorded in the Acts of the Apostles. Historically trailing the earlier Holiness Movement, they were at home with a two-stage theology of regeneration and spirit baptism. In an attempt to reduce their theological emphasis to four simple points, some claimed to be four-square in their creed. They highlighted Jesus as Saviour, Baptiser, Healer and Coming King.

Whatever might be said of this simplistic theology, historians acknowledge that Church growth in the twentieth century would have been severely curtailed had it not been for Pentecostal preachers, evangelists, and missionaries.

Much to the Pentecostalists' surprise, the dawning of the Charismatic Movement, far from bringing errant, conservative Christians into their fold, had the effect of spreading the Pentecostalist claim for a resurgence of the *charismata* into the main-stream denominations. The two movements did not, and have not, fused. For three decades they have lived side by side with greater or lesser degrees of toleration and respect. Charismatics, far from being homogenous, have in their groupings produced as many segments as their Pentecostal cousins.

What has all this to do with a book on Martyn Lloyd-Jones's philosophy of preaching? His ministry straddled the rise of these groups. The very nature of the man and his commitment to revival meant that he could not be a disinterested spectator. His concerns caused him always to listen sympathetically, though objectively, to reports of anything which might savour of a genuine outpouring of the Holy Spirit.

Twice, at least, George Jeffreys, principal and founder of the Elim Pentecostal Church (one of the larger Pentecostal groups in Britain) and a fellow Welshman, sought him out. The former occasion was at the beginning of Lloyd-Jones's ministry at Aberavon and the latter on a Whitsunday morning in the 1960s, toward the end of Jeffreys's life when he attended Westminster Chapel. At the close of the service the two Welshmen conversed. Dr. Lloyd-Jones had been preaching from the second chapter of the Acts of the Apostles, emphasising his belief in the baptism of the Holy Spirit as an experience distinct from salvation. Jeffreys said to one of his colleagues, while in DML-J's vestry, 'You see I always told you Dr. Lloyd-Jones was one of us.'

The Doctor interrupted, 'But I do not teach that the Baptism of the Spirit must be accompanied by speaking in tongues!' 'Neither do I', responded George Jeffreys.[2]

A few years later, some of the young leaders of the Charismatic Movement (particularly within the Church of England) asked Lloyd-Jones for counsel. They had experienced what they considered to be the Baptism of the Spirit and wished to discuss the implications with him.[3]

Alongside the burgeoning Pentecostal and Charismatic Movements was another that did not capture the headlines of the religious press. We refer to the revival in interest being shown in Reformation theology. The writings of the Puritans and the men of the Great Awakening were now being sought. In the United Kingdom, this was encouraged and stimulated by Dr. Lloyd-Jones and Dr. Ernest Kevan, who became the first principal of the London Bible College. Many younger preachers-in-training were to discover the truth in DML-J's and Kevan's assertions that the Reformers were not dry, cerebral theologians but experiential in their approach to doctrine. The works of John Calvin, Jonathan Edwards, George Whitefield, John Owen, Richard Sibbes and Thomas Goodwin, to name but a few, were increasingly read. The claim that Pentecostalists alone knew the dynamic of the Spirit could be contested. God had not by-passed Christendom from the first to the twentieth century!

Interest in the doctrine of the Holy Spirit spiralled. Lloyd-Jones was God's man in one of London's most influential pulpits for such a time. As early as the 1950s he was pleading for Christians—and especially for preachers—to consider carefully and humbly the doctrine of the Holy Spirit. Though he did not then, nor subsequently, espouse Pentecostalism,[4] he reacted strongly to a conservative theology which seemed to him to deny de facto the immediacy of the Spirit. The consequence for the ordinary Christian was bad, it stunted growth. For the pulpit, it was disastrous. The danger could be that men preaching Sunday by Sunday might be so academic in striving for theological perfection and polemical ability that they were grieving the Spirit by their lack of openness. Thus they were forestalling what British Christendom needed more than anything else—revival![5]

Lloyd-Jones can be perceived as a type of John the Baptist, crying for an unbiased handling of Scripture especially on the doctrine of the Spirit. His sermons on revival[6] registered his heartbeat. In 1959, the year that commemorated the centenary of the British revival, which had its parallels in various parts of the world, he interrupted his long series on the Epistle to the Ephesians in order to deliver these sermons.

It is necessary to bear all this in mind for it is part of the backcloth of Lloyd-Jones's ministry. From it, we should consider his pleas to wait on God for revival and for preachers to seek unction in their preaching.

Later in this volume we shall see how DML-J's sermons reveal that he had a reference grid which was part of a checking procedure to ensure that his expositions were biblically accurate. One of his appeals was to Church History. In other words, he wished to know how his noble predecessors had handled particular passages of Scripture. He was equally interested not just in their expository method but in their personal experience of the grace of God.

CHURCH HISTORY

A reasonable comment on Lloyd-Jones's sermons is that he read much and footnoted little![7] To track down his quotations is not easy. When he preached on the experiential aspects of the doctrine of the Spirit, he delved into the history of the lives of earlier preachers. His posthumously published volume, *Joy Unspeakable*, is replete with historical anecdotes, but, unfortunately, totally barren of references.[8] The same goes for his first volume of sermons on the Epistle to the Ephesians in which there are several addresses on the sealing of the Spirit. Once again he relates the experiences of great Christian leaders of the past.[9]

Most of the historical illustrations were used to buttress Lloyd-Jones's pneumatology. He endeavoured to show that his convictions on the doctrine of the Spirit, far from being novel or an aberration, as some have argued,[10] represented the historic stance of many of the leaders of the Church in its history, especially since the Reformation.

His interest in the experience of the Spirit, doubtless traceable to his background in the Welsh Calvinistic Methodist Church, had caused him to read deeply in the area of historical theology. Few can have quarried so assiduously and found so much 'gold'. Though his excavations largely took him into the realm of the Puritans and preachers in the eighteenth and nineteenth centuries, he also quoted from preReformation men.

He related the story of Thomas Aquinas and how, toward the end of his days, he had a sense of the Holy Spirit's empowering and sealing. He quoted the memorable words of the famous philosopher-theologian and author of The *Summa Theologica* when encouraged to add to it, 'I can do no more, such things have been revealed to me that all I have written seems as straw, and I now await the end of my life.'[11]

He reported the case of John Tauler,[12] a German Roman Catholic priest, who preached in one of the great cathedrals. God suddenly took hold of him, filled him with his Spirit and, as a result, his whole preaching was transformed. This was in the Dark Ages. Even in those times, DML-J reminds us, God had his hand on some men, 'these so-called mystics . . . of that era were burning and shining lights.'[13] He refers to the great Savonarola and in a reference coupled him with Luther. 'You cannot explain him—or Martin Luther either—except in terms of being baptised and filled with the Spirit.'[14]

He graphically recounted the story of Blaise Pascal, a Frenchman from the seventeenth century. Lloyd-Jones calls him 'one of the great geniuses of all time'. Apparently when Pascal died, a piece of paper was found stitched into his shirt. Curiously, Pascal had recorded the day and hour when he had a most remarkable experience of the grace of God. It lasted for two hours. The word he used to describe it was 'Fire'. And he went on to add 'joy, joy, joy, tears of joy'. Subsequently, he retired from the academic world of mathematics and joined a religious community where he wrote his great works, the *Provincial Letters* and the *Thoughts* (*Pensées*). On telling the account, Lloyd-Jones concluded, 'All I want to convey to you, my dear friends, is that we all ought to know something like that'.[15]

It was Dr. Lloyd-Jones's conviction that there had been a shift of emphasis by the Church on the doctrine of the Spirit midway through the nineteenth century. Prior to this, he argued, many of the notable (and lesser known) preachers subscribed to the same pneumatology which DML-J embraced. He believed the Church reacted badly to German rationalism and liberalism. She became academic and defensive. She conceded ground. Sermons were decidedly bookish, written more as essays with an eye to publication than delivery in the power and demonstration of the Spirit in the charismatic way with which Lloyd-Jones associates the preaching ministry. Because the person of the Spirit was largely by-passed, the pulpit suffered. Fire and fervour were traded for style and scholasticism.

His seventh volume on the Epistle to the Romans entitled *The Sons of God* is especially interesting. These addresses were preached in 1960/61—some years before his sermons published in the volume *Joy Unspeakable*. The reference to the date of delivery is important for it puts to flight the notion that there was a drastic revision in Lloyd-Jones's teaching on the Holy Spirit in the closing years of his ministry.[16] If anything, these sermons demonstrate a remarkable consistency.

In a detailed fashion, he presented his case with frequent appeals to history. These sermons contain his longest defence of his views on the sealing or baptism with the Spirit. They are footnoted. Inasmuch as DML-J examined them before they were published, perhaps they have greater significance than those edited and printed after his death. The sermons on Romans represent his considered opinion.

This volume, *The Sons of God*, contains thirty-three sermons which cover a mere eight verses. Eight of his sermons are dedicated to expounding the sixteenth verse of Romans 8; 'The Spirit itself beareth witness with our spirit, that we are the children of God' (*AV*). Three of them are largely occupied with relating experiences from the lives of earlier preachers.

On reading through these addresses, and the ones immediately preceding and following, it becomes clear why DML-J stayed so long with this verse. Twice he used the word 'evidence' to describe his goal. Whether one agrees or disagrees with the case he presents, it is clear that he was definitely convinced that the position he outlined is in line with Apostolic teaching and broadly reflects the belief held by the Puritans and great men of God in succeeding generations.

His case from the perspective of Church History can be summarised thus:

The charge that 'none of the Puritans held this view' was false

He referred to John Preston, John Owen, Thomas Brooks and Thomas Horton. He quoted from the Scottish divine, William Guthrie's volume *The Christian's Great Interest*, where Guthrie asserts:

> There is a communication of the Spirit of God which is sometimes vouchsafed to some of His people that is somewhat besides, if not

beyond, that witnessing of a sonship spoken of before. It is a glorious divine manifestation of God unto the soul, shedding abroad God's love in the heart. It is a thing better felt than spoke of. It is no audible voice but it is a ray of glory filling the soul with God as he is light, life, love and liberty . . . [17]

One would expect Lloyd-Jones also to have cited Richard Sibbes, for whose writings he had a special affection,[18] and Thomas Goodwin. We are not disappointed! DML-J could not resist repeating Goodwin on Ephesians 1:13,

> There is a light that cometh and overpowereth a man's soul and assureth him that God is his, and he is God's, and that God loved him from everlasting . . . It is a light beyond the light of ordinary faith . . . the next thing to heaven: you have no more, you can have no more until you come hither . . . It is faith elevated and raised up above its ordinary rate, it is electing love of God brought home to the soul.[19]

There is an interesting sermon which Lloyd-Jones preached early in his Westminster ministry. It is one of the first series of addresses of his to be recorded[20] and it is on the doctrine of the Spirit. Later, he would qualify certain aspects of his teaching, though his revision is quite modest.

This particular sermon reveals the difficulty he encountered in getting some of his congregation fully to grasp the distinction he was drawing between regeneration and the baptism of the Holy Spirit even in the earlier middle part of his Westminster ministry. Typically, he summarised and repeated the arguments of the previous sermon. He took his hearers back to the days of the Puritans when he claimed that there was a division of views which became two streams of thought on the matter. The one, he believed, was traceable back to John Owen and Thomas Goodwin, the other to George Fox. DML-J had no doubt that George Fox was right in highlighting experience, 'he was on to something'. But it went too far. The error was emphasising experience to the extent that the Bible was viewed at a distance and ultimately not at all. Thus Quakerism today represents 'a vague general benevolence and a good spirit'. The stream that proceeded from Owen's teaching ran the danger, at its extreme, of creating a 'barren intellectualism', a 'protestant scholasticism'. Despite this, Lloyd-Jones believed his case to be irrefutable: among the Puritans, there were those who espoused a pneumatology to which he traced his own.

Some eighteenth century men also held the same belief

In the previous chapter we referred to Howell Harris and George Whitefield. In DML-J's sermons from Romans dealing with the experiential aspects of the doctrine of the Holy Spirit, he highlighted the teaching and witness of Jonathan Edwards. Several times he related the story of Edwards's remarkable encounter with the Lord. On one occasion Edwards dismounted from his horse and commenced his usual daily walk in which he gave time for contemplation. He testified:

> I had a view, that for me was extraordinary, of the glory of the Son of God, as Mediator between God and man, and his wonderful, great, full, pure and sweet grace and love, and meek and gentle condescension. This grace that appeared so calm and sweet appeared also great above the heavens. The person of Christ appeared ineffably excellent, with an excellency great enough to swallow up all thought and conception—which continued, as near as I can judge, about an hour; which kept me the greater part of the time in a flood of tears and weeping aloud. I felt an ardency of soul to be, what I know not otherwise how to express, emptied and annihilated, to lie in the dust and to be full of Christ alone; to love him with a holy and pure love; to trust in him; to live upon him; to serve and follow him; and to be perfectly sanctified and made pure with a divine and heavenly purity.[21]

In DML-J's early sermon in which he referred to Owen and Fox in particular, he then went on to speak about Jonathan Edwards. His estimate of Edwards knew no bounds, 'possibly the greatest mind the world has ever known . . . certainly the greatest brain that America has ever known'. Later he would refer to him as 'that mighty genius, that spiritual giant . . . 'One of the outstanding characteristics of Edwards was the way in which he held on to the best in both schools. He was a man who knew how to distinguish between the work of the Holy Spirit and 'the carnality which simulates it'. His book *The Religious Affections* [22] is irrefutable evidence which proves the point. Edwards went to neither extreme. He expounded the position which Lloyd-Jones too adopted. In his writings, 'we find the same plain and unmistakable fact' about the Baptism of the Spirit. Edwards taught that to believe was one thing, and this 'sealing of the Spirit', this 'Spirit bearing witness with his spirit' was something different.[23]

*In the nineteenth century Charles Simeon (whose life-span
bridged the latter years of the eighteenth century) shared his
pneumatology as did C. H. Spurgeon*

Dr. Lloyd-Jones claimed alongside these other proponents such as
Robert Haldane and J. C. Philpott.[24] In a remarkable sermon in which
he deals with the experience of Apollos who was ministered to by Aquila
and Priscilla, Lloyd-Jones had occasion to quote from Spurgeon. DML-
J sustained the proposition that there are 'stages' in Christian experience. Basically he was defending his position about the baptism in the
Spirit. Spurgeon taught that 'the difference between these two stages is
greater than between the non-Christian and the Christian in the first
stage'.[25] DML-J commented that this is a serious statement but 'it is very
true'.

Other telling quotations reveal C. H. Spurgeon distinguishing
between those in his congregation who lacked full assurance and those
who did not. His advice to the former was that they should present this
request before God. 'Write my name not only in Thy heart but may it
be as a signet on Thy heart that I may see it.' He went on to speak of
those who, though they have been loved by Christ from all eternity, as
yet 'have never had the seal of the Spirit to witness within that they are
born of God. While their names may be in His heart they have not seen
them there as a seal upon his heart . . .'[26] We will have occasion to return
to Spurgeon's pneumatology later.[27]

*The experience was witnessed to by those from a different
theological perspective*

DML-J argued that both Calvinists and those of Arminian persuasion
testified to it. Somewhat ruefully, Lloyd-Jones explained he had
mounted this aspect of his inquiry 'in order to deal with the theologians'.[28] He made a great deal of the testimony of John Wesley and his
experience in Aldersgate Street, London on May 24th, 1738. Someone
read the preface to Luther's commentary on the Epistle to the Romans
in Wesley's hearing. He was deeply affected and uttered the now famous
words, 'my heart was strangely warmed . . .' He was given an assurance
that Christ had died for him and he was reconciled to God.

Earlier, Wesley had gone as a missionary to Georgia. On his return,
there was a dreadful storm in the Atlantic; Wesley was afraid, but his
fellow Moravian passengers were not. John Wesley was convicted and
he had to admit, 'those people have got something I have not'. They
were truly Christian. Under their instruction, Wesley heard about justification by faith. Thus informed, he came to London. At Aldersgate

Street, what he had seen with his head he now felt in his heart. At first he thought that the profound experience the Lord gave him there marked the occasion when he became a Christian. Later, in 1770, looking back with greater wisdom, he put a significant footnote in the page in his diary which recounted the incident. He now realised that he had been a Christian before. But, in the centre of London he received full assurance. The theological explanation that he proffered contained the declaration, 'I was a Christian before but I only had the faith of a servant, but not the faith of a son.'

Judging from the number of times DML-J made reference to D. L. Moody's experience of the Holy Spirit while the American evangelist was in New York, he was very impressed. He was particularly influenced by the testimony Moody gave to the greater blessings following the same sermons preached after what Moody called his baptism in the Spirit than before. DML-J commented, 'the same sermons and yet they were not the same sermons. There was this demonstration of the Spirit and of power. It is the same with many others.'[29] Thus, Lloyd-Jones felt that such testimony underlined the need to call men back to what he believed to be the older and biblically correct pneumatology. To the name of Moody was added that of Charles G. Finney. Though Lloyd-Jones contested Finney's teaching on revival[30]—a mechanical view which claimed that if certain criteria were fulfilled revival would automatically follow—he did not challenge Finney's account, in his biography, of being baptised in the Spirit.

What is more, the experience crossed the denominational and what might be called the psychological barrier

Lloyd-Jones held it to be significant that Baptists and Presbyterians on both sides of the Atlantic as well as Congregationalists bore testimony to the sealing of the Spirit as a distinct work following conversion. Moreover, it transcended differences of personality. The temperaments of many preachers whom he cites were very contrasting. Nonetheless they had the experience as a common denominator.[31]

It was the position of the early brethren

It might be considered surprising that this was part of Lloyd-Jones's case when it is remembered that he believed that the brethren had an unfortunate influence on the ministry of preaching. He believed the idea that all men might participate was both unscriptural and lowered the quality of preaching.[32] But it should be noted that he had respect for J. N. Darby whom he sometimes describes, as he did Spurgeon, as 'the great'.

Not only does he cite Darby on the sealing of the Spirit[33] but also C. H. Mackintosh[34] as well as William Kelly.

In addition to all this, he argued that the liturgical practice of the Episcopalian Churches added weight to his convictions. Such denominations baptise their infants. Later, those who have been baptised are advised to present themselves for confirmation. This practice is defended (though not by DML-J) on the basis of the two-stage passages in the Acts of the Apostles which suggest that people became believers and then subsequently received the Holy Spirit. Thus, the bishops laid hands on the candidates. The infilling of the Spirit is invoked. Although nothing observable happens, this is not the point, for Lloyd-Jones wished to demonstrate that, embedded in the liturgy of these historic churches, is the belief that more is to be received from the Holy Spirit than occurred at infant baptism.[35]

On surveying the evidence, Dr. Lloyd-Jones felt he was on sure ground. He confidently believed that his appeal to doctrinal history confirmed the deductions he had made from the Scriptures. He believed that there was a 'strange and curious unanimity with regard to the character of the experience of the witness of the Holy Spirit'.[36] By making such an assertion, he was not claiming that all his forebears agreed with him but that there were a good number who did. Thus he refuted the charge that his approach to the doctrine of the Spirit was novel. Rather, he claimed, he was appealing for a return to the old paths.

> . . . many imagine that what I have been saying in exposition of this verse is something new and strange. I want to show, therefore, that, far from being an innovation, it has been taught regularly throughout the centuries; and it is chiefly in this present century that it has dropped into the background, and has been neglected and forgotten. I do not hesitate to assert that the main explanation and cause of the present state of the Christian Church—and I am referring particularly to Evangelical churches—is the neglect of this doctrine. . . .[37]

We have mentioned the cautions of some who are positive and the criticisms of some who are negative concerning Lloyd-Jones's pneumatology. When we get to his volume *Joy Unspeakable* we might, as we remarked earlier, have wished for more context and a few footnotes! But we must bear in mind that he was preaching, not delivering lectures nor preparing manuscripts for a future book. Whatever qualification may need to be placed against some illustrations, Lloyd-Jones's main arguments are surely substantiated. There were among leading Christians of former generations:

Many who had remarkable experiences of the Holy Spirit's enabling

Some who definitely theologised their experience in what might be termed a two-stage fashion.

Though Lloyd-Jones's personal views may be considered as a refinement or development of the thought of his predecessors,[38] in no way can it be proven that he was adrift from the beliefs of many of the Puritans or eighteenth-century men. His reasoned, historical position demands careful attention and should not be peremptorily dismissed.

Following Dr. Lloyd-Jones's sustained preaching style, having looked generally at his historical position, we must now move to the particular and consider his own experiences and the manner in which he evaluated them!

PERSONAL EXPERIENCES

On the grounds of what we have seen above, it is justifiable to research Lloyd-Jones's own encounters with the Holy Spirit. After all, he placed a premium himself on researching and recounting the experiences of others and the effect such had on their ministry. Also, if unction is one of the consequences of the baptism in the Spirit, it is necessary to attempt a review of the effect of this experience in DML-J's ministry. We need to raise several questions. When did he first experience unction in his preaching? Was this subsequent to a personal experience of the Holy Spirit? When was this experienced? Are there differences in his sermons before and after his baptism in the Holy Spirit? How is this detectable in his sermons?

Mounting such an enquiry is far from easy because of his reluctance to speak about himself or make personal references in the course of his sermons. But from several deposits of information, not least the two-volume *Biography*, the following picture emerges.

DML-J experienced at least two dark patches in his ministry. The accounts are found in Volume 2 of the *Biography* which is appropriately entitled *Martyn Lloyd-Jones, The Fight of Faith*. The first episode is of particular interest. It occurred in 1949. The Lord took him through a period of extraordinary temptation and conflict. Afterwards he was lifted up and given an experience of the nearness of heaven. Murray tells us, 'He was brought into a state of ecstasy and joy which remained with him for several days.' He had a consciousness of the presence and love of God which seemed to exceed all he had ever known before. Similar incidents in the lives of Thomas Goodwin, Robert Bruce, John Flavel and Christmas Evans are mentioned.[39]

Though the term 'baptism in the Spirit' is not employed by his biographer to describe the experience, in the 1970s, during a meeting of the Westminster Fraternal, Dr. Lloyd-Jones made reference to what is described in the book and used this terminology to identify it. Some believe that the experience became a watershed in his ministry and from then onwards a perceptible shift is recognisable.[40] His preaching became less cerebral and more experimental.

THE EARLIEST YEARS

However, we must be careful. In order to obtain as full a picture as possible of DML-J's experience of the Holy Spirit and the resulting further equipment for ministry, we need to go to the beginning of his preaching career and the events which led to him leaving the medical profession.

He trained as a doctor of medicine in London. Generally, he attended Westminster Chapel once on a Sunday and benefited from the ministry of Dr. John Hutton. On one occasion Lloyd-Jones agreed to address a meeting held in Charing Cross Chapel. This was in March 1926. He was to speak on Puritanism. Significantly, he argued that Christianity should exist not in belief only but in 'vital force'. It 'does not merely improve a man but rather completely changes him'. He went on to affirm that this type of Christianity is not to be found outside 'the baptism in the Holy Spirit' and a personal experience of God.[41]

We would not wish to read more into his reference to Spirit baptism than is intended. However, incidents which followed shortly after this need to be borne in mind. Murray records how, at the end of his life, Dr. Lloyd-Jones reminisced about those earlier times.

Although we have referred to two crises in Lloyd-Jones's ministerial career there had in fact been an earlier one. This preceded his entry into the ministry and, indeed, was the reason for it. In other words, it occurred as he was contemplating the call to be a preacher.

In later years, DML-J never hinted that he had sacrificed anything when he left the medical profession. Quite the contrary; to enter the Christian ministry in God's sovereignty is a great honour. Nonetheless, the decision to quit medicine was far from easy. He was being tugged in two different directions. Speaking of his experience many years later he recalled,

'I literally lost over twenty pounds in weight.' Some of his friends suggested that he should compromise and continue in medicine with occasional preaching assignments. He recalled, 'I tried that, but it did not satisfy.'[42]

Coupled with this struggle was an even graver issue. He felt unworthy to be a preacher of the Gospel. It was at that critical time, on the threshold of withdrawing from his career in medicine, that he was granted a profound experience of God's grace. In the eventide of his life, DML-J remembered what had happened to him when he was still a young doctor:

> I must say that in that little study at our home in Regency Street, and in my research room next to the post-mortem room at Bart's, I had some remarkable experiences. It was entirely God's doing. I have known what it is to be really filled with a *joy unspeakable and full of glory*.[43]

He went on to add:

> Whatever authority I may have as a preacher is not the result of any decision on my part. It was God's hand that laid hold of me, and drew me out, and separated me to this work.

Again, we do not want to fall into the trap of reading into this more than is warranted, but it does seem the timing of the event and the retrospective comments are significant.

In later years, Lloyd-Jones would argue that the Apostle Peter's reference to 'joy unspeakable and full of glory' is a term which is descriptive of the experience of the baptism in the Spirit. He would sometimes warn preachers against diluting the verse. It must be taken at face value, for it means what it says. We must not bring it down to our level of our own particular present-day experiences. The verse describes what members of the early Church generally knew.

Was it not providential that at such a critical time in DML-J's life he should be so singularly blessed? Cannot this be interpreted as the Lord's seal and anointing on him for what was to lie ahead? Is not this the reason for the success which was to meet him when he returned to his home country?

HIS MINISTRY IN WALES

In 1926, much to the amazement of many of his colleagues, Dr. Lloyd-Jones determined to leave his work as assistant to Lord Thomas Horder and his rooms at Harley Street in order to take on the pastorate of a small church in his native South Wales.[44] His church was to be at Aberavon. Such a stir was caused that one newspaper for December 14th carried the headlines 'Leading Doctor turns Pastor: Large income given up for £300 a year'! His wife, Bethan, recollects that when his decision was made known, everybody did their best to dissuade him, from fellow doctors, family, friends, to his own minister!

A remarkable exception was the weekly paper, *John Bull*, which someone sent to me. Under the heading, 'From palpitations to pulpitations', it had a statement beginning, 'Dr. Lloyd-Jones, a brilliant young heart physician . . .' and under that as comment: 'Hats off to Dr. Lloyd-Jones'![45]

His time in South Wales was extraordinarily fruitful. Congregational strength soared tenfold from the original eighty worshippers who greeted him when he entered the Sandfields' pulpit. The membership went through the five hundred limit. On one evening, forty people were baptised. Lloyd-Jones did not baptise by immersion, nor did he baptise infants. He sprinkled baptismal candidates on confession of their faith, a practice he maintained throughout his pastorates.

His ministry coincided with a period when the whole area had been sucked into the vortex of a depression. There was social unrest and a great deal of poverty. Men and women in the mining villages were paying more attention to the heralds of Marxist-Leninism than the preachers in the many chapels generously scattered around the valleys. It is arguable that one of the factors which saved South Wales from Communism was the forceful ministry of Lloyd-Jones. Indeed, the local Communist party official was converted and became a member of Lloyd-Jones's church!

The success of his preaching grew more pronounced. Murray was driven to use the word 'revival' in order to describe it.[46] Revivals can be local as well as national. The effects of the 1904 revival had been relatively short-lived. The after-glow had long since faded, and Wales was spiritually barren. However, in Aberavon, singular blessing was known. A type of preaching was heard which was quite rare. The 1904 revival was not noted for its preaching. This may be one of the reasons why it was ephemeral and not comparable with the great revivals of previous centuries.

Murray contrasts the ministry of Lloyd-Jones with that of his contemporaries, noting, 'Most of the preaching which Dr. Lloyd-Jones had heard throughout his life had only convinced him what he must not do'.[47]

A reading of his earliest book of sermons gives a sample of the fare which his growing congregation was to know.[48] They not only provide an insight into the early years of his ministry but are, as the publisher's blurb claims, 'examples of what preaching ought to be'.

One journalist, tempted to write a story on Lloyd-Jones, having heard of his departure from medicine, gave a fascinating account of his experience. In July 1927, he attended the church in Aberavon and referred to Lloyd-Jones's 'great zeal'. The mere curiosity which had compelled the reporter to attend the church was swept away. He apologised to his readers that his reported words of Lloyd-Jones's address were 'but a weak picture of the originals'. On the other hand, he says, the preaching contained 'the words of one who has felt himself forced to speak by a greater than human power'.

We referred earlier to George Jeffreys, the Pentecostal pioneer preacher who was attracting large crowds throughout the United Kingdom. He visited Aberavon and spoke to Dr. Lloyd-Jones after the service. Principal Jeffreys, as he was known, was unwell at the time and was recuperating in his native Wales. Lloyd-Jones had never met him but noticed this rather distinguished-looking person in his congregation. Jeffreys had been so moved by DML-J's ministry he told him 'it was a sin to have preached that sermon *here*'. The Doctor was bemused. He was not aware of any error or heresy in what he had declared. However, Jeffreys's point was that the message was so powerful, it deserved a wider audience. Lloyd-Jones asked where it should have been preached and was told the venue should have been the vast Royal Albert Hall, London (which Jeffreys filled many times). If Lloyd-Jones would agree to go there, the evangelist would guarantee to fill it. DML-J declined the offer but related the story, in later years, with much warmth.[49]

It seems quite evident, on reading a selection of his early sermons, hearing the testimonies of a reporter and another famous Welsh preacher, as well as considering what took place in terms of church growth, coupled with the fascinating accounts of conversion recorded by Bethan Lloyd-Jones,[50] that his ministry was attended with great power, even from the earliest days. The evidence surely leads to the conclusion that an unusual unction was on DML-J's preaching and that this, in part, is the explanation for its remarkable fruitfulness. In his later years, though his ministry in London was to be significantly blessed, it is arguable that the touch of revival was more characteristic of the Welsh than of the Westminster pastorate.

WESTMINSTER

In the first part of his London ministry, we have the assessment of some-one who was to become a close associate of DML-J. It is of significance because the testimony comes from a fellow preacher and theologian. We refer to Dr. James Packer.

Just before the trauma and blessing of 1949, DML-J spent many Sunday evenings preaching through the eleventh chapter of Matthew's Gospel. These sermons have been subsequently published.[51]

Packer was a regular evening worshipper at the Chapel. Lloyd-Jones's preaching, both in content and style, made a marked and indelible impression on him. Indeed, he asserted that all he ever learned about preaching came from that period.[52] The many references to Lloyd-Jones in Packer's books reveal the impact he made on the younger man. He gives a graphic description of his mentor's pulpit ministry at that time.

> The sermon (as we say nowadays) blew me away . . . He worked up to a dramatic growling shout about God's sovereign grace a few min-utes before the end; then from that he worked down to businesslike persuasions calling on needy souls to come to Christ . . . I went out full of awe and joy, with a more vivid sense of the greatness of God in my heart than I had known before . . . The thunder and lightning; the gestures—kneading fists representing perplexed philosophers, the vibrating arm with open hand marking God's descent in grace, the right-angled turns to point to heaven and hell (one side of the church for each, and always the same side): and the electric impact of those trombone-sforzando shouts about God . . . [53]

Even if words are inadequate to describe unction—and you can't get 'the lightning and the thunder'[54] on to the page—we are indebted to Packer for a creditable attempt to supply us with an insight!

It was after these sermons were preached that Lloyd-Jones went through what the Puritans called 'the dark night of the soul'.[55] Eventually, the pain and depression gave way to overwhelming experi-ences of God's grace. We have already intimated that these have been identified as the baptism in the Spirit. But what about the experience(s) in 1926?

We need to bear in mind that Lloyd-Jones's pneumatology allowed for more than one personal baptism in the Holy Spirit. There can be ebb and flow in spiritual experience. He reminded us that the Apostle Peter was baptised on the Day of Pentecost and preached with great power. A few days later, a similar experience was granted him. Significantly,

DML-J commented: 'It is obvious therefore that this is something which can be repeated many times.'[56]

It is reasonable to interpret Lloyd-Jones's own experiences from within the categories that he sets down. They comfortably fit into his theological scheme.

There can be no doubt that he had known the peculiar afflatus of the Spirit powerfully resting on him during his time in Wales. Nothing else explains the extraordinary and wonderful blessings which accompanied his preaching at that time. Nowhere, as far as we are aware, does Lloyd-Jones claim that his experiences in 1949 were so outstanding they were incomparable with anything he had known before. From the outset of his ministry he had known a great endowment of 'power from on high'.

REVIEW

In this chapter we have attempted three things: to describe in part something of the backcloth of Dr. Lloyd-Jones's ministry as it reached its heights in London; to summarise his conclusions when assessing the testimonies in historical theology of his forebears and simply to set down his own experiences of the doctrine of the Spirit. This has been done factually rather than critically. We now proceed to examine more closely and in greater detail his conception of unction. As we have conceded, not all will agree with his doctrinal formulation of the experience of the Holy Spirit. Reluctantly, we move into the area of controversy. DML-J passionately believed that unction in preaching was one of the consequences of the baptism in the Spirit. If we are defective in our theology, he affirmed, we are sure to be deficient in our preaching.[57] However, our main objective is not to major so much on points of theological disagreement but to unearth helpful principles for preachers who desperately want to know more about being borne along in the power of the Holy Spirit as they preach to their congregations Sunday by Sunday.

3

Unction

Seek Him! Seek Him! What can we do without Him? Seek Him! Seek Him always. But go beyond seeking Him; expect Him. Do you expect anything to happen to you when you get up to preach in a pulpit? . . . Seek this power, expect this power, yearn for this power; and when this power comes, yield to Him. Do not resist. Forget all about your sermon if necessary. Let him loose you, let Him manifest His power in you and through you.[1]

Martyn Lloyd-Jones

The Doctor had a massively commanding personality disciplined voice and great facility of expression. But he never strove for effect. All was perfectly natural.

Two other qualities of his preaching remain indelibly in the memory. First, expression. He acted all his life on the principle that the heart can only be reached through the head. Hence the relentless argument with unceasing endeavour to win the consent of the intellect. Yet his sermons never became lectures. The truth quickly ignited his own soul: and he, as quickly, communicated the fire to his audience.

The second thing was the persistent, remorseless application . . . His sermons were direct to what he saw: to the errors to which men were prone, the moods to which they were liable and the false refuges in which they sought security. 'Preaching', he said, 'is the highest and the most glorious calling to which anyone can ever be called?'[2]

Donald Macleod

W e pick up again and attempt to come closer to the word 'unction'
as Lloyd-Jones understood it. What is the nature of this power
that rides so high in his estimation?

Dr. Lloyd-Jones's theology of the Spirit has been the subject of one
in-depth study[3] and several critical essays and articles to which we shall
refer. His pneumatology is pivotal to his longings for, and conception of,
unction. He believed unction prompts greater boldness, clarity and
power in preaching. If the latter are the consequences, the former is the
cause. At one point he detailed benefits which flowed from the baptism
in the Holy Spirit and continued: 'The next thing I hasten to emphasise
is the effect of the "Baptism with the Spirit" upon the speech of men, by
which I really mean preaching'.[4]

As we have noticed, he sometimes employs the technical word *afflatus* as a synonym for unction. But what does he really mean by this?
Fortunately he tells us.[5] He described it as an 'accession' or 'effusion of
power'. This affects the preacher, lifting him out of himself and giving
him abilities which are not naturally his as he discourses. Several deductions can be drawn from a detailed consideration of Lloyd-Jones's
teaching and scattered references to the divine empowering in the sermons he preached over more than forty years.

Unction is not a permanent possession

Some may experience it more than others. But none can assume it. If
unction has been received once, it is to be sought again. Lloyd-Jones
would take us, among other examples, to the experience of Peter. As the
result of the Holy Spirit's effusion on the Day of Pentecost, he was
enabled to preach with great power. In a later chapter, we see Peter and
John before the Sanhedrin. They were arrested because of their preaching ministry. When Peter was called to give an account, the narrative
continues, 'Then Peter, filled with the Holy Spirit, said . . .' (Acts 4:8).
He had known unction when he preached on the Day of Pentecost. But
now he needed a fresh supply for the current situation.

Similarly, when Stephen was appointed a deacon with six others, a
key quality for the office was that the men must be 'full of the Spirit'
(Acts 6:3). Faced with the critical circumstances which brought about
his martyrdom, Stephen received a further supply of the Spirit's
dynamism (Acts 7:55).

A favourite story of Lloyd-Jones's helps to fix the point. He spoke
of a native countryman, David Morgan. This was at the time of the
Welsh Revival in 1859.[6] He had been a carpenter and lacked training as
a preacher. He had known a faithful but fairly unremarkable ministry.

Then, one day, he had an experience of the Holy Spirit. He told a friend about it, 'I had felt power in the service but I went to bed that night David Morgan. But,' he said, 'you know, when I woke up the next morning, I realised I was a different man. I felt like a lion, I felt great power.' He began to preach with tremendous authority. This continued for a considerable time. Then he said to this same friend, 'One night, I went to bed filled with this power that had accompanied me for two years, I woke up the next morning and found that I was David Morgan once more.'

The illustration is an unusual one, but it does help to fix in our minds the conviction which Lloyd-Jones held that this bestowal of power cannot be taken for granted. There is an ebb and flow. Like the gifts of the Spirit, it is not given as a permanent possession.

> I often say that the most romantic place on earth is the pulpit. I ascend the pulpit stairs Sunday after Sunday: I never know what is going to happen. I confess that sometimes, for various reasons, I come expecting nothing; but suddenly, the power is given. At other times, I think I have a great deal because of my preparation: but, alas, I find there is no power in it. Thank God it is like that. I do my utmost, but He controls the supply and the power, He infuses it.[7]

This leads us on to underscore a further emphasis which Lloyd-Jones made about unction.

Unction is dependent on a 'given' element[8]

In other words, this effusion hinges entirely upon the sovereign will of the Holy Spirit. He may grant it, he may not. It is utterly at his discretion. Receiving it once does not mean you can bank on it the next time. Leigh Powell made the observation when reflecting on DML-J's ministry:

> At times, often toward the end of the sermon, he seemed to be hovering, waiting for something . . . sometimes the wind of the Spirit would come and sweep us and him aloft and we would mount with wings like eagles into the awesome and felt presence of God.[9]

The point is perceptive. In the process of delivering the message, he was yearning for the afflatus of the Spirit to fall on him. Then he would soar and deliver the sermon with a volley of words and argumentation stimulated and empowered by the anointing, with the consequence that the congregation was often transfixed. Boldness and authority are always present when the Spirit's dynamism is in operation. DML-J continually longed for this experience. On one occasion, he made reference to the 'heavenly presence' which he felt during the course of his preaching.[10]

Unction is not impeded by the weakness of the preacher

The weakness here can be descriptive both of physical appearance as well as of a stuttering tongue. DML-J once remarked how God used 'ugly' men in a remarkable way! He took us to Paul's Corinthian Epistles. Here, the Apostle recognised his feebleness both in his speech as well as his appearance (2 Cor. 10:10). He admitted to his trembling, fear and speech patterns which lacked natural eloquence. Nonetheless, his recollection of his time of ministry at Corinth caused him to assert that his preaching was 'with a demonstration of the Spirit's power' (1 Cor. 2:4). This is a very important claim. Indeed, Lloyd-Jones took it to be a 'controlling statement' for the whole subject.

The effusion works through, or in spite of, the speech of a man who, by his own confession, was not a natural orator and had no desire to train in the same fashion as the rhetoricians of the day.

This deduction finds further support in the first chapter of Colossians. Paul referred to his attempts to proclaim the good news about the Lord 'admonishing and teaching everyone with all wisdom' (v.28). As a preacher, Paul did his best, 'to this end I labour'. Encouragingly, he was able to add, 'struggling with all his energy, which so powerfully works in me' (Colossians 1 v. 29). The energy is the Spirit's dynamism which, arguably, is the substance of which unction consists.

The need for unction confirms that there is more to preaching than speaking![11]

Dr. Lloyd-Jones distinguished between the sermon and the act of preaching. The former might be well prepared and laced with good material, but that does not guarantee an effective and powerful delivery. When Paul wrote to the Thessalonians, he recalled the time when he was with them in the same way he had reminisced when writing to the Corinthians. He remembered the nature of his preaching. This had been 'not simply with words but also with power, with the Holy Spirit and with deep conviction' (1 Thess. 1:5). The vital statement is 'not simply with words'. A successful preaching goes beyond speaking out.

DML-J often stressed this. Occasionally, he ran the danger of putting so much emphasis on the dynamic of the Spirit in the act of preaching that an outsider might feel that this was all he had in mind.

It was a calculated risk. He knew he was taking it and might be misunderstood.[12] But he was correcting what he felt to be an imbalance in modern philosophies of preaching. Both by his frequent pleas and by his own diligent example, he laid solid stress on the need to work hard at sermon preparation and to expect the Spirit's unction.

To say that preaching requires words is to state the obvious: thoughtfully prepared concepts, ideas and speech patterns are the substance of which sermons are made. But diction, articulation, quality of thought and form all added together are not enough. The total approximates to 'word only'. More is to be expected. Essentially this was what Paul was saying in his Thessalonian letter. He was grateful that his ministry was effective because of the power of the Spirit which accompanied it.

Lloyd-Jones emphasised Paul's point and advised preachers that as Sundays approach they should give careful attention to the preparatory groundwork, but they ought also to seek for the Spirit to own what is to be declared:

> The man should prepare his two sermons and put all his abilities and knowledge into them; but he should realise that unless the Spirit comes upon them, they will be of no avail. The Spirit generally uses a man's best preparation. It is not the Spirit [I]or preparation; it is preparation *plus* the unction and the anointing and that which the Holy Spirit alone can supply.[13]

In the grace of God unction may still flow when the preparation is hurried and inadequate

Dr. Lloyd-Jones referred to a visit to England undertaken by Samuel Davies and Gilbert Tennent. Their purpose was to raise money for a newly-formed college. The journey was so terrible they thought they would be shipwrecked. When they got to London, they wanted to hear Whitefield. They were delighted to learn that he was in town and went to listen to him the following morning. In his diary recording the event, Davies was to write, 'It became clear to me quite soon in the service that Mr. Whitefield must have had an exceptionally busy week; obviously he had not had time to prepare his sermon properly . . . from the standpoint of construction and ordering of thought, it was very deficient and defective; it was a poor sermon'. 'But', Samuel Davies continued, 'the unction that attended it was such that I would gladly risk the rigours of shipwreck in the Atlantic many times over in order to be there just to come under its gracious influence.'[14]

We emphasise that Lloyd-Jones was not advocating slovenliness in preparation, but there are times when the preacher may go less prepared than he would wish into the pulpit and yet still deliver a very powerful address. Unction is not a reward even for hard work, however laudable the discipline is.

Unction causes the preacher to 'burn'

'Preaching', exclaimed Lloyd-Jones, 'is theology coming through a man who is on fire'.[15] The best description is 'Logic on Fire! Eloquent Reason!'[16] The combustion and blaze depend on unction for ignition. As Elijah awaited a fire-bolt from heaven to set ablaze his well-prepared and deliberately water-drenched offering, so the preacher longs for an empowering on his preaching. In the pulpit, there are choice times when the occupant knows that he is being energised in a special way; he has a great authority and winsomeness.

There is an interesting reference, though of a different sort, in the Book of James to the damaging and fearful power of the tongue. We read, '[It] also is a fire . . . it corrupts the whole person, sets the whole course of his life on fire, and is itself set on fire by hell' (3:6). It seems to us that this is the very antithesis of the unction we are seeking to define and declare. But negative examples can be helpful by providing us with a stark contrast. A tongue ignited with holy fire is what the preacher wants: reason ablaze!

Oswald Sanders writes eloquently of such an anointing resting on the cousin of the Lord Jesus.

> Immersed in the oil of the Spirit and touched by the fire of God, his life became incandescent. The secret of his effectiveness lay in the fact that his whole personality was dominated and inter-penetrated by the Holy Spirit.[17]

Sanders is, of course, speaking of John the Baptist. In so doing, he gives a description, if not a definition, of a man who preaches with unction—the penetration and domination of the personality by the Spirit.

Even the most experienced and godly preachers will still need further instalments of unction for specific tasks[18]

Lloyd-Jones takes us to the Apostle John for an example. He was essentially a spiritual man. As we shall remind ourselves later, he wrote of unction in his first epistle. John was present when the Lord breathed his Spirit upon the disciples in the Upper Room. He was also among the one hundred and twenty who waited for the Promise of the Father some weeks later. In addition to this, he testified, in the opening chapter of Revelation, to another anointing. In front of him was the task of relaying to the seven churches of Asia the message of God. But Lloyd-Jones felt it was significant that even John, having served the Lord so faithfully over such a long period of time, when faced with the challenge of storing up and delivering the message of the Book of Revelation, needed further help. This was given. Thus John declaimed, 'I was in the Spirit on the Lord's day' (Rev. 1:10 *AV*).

Unction involves the congregation

Dr. Lloyd-Jones had a high estimation of his congregation. That he loved and appreciated his people is obvious from the endearing way in which he sometimes refers to them. In addition to his comment that one cannot preach in 'cold blood' is the implication that you cannot preach without a congregation! In these days of media communication, the point is not as absurd as it seems. To speak in front of a camera or microphone without the presence of a congregation is not preaching.

> The very presence of a body of people in itself is a part of the preaching . . . It is not a mere gathering of people; Christ is present. This is the great mystery of the Church. There is something in the very atmosphere of Christian people meeting together to worship God and to listen to the preaching of the Gospel.[19]

The fact that the Bible is used and exposition is attempted does not qualify it to be rated as preaching. The presence of a congregation is vital. There is an interaction between the pulpit and pew. The preacher needs his hearers' empathy and prayers.[20] On one occasion DML-J challenged his congregation to appreciate their importance in the area of intercession, 'How much time do you give to praying that the preachers of the Gospel may be endued with the power of the Holy Ghost? Are you interceding about this? Are you concerned about this?'[21]

He narrated an incident which was probably a rare piece of autobiography.[22] It involved successfully preaching a sermon to the home congregation and repeating it a couple of weeks later in a different church. There was no transfer of success and blessing despite the fact the same material was in use. What is the explanation? After all, on the first occasion 'your little sermon was taken up and you were given this special unction and authority in an unusual manner, and so you had that exceptional service'. Two possible reasons are proffered, (i) it wasn't much of a sermon after all and on the latter occasion you were relying on it without the special effusion of the Spirit or, (ii) the unction had actually rested upon your hearers. The first time you received something from them. But on the following occasion, there was no exchange between the listeners and yourself.

The preacher should receive something from the congregation. There is an interplay, action and response, and this often makes a very vital difference . . . the responsiveness and eagerness of his congregation lifts him up and enlivens him. He is to be open to this and looking for it. Otherwise, he may 'miss one of the most glorious experiences that ever comes to a preacher'.[22]

REVIEW

Our eight points should have helped us to see what are some of the general characteristics of unction which Dr. Lloyd-Jones emphasised. Basically, unction is what propels the preacher along. It makes the act of preaching special. This is not to say that unction is not given in the course of sermon preparation. An anointing can come as the preacher's mind and heart are enlivened and warmed when in the study.

Now we proceed to examine what the New Testament has to say about our Lord and the disciples as they embarked on the preaching ministry.

THE EXPERIENCE OF OUR LORD

Lloyd-Jones took the ministry of our Lord as an anchorage. The Saviour commenced preaching in his hometown of Nazareth. He was given one of the scrolls of the Old Testament which contained the prophecy of Isaiah. Deliberately and pertinently he opened it at the sixty-first chapter and, in the hearing of the worshippers, read out, 'The Spirit of the Lord is on me, because he has anointed me to preach good news to the poor . . .' (Luke 4:18).

Handing the scroll back to the attendant, as was the custom in his time, he then sat down and began to preach. His opening statement was nothing short of sensational. In it, he twice made the claim that Isaiah's prediction had just come true, 'Today this scripture is fulfilled in your hearing' (v. 21).

All this occurred after our Lord had been baptised by his cousin John in the waters of the Jordan and had known the descent of the Spirit. This was visibly attested by the dove which settled on him (Luke

3:22). Then he was driven into the wilderness. There he endured a fast for forty days and nights which culminated in the temptations. He went into the wilderness 'full of the Holy Spirit' (Luke 4:1) and returned to his native Galilee 'in the power of the Spirit' (v. 14).

In his local synagogue, he described what had happened to him by quoting the verses from Isaiah—he had been anointed with the Spirit.

In our excursion into the Old Testament, we recalled that anointing was something done to priests and kings as they were ordained into their respective calling. The threefold offices of prophet, priest, and king converge in the person of the Lord Jesus. The three streams flow into the one river. So our Lord is the King who is greater than Solomon (Luke 11:31), the great High Priest superior to Moses and his household (Heb. 3:3; 4:14) and the great Prophet through whom God spoke his final message in the 'last days' (Heb. 1:2).

For Lloyd-Jones, a fundamental question is how the descent of the Holy Spirit upon our Lord affected his subsequent ministry. In case some of our readers still feel that his position changed toward the end of his preaching career,[24] it is interesting to note that there are references to his tackling this issue both in his early and later works. For example, at a conference of students in Canada in the early 1950s, he was asking the same question and giving the same answer as he did in his later sermons from John's Gospel. In both, the similarity of thought, argument, conclusion, and even language is quite remarkable.[25] He noted that the Lord did not preach before his baptismal experiences. He needed the baptism in the Spirit to launch him into his public, preaching ministry.

DML-J stiffened his conclusion by taking us to the occasion when reference is made to the sealing of the Lord by the Holy Spirit. He considered that the sealing and the Baptism of the Spirit are synonymous.[26] Following on from the feeding of the five thousand, the next day the Lord mentioned the miracle. But he made more than just an aside to his disciples. He spoke of what his Father had done for him. 'Do not work for food that spoils, but for food that endures to eternal life, which the Son of Man will give you. On him, God the Father has placed his seal of approval' (John 6:27).

Lloyd-Jones is again quite consistent with the teaching he gave earlier when preaching his sermons on the Ephesian Epistle. The sealing of the Son was marked by the descent of the Holy Spirit. He argued that God the Father sealed the Son at the Jordan when he sent the Holy Spirit upon him, 'there he received the Spirit in fullness'.

Although He was still the Son of God, eternal and co-equal with the Father, he had limited Himself, He had come in the form of a servant, and before He could do His work as the Son of Man and as the Saviour, He needed the power of the Holy Spirit . . . This is surely most helpful as we come to consider the meaning of this term with respect to ourselves. It obviously must mean for us what it meant for the Lord Himself. It means that we can be authenticated, that it can be established by intelligible signs that we are indeed the children of God . . . [27]

DML-J approved Bishop Westcott's definition on sealing. It means 'solemnly set apart for the fulfilment of a charge and authenticated by intelligible signs'.[28] This is precisely what had happened to our Lord at his baptism. The experience was vital for him. In effect, it launched him into his public ministry.

Lloyd-Jones built on this. If such an endowment of power was necessary for the Son of God, how much more will it be needed by the ordinary believer and especially those called to the preaching ministry!

Our Lord himself could not act as witness and as preacher and as testifier to the Gospel of salvation without receiving this endowment of the Spirit. And that, I hope to be able to show you, is the purpose of the Baptism with the Holy Spirit.[29]

Speaking in a slightly different context when preaching one of his addresses on the Ephesian Epistle, he made reference to the Lord's baptism in water and in the Holy Spirit.

. . . He was baptised by John in the Jordan, and was setting out on his public ministry to do His work as the Messiah. The Holy Ghost descended upon Him in the form of a dove. He is now equipped. He is sealed by the Father, He has been anointed by the Spirit to preach and to carry on the work of redemption.[30]

Lloyd-Jones here reflects the view of Thomas Goodwin. The Puritan saw in the sealing of Christ, the work of the Trinity. Goodwin took his readers to 1 John 5:7 (*AV*). He remarked,

'There are three in heaven that bore witness that Jesus Christ is the Son of God . . . all three witnesses concurred then at his baptizing; and thus was Jesus Christ our Lord and Saviour then sealed. Would you have me speak plainly? Though he had the assurance of faith that he was the Son of God, he knew it out of the Scriptures by reading all the prophets . . . yet to have it sealed to him with joy unspeakable and glorious by the witness of all the three Persons, this was deferred to the time of his baptism. He was then "anointed with the Holy Ghost" . . . '[31]

This launched him into his three-year preaching ministry. In another of his volumes, Goodwin concludes: 'The Spirit was he that made him a preacher of the Gospel to utter things which man never did and to speak in such a manner as man never did.'[32]

CRITIQUE

This view has not gone unchallenged. In an article on Lloyd-Jones's pneumatology, Professor Donald Macleod criticised his premise. He cautioned that DML-J had not taken sufficiently into account the uniqueness of Jesus Christ. Our Lord is so different from us he cannot be our model. With eloquence the argument proceeds:

The difference between the sinless Son of the eternal God and our-selves is so vast, we should hesitate to draw conclusions which are hasty and prove to be indefensible. 'He knew no sin', 'no deceit was in his mouth': all that plagues us never contaminated him. His unique experience can hardly become a platform for our own.[33]

Furthermore, Macleod continues to argue that, at his Bar Mitzvah, our Lord was fully aware of his relationship with God. He firmly, but cour teously, replied to Mary and Joseph when his mother reproved him after he was missing in Jerusalem, 'Why were you searching for me? Didn't you know I had to be in my Father's house?' (Luke 2:49). Jesus empha-sised his divine paternity. He was clear in his perceptions even at this early age—thus the impact he had made on the religious leaders in the Holy City (v.47).

Moreover, our Lord's conception and birth were a result of the miraculous working of the Holy Spirit (Luke 1:35). Surely, he was no less blessed of the Holy Spirit than his cousin John. And we are told that the Baptist was filled with the Holy Spirit even from birth (1:15).

Putting all this together, Macleod affirms that we are on shaky ground if we claim support for a definite two-stage approach to the experience of the Spirit from the example of our Lord. The ground is even less able to hold the weight of this reasoning if we attempt to make our Lord's experience a blueprint for our own.

We confess that we have come across nothing in Dr. Lloyd-Jones's sermons where he deals with this view head-on. Nonetheless, there are pointers to indicate what his rejoinders would have been.

Of course, he recognised that our Lord was both the Son of God and the Son of Man. He was divine and he was human. His humanity was very real and we must always consider this in the light of the spiritual experiences through which he passed.

> He had lived as a man, he had worked as a carpenter, but now at the age of thirty, he was setting out in the ministry, and—here is the teaching—*because he had become a man and was living life in this world as a man* , though he was still the eternal Son of God, *he needed to receive the Spirit in his fullness , and God gave him the Spirit.*[34]

Years before Lloyd-Jones preached that, he addressed the same issue at the Canadian students' conference to which we have referred.

He was speaking about the authority of the Holy Spirit in the ministry of the Lord. He realised that the commencement of the Lord's ministry is 'unique'. Here is Jesus Christ depicted as being filled with the Holy Spirit in order that he might fulfil his role as Messiah. Lloyd-Jones took his audience to John's Gospel 'God giveth not the Spirit by measure unto him' (John 3:34 *AV*). The Doctor recognised the difficulty of grasping what has happened, bearing in mind who the Lord is. He confessed:

> This is a mystery, but it seems clear that even the Son of God (for the purpose of his mediatorial work on earth) could not have done the work that had been given Him to do unless the Father had thus 'given' Him the Holy Spirit. Jesus Christ was still the second Person in the blessed Holy Trinity, but He had laid aside the insignia of His glory . . . that is why he had to pray . . . [35]

He reasoned his case further and tied it in with his understanding of Acts 10:38 which speaks of God's anointing his Son. The only conclusion he feels is that the Lord could not have done his work had he not received 'the authority, the anointing, this unction which the Holy Ghost alone can give'.[36]

Moreover, DML-J would have had the right to ask those who differed from him how they theologised the account of the descent of the

Spirit on the Son of God bearing in mind what immediately followed. Why do the evangelists emphasise the ministry of the Spirit at the beginning of the Lord's public preaching? Why did he not preach before the Holy Spirit came upon him in this remarkable way? Is it not reasonable to suppose that the evangelists were implying that something of great significance had happened to him, which was to have a parallel in principle, if not in degree, with the experience of the disciples on the Day of Pentecost? As he was anointed with the power of the Spirit, can we not take his example, in some way, as a pattern for ourselves?

THE EXPERIENCE OF THE DISCIPLES

In consecutive chapters, Luke records two occasions when our Lord sent out groups of disciples to 'preach the Kingdom of God'. At the beginning of the ninth chapter, the evangelist notes the instruction which they were given. They were told not to make provision for their itinerary. If they were not well received, they were to symbolise the rejection and that they had fulfilled their responsibility by shaking the dust from off their feet. In the following chapter, information is given of seventy-two men who were sent out in pairs. They, too, registered the reception they received. They preached about the kingdom. As with the first group, their preaching was accompanied by miraculous phenomena.

Despite all this experience, they were still not reckoned to be sufficiently qualified to take up the preaching ministry directly after the resurrection of the Lord.

Charles Spurgeon made reference to these preliminary preaching tours and the disciples' efforts at ministry prior to their Pentecostal experience. He claimed he had 'not the slightest doubt' that their attempts at ministry were crude and incomplete. He reasoned that they showed more of 'human zeal than of divine unction'. His argument is basically one from silence. He believed that had their preaching been significant there would have been a permanent record. He contrasts these itineraries and the lack of information with what happened on and after the Day of Pentecost: 'no sooner had the Holy Spirit fallen than Peter's first sermon is recorded, and henceforth we have frequent notes of the utterances of apostles, deacons and evangelists'.[37]

If we continue in the Gospel of Luke for a while, we note specific instructions which were given to the disciples regarding their future ministry. They are very plain, quite detailed, and highly significant. They are found in the account of the last resurrection appearance recorded by the gospeller (Luke 24:44-9).

When Lloyd-Jones commented on this, he prefaced his remarks by acknowledging this 'as (one of) the most important passages which deal with this matter' and continued:

> . . . here we have men who, you would have thought, were in a perfect position and condition already to act as preachers. They had been with our Lord for three years; they had heard all His discourses and instructions; they had seen all His miracles; they had the benefit of being with Him, looking into His face, and having personal conversation and communion with Him. Three of them had witnessed His Transfiguration, all of them had witnessed the Crucifixion and the burial, and above all, they were all witnesses of the fact of His physical resurrection.[38]

Because Lloyd-Jones put such an emphasis on the passage we pause to examine it and its parallel in the Acts of the Apostles in some detail.

LUKE 24 AND ACTS 1

The narrative follows on from when the Lord had appeared to two disciples on the Emmaus Road. These recounted what had happened to the other eleven in Jerusalem. The Lord suddenly appeared. He drew attention to his hands and feet, then he asked for something to eat. They gave him broiled fish. What follows next, for our purposes, is highly significant. We emphasise certain steps in the information and instructions contained in the passage.

- The Eleven were *given spiritual illumination*: the Lord 'opened their minds so they could understand the Scriptures'.
- The claim was made that *recent events had fulfilled the prophetic scriptures*, 'Christ will suffer and rise from the dead on the third day.'
- *The heart of the Gospel was isolated*, 'repentance and forgiveness of sins'.
- *The method of communication* in which the disciples were to be involved was identified 'this will be preached in his name'.
- *The initial location and then the widest parameters of the preaching ministry were defined* 'to all nations, beginning at Jerusalem'.
- *The disciples' unique qualification was recognised*, 'you are witnesses of these things'.

Recall DML-J's statement. He reckoned that at any ordination service such candidates would be considered well qualified to be sent out into the ministry. But our Lord deliberately put a brake on them. Something else was necessary. Notwithstanding the practical apprenticeship which they had served for three years and the completed itineraries, before public ministry could commence, they were told by the Lord to wait in Jerusalem until they received 'what my Father has promised'. Only when this had been experienced would they be equipped for preaching. Then, and only then, could they commence preaching. The 'endowment' would be like putting on a cloak, 'clothed with power from on high.'

We draw parallels from this account in Luke's Gospel of a resurrection experience and his summary statement of the same incident in the Acts of the Apostles 1:4-9:

- *The disciples were told not to leave Jerusalem* but to wait for 'the gift my Father promised, which you have heard me speak about'.
- *John's baptism in water is juxtaposed with the baptism in the Spirit* which will be experienced in a few days' time.
- *They were encouraged to be more interested in receiving power* for ministry than details of any prophetic programme: 'it is not for you to know the times or dates the Father has set by his own authority'.
- *Power will be the consequence of which the promised blessing will be the cause*: 'you will receive power when the Holy Spirit comes on you'.
- *The nature of the task is defined*: 'you will be my witnesses'.
- *The commencing point and the furthest goals of the future ministry are set*: 'in Jerusalem, and in all Judea and Samaria, and to the ends of the earth'.

After our Lord's ascension the disciples were told not to remain staring into space from the Mount of Ascension. An assurance was given that the Lord who had disappeared from view would return in the same way as he had departed. Then they retraced their steps to Jerusalem and faithfully obeyed the instructions they had received. The Spirit came to equip them so that they could rise to the colossal responsibility which had been entrusted to them. They were to take over where the Lord had left off. They were to be *his* preachers continuing *his* preaching in *his* power—competent as ministers of a new covenant (2 Cor. 3:6).

The similarity between the accounts of the disciples' endowment of the power of the Holy Spirit and that of our Lord is most striking. Yet, even if the argument can be sustained that the Lord's case is unique because of the nature of his person and, therefore, cannot be adjudged as normative, what are we to make of the carefully described experiences of his followers prior to their commencement of a very blessed preaching ministry? Is their experience to be considered simply as descriptive and not prescriptive? If so, on what grounds is this argued? Are we warranted in adopting this interpretation from the text? Are there qualifying passages which make such an assertion? If so, which are they? Moreover, why are there several passages in the Acts of the Apostles containing a description of a second work of the Holy Spirit, which could well be described as the Baptism of the Spirit, having similarities with the outpouring depicted in the second chapter of the book?[39]

Though we have formulated the questions, they are basically not ours. They are there explicitly and implicitly in the astonishingly large number of sermons which Dr. Lloyd-Jones preached on the Holy Spirit.[40]

He had a high estimate of Scripture as a whole, believing it to be the inerrant Word of God. But it is interesting to consider his assessment of the Acts. This book stimulated him to expect great things from the Lord. It describes the Church in a condition of revival. It pictures the Church as he hoped and prayed she would be. It portrays preachers as they successfully presented the Gospel with great power and authority. It projected the image of a dynamic community, the most powerful organism in the world, declaring the Word of God and forever pushing out the frontiers of the Kingdom.

He claimed, in contrast to its modern counterpart, that the essence of New Testament Christianity was its warmth. This, he reckoned, was 'invariably the result of the presence of the Spirit'. He valued the Acts of the Apostles as 'the most lyrical of books'.[41] He exhorted believers to live in it, reckoning it to be 'the greatest tonic that I know of in the realm of the Spirit'.

Lloyd-Jones prayed for a return to the days of the Acts. More than anything else, he wished to witness an outpouring of the Spirit which would lead the Church into revival. He wanted preachers to be powerful in their proclamation with ministries set ablaze by the Spirit's anointing. He never undervalued study and was meticulous in his own preparation, but he argued that, though a man be ever so diligent in his research and learning, if he did not experience the anointing of the Spirit resting on him, he would not know success.

Listen to him as he made the point in his early addresses from the book of Romans:

> You can have a highly educated, cultured ministry, but it will be useless without this power. You can have men who can speak and

expound learnedly, and do many other things, but, if this power is not present, it will end in nothing better than entertainment.[42]

This is a recurrent note in Lloyd-Jones's writings. He held that a man's ministry could be impoverished by an inadequate pneumatology. He gave the last chapter of his book *Preaching and Preachers* to declaring and defending this conviction.

He considered revival to be a phenomenon when multitudes of people are baptised in the Spirit on the same occasion.

I would define a Revival as a repetition in some degree, or in some measure, of what happened on the Day of Pentecost . . . It is a pouring out, or a pouring forth, of the Spirit of God upon a number of people at the same time. Sometimes it has involved one church, sometimes a district or a neighbourhood, sometimes a whole country.[43]

Power in the pulpit is invariably an accompaniment of revival. The Church as described in the Acts of the Apostles is in revival. Thus, at the beginning of the Christian era, the preachers were highly successful; many converts were won, and local churches established.

DML-J believed the reason for the barrenness and sterility which have marked much of modern Christendom is the failure to respond to the lessons which should be gathered from the initiation of the disciples into the preaching ministry.

CRITIQUE

What are we to make of all this? Certainly Lloyd-Jones's challenge deserves consideration in the light of his own success and the awareness recognised by many of a very special anointing which rested on his preaching. Had he been prepared to accept that his ministry was impressive, he would have attributed it to no other reason than the one which we have been presenting.

But is his appreciation of the disciples' experience and of subsequent deductions which he draws concerning the Baptism with the Holy Spirit accurate? It seems that the only way his view can be disputed is by falling back once more on the view that, as with the Lord, they were a special case and are to be placed in a category on their own. Their experience, in a sense, is unique. The Acts describes the birth of the Christian Church. The period through which it passed was transitional. The conclusion of the Apostolic era and the completion of the canon of Scripture saw the end of the first phase. After that, 'normal' church life emerged.

The argument continues that if the Baptism of the Spirit, as taught by Lloyd-Jones, is so vital why is there no evidence of believers being encouraged to seek after such an experience?[44] Moreover, it could be argued that Acts is a historical rather than a didactic book. Therefore the reasoning runs that we cannot safely draw our theological system from it. We should look to the epistles rather than to the Acts in order to formulate our theology.

The danger with such a critique is that it could be tantamount to questioning the authority of one of the canonical books. As part of the New Testament corpus, does the Acts not command equal respect with the other books?

What is more, if the Acts describes a stage which is purely transitional, and yet the picture it presents is one of revival, there is no place left for a theology of revival.[45] To pray that the Church should return to a situation conceded as temporary would be to speak out a nonsense prayer.

If the account in the Acts is to be considered as transitional, the expository preacher should be very careful when referring to this book as he deals with the epistles. But the Acts gives the historical backcloth of the early Church as it paints in the context and radiates the atmosphere. Surely the insights and cameos of church life and evangelism recorded in this book are the dimension from which the letters emerged. A failure to interpret the latter from within the surrounds of the Acts is comparable to the unframing of a masterpiece, or the removal of the visual in a documentary leaving only the sound.

Peter Masters strongly condemned what he believes to have been Lloyd-Jones's unthinking criticism of cessationism.[46] This term describes those who consider the charismatic gifts of the Spirit ceased at the conclusion of the Apostolic era and who generally deny what they call a two-stage experience of the Holy Spirit. For cessationists, conversion and the Baptism of the Spirit denote the same thing, our initiatory experience into the Kingdom of God.

DML-J expressed himself strongly when dealing with this subject. It was a theme to which he often returned in the closing years of his ministry. But it would be wrong to conclude, as Masters implies, that he shifted his opinion in later years as a panic measure because little was happening in the dry, reformed circles from which he had emerged.[47] As we have seen, he was teaching the Baptism of the Spirit as a definite second experience by the early 1950s!

The reason he declared his opinions so forcefully was that he considered the issues at stake to be very high. Remember, he believed that an inadequate pneumatology has a deleterious effect on the pulpit and is responsible for what he considered an intellectualism devoid of Holy Ghost power. Though he was outspoken, as we have noticed, hyperbole is a feature of Lloyd-Jones's style.

It is grossly unwarranted to accuse DML-J of shallow thinking. He was never 'puny and inadequate' in his reasoning let alone 'silly'.[48] Though he rejected an absolute cessationist position, in practice, his stance was not far off those whom he criticised and from whom he has received much rebuff. He *did* assert that *certain* aspects of the Acts record were foundational and would not be repeated.[49] The obvious example is that of the Apostles themselves. With the inclusion of Paul in the list, the Twelve have a unique place in the Church. None would add to their number: the signs of their Apostleship were noted in the miracles which they performed.

Furthermore, Lloyd-Jones felt the ministry of prophet[50] and evangelist[51] to be in the same category. He did not reject speaking in tongues as a possible modern endowment of the Spirit, but he seemed to have some reservation about its recent manifestations and, most certainly, about the methods employed by some to help people become glossolalic.[52]

As for evangelism and prophecy, the ministries continue, but only within the Spirit's sovereignty. There does seem to be a revision of his thought here.[53] In the Ephesians series, he came close to suggesting that the gift of prophecy has ended because there can be no further revelation. But, as we shall see,[54] he later came to appreciate an affinity between preaching and prophecy.

Lloyd-Jones believed that miracles of the standard of the Acts of the Apostles could recur, particularly at the frontiers of the Kingdom, and possibly as things get more bleak toward the end of the age when evil forces will be even more aggressive. But generally, in days of revival, these phenomena have been unusual and rare.

> During those great periods of revival which have come periodically in the history of the Church, the phenomena consisted not so much in the working of miracles or healings as in extraordinary power of preaching and extraordinary depth of conviction and an unusual element of joy and exultation.[55]

DML-J was criticised for arguing so forcefully for the need of unction seemingly to the exclusion of all else. Peter Masters makes an assessment of him at this point, 'all that mattered was that the preacher should have an unction and an anointing of the Spirit, and every blessing would then follow'.[56] He went on to suggest that Lloyd-Jones failed to encourage his congregation in personal evangelism. All they had to do was to turn up faithfully and hear him preach.

There is substance in the criticism that DML-J did not train people in personal evangelism in the way that Masters and Kendall have attempted with their respective congregations. He ran no seminars for this type of activity. An editorial about him when he terminated his ministry at Westminster commented, 'He was hesitant, too, of putting over-much emphasis on personal work or counselling, holding that such activity' goes up when preaching goes down'.[57] He indicated his strong reservations about organisations like Evangelism Explosion.[58] Nor did it seem to occur to him to build up a team to work beside him, let alone get himself a permanent, personal aide. The ministerial assistants he had preached rarely—even men of the ability of Herbert Carson.[59]

Nonetheless, the fact remains that hundreds of people came to the Lord as a result of Lloyd-Jones's preaching and brought friends to hear what he had to say. Even though he seemed apprehensive about people going from door to door, or engaging in tract distribution, an army of people made their way into the Christian ministry as preachers and missionaries because of his influence. Hundreds of students were affected in their own lives and testified to their contemporaries. The growth of the Inter-Varsity Fellowship and the Christian Medical Fellowship, among other groups, is evidence of the persuasive powers and fruit of Lloyd-Jones's ministry.

It was DML-J's practice to have a gospel service each Sunday evening. He never called men and women to the front of the church to register their assent to an invitation, but he could hold his own with any modern evangelist in sounding the clarion call of the Gospel and urging the people to make a positive commitment. Though he was a confessed Calvinist, he would have warmed the heart of many an Arminian in his appeal to the will of his hearers!

Not to see the effect that his evangelistic heart had in inspiring others to a life-time activity reveals a lack of information, or a failure to deal adequately with the facts meticulously recorded by his biographer. Lloyd-Jones did often assert that more was achieved in revival in five minutes than we can do in forty years. But this, of course, is true.

To draw the conclusion that his congregation was passive and evangelistically inert is to claim too much. Westminster Chapel continued to pull in the crowds at a time when church-going was as unfashionable in the United Kingdom as it is thirty years on and when the doctrinal stance of Lloyd-Jones was shared by few preachers.

The multitudes who came to the Chapel were tangible evidence bearing out Lloyd-Jones's assertion that people gather to hear preaching which has the unction of the Spirit.[60]

REVIEW

We may summarise Dr. Lloyd-Jones's position by stating that he believed passionately that Apostolic power for preaching the Gospel is still available within God's sovereignty today. The Acts depicts the Church with preachers on fire; preachers who are given a great boldness and authority. In a word, they had unction. This alone accounts for their astonishing success, which has been repeated in periods when the Spirit of God has been poured out upon the Church. The supply can still be tapped.

Such should be earnestly requested by every minister. The exciting atmosphere of the 'lyrical' Acts of the Apostles with its manifold examples of the Spirit at work in the preaching ministry producing what the Authorised Version calls 'seasons of refreshing' can, in the sovereignty of God, be recaptured. The history of revival furnishes us with undeniable proofs. My enquiries now take us to the pivotal question of how this unction may be received. And I shall preface this by taking a sideways look at another issue which is both controversial and illuminating.

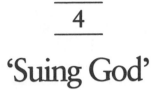

4

'Suing God'

You that are believers, wait for a further promise of the Holy Ghost as a sealer and sue it out with God . . . Sue this promise out, wait for it, rest not in believing only, rest not in assurance by graces only; there is a further assurance to be had.[1]

Thomas Goodwin

There is all the difference in the world between preaching merely from human understanding and energy, and preaching in the conscious smile of God . . . [2]

I take leave to say in all humility, that there is nothing more blessed under heaven than to know something of the power of the Holy Spirit. I am sorry for those who have never known it as they have preached and tried to expound the Scriptures. There is an almost inexpressible difference between preaching in one's own strength, and preaching in the power of the Spirit. This can happen also in conversation, and in all the activities and endeavours of the Christian [3]

Martyn Lloyd-Jones

The most humbling and wonderful experience for any preacher as he enters the pulpit is to know that God is with him. The most frightening for him is to be in the pulpit and feel that he is on his own.

79

There is a significant term used by the Hebrews to identify when God speaks—the *bat qol* (literally 'daughter of the voice'). At least twice, the voice of God was heard when our Lord engaged in his public ministry. At his baptism, the declaration was made, 'You are my Son, whom I love; with you I am well pleased' (Mark 1:11). On the Mount of Transfiguration, the three close companions of the Lord heard it again, 'This is my Son, whom I love. Listen to him!' (Mark 9:7).

To bring pleasure to the Lord in the discharge of his message is the goal of the preacher. To enter the pulpit as Moses descended from Sinai with the radiance of God upon him must surely be the preacher's greatest desire (Exod. 34:29-35). The smile of God upon the messenger conveys the signature of God upon the message. Moses experienced this priestly blessing in some measure, Paul testified to its increase (2 Cor. 3:18), our blessed Lord knew it absolutely. Preachers need to seek it always.

If unction is power which comes from the throne of God, it must authenticate the preacher's preaching. It is not claiming too much to say that this is why Pharaoh believed and acted on Joseph's message, though arguably eight years would have to elapse before the Hebrew could produce empirical verification about the interpretation of Pharaoh's dreams. The pagan king recognised Joseph's anointing. Was not this why Herod was constantly drawn back to listen to John the Baptist even though the strangely dressed preacher had a message which cut into him? Unction occurs when God makes his face shine on the preacher. And the power of the anointing can be felt by those who hear the message. Unction may well be defined, in the words of Lloyd-Jones as the smile of God upon the preacher. The world always needs preachers on whom God has smiled and is smiling.

In this chapter, it is our goal to make clear what the preacher can do to ensure that he is in the place where, in the language of the Authorised Version of our Bible, the Lord will 'lift up the light of his countenance' upon him and 'give him peace'. Immediately it must be said that there is no simple formula. Lloyd-Jones offered no easy equation which, if worked through, would produce the desired results. Unction, like revival, rests within God's sovereignty. When preaching on revival, DML-J declared, 'You cannot stop a revival any more than you can start it. It is altogether in the hands of God'.[4]

There are, however, further matters which must detain us a while. We have to determine how, with his pneumatology, he interpreted a text which, at first reading, seemed to threaten his position.

THE UNCTION OF 1 JOHN 2:20, 27

Lloyd-Jones was aware that he might well be criticised by referring his teaching to the statement of John in his first epistle. When seeking to establish the meaning of the Greek words translated 'anointing' or 'unction' (AV) as used in the New Testament, it will be remembered that we cited this reference.[5] In this instance the word *chrisma*[6] highlights not the action but concentrates on what happens to the person who has been blessed. The Apostle states:

> But you have an anointing from the Holy One, and all of you know the truth.
>
> As for you, the anointing you received from him remains in you and you do not need anyone to teach you

Here, therefore, is cause and effect; the cause is the anointing, the effect is knowledge of the truth. The issue will come into focus as we raise a few questions.

Is not this descriptive of the believer at the point of conversion? Don't these verses employ the word 'anointing' to describe the initiation into the New Birth? Don't such texts demolish Lloyd-Jones's position? Doesn't his teaching affirm that unction is a blessing which flows from a person's being baptised in the Holy Spirit?

To help us as we come close to the text, we lift out several points in order to clarify the meaning:

- The anointing comes from our Lord; *the Holy One; him.*
- It is made available to every believer and not just the leaders or a group within the Church; *you* (plural), *all; as for you.*
- The anointing promotes an illumination; *the truth.*
- The illumination is completely sufficient; *all* of you know the truth; *you do not need anyone to teach you.*
- Careful study of the Epistle makes it plain that John was writing to warn the Church against the Gnostics.

Gnosis is the Greek word for knowledge. The Gnostics were a group who defected from the Christian community (2:19), claiming they had received superior revelation. They represented a threat to the purity as well as the harmony of the Church.

Countering this, John argued for the adequacy of the Christian faith. It is a complete revelation. Nothing else is to be added. Nothing else is necessary. The Gospel contains all the potential for the life of godliness which Christians are to pursue. As the believer embraces the faith he is given unction—'you have an anointing from the Holy One'. Without it, he cannot be classed as a Christian at all.

However, Dr. Lloyd-Jones claimed that this anointing, so vital to conversion, has nothing to do with power for service, authority in preaching, or boldness in witness. He reasoned that this verse describes something that is non-experimental. 'It is the first rung on the ladder of assurance.' But there is more. He taught that there are two further levels of assurance, the third being the sealing or Baptism of the Spirit.[7] He declared, 'clearly this sealing with the Spirit does not apply here because you can have this unction and spiritual understanding and still not know this sealing'.[8]

There are two significant occasions where this anointing is illustrated in the course of the Gospel record. DML-J explained how he interpreted 'this unction and the spiritual understanding'.

There is the experience of the two on the Emmaus Road. They had enjoyed the inestimable privilege of listening to a long Bible study given to them by the Lord. We read that 'beginning with Moses and all the Prophets, he explained to them what was said in all the Scriptures concerning himself' (Luke 24:27). He responded to their request to stay with them longer while at Emmaus. During the breaking of bread we read, 'Then their eyes were opened and they recognised him' (v. 31). They testified to a strange warming of their hearts during the preceding discourse. And from their subsequent action it is perfectly obvious that they had been given insight. What they apprehended and believed they went to share with others (vv. 33-5). Observe how Luke carefully recorded that 'their eyes were opened'. Something was done for and to them. This was the anointing. It was a reversal of their previous condition clearly described earlier in the chapter.

Then there was the occasion when our Lord appeared to the Eleven. After inviting his disciples to touch him and establish that he was not a ghost, he showed them the wounds he received when crucified. Next, he ate in their company. Following this, he directed their attention to the Old Testament. At this point, we read, 'Then he opened their minds so they could understand the Scriptures' (Luke 24:45). Lloyd-Jones continued, 'They received it; and they could not have received it without the enlightenment by the Holy Spirit; but still they had not received the special blessing which came to them on the day of Pentecost.'

Thus, he claimed, this enlightenment corresponds to the initial anointing of every believer—'unction from the Holy One' (*AV*)—to which John refers. Thus, also, he disengaged it from the subsequent, powerful Pentecostal experience of Spirit baptism.

DML-J saw a parallel between such incidents and the teaching of Paul. In the second chapter of the First Corinthian Epistle, the Apostle dealt with the intransigence of those whom he called 'the rulers of this age' (v. 6). Why did they not respond to the Gospel? In the previous chapter, Paul had asserted that the Cross was a stumbling block to the Jews and foolishness to the Gentiles. The reason for this was that they had not entered into 'God's secret wisdom, a wisdom that has been hidden' (1 Cor. 2:7). Drawing from Isaiah 64 and 65, he concluded that 'God has revealed it to us by his Spirit' (v. 10). Paul reasoned closely that there needs to be an illumination granted by the Holy Spirit so men can apprehend spiritual truth. In other words, this anointing is an essential aspect of conversion. The man who was blind now sees! He is given eyesalve by the Holy Spirit (Rev. 3:18).

This is how Lloyd-Jones understood what Calvin termed the *testimonium Spiritus internum*. In one of his earlier books, DML-J argued that the Corinthian passage affirmed this.

> It is only as the result of the work, and *the illumination of the Holy Spirit* within us that we can finally have this assurance about the authority of the Scriptures. This is just to say, in other words, what the Apostle Paul states so clearly in 1 Corinthians 2:14 'the natural man receiveth not the things of the Spirit of God: for they are foolishness unto him: neither can he know them, because they are spiritually discerned' (*AV*).[9]

Here Lloyd-Jones rested his case. The reference to unction in the Epistle of John has to do with our initiation as Christians—the moment when we see the light. As we have noted, this is what he perceived to be the first level of assurance. It is an anointing or unction which brings understanding. As a result, 'certain ignorant, more-or-less illiterate people have been able to discriminate between truth and error much better than the great doctors of the Church. They were simple enough to trust to the "anointing", and thus they were able to distinguish between things that differ'.[10]

Not everyone, however, will be as convinced as DML-J that entry into the Christian Faith, what the Apostle John terms an 'anointing', is entirely non-experiential. John Calvin taught that the Baptism of the Spirit was the initiation into the Christian Faith. He believed this to be a 'secret' work, yet it brings immediate assurance and joy as it had to the two on the Emmaus Road. To a degree then, it is experiential.[11] John Owen took a similar view.[12]

Lloyd-Jones's case still holds, even if it is conceded that an experiential element is involved. Many believers who would testify to a felt experience of salvation—an awareness which goes beyond what A. W. Tozer called 'a mere deduction from the text'[13]—yet long for an overwhelming encounter of God's grace and empowering. Dr. Lloyd-Jones believed the Apostle Peter was describing the consequence of such when he referred to Christians being 'filled with an inexpressible and glorious joy' (1 Pet. 1:8). He thought it was significant that Peter observed how the prophetic ministry of the Old Testament era had been fulfilled and developed in the New Testament period by 'those who have preached the Gospel to you by the Holy Spirit sent from heaven' (v. 12). This, he believed, refers to the particular unction which rested on the proclaimer of the Gospel (to differentiate it further from the 1 John 2 unction).[14]

THE MESSAGE

As we have seen, Dr. Lloyd-Jones's pneumatology influenced his views and approach to preaching. Not all will agree with his formulation of the doctrine of the baptism in the Spirit. He believed, as we have noted,[15] that there is a great difference between preparing an address and preaching it in the power of the Holy Spirit. The former may demand intellectual ability, a knowledge of the Bible, a good command of the English language, but it does not necessarily constitute a powerful declaration of the Gospel which will transform lives.[16]

He expresses this point strongly with a personal reference in one of his sermons on revival. He had been referring to the verses from Peter which have just occupied our attention:

> Men can preach, alas, how well I know it. A man can preach without the Holy Spirit; I can expound the word with intelligence, but that is not enough. We need the demonstration of the Spirit and of power ... *What a man can never do is what God does.* The Holy Ghost sent down from heaven, the descent of power, this uniqueness, this special manifestation of the presence, and of the power of God.[17]

Ideally, preaching is delivering a message. He believed that there should be a return to this concept. He eschewed the word 'address', vilified the term 'quiet talk'[18] but believed that the term 'message' appropriately describes what the preacher is about. He is a herald bringing a communication from the throne of God which demands a hearing and a response. 'Scripture has to be fused into a message with point and power', the sermon must move people, giving them a sense of the glory of God. Thus, it is necessary to bring the message and deliver it in 'demonstration of the Spirit and of power'.[19]

The prime responsibility of the preacher is to determine what the Holy Spirit wants to say to his congregation from that passage. The preacher will be open to returning to the verse several times. He is not commenting on a text, he is expounding Scripture with a view to the needs of his pastoral charge. There is a fundamental difference between writing commentaries and preaching expository sermons which may later be encapsulated in a book.[20]

It is this desire to recapture both the urgency and the authority which should be the hallmark of preaching that caused Lloyd-Jones to emphasise the necessity for unction so strongly. If there is a degree of overstatement in his views, it is surely pardonable when something vital has been woefully overlooked. It takes effort to push a heavy pendulum that has become stuck back to its normal position. He wanted to restore a balance.

He believed that, however educated and cultured the ministry might be, without the power of the Spirit, it would be useless. 'You can have men who can speak and expound learnedly, and do many other things, but if this power is not present it will end in nothing better than entertainment.'[21]

THE ADVOCATE AND THE WITNESS

It is therefore the power of the Spirit that transforms a man who seems to have a clinical detachment from his subject matter. The endowment causes him to become passionately involved in declaring his burden. The distinction, Lloyd-Jones argued, is illustrated in the character of an advocate in contrast to a witness. The latter gives testimony to what he has personally experienced. He is involved in his subject matter. The advocate reflects what he has been told. It is second-hand. He is at a disadvantage. The person who is able to say what he saw, and thus relate the experience graphically, is better qualified to speak than the person who relates on behalf of another what he has been told. The preacher must see himself as a witness. This will make his ministry compelling, giving it passion, fervour and persuasiveness.[22]

In our preaching we must have this baptism or we fail. We may preach as advocates, but not necessarily as witnesses. Have we a greater experience of the presence of God than the Old Testament saints had? If not, why not? We should have.

PROPHECY

We promised in the closing paragraph of our last chapter to take a side-step and to look at a controversial issue. We refer to prophecy as an assured spiritual gift for today. In light of the current debate[23] on this, it will be helpful to enquire into Dr. Lloyd-Jones's views on the subject in relationship to preaching. If it is admitted that charismatic gifts can be granted throughout the Church Age then, obviously, claims will be made by some people or groupings to have received such engifting.

A number of reactions to this can be anticipated. Cessationists will immediately dismiss the claims. Non-critical people may find themselves almost at the mercy of those asserting prophetical gifting. Some will warn that prophecy brings the danger of a 'hot-line', more dramatic and more authoritative than preaching. Those who are in a middle position between stark cessationism and rank gullibility will need to judge the claimed, inspirational messages that they hear or that are brought to them.

Why should a work on the preaching method of Martyn Lloyd-Jones investigate, in part, this subject? There are at least four reasons and possibly a fifth:

- He was not a cessationist, in principle. But our earlier comments deserve attention.[24]

- He was absolutely committed to the necessity of preaching, the authority of which is enhanced as the preacher is borne along by the power of the Holy Ghost.

- He was identified with Reformation theology. Among the reformers, Calvin referred to preaching as prophecy. William Perkins, who wrote the first book in English on preaching, called it *The Art of Prophesying*.[25] With some qualification, as we shall see, Lloyd-Jones inclined to the view that there is a bond between preaching and prophesying.

- On one occasion, he expressed in a compelling fashion his disenchantment with the worship patterns of most churches including his own. Ideally, there should be a pronounced participatory element in worship.[26] This may include prophecy.

- The final, more tentative, reason which we put forward is that there are some who believe the position they have embraced in regard to charismatic gifts is but a further development of the views held by Lloyd-Jones.[27]

One of the first direct comments on record made by Lloyd-Jones in this area was at a private meeting he addressed in 1941 . He identified what he felt to be weaknesses in evangelicalism. He spotlighted several main items before coming to three sub-points. He referred to the legacy of D. L. Moody (for whom he had expressed admiration as well as criticism).[28] He was concerned that something less than a biblical idea of an evangelist had emerged: a layman who cracks jokes, sets people at ease, rides high on personality, and incorporates an appeal into his technique. Another of his sub-points was the Keswick 'higher-life' movement with its 'give up, let go and let God' appeal. But first place in his warnings was given to the overspill of influence from Edward Irving's Catholic Apostolic Church.

Irving was a defrocked minister of the Church of Scotland. He had become a celebrated preacher in London—'by many degrees the greatest orator of our times'[29]—in the nineteenth century and achieved notoriety as the result of the manifestation of spiritual gifts in his church.[30] Irving had interacted with J. N. Darby and the leaders of the Brethren Movement. The common denominator was not Irving's views on the *charismata*, but, rather, his novel, defined and exciting views on the Second Advent.[31] It was the eschatology of Irving which was to make an impact on Christendom through the Brethren. Murray comments, 'all the salient features of Darby's scheme are to be found in Irving . . .'[32]

However, it was not his eschatology (nor his pneumatology) which brought Irving under the censure of his denomination, but his Christology. This was considered heretical and led to the suspension of his ministerial licence.[33] But it was his views on the resurgence of spiritual gifts in addition to his outstanding preaching ability which earned him fame and are significant for our purpose.

Lloyd-Jones attempted an evaluation of the aftermath of Irvingism in this respect. He reckoned that:

> The availability of gifts of prophecy (which) lessened the need for scholarship. A rich and accurate knowledge of Scripture was essential unless the Early Church's charismatic gift of prophecy, in the form of new knowledge, was restored as Irving believed was happening in his time.[34]

Here DML-J seems to be suggesting that prophecy per se must be revelatory. Its original function was to compensate members of the early

Church for not having the benefits of a full Bible which later believers would enjoy. Any claims for the restoration of the gift of prophecy appear to imply the need for additional revelation. Such aspirations and, indeed, practices weaken the Church as they undermine the doctrine of the sufficiency of Scripture. Thus Lloyd-Jones's warning on the dangers of Irvingism.[35]

Seventeen years later, during the course of his series from Paul's Epistle to the Ephesians, he referred to what are sometimes called the ministry gifts with which the risen Lord has blessed his Church (4:11-14). In doing this, DML-J also took a sideways glance at the related passage in 1 Corinthians 14 where the Apostle declares, 'Let the prophets speak two or three, and let the other judge. If anything be revealed to another that sitteth by, let the first hold his peace' (vv. 29-30 AV).

We pose two questions. How did Lloyd-Jones interpret this? What did the people referred to in Corinth actually experience?

He believed that a revelation or message or some insight into truth was given to them. As a result of this, these engifted Christians were able to make utterances which were of benefit and profit to the Church.[36] However, this was a temporary expedient. He reasoned in a similar fashion, as he had in 1941, that in the first century the canon of Scripture was not complete, 'the Truth had not yet been expounded in written words'. Thus the gift was necessary. However, once these New Testament documents were written, the need was met.

He warned that preachers should not enter pulpits purporting to have received revelations on a par with Scripture. Rather, they should claim to be men who have read the Word and have prayed and believe as a result that the Holy Spirit has illuminated and enlightened their understanding. Thus they are equipped with a message for the people.[37]

He felt his conclusions about the cessation of the office of a prophet found further support from the absence to any reference to prophets and prophecy in the pastoral epistles, which were written at a later date than the others.

However, even in these sermons, he did not believe that one could be overconfident. 'The whole question of prophets is a difficult subject, and one must not speak too dogmatically about it'.[38] His later position evolved from the former one[39] which he seemed to find experimentally too restrictive, lining up neither with his further studies in the Scriptures, nor the story of the Church down the ages.

He began to state that 'prophesying' brings us nearer to understanding what the elements of true preaching actually are—a word from God. 'But to me, when a man is truly preaching, he has been given a message. What he has himself acquired as the result of his study of the Scripture and his understanding of a passage this is taken up and *it becomes prophetic utterance.* He is speaking in the Spirit, "in demonstration of the Spirit and of power"' (1 Cor. 2:4 AV).[40] On another occasion, he was to say, 'I believe spiritual gifts can be superimposed on a natural gift'.[41]

Edwin Hatch's Hibbert lectures of 1888 made an impression on him. He referred to them when delivering his addresses on preaching at Westminster, Philadelphia, in 1971. Hatch argued that the influence of Greek rhetoricians had a deleterious effect on preaching. They approached it as an art. Form and structure were all-important. This lessened the concept of freedom and spontaneity. DML-J records Hatch as saying that 'Christian men received messages through the Holy Spirit and got up and delivered them without premeditation, thought or preparation. They had no form, no sermonic form, about them, but were isolated statements . . . there are indications of this in 1 Corinthians 14 and in other places.'[42] Dr. Lloyd-Jones reasoned that there is a great deal of truth in this argument, 'one can see this pneumatic, this prophetic element.'[43] He was fearful that preoccupation with form and symmetry may reduce the 'charismatic' factor. For him, as we are seeing, freedom is essential in the act of preaching. Nonetheless, he believed that the New Testament does indicate that there is a structure in the sermons it records. For example, Peter's discourse on the Day of Pentecost was not a series of disconnected remarks. Similarly, the defence of Stephen reveals an outline, 'he knew where he was going to end before he began and he leads on to that' (Acts 7). He argues that the same can equally be said of Paul's address in Antioch of Pisidia (Acts 13), 'he was speaking to a plan, or, if you prefer it, he had a kind of skeleton or outline. There was certainly form to that address'.

The Word and the Holy Spirit, he believed, generally went together.[44] The Spirit gives the Word and he uses it. But he did not rule out the possibility that the Spirit can speak independently of the Word. This, however, would be the exception and not the norm. In the process of the exposition and application of Scripture the preacher might be so empowered by the action of the Holy Spirit upon his faculties that his preaching would be elevated above the ordinary. For an experience like this, Lloyd-Jones did not balk at using the word prophecy to define it.

A preacher is taken up; he is in this realm of the Spirit, and God is giving a mesage through this man to the people. It is not an inspired utterance in the sense that the Scriptures are, but in another sense, it is an inspired utterance because the Spirit is giving it and using it. Thus a vital element in preaching is a reliance on the Holy Spirit.[45]

In 1973, DML-J evaluated the experience of Howell Harris in an address, to which we have already referred,[46] given at the Puritan Conference, Westminster, London. He was driven to make some very interesting and pivotal observations. As we noted, an endowment of power sometimes rested on Harris' ministry, 'the power came down'.[47] It illustrates the dramatic and vital elements which are sometimes present in preaching. Lloyd-Jones tells us that a man cannot preach in what he calls 'cold blood'. Such a notion, he asserted 'is impossible, he can utter a sermon, he can read or write an essay, but he cannot preach in cold blood'.[48] Certainly Harris did not. How then are Harris's experiences to be theologised? DML-J both raises and answers the query:

> I ask a question at this point. Was not this what the New Testament calls prophesying? Was this not the prophesying that we read of in 1 Corinthians 12 and 14? I would venture the opinion that it is. This is a man delivering what is given to him. It is not *revelation* but *inspiration*.[49]

He felt that this 'pneumatic element' was a component in the views and preaching content of some of the Reformers. Professor David Schuringa brings to attention Calvin's probable use of the word prophecy in this context.[50] DML-J hinted at this when he commented, 'it is interesting to observe that Calvin preached from notes or in an entirely extempore fashion' and immediately Lloyd-Jones continued 'I came across something recently which I had not realised before . . . It is that some of the early Baptists in this country not only did not believe in reading sermons or reciting them; after having read the Scriptures, they would shut the Bible as they began to preach. Their view of preaching was that it was a kind of exhortation, something similar or comparable to the idea conveyed by 'prophecy' in 1 Corinthians 14.' He quotes Thomas Helwys:

> They, as partes or means of worship, read chapters, Texts to preach on and Psalms out of the translation; we already in praying, so in prophesying and singing psalms, lay aside the translation, and we suppose that will prove the truth that all books, even the originals themselves, must be laid aside in the time of spiritual worship, yet still retaining the reading and interpreting of Scriptures in the church for

the preparing to worship, judging of doctrine, deciding of contraries
as the ground of faith and of the whole profession.[51]

Lloyd-Jones interpreted this as meaning that when they read the
Scriptures in a public service, they would give a brief exposition of it
verse by verse. But when they came to preaching, they seemed to leave
that on one side and turn to some kind of prophetic utterance. He
offered some qualification, especially when referring to later Baptists
who 'seem to have been carrying the prophetic element in preaching to
bounds which some of us might question'. But, significantly, he adds,
'at any rate, it is surely something that should make us consider again
whether our preaching should not contain more of this prophetic
element'.[52]

The concept of being taken up and borne along while receiving
inspiration was not foreign to Lloyd-Jones's own experience.
Occasionally, he made reference to such events. Away from the hundreds
who thronged Westminster Chapel, he would pray for the same passion
and fervency when he preached to a handful of people in a Welsh chapel.
Mari Jones remembered an occasion in her chapel. She recounted how
at home after the service 'he asked whether we were conscious of the
heavenly presence. He felt it was not his effort, but rather, he watched
someone preaching by his side.' She added that it was for this anointing
that he yearned.[53]

The experience was not dissimilar from that of his pulpit heroes—
George Whitefield and Howell Harris. Whitefield actually believed at
times that the Spirit was speaking directly to him, something that troubled Edwards.[54]

Inspirational blessing in this fashion brought some remarkable consequences. Lloyd-Jones reports on one occasion how he met a man who
remembered the revival of 1904 and 1905 in Wales. He related what
happened to his own minister. He had pastored this particular church
for a number of years. He was an able man who preached a good and
sound sermon, but he was always halting and hesitant. 'He coughed a
lot, and was a poor speaker in every respect, apart from his subject matter.' One day, he attended a presbytery meeting, something which he had
done on similar occasions many times. At that presbytery, numbers of
other ministers were giving reports of the events which had been taking
place in their churches during the revival. This man listened, and he
came back to his own church completely transformed as a preacher. He
went into his pulpit the next Sunday. His congregation could scarcely
believe that he was the same man. All the hesitation had gone, all the

impediment had disappeared. He spoke with freedom, with authority, and with a power such as they had never known from him before.

It is possible that a preacher can be given insights into what is going to happen. There was the case of the famous Covenanter, Alexander Pedan. DML-J believed it to be beyond dispute that he had the power of foreknowledge and was able to prophesy. He added that the records are authentic and can be read in two great volumes of selected biographies edited for the Wood Row Society.[55] He adduced further testimony,

> I knew a man whose minister had this gift, in the revival of 1904 and 1905. It disappeared completely afterwards, but while the revival lasted he was told beforehand of something that was going to happen in his Church, not once, but morning by morning. He would be awakened out of his sleep at half past two in the morning, and given direct and exact information of something that was going to happen during that day, and it did happen. That is another part of this mental phenomenon.'[56]

One of the most interesting, though lesser-known occasions, when Dr. Lloyd-Jones expounded his views on prophecy occurred when he was preaching from the passage in Romans 12 which refers to charismatic gifts. He was quite specific in dealing with a particular verse: 'We have differing gifts, according to the grace given us. If a man's gift is prophesying, let him use it in proportion to his faith (v. 5).

He asks 'what is this gift of prophecy?'. He tells us that it doesn't mean that a man has the gift of expounding the Old Testament Scriptures as Luther and Calvin believed. (He reckoned that the Reformers were reacting to the teaching of the Anabaptists and their claims for a resurgence of the *charismata*). Neither does it mean the gift of foretelling the future. Rather, 'it is a direct inspiration of the Holy Spirit. It is a person receiving inspiration from the Holy Spirit.' The consequence is that 'they will be able to give a word from God or the Word of God, if you like, to the church'. He further defines prophecy, 'it is the inspired delivery, warning, exhortation, instruction, judging, and making manifest the secrets of the heart'. The gifted person is able to pass on the word of God to the Church and to individuals in the Church.

He is quick, however, to add a cautionary, qualifying note. He warns against 'directional prophecy'. By this, he seems to mean detailed instructions for an individual on a specific matter.[57] He quotes Donald Gee for support. Gee taught against any trends to give personal prophecies, for example, in the case of marriage, moving home, and the like.[58]

He asks further what the distinction is between prophecy on the one hand and teaching and preaching on the other.

> The difference can be put in one word and the word is *immediacy*. It is a word that is given to him, that comes to him. Preaching and teaching are not like that. The preacher and the teacher is the man who takes time to study. He takes time to think, to prepare. He arranges his matter. He has got order, he has got system. That's the truth about preaching and teaching. A preacher and teacher should never enter the pulpit and trust to the immediacy of the moment. That's not preaching and teaching, but that's prophecy. Prophecy is something that is given to a man immediately and directly.[59]

Another difference is that women can be involved in a prophetic ministry. This is clear from the example of Philip's daughters and the fact that in the listing of the gifts in 1 Corinthians 12 and 14, no restriction is placed on women. Lloyd-Jones, no supporter of women's preaching ministry in mixed congregations, argued, however, that they are able to use this gift in a public manner.

We attempt a summary of Lloyd-Jones's position.

- The office of prophet no longer remains. With that of an evangelist and an apostle, it was part of the foundation of the Early Church and had not been reinstated.
- The prophetic element, nevertheless, can still be looked for particularly in preaching. Lloyd-Jones had known this himself.
- Unction and the prophetic are closely woven. The latter is an outflowing of the former.
- When a man is being used in a prophetic manner, he may be given a facility in speech which he does not normally have.
- The prophetic endowment may have a predictive component.
- The inspiration lifts the sermon on to a higher plane, but it is never revelatory in the sense of adding to what has already been received. Rather, it has the effect of applying in a powerful and effective fashion what is contained within the text of Scripture.
- DML-J believed that this prophetic enabling could be experienced by ordinary members of the congregation and should be shared for the benefit of the total church body.[60]
- Women can be involved in this ministry.[61]

With the above qualifications in mind, it is clear that in Lloyd-Jones's estimate the term 'prophesying' brings us to a closer understanding of what biblical preaching consists.[62]

All this taken together, however, is a long throw from practices in some, though not all, present-day charismatic circles. The custom of speaking in the first person singular as though an individual was, without qualification, declaring the Word of God on a par with the Old Testament prophets and New Testament apostles would have been unacceptable to DML-J. Such a procedure threatens the doctrine of the sufficiency of Scripture and, by implication, rules out the possibility of judging the prophecies, an important qualification which the Apostle Paul emphasises (1 Cor. 14:29).

One area where Dr. Lloyd-Jones singularly fails to help us is in the practical outworking of his teaching. By this, we mean that if prophecy can occur outside the ministry of preaching and be practised by members of the congregation, what is the context in which this can happen? Certainly it was not in the somewhat inflexible worship pattern of Westminster Chapel. The same critique must be made of Dr. Lloyd-Jones's sermons on worship both in the Romans' and the Ephesians' series, to which reference has been made. Outspoken about his dissatisfaction with the style of worship at Westminster, he made no move to change it, though it was certainly within his influence to have brought about modifications to allow for what he believed should have found expression.

Lloyd-Jones had inherited, as far as one can gather, the order of service from his predecessor, Dr. Campbell Morgan. We are indebted to Bethan Lloyd-Jones (who became an author when she was over eighty years of age!) for giving us an insight into the informal type of services which her husband, whom she refers to as 'Doctor', encouraged in his Welsh pastorate.[63] It becomes clear that he was accustomed to a more participatory style of worship in the earlier years.

> The church prayer meeting was held on Monday evenings at seven o'clock. After a year or two, it was always well attended, usually somewhere between 200 and 300 people being present. The minister would ask someone to begin with Bible reading and prayer. After a hymn, the meeting would be 'open'—no one was ever called or invited to pray. Doctor felt that the Holy Spirit would inspire and prompt, if we were humble and expectant. If he sensed a break after about a half or three quarters of an hour, he would give out a hymn, and then resume the meeting, and again bring it to a close in another

half hour or so, when silence fell—always allowing a few minutes for the nervous or hesitant, in case they really wanted to pray.

These meetings were blessed beyond words—they were warm and sincere, and we occasionally felt lifted to the very gates of heaven.

The Doctor believed in interfering as little as possible in a prayer meeting . . . Every now and again he would tell us not to make long prayers . . . That was indeed a word in season, for it was not unusual for thirty, sometimes more, sometimes less, to take a public part in a meeting.

RECEPTION

We come now to a key area. If unction is so important in bringing power and a prophetic element to the message—how do we get it? How can we know the priestly blessing upon our ministries? Many a preacher has been driven almost to a point of desperation in wanting to know the answer to this question. Can Lloyd-Jones help us practically? We have sought to sift his addresses and teaching on this subject over the whole compass of his ministry. The following needs to be carefully considered as we remember that a fundamental premise for DML-J is that this bestowal is within the Spirit's sovereignty. It is part of the largesse with which the Lord equips his Church. What, if anything, can the preacher do?

It should be obvious that the first prerequisite admitted by Lloyd-Jones is that the preacher should be a diligent workman

He will not skimp on preparation. He will enjoin the Holy Spirit to enliven his own spirit and mind at this point. Lloyd-Jones underlined the necessity for good groundwork. The Spirit will inform the mind as the preacher studies the Bible. Indeed, he argued that this is most vital when dealing with a difficult passage for exegesis. It is the Spirit who 'illuminates' the Word. Reliance on the Holy Spirit during preparation is essential. DML-J emphasised this at the beginning of one of his addresses from the Sermon on the Mount. He was dealing with our Lord's teaching on the cloak and the second mile (Matt. 5:40-2). It is 'fatal' to rush at these Scriptures 'in an argumentative or a debating mood'. The preacher's own spirit has to be prepared. He has to be in the right attitude. Heart preparation is an essential. He emphasises his point: 'It is not enough to come to Scripture with a mind, however clear, powerful or intellectual. In the understanding and elucidation of Scripture, the spirit is very much more important even than the mind.'[64]

He repeats the advice again in his Ephesians' series of sermons. Referring to the preacher as he enters the pulpit to deliver an address, he asserts: 'his claim should be that he is a man who reads the Word and prays and believes that the Holy Spirit illumines and enlightens his understanding, with the result that he has a message for the people.[65]

In an earlier book, he advises that 'the way to have power' is to study, think, analyse, order, and 'do your utmost'.[66] But on top of this there must be a dependence on the Spirit—preparation plus unction.[67]

He will beseech the Lord to send the Spirit to affirm and empower what he believes should be preached

Lloyd-Jones felt burdened to encourage people to seek for the full blessing of the Holy Spirit. This was basic to his pneumatology. He was following the practice, among others, of Charles Simeon and, especially, Thomas Goodwin. In Goodwin's sermons on Ephesians, which are a model for modern preachers and will profit the serious student immensely, Goodwin regularly exhorted his readers to plead with the Lord for the dynamic of the Spirit. His famous phrase, which DML-J echoed, was 'sue him for it'.

With a similar persistency, the preacher should come before the Lord and ask him to ignite his ministry. On one occasion, Lloyd-Jones permitted himself a rare colloquialism as he made his point reminding us that 'Faint heart never won fair lady' and added, 'of course not!'[68] He continued by issuing the reminder that if we really want something, we are to be persistent and should not be put off. We should keep on even at the risk of making a nuisance of ourselves. 'I say, with reverence, we must become like that in the presence of God if we really understand this and truly desire it. Keep on! Be persistent! Be importunate! 'I will not let thee go!'

We are reminded of Spurgeon's dictum and advice that he gave to his students. They were to go into their studies and prepare as though everything depended on them. This was their mentor's practice. Then, he advised them to do what he did as he ascended the steps into the pulpit and to repeat 'I believe in the Holy Ghost the Lord, the Giver of Life . . .'

The preacher will do his 'spiritual exercises'

Though the preacher is unable to command the Holy Spirit to be with him in an unusual manner while he is preaching, he can so discipline his life that the Spirit will feel comfortable and grace him with special power. Lloyd-Jones spoke a great deal concerning grieving the Spirit.

The preacher must take care not to do this. In one sermon, he warned against 'dampening' the Holy Spirit.

DML-J referred favourably to Whitefield, Wesley, Jonathan Edwards, and Fletcher of Madeley—all great expositors. He said that these men gave themselves to what he termed 'spiritual exercises'.[69] By this he meant self-examination and mortification of the flesh. The result of this was that they entered into the experience of the Baptism of the Spirit, which brought great authority to their ministry.

He clinched the point further. The preacher as a herald should stand in the presence of God in order to receive the message. 'Delivering what has been received first-hand from the Lord' ideally defines preaching. Reception in such a fashion carries with it an authority of which the preacher is aware. This means he may rightfully demand, in the name of God, both a hearing and a response.

The preacher should prepare for freedom in the pulpit!

This is not a contradictory statement.[70] The preacher is to make room for freedom. He will decide not to be so restricted by his notes that consequently he is unable to risk leaving them behind at the Spirit's prompting. To soar on eagle's wings demands a commitment to flight. It requires the preacher to be prepared to leave the ground. Preaching, Lloyd-Jones has told us, has a romance. Part of this is the sheer unpredictability of the event, 'you never know quite what will happen'.

Freedom means that the Spirit will not feel restricted. He won't be grieved because the preacher seems to put more reliance on his studying and the notes with which he has armed himself than on the immediacy of the Spirit. During the act of preaching the Spirit can inform the mind, quicken the reason and reveal aspects of application of which the preacher was totally unaware in his preparation. This should be seized and delivered. And for very good reason, which Lloyd-Jones states:

> There are times when, entirely outside his control, he [the preacher] is given a special authority, special power, an unction which is unusual. And there are good reasons for its bestowal. There are circumstances which he himself is not always aware of, which he only discovers afterwards. Somebody may have come to the congregation who needed a particular message or word, and the preacher, without knowledge on his part, is guided to say something which is just appropriate to that particular state and condition. There is, therefore, this special endowment of power which is called 'the anointing'. *It is*

something that one should seek and covet, it is something for which one should be constantly praying.[71]

It would have been interesting, at this point, to have had Lloyd-Jones's views on Jonathan Edwards's manner of delivery. He recalled how Edwards's practice was to read his script. During the delivery of his sermon, an unusual conviction fell among the people, many writhing in agony as they felt the power of sin and had come to realise the awesome majesty of God. Presumably, Lloyd-Jones would have argued that this demonstrates purely the sovereignty of the Spirit and that normally such an unction does come only as a man is 'free'.[72]

Even when the unction does not flow the preacher will continue and do his best with the enabling that he has

In personal conversation, when asked what we should do when the revival for which we pray does not come, Lloyd-Jones responded, 'we go on!' There are no guarantees given in Scripture about revival. The frequency of the visitation is within the sovereignty of God. This is exactly the case with unction. Sometimes it is there, sometimes it is not. Sometimes it seems not to be there and is! Sometimes the congregation are aware of it and the preacher is not! Such is its romance. But the preacher will always be hoping, praying, expecting to be lifted up beyond himself, given a passion, a train of thought, spiritual insights beyond his usual abilities. If it comes, he will thank God. If it does not, he will still thank the Lord. He is called to do his best, to work within the parameters of his responsibility—diligence in study, godliness in life, faithfulness in prayer. After this he can do no more. He needs to do no more. Like the woman who washed the feet of the Saviour, he has done what he could. He waits for the Lord to take what he has offered and use it, within his sovereignty, for his glory and the extension of his kingdom.

What about the preacher who is not baptised in the Holy Spirit?

This, surely, is an important question which has to be faced. How did Lloyd-Jones deal with it? Many preachers may disagree with his pneumatology and perhaps not be overly troubled about his views on unction. Others, however, may agree but feel they have nothing which accords with the experience which Lloyd-Jones highlights. Do they give up or go on? We have not found any direct statements in his sermons which deal with this head-on. But this does not mean that we are utterly unaware of what would have been his reply to this question. We have recourse to two messages which he brought that throw light on the issue.

The first is found in his treatment of Spiritual Gifts in his Romans' series. We pick up on previous comments.[73] He makes a distinction between what he terms the regular and the more uncommon gifts of the Spirit. He also declares, as we have seen, that a spiritual gift may well be superimposed on a natural gift. A natural gift will manifest itself. A person blessed with a good voice will discover that talent sooner or later. Somewhat puzzlingly, he comments that 'the fact that you cannot be a Christian without having the Spirit of God within you means that each one of us who is a Christian has one of these gifts. But then the Baptism of the Spirit heightens these and adds to them . . . power that we did not have before'.

What he appears to be arguing is that every individual in the Christian community is engifted in some way. Each has a natural gift-ing even at the point of entry into the faith and should seek to realise what this gift is and use it accordingly. The 'natural' gift can be enhanced in its effectiveness by the Baptism of the Spirit. Thus, an ordinary preacher like David Morgan[74] might know what it is to be lifted well beyond his ordinary ability as a preacher. A person in a prayer meeting can be given an eloquence and articulation which is not natural to him. The explanation is that he (or she) might be manifesting the gift of prophecy according to the proportion of their faith.

Prophecy, thus, is distinct from preaching. But it can be part of preaching. Lloyd-Jones affirms, 'I think I know what it is to be teach-ing and preaching and suddenly to find myself prophesying.' And he makes the same comment as we heard him make earlier, 'what I mean is that it is not something you have prepared but at that moment you are given something with unusual force, clarity, and directness because you are uttering and you are listening to yourself because it is not you. So you see, it may come in the middle of a sermon . . . or in a teaching, or something of that kind.' The man who is not baptised in the Spirit can still effectively minister. After all, the preacher who has known this crisis experience is not guaranteed continuous unction. Sometimes, he will know it. Sometimes, he won't. Because he has not received it does not mean that his preaching will be ineffective.

Lloyd-Jones preached a sermon on Apollos. His exposition throws further light on this whole issue.[75] As the sermon unfolds, we are given a thorough evaluation of Apollos' preaching ability. According to DML-J's pneumatology, Apollos had not been baptised in the Spirit. Nonetheless, Lloyd-Jones is fulsome in his assessment and does a superb job in bringing all the biblical evidence to bear. He emphasised that Apollos was 'mighty in the Scriptures', well versed in oral tradition, an eloquent, courageous and effective man. He taught accurately about the Lord Jesus. He was a fervent preacher, 'boiling over in spirit,[76] what they call today—keen'.

The conclusion to which we are driven is that a man without this endowment of power and the accompanying unction can be a very effective preacher. Then why seek for more? DML-J's answer must surely have been that, as a preacher knows more of the dynamism of the Holy Spirit, so his ministry will be even more effective. If this blessing has not come his way, he should still continue with his preaching, not in a state of frustration but in a spirit of expectancy, knowing that either way, the Lord can still use him.

We refer our readers to two significant occasions when DML-J with great passion encouraged his hearers to seek for more power. Remember his conviction that there is a link between sealing and unction. He pleads:

> So I say again, seek it. Be satisfied with nothing less. Has God ever told you that you are His child? Has he spoken to you, not with an audible voice, but, in a sense, in a more real way? *Have you known this illumination, this melting quality? Have you known what it is to be lifted up above and beyond yourself?* If not, Seek it . . . 'Sue Him for it' . . .[77]

And, before a group of students at Westminster Theological Seminary, he both testified and urged:

> This 'unction', this 'anointing', is the supreme thing. Seek it until you have it; be content with nothing less. Go on until you can say, 'And my preaching was not with the enticing words of man's wisdom, but in demonstration of the Spirit and of power'.[78]

As we have noted, Lloyd-Jones eschewed any formula which might be suggested to be generally applicable. Such does not exist. The bestowal of unction, as with all charismatic gifts, remains in the hands of the divine giver. It cannot be worked up or brought down. The Holy Spirit is sovereign. No one should assert that if we do *this*, *that* will follow. Nevertheless, the preacher should constantly be coming before the Lord to request the priestly blessing.

More than anything else, he should want a God who is pleased with him to visit him in the act of preaching with a holy anointing. He should desire that superabundant unction that comes from above and, therefore, sue God for it. And when he has it, he knows that this side of heaven there is nothing more wonderful than to preach with the Lord God Almighty smiling on him.

REVIEW

One man who always wanted power from on high to descend upon his preaching was the Apostle Paul. Amazingly, and with great humility, he asked his own converts to intercede for him. 'Pray also for me', he asks one of the Christian communities, 'that whenever I open my mouth, words may be given me so that I will fearlessly make known the mystery of the Gospel . . .' (Eph. 6:19).

Though an experienced and highly successful preacher at the time of writing, Paul still invoked the intercession of others for an endowment of power as he expounded the Word of God. He could not take for granted the holy anointing. It is to this most remarkable of men that we now turn as we seek to explore the sway he had on Martyn Lloyd-Jones.

5

Pauline Influence

Take the Apostle Paul, this outstanding genius, this most learned Pharisee, this erudite man.[1]

Oh, Christian church, what has happened to you? How can you ever have forgotten these blessed words and the example of the great Apostle?[2]

I am here to try to discover and to expound what the Apostle Paul has actually written. If you like at the end to disagree with him, that is your responsibility. My responsibility is to make clear and plain, as far as I can, what the Apostle has said, and I do appeal to you to listen to him before you begin to talk about your own opinions.[3]

Martyn Lloyd-Jones

Martyn Lloyd-Jones highly esteemed the Apostle Paul. This is obviously by the way in which he repeatedly referred to him—'the great Apostle', 'the master debater', 'the incomparable'.[4] His aim was to present the teaching of Paul as accurately as possible, to step inside the Apostle's mind and heart and to expound what he was saying. He recognised that Paul was inspired and thus argued that what the Apostle asserted needs to be treated with care and respect. Paul was not a philosopher whose opinions are open for debate. Rather, he was a man through whom revelation was funnelled. What he received is authoritative and inerrant. His words are not to be filtered and qualified, they are to be received and applied.

Dr. Lloyd-Jones endeavoured to reflect the teaching of Paul. He did not feel the term Calvinist was particularly helpful, and, therefore, he hardly used it.[5] It is enough to see both Calvin and Augustine standing in line with Paul. The former two can be critically analysed. Paul is in a different category. When preaching through the First Epistle to Timothy, Lloyd-Jones made his position unmistakably clear:

> I am simply a little expositor of this Word, and if you can prove to me that I am doing any violence to what the great Apostle teaches, I will give in and admit that I am wrong.[6]

Perhaps he never, in his ministerial career, expressed himself so forcefully on this subject as he did in a sermon on a verse from First Corinthians. He spent the major part of his time dismantling the argument that Paul had somehow modified the teaching of the Lord Jesus and, therefore, the reader should employ caution and qualification in interpreting Paul.[7] For Lloyd-Jones, such a notion is untenable. Paul's writings are canonical. They carry the imprimatur of the Holy Spirit and are to be received as oracles from God.

Haddon Robinson contrasts the content of prophecy in the Old Testament with the fare set before the people by preachers ministering in a post-testamental period. He said, 'in human terms their ministry originated the Word of God whereas ours derives from it . . . they wrote the Bible, we preach it'.[8] This echoes Lloyd-Jones's view on the Pauline Epistles. The Apostle did not declare what he had researched, he delivered what he had received. The difference between the two concepts is enormous. The source of Paul's Epistles is divine and their contents should be treated accordingly.[9]

It goes without saying that not all of DML-J's contemporaries shared his conviction on Paul's Epistles. William Barclay was in difficulty over divine sovereignty and Paul's 'lump of clay' analogy in Romans.[10] C. H. Dodd also had problems with Paul, one area of disagreement being the way in which the Apostle handled the obduracy of Pharaoh when the Egyptian king refused to let the ancient Hebrews leave Egypt.[11] Paul said that God had hardened his heart (Rom. 9:17-18). Dodd, along with modern liberal scholars, reckoned

Paul to be wrong. God's alleged actions would be incompatible with his character.

DML-J was dismissive almost to the point of being contemptuous of such criticism. He took Dodd to task for asserting that Paul was guilty of 'an unethical determinism'. Lloyd-Jones commented:

> Here is a man who does not hesitate to set himself up as a greater authority on ethics and the love of God than the Apostle Paul ... The commentator is a greater man, a greater mind, a greater spirit and a greater saint than the Apostle, and he looks on as a judge. He says, 'Now the Apostle at other times, of course, has this wonderful conception of the love of God, but in order to score a debating point over true Jews, he has let himself down here.'[12]

DML-J's opinion of Paul's intellect, even putting aside claims for divine inspiration, compelled him to dissent from the view that the Apostle could have been guilty of self-contradiction. Lloyd-Jones reckoned that criticism of Paul came from those who believed themselves to be theologically more competent than the Apostle. They claimed a 'superior position'. They dealt with Paul in a patronising way, expressing their sorrow for the inadequacy of his argument.[13]

Dr. Lloyd-Jones was gripped by the content of Paul's teaching. He immersed himself in it. Elizabeth Catherwood is not claiming too much when she says of her father, 'But on the New Testament, on the Epistles of Paul, he was matchless'.[14] What perhaps has not been so widely recognised is the way in which he was influenced by the Apostle himself, his personal traits, abilities, and demeanour. He makes his position quite clear:

> I must confess that I am charmed by this man and everything he does. I admire his methods. I like his style. I am drawn to his way of doing things. But particularly, and above all else, I admire his great pastoral heart ... his burning desire was to help the churches.[15]

In measure, DML-J sought to reproduce Paul's teaching technique. Our aim, now, is to explore the influence Paul's personality and preaching style had on him. There are many significant volumes on the theology of Paul but little, as far as we know, on the presentation of his teaching coupled with an examination of his temperament. So we turn the spotlight away from Paul's *material* to the man himself and his *method* as Martyn Lloyd-Jones seemed to recognise and absorb it.

PERSONALITY

Delivery and personality are interwoven. We consider aspects of the personality of Paul and the way in which they appear to have inspired Lloyd-Jones. As we have seen, he was very concerned lest personality be projected in a fashion which brings abuse to the act of preaching. He recognised that the preacher must not be a bland man without character. He must be able to speak out in a meaningful fashion. It was the abuse of personality which alarmed him. Certain aspects of a preacher's nature may have to be checked or refined in order to enhance and not detract from his preaching ministry. What needs to be pruned? What should be encouraged? These rarely faced questions are ones for which we shall endeavour to find some answers.

INADEQUACY

When we focus on Paul, we find that he used language paralleled by the already cited sentiments of James Thornwell and Martyn Lloyd-Jones.[16] These men were quick to point out the weaknesses in their respective ministries. What we hear from Thornwell and DML-J is but the echo of Paul's drum beat. And that in turn, as we have discovered, throbs through the experiences of men in the ministry in Old Testament times. The call came from the Lord. Their reaction was the feeling of unworthiness and inadequacy.

When Paul arrived at the seaport of Corinth, he was fully aware of his limitations. With some nostalgia, he recalled the occasion:

> I came to you in weakness and fear, and with much trembling. My message and my preaching were not with wise and persuasive words, but with a demonstration of the Spirit's power, so that your faith might not rest on men's wisdom, but on God's power (1 Cor. 2:3-5).

Literally, the word weakness means 'strengthlessness'. Paul knew what it was to lack energy (2 Cor. 12:9). Astonishingly, he employed the same term to convey his understanding of the death of our Lord at the human level, 'he was crucified in weakness' (13:4). He referred to this in his earlier epistle, speaking of the weakness of God (1 Cor. 1:25)! How weakness and omnipotence can live alongside each other is beyond Paul's brief to explain. He is out to secure the premise that God in his grace and sovereignty delights in taking weak men in order to demonstrate his power (1 Cor. 1:27).

This is how we understand the summons of our Lord to Peter, '"You

are Simon son of John. You will be called Cephas" (which, when translated, is Peter)' (John 1:42). There is an implied difference between what
the disciple was and what he would become! A deficiency, when
acknowledged, can become the crucible in which God works a divine
alchemy. The result will be explained only in terms of God being at
work! Preachers need to recognise this.

Listen to Dr. Lloyd-Jones, on one occasion, when he was ministering in Scotland. He was aware that he had run into criticism about his
professional competency:

> As you have been told, I am not a professor. There are some who say
> that I have ceased to be a physician. And I fear that the majority of
> my brethren refuse to regard me as a theologian. But, like another,
> who once lived on the face of the earth, I can positively say that 'I am
> what I am by the grace of God'. And it is in that capacity and in that
> way that I stand before you and speak this evening.[17]

Paul was aware that he had been criticised both about his physical
appearance and his diction (2 Cor. 10:10). He conceded that he was not
a 'trained speaker' (11:6), and his poor performance was not exceptional. In his later Epistles to the Thessalonians, he recalled his preaching style, remembering that he did not preach 'simply with words'
(1 Thess. 1:5).

The Apostle's self-effacing comments made an indelible impression
on Lloyd-Jones. They fixed his unswerving views on preaching: what in
essence it is, how it is to be approached, on what it depends, and what
methods should now be employed to help draw a congregation together.
For him, the drumming up of interest in church services by posters,
press-briefings, and the like was totally unacceptable. Nothing in the
strategy of Paul, he thought, gives warrant for such measures. This
prompted him to make statements which, though revealing his own convictions, were hardly calculated to make him favoured in some quarters:

> I am afraid that the Apostle would not be a popular, modern evan-
> gelist. It seems that he was not much to look at. We are told that he
> was a short man, bald-headed with a hooked nose, and that he had a
> horrible inflammation of his eyes, an ophthalmia, which made him
> utterly repulsive to look at.[18]

The preacher is ever to appreciate his utter inadequacy to respond to his
God-given call. This will ensure he remains dependent on the Lord for

enabling. Though he may glory in the office of preaching, he must realise that he is 'less than the least of all saints' and, apart from the grace of God, he has nothing of which to boast.

SUBMISSION

Dr. Lloyd-Jones took Paul's assertion, 'For God is my witness, whom I serve with my spirit in the Gospel of his Son . . .' (Rom. 1:9 *AV*) as illustrative of the Apostle's attitude in his approach to the ministry. It bespeaks a humility and necessary submission to the Holy Spirit. His goal was not to 'put his personality over': quite the opposite. Paul wished to be eclipsed.

The preacher should never aim to draw attention to himself. To do so is to fall foul of Paul's stated maxim 'we preach not ourselves but Christ Jesus the Lord'.[19] Thus, DML-J's assertion, 'When I preach, I do not tell stories about myself or anybody else, I do not just make people sing choruses and try to work them up—I *reason* with them.'[20]

The purpose of Lloyd-Jones's caution was his concern to avoid promoting a following whose loyalty was to him or drawing attention to himself and his background.[21] Significantly, he went on record affirming he had 'almost vowed' never to mention anything medical in the pulpit.[22] When he did so, he felt an unhealthy interest quicken the congregation. He was fearful of it, because it represented concern for the wrong thing. 'Congregations often spoil preachers', he declared, referring to the fact that people in the pew want the pulpit occupant to be more personal than he should be. The danger is that they may pay more attention to the preacher than his preaching.

TEMPERAMENT

Dr. Lloyd-Jones believed that curbing the temperament was 'probably the greatest problem that the mighty Apostle Paul ever had to face'. Paul was a man of 'vivacity, eloquence and enthusiasm'. Circumstances could carry him away. DML-J found evidence for his diagnosis in the infrequent, autobiographical passages in the epistles. Paul was often tempted by depression—'without were fightings, within were fears'. He referred to Paul's sensitivity, believing him to be a highly-strung man who could be hurt by the Corinthians from whom he demanded and expected love but did not always get it.

Lloyd-Jones rejected the notion that conversion changes the temperament, though it should refine it. He clearly expressed his belief, 'the fundamental elements in our personality and temperament are not changed by conversion and by re-birth . . . the man himself, psychologically, is essentially what he was before.'[23] Thus, he found a common denominator between Saul of Tarsus in his unconverted days and Paul the Apostle. As a former persecutor of the Church, Saul was violent beyond all others. In all spheres, he was at the top; the outstanding student of Gamaliel, surpassing his contemporaries in conforming to details of the Mosaic Law and the Tradition of the Elders; in his zeal he was the arch-persecutor of the Church.

When he became an Apostle, the same characteristics showed themselves. His preaching was not that of a gentle, quiet man, rather, he preached with all the intensity of 'his mighty, emotional nature'. He knew what it was to weep, to be fearful, and to be downcast.[24] DML-J hammers in the point. Paul's temperament *per se* did not change.

Dr. Lloyd-Jones argued that this is a principle which can be generally applied though we sometimes fail to appreciate it. 'When, for some reason—perhaps physical or perhaps due to overwork—the vivacious side is slowed down and the melancholic side tends to take over, we imagine that we are in bad and sad spiritual condition.'[25] The explanation lies within the complexities of our personalities. We should know and come to grips with our personality traits. This is particularly true for the preacher. He must curb excesses. Paul is a model.

HUMOUR [26]

DML-J examined the Apostle's attitude to frivolity. He could not conceive of Paul's ever being 'glib' or 'light-hearted'. When advising younger ministers such as Timothy and Titus, Paul tells them to be 'grave' and 'sober' and serious.[27] The weight of responsibility was heavy on Lloyd-Jones. The message is solemn and is to be preached in a conducive fashion. He revealed his inner self on one occasion when he confessed to his congregation, speaking about the Scripture passage he was expounding, 'it is not an easy thing to spend a week with a text like this'.[28]

There is hardly a trace of humour in Lloyd-Jones's sermons. He rarely expressed himself in a light fashion when preaching.[29] Anything that verged on humour was unconscious, as on the occasion when he suggested to his congregation that an explanation for the Second World War was—at the human level—possibly attributable to Hitler's thyroid gland! The laughter which was heard was hardly appreciated by the preacher. For him, the point was serious. He was demonstrating how a person's chemistry and metabolism, to some extent, affect his personality. In turn, this can be used as a tool in the Devil's hands to transform them into something grotesque. Sometimes laughter on the part of the congregation earned them the preacher's rebuke.[30]

SENSITIVITY

Lloyd-Jones was impressed by the sensitivity of Paul, especially with regard to his own nation. In Romans 9-11, Paul devotes three chapters to establishing the position of the Jews in the sight of God. DML-J assesses Paul's approach:

> Paul does his best for the Jews in every way. He does not start off here, when he comes to the quotations, by giving the Scriptures which show that they are going to be pushed out and punished and so on. No, he leaves that as long as he can, so he takes up the admission of the Gentiles first. He is sparing his fellow-countrymen; he does not rush at any condemnation; he is trying to win them, trying to persuade them. He enjoys being positive. He has got to prove his case with regard to the Jews, but he seems to postpone it as long as he can. From which I deduce that the Apostle was not only a great man and a great debater, a great logician and teacher, but also a very great gentleman.[31]

The chapters reveal 'the delicacy, the sensitive nature, and character of the great Apostle and his tenderness'.[32]

This, again, contrasts with the untenable assumptions of the Apostle's critics. Moreover, Paul's sensitivity is seen in the way that he responds to the leadings of the Spirit. Though the Apostle had an obviously strong wish to visit the capital he was prohibited from going.[33]

TEACHING METHOD

As we have observed, Lloyd-Jones was cautious about books on homiletics. The reason behind this was his belief that many such books regard the construction of sermons as an art or a craft to be learned. This is an incorrect and harmful approach. A man cannot be crafted into being a preacher. 'Preachers (and pastors) are born not made.'[34] They are fitted for office through talents with which they have been endowed rather than by skills that have been acquired. Moreover, he found the way in which the Apostle Paul presented truth was at variance with the fashion in which homileticians teach their students.

Alliteration

Paul did not construct his letters with three or four alliterated points, followed by carefully planned subdivisions. Some have tried to infer such an arrangement from the epistles. But this is induction rather than deduction. Effectively, they leave us with an analysis which they have imposed on to the text rather than something which has been accurately read out from it. Such endeavours run the risk of sacrificing truth on the altar of ingenuity.

DML-J had no great affection for alliteration and could be quite critical of it, especially when it was contrived. 'We not only have our points, our numbers, but we will insist on having alliteration as well, as we almost force the truth into our little system of five p's and five s's, or whatever it is.' He went on to say that, though it might look neat, it might well be 'the neatness of death'.[35]

There were times, however, when Lloyd-Jones found that his passage opened up in a threefold fashion. But these were rare. His point is not a total shunning of alliteration: artificiality is what he rejected. To twist and force a text or passage into a preconceived shell is wrong. It distorts the message though it may enhance the reputation of the preacher for his cunning use of words.

This point is important. Lloyd-Jones did not need alliteration to hold the attention of his congregation. He had a natural eloquence and a clear and sharp mind. Preachers who maintain the alliterative mode of presentation should, however, ask if their treatment is justified by the text. What is being gained by the style they are adopting? Assuming the Pauline epistles are being expounded, they should enquire, 'Is this what the Apostle was actually conveying? Does it represent his emphasis? Is my method distorting his message?'

Exposition

Why did Lloyd-Jones spend so much time going through the Pauline epistles in so much detail? Can one really justify several years of Sunday mornings on the Epistle to the Ephesians and eleven years of Friday evenings on Romans?

The truth is that DML-J's expository style, he believed, was derived rather than contrived. Paul spent twenty-four months preaching at Ephesus. Every day he addressed people, first in the synagogue and then in the lecture hall of Tyrannus. The influence of his ministry was widespread throughout a huge area (Acts 19:10). Any computation of the total teaching time given to the Ephesian believers leaves us with a very big figure. The Apostle spent a huge number of hours carefully teaching. Where do we go to find an account of what he had to say? And how should preachers treat the material that has been recorded?

We must take our enquiry to the Epistle to the Ephesians. Herein is Paul's distilled wisdom; a summary of the messages which he delivered as he was empowered and enlightened by the Holy Spirit in Tyrannus' academy. Paul's material is found in the epistle in a concentrated form. The expositor's task is to immerse himself in it. He is to ask for the Spirit's enabling as he takes stock of the immensities and plumbs, the profundities of the Apostle's thought in order to make it plain to his audience.

In a rare piece of autobiography, not without gentle humour, DML-J spoke of an occasion when someone suggested to him that Paul might be amazed at what he had got out of his letters! (This was a friend of Lloyd-Jones's who daringly referred to the length of his expository series.) The Doctor recalled the incident sometime after the man's death. Characteristically, the point was turned on its head. DML-J significantly commented: 'Poor man! Now my friend has discovered that the Apostle Paul is amazed at the little that most people, and I with them, get out of his great Epistles!'[36]

He clearly appreciated that what we have in the epistles is but a sample of Paul's ministry. When DML-J commenced his long series on the Epistle to the Romans, he compared its size to that of the Ephesian letter. Unlike the city of Ephesus, Paul had not been able to visit Rome. He did, however, desire to have conveyed to the Roman Christians 'some spiritual gift, to the end ye may be established' (1:11 *AV*). He was referring to the epistle designated for them. It contains his teaching. Romans is a masterpiece of Pauline doctrine and reasoning. Receiving this would enable the readers to be 'strengthened', 'built up', 'made more secure', 'made firm'. Had Paul been able freely to visit Rome, he would have spent lengthy periods with the believers. He would have expounded the doctrines of the faith in an expanded and leisurely fashion.

The Epistle to the Romans represents the concentration of Paul's inspired theology. As such, it demands careful and thoughtful study. The expositor who hurries through the epistle does it an injustice. Some teachers run this danger. The treatment too often accorded this and all the epistles is tantamount to implying Paul might have delivered them in one afternoon! Such an approach fails to take into account the work and thought Paul put into them. Speaking of the Epistle to the Romans, Lloyd-Jones declared, 'My friends, this is a synopsis!'[37]

The task of the preacher is to spend time in mind and heart preparation so that he might present the truths of the epistles with a degree of inspiration and unction. He will expound the teaching, applying it to the felt need of his congregants. He will do this slowly and with great care. Relentlessly and typically, DML-J further secures his point:

> The Apostle would have taken months to expound fully what he says here in this short compass, so that when we go to study the Epistle to the Romans we do not just go through it lightly and superficially. *It is our business to try and do what the Apostle himself would have done if he had been in Rome.* In other words, our consideration of the Epistle to the Romans must be a very long one. That is why, too, you must have noticed that any commentary you have ever seen on the Epistle to the Romans is very much longer than the Epistle itself.[38]

Remember that Lloyd-Jones believed the spiritual gift Paul wished to impart to the Romans (1:11) was the opening up of the Scriptures. He linked this to a verse from John's Gospel. In the high-priestly prayer, our Lord requested that the Church might be sanctified through the truth. He then asserted, 'thy word is truth' (17:17 AV).

This is fulfilled through the preaching ministry as the congregation are thus 'sanctified through the truth'. Such a conviction raises the preaching ministry to incredible heights and brings to the preacher a great sense of responsibility. In the sovereignty of God, he is being employed to realise a request made to the Father by the Son of God! It is imperative for the preacher to take great care in reaching into the depths and endeavouring to scale the height of the Scriptural revelation of God and adequately explaining this to his congregation.

This was Paul's acknowledged goal. It became the consuming force in DML-J's life. The privilege of being a preacher prevented him from ever referring to how much he had surrendered in order to enter the ministry. He was a man with a call from God. The one thing needful was to rise to the challenge and so to preach that when one had finished the congregation were left with a sense of God.

Literary freedom

There is a form and a plan in Paul's epistles. Close examination reveals the foundations and girder work on which the main thesis was built. But the Apostle's method was never his master. He was not a slave to his schema. The observation is important. When its significance is grasped, a number of puzzling items concerning Paul's style and the development of his argument fall into place.

There were times in Paul's writing, when the main point led to a sub-point which then took on the stature of the main point. Commenting on the opening verses of the Roman Epistle in which Paul sets down his first point but fails to register the following ones, Lloyd-Jones asserts: 'Here is a man, you see, who sets out to say a number of things—one, two, three and so on; he starts with the first and then off he goes, and forgets that he ever said "first" and he never comes back to it.'[39]

Paul did not revise or refine this, let alone offer an apologia. The stimulus behind the switches and changes was the unction of the Spirit. Thoughts and concepts raced through his head. Sometimes his pen failed to keep up with the flow of thought. This resulted in a style that is not always polished and where there are grammatical errors. But the epistles are not intended to be literary essays. They are, however, theological masterpieces which have changed the lives of innumerable people all over the world.

To ride roughshod over the rules of grammar is known, in Britain, as 'breaking the Queen's English'. The technical term is 'anacoluthia' to which Lloyd-Jones repeatedly refers. Despite what DML-J describes as the Apostle's 'giant intellect', Paul is so carried away at times that he breaks the rules of both grammar and form!

Dr. Lloyd-Jones referred to this on one occasion in a sermon from the Ephesians series.[40] He spoke of the criticisms levelled at Paul's literary form. It is said that the Apostle lacked a chaste, pruned style. He was ornate and multiplied his adjectives, he repeated himself, he crowded epithet upon epithet. Having started a line of argument, he allowed a word to set him off, and he became so carried away and fired by it that he interposed praise to God. He seemed to forget what he had set out to say and then returned to it. Sometimes he forgot to do so and left a sentence unfinished. Lloyd-Jones commented:

> Some of the pedants who are trying to translate him today accuse him
> of being guilty of what they call inconcinnity and anacoluthia—inel-
> egancies of style and incomplete sentences. The explanation is that the
> Apostle was moved and carried away by the truth![41]

All this, for Lloyd-Jones, far from being a black mark to set against the Apostle, reveals the measure of his spirituality. He asserted that Paul was not 'a mere littérateur'. 'Syntax and sentences are not his chief concerns.

He was interested in the truth.' When a matter gripped his heart and he felt constrained to praise the Lord, he indulged himself. He did not consider it necessary to stop and round-off, let alone polish, what had been said:

> Now, the Apostle was very guilty of that—unfinished sentences! Or if he does not actually leave them unfinished, he will throw in a tremendous digression, and then will suddenly remember, and back he will come and finish his sentence. An appallingly bad style, you say? I thank God for it.[42]

Style and system should bow to the greater claims of passion and praise. This ought to be the case for all preachers. Urgency, feeling, aspirations of love and devotion do not threaten clarity and doctrinal accuracy when the preacher has a mind sharpened and a heart warmed by the Spirit.

This was the case with both Jonathan Edwards and George Whitefield. Lloyd-Jones reckoned Edwards to be, among others, 'an atrocious stylist'.[43] And, as we have seen, he quoted approvingly the remark concerning Whitefield's 'noble negligence'.[44] James Packer stated that this description was first used to sum up Richard Baxter's writing; he added that the term 'fits Dr. Lloyd-Jones' transcribed sermons and lectures admirably; persuasive man-to-man clarity . . . no attempt at verbal elegance was ever made'.[45]

Form and order

Tricks of homiletics were repugnant to Lloyd-Jones. This does not mean he had no interest in structure. The reverse was the case. But form in a sermon is to be the preacher's servant and not his superintendent. The infrastructure of Paul's Epistles—what Lloyd-Jones, in referring to his own style, would call his skeletons—is quite clear. It demands hard work. The skeleton needs flesh, tissue, muscles, clothes! The preacher prepares in the hope that the Holy Spirit, both at the point of preparation and delivery, will help him to achieve this.

Thus, Dr. Lloyd-Jones encouraged us to study Paul's method. He claimed nothing is so entrancing as to watch the working of a great mind. The Apostle was never clumsy nor untidy except when he was lifted to ecstasy and could not find the language, let alone the grammar, to allow him to put his thoughts into adequate words! What emerged from his pen was not a jumble of random, disconnected thoughts. He did not just write the next thing that came into his mind.

Rather, the Apostle had a plan, a scheme; he is always orderly. And this is something that those who preach should learn from him. Do not imagine that you are giving a manifestation of spirituality by not having order in your sermons or your addresses or your Sunday school lessons. It is not a hallmark of spirituality not to have order. It is the exact opposite. Here is this mighty man filled with the Spirit of God, and yet, observe the order, observe the arrangement, observe the logic and the sequence, observe how he marshals his evidence and presents his case.[46]

To help us understand Paul's strategy further, Lloyd-Jones sometimes used an illustration from great music composers. Their compositions have themes; there are the main and the subsidiary ones. The latter are called the leitmotifs. During the course of the symphony, they will keep recurring. This is, of course, not accidental. It is deliberate on the part of the composer who wishes to return to them. He has his total composition under control. It follows his scheme. So it is with the Apostle as he writes his epistles.[47]

DML-J applied his illustration as he endeavoured to give a comprehensive view of Romans, chapters 9-11 . In the process, he reviewed the chapters. The main theme, he believed, is the absolute sovereignty of God which nothing can thwart. But there are lesser ones—(i) the tragedy of the Jews as rejectors of Christ, (ii) God's sovereignty in the matter of election and, (iii) the vindication, by reference to the Old Testament, of the Christian claim that salvation is for all, Gentiles as well as Jews, on the basis of saving faith.

The main theme dominates. Paul keeps returning to it, but he also mentions, develops, leaves, and returns to the subsidiary ones—as does the music composer. It is important to grasp this aspect of Paul's style. Failure to do so will run, for the expositor, the risk of obscuring Paul's teaching as the preacher presents it to his congregation.

Paul stated an argument, moved outwards, then back, took up a further sub-point, returned to the first, and so forth. All expositors need to appreciate this and determine to 'go with the flow' of Paul's method in order to secure accuracy of exposition.

A further example of this is found in DML-J's sermon in which he dealt with the complexities of the doctrine of election. He is expounding the statement 'the elder shall serve the younger'. He then moves on to the further quotation of Paul's from the Old Testament, 'Jacob have I loved but Esau have I hated' (Rom. 9:10-13).[48]

Logic

Lloyd-Jones's diagnostic method can be traced back to his medical training. But this was not the only influence. At a broader level it should be remembered that when he was at the peak of his ministry, the philosophy of Logical Positivism was arousing great interest and a considerable following in Europe. DML-J was essentially a logical preacher. Our argument is that, providentially, he exercised his ministry at a time when there needed to be an influential pulpit, the occupant of which presented a coherent, positive, and diagnostic approach to the Scriptures, and was equal to all attempts made to ridicule a conservative view of the Bible.

Paul had a logical mind. There is much compelling evidence warranting the conclusion that his teaching method was that of the diagnostician. The analysis of language, the laying down of propositions, the building of a super-structure were the Apostle's stock-in-trade. Lloyd-Jones seized on this. It has much in common with his own training. The analytical approach has Apostolic sanction! Dr. Lloyd-Jones was reproducing the established pattern of his great mentor in his presentation of sermons. DML-J argued, in his series on the Sermon on the Mount, that, once a basic commitment to the faith is made, what follows is essentially a logical system. 'The Bible is full of logic and we must never think of the Christian faith as something purely mystical . . . Christian Faith is essentially thinking.'[49]

Commenting on Romans 5:10 DML-J says: 'This is how Paul puts it. "if [I like that 'if', I like the logic of the New Testament] when we were enemies, we were reconciled to God by the death of his Son, much more, being reconciled, we shall be saved by his life.' . . . Can you refute that logic?'[50]

DML-J pressed the argument when delivering a sermon in London toward the close of his ministry, calling Anselm as a further witness of a preacher who was logical in his sermon presentation.[51] He reminds us in his Romans' series that the 'Apostle continues the great argument of this section of the Epistle. He goes on from point to point, from step to step. He makes a statement and then proves it; then he takes up another and again demonstrates and proves it.'[52]

This, of course, is not originally Pauline. The use of cogent, close reasoning is traced back to the ministry of our Lord. Lloyd-Jones delighted in referring to the teaching method of the Saviour. In the Sermon on the Mount, DML-J is preaching on the verse, 'Lay not up for yourselves treasures upon earth . . . But lay up for yourselves treasures in heaven' (Matt. 6:19-20). Carefully, our Lord argues out the case for preferring celestial to temporal investment. The Son of God reasons with us for our benefit, 'He stoops to our weakness, mighty as He is, and He comes to our aid and supplies us with these reasons for carrying out His commandment.' DML-J continues, 'He works it out for us in a series of logical propositions.' The Lord's motivation was twofold. He was anxious to help us for the subject matter is so grave.[53]

Anticipation

This follows on from the use of logic. We see how, in presenting his argument, Paul ensured that he was familiar with the position of his antagonists. Sometimes he imagined them to be present as he wrote. We 'hear' them putting up their objections, advancing their propositions and thereby declaring their position. The opening chapters of the Epistle to the Romans furnish several examples (3:1, 3, 5, 7-9). Having allowed his opponents a platform, Paul then felled their argument with several blows.

A further case is the brilliant fashion in which he explained how Abraham's favoured position before God rested on the faith that he showed in the Lord prior to the act of circumcision. The whole of the fourth chapter of the Epistle to the Romans is dedicated to establishing the point. Typically, Paul started off by citing his opponents' complaints. They believed that Paul's teaching about saving faith was shipwrecked on the experience of Abraham. He was justified by works. If this is the case 'he had something to boast about' (4:2).

Paul opened up the historical field and also brought into the picture the experiences of David. Thus, he reviewed the lives of two of the leading Hebrews of all time. Paul explored the circumstances which led to the declaration of Abraham's righteousness before God. Was it prior or subsequent to the act of circumcision? (4:10). Having established the facts he made his conclusion that Abraham was pronounced righteous *before* he was circumcised. The assertion about Abraham was made solely on account of his believing God and taking him at his word. Therefore, he is designated 'the father of all who believe but have not been circumcised'.

Here then is Paul, a Jew of great scholastic ability, driven to the conclusion, by the relentless application of logic, that the founder of the Hebrew nation is also father to all who exercise a similar faith! He hammers home the subsidiary point which stems from his main premise—circumcision is primarily spiritual and not physical. The religious significance is of greater import than the surgical incision. Indeed, a Jew could submit to the cut but entirely annul its meaning by failing to have the appropriate heart attitude. This would leave him in a state of uncircumcision! The principle can be reversed. An uncircumcised Gentile with the right attitude is reckoned as circumcised, thus qualifying him to participate in covenantal blessings.

This stunning piece of logic is not only reproduced throughout the Pauline epistles, but the method is a feature of the teaching style of DML-J. He, too, would cite the position of his opponents, erect their propositions and then, with a measure of satisfaction, knock them down. To the hearer, the method is compelling. It arouses and retains his interest. It helps him also to think through his position clearly. Paul was a great debater. He anticipated and out-manoeuvred his opponents.

> It is a part of the business of any teacher to try to forestall difficulties and problems that will arise in the minds of those who are listening to him. It is a very poor teacher who just makes a positive statement and leaves it at that. The test of a good teacher is the number of negatives he uses; and, furthermore, the number of possible objections that he deals with before people have even thought of them.[54]

To be anticipatory, logical, and positive is to be Pauline. The Apostle's method should be followed. Thus, Lloyd-Jones comments, 'let us try to learn from this man how to conduct an argument'.[55]

Often, in controlling discussions, as well as in the pulpit, DML-J would demonstrate this approach. He showed how, on the premise someone put up, 'A would lead to B which would lead to C. Is this what the contributor meant to imply? Did he not see the point? Would he revise his opinion as a result of seeing where it would lead? You see, if you say that, then this is what is bound to follow'[56] . . . shades of the Apostle. To get an individual or a congregation to think Christianly by a process of anticipation and deduction is to continue a well-tested method.

But anticipating the opposition's position and reducing it by a series of negatives is not enough. Negatives generally should be followed by positives. The clearing of the ground gives way to the erection of a building. We will enlarge on this aspect of Lloyd-Jones's method in a later chapter.[57] But the point needs securing that he was actually reflecting a definite teaching technique of both Paul and that of our Lord.

THE HOLY SPIRIT

We have discussed at length the concept of unction produced by the afflatus of the Spirit resting on the preacher. Without back-tracking, it is needful to see this illustrated by coming close to the Apostle Paul.

Lloyd-Jones believed the Apostle was impelled by the Spirit not only in his preaching but in the composition of his epistles. They are, in effect, written sermons, but cast in sermonic and not essayist style.[58] By now, the difference should be quite clear. They are composed to convey a message which cannot be orally proclaimed because of Paul's absence from those to whom he is directing his letters. Paul is more concerned to be borne along by the Spirit in what he has to say than to produce some stylish treatise.

Thus, Lloyd-Jones gave one of his typical, comprehensive, surveys of the Apostle's argument as he approached the Epistle to the Romans. He brings us to Paul's choice assertion that 'All things work together for good to them that love God.' And then he sought to show how Paul's heart was so warmed by the goodness, grandeur, and consistency of God's love toward the believer that *'he lets himself go'*[59] with a series of 'tremendous challenges and questions'.

The phrase I have italicised is important. It sums up what Lloyd-Jones felt about the spontaneity and exuberance which came through even in Paul's writings, which he felt was often lacking in modern pulpits, thus contributing to a dead orthodoxy. Elsewhere, he writes: 'Paul was much more concerned about what he said than the way in which he said it . . . The Apostle never cultivated 'art for art's sake . . .'[60]

To take such liberties is to secure the freedom of the Spirit. To be decorous and controlled, to associate 'true scholarship' with a lack of animation, to engage in a quest for quietness without passion is wrong. It grieves the Spirit, bores the people, and is the reason why so many churches are empty.

Lloyd-Jones tells us that Paul's 'heart was as big as his brain'.[61] Thus, he continues, in Paul's writings, 'his heart seems to control him at the expense of his mind'. DML-J is commenting on Paul's neglect of form in favour of fervour. He presses his case and warns against the 'lifelessness of mere form without a living substance within it!'

There are times when the power of the subject matter so warmed Paul's heart and deeply moved him that he felt impelled to break out into doxology and praise. This was not part of the argument. Stylists might feel such eruptions were unnecessary. On the contrary, Lloyd-Jones argued, they represented freedom in the Apostle's approach.

DML-J taught the essentiality of a preacher's being free. Without liberty, he is unable to proclaim his message adequately. After all, he is not an academic philosopher concerned to reason in a cold, dispassionate fashion. The message and the messenger cannot be separated. The proclamation and the proclaimer intertwine. There is a sense in which true preaching requires the message to be incarnated in the man. The great violinist, Yehudi Menuhin, was once asked the reason behind his genius. He offered a one-word explanation—surrender. The violinist surrenders to the violin. Thus, the preacher surrenders to the message. The delivery becomes the only thing in the world for him at that time.

This sort of preaching, though prepared in the head, has, on delivery, to flow from the heart. Sometimes Paul gave vent to his emotions in passionate praise. In the quality of his doxologies his inspiration soared to incredible heights as he was given a vista of the splendour and grandeur of God's person and plan.[62] Paul would take off! In his book on preaching DML-J refers to such occasions:

> Again, I would refer to those eloquent flights of the great Apostle Paul in his Epistles. He never set out to produce a literary masterpiece. He was not even concerned about literary form. He was not a literary man; but when the Truth took hold of him, he became mightily eloquent.[63]

It must be said that the idea of the truth possessing and controlling shows great insight. It penetrates a little more the meaning of unction. Lloyd-Jones goes on to comment that when eloquence is so produced, it is one of the best handmaidens of true preaching. Thus, the preacher should always be wishing for such experiences in his own ministry.

CHRISTOCENTRIC

A feature of Paul's epistles is the way in which they immediately introduce the reader to the person of the Lord Jesus Christ. True preaching must have Christ at its centre. Spurgeon's aim in handling any text was to make tracks to the Lord Jesus and his Cross. As all places in Britain can be linked into a route that enables the traveller to reach London, so the preacher will take every opportunity to move his argument from the circumference to the centre. He will bring the hearer to the Lord. DML-J comments about Paul:

It does not matter at all what the occasion is; he cannot begin writing without at once introducing us to Jesus Christ. To Paul, He was the beginning and the end, the all-in-all . . . You will find that in this introduction the Apostle mentions Him at least five times. I had occasion to note recently that in the first fourteen verses of the Epistle to the Ephesians he mentions Him fifteen times . . . he must keep on mentioning the Name. He uses the terms 'Jesus Christ', 'the Lord Jesus Christ', 'Christ Jesus our Lord', and so on. Watch him in his Epistles, he is always using the Name, and it evidently gives him great pleasure to do so.[64]

Love for the Lord is part of the stuff from which unction comes. People become lyrical when they deeply appreciate the person or the concept about whom or which they are speaking. They move to the point where they feel that the object they are endeavouring to praise or describe is almost beyond their reach so to do. Nonetheless, they try. They strive. They reach out.

It was when George Frederic Handel had his great vision of the Lord God in heaven that he was inspired to write his great oratorio, *The Messiah*. At a much higher level, the great Apostle was stretched to find the words which could bear the weight of what he endeavoured to convey about the greatness and grandeur of God. His love for his Lord was boundless. It is this that causes his letters to be so moving. The emotion seems to come through and to grip us also.

The very Name of the Lord Jesus Christ always moved the great Apostle and seems at times to make him forget his argument and his logic for a while. He bursts out repeatedly into a hymn of praise and of thanksgiving; yet, we note his great humility, his self-deprecation, his self-abasement.[65]

REVIEW

The influence that Paul had on Lloyd-Jones's preaching style can hardly be exaggerated. Possibly DML-J was not unlike Paul physically. Certainly, he consciously modelled his teaching style on that of the Apostle and became one of the greatest expositors of Paul's epistles. We pause to introduce one further thought which will position us for our next chapter.

Paul had one all-embracing concern. It was to live for Jesus Christ, to die daily, to surrender all, to run the race and complete his life's work.

A. W. Tozer well describes such a goal as the 'pursuit of God'. It is appropriate for us to become personal once again in our researches and attempt what, for a private man like Lloyd-Jones, is no easy task—to lift the veil on his own spiritual disciplines, to try and track the course of his own pursuit after the Lord.

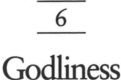

6

Godliness

My dear friend, the only way to live life, the only way to die, is to know Jesus Christ, to believe in him. I know him in whom I have believed.

I believe that he is very God and very man. I believe that he came from the glory of eternity and was born of the Virgin Mary. I believe he demonstrated and manifested his deity in his miracles of power. I believe that when he died on the cross, he was dying in order that I might be forgiven. I believe that he was smitten with the stripes that were meant for me and that I so richly deserve.

I believe he made his soul an offering for sin. I believe that he did so in a perfect manner and that he has rendered a complete satisfaction to every demand of a holy God and of a holy law. I believe that he arose literally from the grave in the body—the same body, but one that was changed and glorified. I believe in the literal physical resurrection—I have no gospel apart from it, for I would not know that he had conquered death apart from this. I believe in the literal physical resurrection, whatever modern science may say.

I believe that he ascended into heaven in the sight of his assembled disciples ten days before the day of Pentecost at Jerusalem on Mount Olivet. I believe they saw him passing through the heavens. I believe that he sent the Holy Ghost on the day of Pentecost.

*I believe that he will come again to receive those of us who
believe in him unto himself, to judge the whole world in righteousness and to set up his eternal kingdom. That is what I
believe.* [1]

Martyn Lloyd-Jones

D ML-J uttered what in effect was a personal, credal statement as he
preached through one of his sermons from the Epistle to Timothy.
The lengthy extract is informative on several counts. It clearly reveals
his theological position. It is vibrant with that sort of confidence and
authority which is often lacking in preachers but is actually what people need to hear. 'Share your certainties, I have enough doubts of my
own', is more often than not the plea of the unchurched engaged in the
pursuit of truth. Moreover, it is an example of close reasoning and the
distillation of conviction, preached in an unscripted fashion and
prompted by the Holy Spirit's afflatus. Unction can quicken a preacher's
mental faculties in an extraordinary way.[2]

'The only way to live life, the only way to die is to know Jesus
Christ'—this is a pivotal testimony from DML-J, summing up his
approach to life as a minister of the glorious Gospel. His advice to others reveals, as is often the case, what were also his personal goals.

The obvious needs restating. There is more to preaching than
preaching. The preacher should complement the preaching as a frame
sets off the picture. A picture can be removed from a frame or be placed
in one that does not do it justice; either way, the picture remains but the
circumstance is unfortunate. Ideally, a picture needs a suitable frame. So
the preacher's disposition and quality of life should complement the
ministry.

No book on a minister's philosophy of preaching is complete without pausing to look at the preacher himself. DML-J states the point
clearly, 'The preacher must be a man who is characterised by spirituality in an unusual degree . . . The preacher's first, and most important,
task is to prepare himself, not his sermon.'[3]

We take time to come up close to Dr. Lloyd-Jones not only as a
preacher but as a godly man. And we shall attempt this by considering
basically some of the content of his preaching. In other words, we shall
look at what he said over the years as he ministered to others. This will

help us for not only will it give evidence about his own spirituality but, at the same time, it will focus further on his preaching and application—the basic goals of our overall thesis.

Some preachers concentrate exclusively on their sermons. Even the prior call to holiness is by-passed. Charles Spurgeon tells of the most extreme case, the man who 'preached so well and lived so badly, that when he was in the pulpit everybody said he ought never to come out again, and when he was out of it, they all declared he never ought to enter it again'.[4]

Lloyd-Jones, in a lecture to the Christian Medical Fellowship, once commented about the tragedy of a man whose gravestone read, 'John Jones, born a man, died a grocer'.[5] He argued that a man is not to die as a grocer, or a doctor, or even a preacher. He is to die as he should have lived, a God-fearing man.

We pause to reflect briefly on a couple of his forebears who lived in differing centuries, both Scotsmen, and who, we believe, had characteristics in common with DML-J. Then we focus on him again.

SAMUEL RUTHERFORD (1600-61)

Samuel Rutherford was more than a preacher. He was a divine.[6] This old-fashioned term still has much to commend it. A person so described makes 'the pursuit of God', his life-long quest.

Anne Cousin was affected by his ministry in Scotland. From him, she had learned so much. He was a pastor in a place called Anworth by the Solway. He was arrested for preaching and, after a period in jail, was summoned to appear before the king. He died before being able to respond to the charges brought against him. Many of his choice phrases made an indelible impression on Anne. She assembled them together. As a result, she wrote one of the greatest Christian hymns, 'In Immanuel's Land'. The original rendering has nineteen verses. Each gives an insight into the preacing of Rutherford.

To aim solely to be an orator or an essayist is to fail as a preacher. Such never rank as 'divines'. To live to preach may seem a worthy object. Actually, it is myopic. Preachers are to live and die for the honour of God, ideally to pour out their lives as a living sacrifice.

When Rutherford was robbed of his pulpit and imprisoned, his faith did not fail. Neither did he feel that his life's purpose had been thwarted. Severed from his pulpit, he could not be separated from his Lord. Preaching was not the only thing for which he lived. Anne Cousin spoke for him as she relived his experiences and evaluated his sermon material.

E'en Anworth was not heaven
E'en preaching was not Christ
And in my sea-beat prison
My Lord and I held tryst:
And aye my murkiest storm-cloud
Was by a rainbow spann'd
Caught from the glory dwelling
In Immanuel's land.

Dr. Lloyd-Jones, in the closing part of his life, was to say, 'our great danger is to live on our activity; the ultimate test of a preacher is what he feels like when he cannot preach'.[7] He was effectively repeating what he had said in previous sermons. For example, he warned, when preaching from the Sermon on the Mount, 'I have seen men who have been indefatigable in the work of the kingdom suddenly laid aside by illness, and scarcely knowing what to do with themselves.'[8]

The statements are revealing. They demonstrate his inner convictions. The preacher should be engaged in an ever-deepening relationship with the Lord. When he, perchance, is no longer able to function as a preacher, he will still be able to go on enjoying the fellowship of the one whose company he has sought down the years.

James M. Gordon is on target when he declares that for Lloyd-Jones 'preaching and spirituality were inextricably linked'.[9] The man who preaches what he does not constantly experience is, at best, an actor and, at worst, a charlatan.

ROBERT MURRAY MCCHEYNE (1812-43)

He, too, was a divine, who impressed and challenged Lloyd-Jones despite the fact that the Scottish preacher died when he was scarcely thirty years old. DML-J reminds us that when McCheyne entered the pulpit, his spirituality was so evident, his congregation would weep.[10] The Scotsman declared his approach to the ministry in one of the finest lines ever spoken by a pastor: 'My people's greatest need is my personal holiness.'[11]

Further testimony to his godliness is found in a little-known book detailing the ministry of Duncan Matheson. The author recalled an occasion when, before setting out as a missionary to Turkey, he heard McCheyne preach. He remarked on the obvious holy deportment of the preacher, 'eternity stamped upon his brow'. He went on to say, 'I think I can yet see his seraphic countenance . . . and hear his sweet and tender voice. I was spell-bound, and could not keep my eyes off him for a moment.'[12]

Lloyd-Jones agreed that there must have been something about the Scotsman's face, and the conviction which his hearers possessed that he had come from God so that 'he was already preaching before he opened his mouth'.[13]

Paradoxically, the more holy the man, the more sinful he considers himself to be. There is, however, a glory which emanates from the throne of God. It can be infused. Though hidden to the recipient, it is as apparent to others as was the shekinah glory which caused Moses' face to shine with a lustre that both astonished and terrified the onlookers as he descended Mount Sinai (Exod. 34:29-35).

It is appropriate for a congregation to look for this from the man who commands their attention each Sunday. Afterall, he cannot preach on the supremacy of God without experiencing that supremacy in his own life. Thus, the godly preacher becomes a medium through which God reveals himself to the people. As God incarnated himself in the Lord Jesus, so he speaks through the words of the expositor whose desire is to reveal him. Greidanus states 'the only proper authority for preaching is divine authority—the authority of God's heralds, his ambassadors, his agents. Heralds and ambassadors . . . do not speak their own words but that of their Sender.'[14]

The words which are to be delivered should affect the preacher himself. An unknown writer has expressed the impact that a preacher's demeanour had upon him.

> For me 'twas not the truth you taught
> To you so clear to me so dim
> But when you came to me you brought
> A sense of him.
>
> And from your eyes He beckons me
> And from your lips His truth is shed
> 'Till I lose sight of you and see
> The Christ instead.

In his book on preaching, Haddon Robinson comments, 'Men and women must get past the preacher to the Saviour.' He adds, somewhat wryly and in parenthesis, 'or perhaps the Saviour must get past the preacher to the people!'[15]

MARTYN LLOYD-JONES

He would not have placed himself in the category of Rutherford or McCheyne. From conversion to homecall, his self-estimate was that he was simply a sinner found by a merciful God. One of his favourite hymns has the line 'A debtor to mercy alone'. At the end of his ministry at Westminster, he was to sign his farewell letter, 'your privileged and unworthy minister and friend'.[16] Some years later, when terminally ill, he was visited for the last time by Vernon Higham, a Welsh minister who had known him for years. As his compatriot left, DML-J called him back for a final word, 'Remember', he said, 'I am only a sinner saved by grace'.[17]

A man sent from God is aware of a great burden. He trembles because of the momentous consequences that he believes flow from his ministry.[18] Arguably, the private life of a politician or lecturer is of no concern to the general public. But this cannot be said of the preacher.

Although ministers of the Gospel differ in their personality and style, 'the individuality of preaching must be contextualized in holiness of life.'[19]

Those who live with us know us best. Thus, the estimate of Bethan Lloyd-Jones is highly significant and must be carefully weighed. 'No-one will ever understand my husband unless they first of all realise that he was a man of prayer and then an evangelist.' Her comment adds further weight to another of McCheyne's pronouncements, 'a man is what he is on his knees and nothing more'.

Geoffrey Thomas, a lawyer greatly influenced by Lloyd-Jones, testified to the godliness he registered when with him:

> There was nothing forbidding and no hint of condescension in the great preacher (DML-J). One felt in his presence that he was a man who obeyed his oft-quoted injunction 'Take time to be holy'. Thus, his bearing was one of benign calmness and kindly gravity, and one occasion on calling at his house at Ealing, I thought he had come straight from the presence of God. Indeed, at my very first interview with him as a pastor, I felt, as he showed me to the bus on the way home, a sense of calm by being in his presence.[20]

KNOWING GOD

A feature of Dr. Lloyd-Jones's ministry, which has escaped reference thus far, was his tendency to quote hymns. He had a wide-ranging knowledge of these which probably is traceable back to his boyhood and the 'singing festivals' common to the denomination in which he was brought up.[21] Most of the hymns he quotes are of an experiential nature. They were born out of revival and are descriptive of profound, religious experiences. They also seemed be expressing for him what he had personally known. One favourite to which he often refers was by William Williams:

Tell me thou art mine dear Saviour
Grant me an assurance clear
Banish all my dark misgivings
Still my doubting, calm my fear:

O my soul within me longeth
Now to hear thy voice divine,
So shall grief be gone for ever
And despair no more be mine.[22]

The verse summed up his deepest longings. During a period of depression following an illness, he once said that, when he found it hard to even read his Bible, the thing which helped most was simply to go through, in his mind, the hymns that he knew so well.

Possibly more than any notable minister this century, Lloyd-Jones preached experiential theology.[23] Within it can be heard his own cri de coeur. He frankly states his position in another biographical reference, which, interestingly enough, followed on from his dynamic experience of the Holy Spirit:[24]

I remember when I was a child that I had great difficulty in deciding what to wish for or what to choose when someone asked me to do so. But I do not have any difficulty with this request to state my desire for 1950. Before everything else my chief desire is 'so that I should know Him'. Nothing surprises me so much as I look back as seeing the tendency to be satisfied with other objects. I do not refer to sins so much as to the 'poor idols of the earth' or to backsliding. It is so easy to satisfy oneself with truths about the person. What gives more pleasure than theologising and being doctrinal about the faith, and even defending the faith? We are all ready to try to obtain and thirst after special experiences—assurance of forgiveness and salvation, being freed from special sins, experiencing joy and peace, being able to live the full life and so on. All these things are part of the heritage of the Christian, but he must not live on them and be satisfied by them. To know Him properly is a life full of peace.[25]

It is in his Ephesians' series perhaps more than any other that Lloyd-Jones attempted a comprehensive treatment of what he believed it really meant to know God. The urgency discernible in the sermons, even in printed form, indicates his deep conviction. Implicit in them is his own experience. In one of the earlier sermons, he typically confronted his congregation with a triplet of questions: 'Is God real to you? When you get on your knees and pray, do you know that God is there, do you realise His presence?'[26]

Lloyd-Jones then moves on into a daring area of experiential theology. A fairly full study of his messages might lead the student to believe that the most wonderful experience this side of heaven is the baptism in the Holy Spirit. Indeed, at times, Lloyd-Jones seems to assert this.[27] But in these sermons, he details the ultimate—the fullest knowledge of God which is obtainable for the believer:

> This is something beyond believing, beyond trusting, even beyond being sealed with the Spirit. The difference is that in the sealing with the Spirit, we are given to know that we are His; the Holy Spirit 'bears witness with our spirit that we are the children of God' (Romans 8:16). It is God saying to us, 'Thou art my son, my child'. Is there anything beyond that? Yes; to know God Himself! That is the summit, the 'summum bonum'. It is wonderful to know that I belong to God; it is an infinitely greater privilege and blessing to know God Himself.[28]

He confronted his congregation further, this time with four questions about their personal walk with the Lord. He reminded them of the book *The Practice of the Presence of God*.[29] He recalled that the author, Brother Lawrence, taught that such an experience is possible even when in the kitchen washing dishes and performing the most menial tasks.[30]

DML-J takes up the whole theme again when preaching from the third chapter of Ephesians. The penultimate sermon is entitled 'The Fullness Experienced' and gives a clear statement of what it means to seek God.[31]

PUBLIC WORSHIP

The spirituality of DML-J was to affect many people. At times it was felt and, in a sense, visible. There were those in the congregation who took note and registered it. Packer's testimony to Lloyd-Jones when he first heard him in London in 1948 is poignantly impressive, 'I went out [of Westminster Chapel] full of awe and joy and with a more vivid sense of the greatness of God in my heart than I had known before.'[32]

In the morning, the congregation commenced with the singing of the Doxology. This was followed by a short prayer, hymn, Scripture reading, a further hymn, a long prayer, notices, a hymn, the sermon, a final hymn and, to conclude, a benedictory prayer. Lloyd-Jones conducted the services entirely himself. The only other person to grace the pulpit at some part of the service was the church secretary. Had others participated and spontaneous contributions been allowed, however, one loss would have been the regular way in which DML-J, at great length, interceded before the Lord on behalf of the people. It was here that expressions and sentiments would flow freely with many similarities, as well as variations, week by week.

It is a pity that another 'Anne Cousin' has not selected the choice phraseology that often studded the prayers. One waited for the references to 'Almighty God our Heavenly Father' and the recognition of the sovereignty and majesty, holiness, power and mercy of the Lord to whom the prayer was being addressed.

The regular listener knew that against this would be set the futility and finitude of Man in his great confusion and need. Allusion would surely be made to the fleeting nature of life and the frailty of humanity—'our short, uncertain, earthly life and pilgrimage'.

The pained intercessor pleaded on behalf of men who, in their foolishness, live as though they would continue for ever, mindless of death and the oncoming judgment. The elderly would be mentioned, the 'aged and infirm' as well as the sick languishing on 'beds of pain'. Often reference would be made to Christian people who might be in danger of losing their faculties. His concern was that they would not forfeit their sense of the presence of God and the assurance that all was well with their soul.

Clearly, the minister was the pray-er. Yet, it was obvious that he was praying on behalf of his congregation. He was their spokesman. Personal pronouns gave way to plural. People were prayed for in general categories with no specific mention of individual church members. The congregation was invariably reminded that 'we come into Thy holy presence, O Lord, to worship Thee . . .'[33] And often one could feel the warmth in the acclamation, 'O Lord, *our* Lord . . .'

Pulpit prayer was never perfunctory. To the hearer it seemed as though the pray-er was toiling hard. He wished to read the mind of the Spirit and pray accordingly. There is an example of an occasion when an unusual intimation seemed to be given to him of the circumstances of a man who entered the chapel after the service had begun. On a later occasion, DML-J reflected on the incident.

A Welshman, a convert from the days of Lloyd-Jones's early preaching, who had fallen into a dreadful life of prodigality, determined to end it by throwing himself from Westminster Bridge into the Thames. Before he did so, a thought flashed through his mind that the Doctor would be just entering his pulpit for his evening service. So, he decided that he would go and listen once more before putting an end to his life. He made his way to Westminster Chapel in about six minutes. As he got through the front door and walked up the stairs into the gallery, he heard the words 'God have mercy upon the backslider'. DML-J was engaging in his pulpit prayers. The words stood out and radically affected the man. He repented, was restored to the Lord, and eventually became a deacon in a London church.[34]

ADDRESSING GOD

The doctrine you believe will shape the prayers that you offer. Someone has criticised certain trends in evangelicalism and what they perceive as an over-developed familiarity with God as a confusion of the Almighty with the all-matey. The fault lies in the worshippers' perception of God.

Dr. Lloyd-Jones held God in awe. His very name should be an object of reverence. He reminded his congregation that the Jews would not voice the name of Jehovah: it was so sacred. A substitute was employed. He bemoaned the fact that the sense of awe appeared to be lacking in some circles. 'The very thought of God in His transcendence, in His majesty and infinity, and in His glory should humble us. We should speak of Him with reverence and with godly fear.'[35]

Lloyd-Jones spoke about his approach to praying in public by, first, admitting to what he called 'the process of exclusion'. When engaging in public prayer, the pray-er must 'forget the congregation in a certain sense'. He is not speaking to them but to God. He is leading in prayer, 'so I have to shut out and forget people'. Second, he needs to 'shut out and forget himself'.[36] What he meant by this is that the person praying from the pulpit needs to be absolutely preoccupied with what he is doing, fastening his mind on God and becoming sensitive to the impulse of the Holy Spirit in order that he might pray effectively. Third, the thought of anyone thanking the preacher for praying is abhorrent. 'Public prayer should be such that the people who are praying silently and the one who is uttering the words should be no longer conscious of each other, but should be carried on the wings of prayer into the very presence of God.'[37]

Not only is this discovered in the fashion in which he prayed but also the vocabulary he employed. Each person of 'the blessed Trinity' would be invoked. The prayers would be to the Father through the Son and by the Holy Spirit.

Scour his volumes of sermons, listen to his tapes, some of which include his final pulpit prayers: never is he found indulging in familiarity as he addresses the Lord. Familiarity and intimacy, of course, are not synonyms. The latter can and should be present when a man is pleading with the God whom he loves and worships.

There is a revealing comment in one of his sermons. He refers to the respect which should be part of the attitude of the pray-er. One Friday evening he stated:

> . . . the more we know God and the more truly pious we are, the less inclined shall we probably be to use in prayer such phrases as: 'Dear God'. Rather we shall be more inclined to say, with the Lord Jesus Christ, 'Holy Father'. The more we realise something of the being of God, the more we realise the importance of treading carefully. You remember what God said to Moses, when He appeared in the burning bush, and Moses was approaching to investigate: 'Put off thy shoes from off thy feet, for the place whereon thou standest is holy ground'. That is it—reverence and godly fear because of His majesty.[38]

Frequently in his preaching, he referred to the Son of God as 'Our blessed Lord and Saviour Jesus Christ'. For him, the fact that the Father had bestowed on the Son the 'name that is above every name' was ever a delight. There seems to be a felt joy and surge of pride in the very way in which he mentioned the Saviour. To hear it with his Welsh accent and sometimes to see his face light up as he did so was to see someone enraptured with the Lord.

His respect for the person of God was such that he did not believe it was right to question the fairness of God. Any temptation toward this should be resisted. The example of Job is to be copied; a hand should be placed over the mouth as the pray-er appreciates the character of the One to whom the prayers are being addressed.[39]

A student of Dr. Lloyd-Jones's preaching would be well advised to acquaint himself with a selection of his public prayers[40] so that he will have the advantage not only of hearing the content, but feeling the passion and pathos of the intercessor.

Dr. J. H. Jowett, a former minister at Westminster, sounded out a warning concerning public prayer:

> There is nothing more dreadfully unimpressive than extemporary prayer which leaps about on the surface of things, a disorderly dance of empty words, going, we know not whither—a mob of words carrying no blood, bearing no secret of the soul, a whirl of insignificant expressions, behind which there is no vital pulse, no silent cry from lone and desolate depths.[41]

On this basis, he would have had no quarrel with his successor whose prayers were often tinged with soul-blood as, from the depths, he sought the Lord for his people, for the Church as a whole and for the nation.

PERSONAL PRAYER

In keeping with his strictures about the abuse of personality and his reluctance to make public disclosure about himself, it might seem that to write on the personal prayer life of Lloyd-Jones would be difficult, if not impossible. This is not the case. Spirituality cannot be hidden. The Apostle Paul, albeit in a slightly different context, refers to the decaying of the outward man and the rejuvenation of the inner. Both are obvious to the sensitive observer. Neither can be totally eclipsed.

Lloyd-Jones made a statement parallel to those of McCheyne:

> When a man is speaking to God, he is at his very acme. It is the highest activity of the human soul, and therefore it is at the same time the ultimate test of a man's true spiritual condition. There is nothing that tells the truth about us as Christian people so much as our prayer life. Everything we do in the Christian life is easier than prayer.[42]

He believed that God-consciousness was a fact of life. It is there innately. Even the 'so-called atheist has it'. He may argue against it, but this is because 'he does not want to believe in his mind what something within him keeps on asserting'.[43] He appealed to archaeological research to substantiate the point that all primitive tribes had a sense of the Supreme God at the back of everything.

There is revealing personal comment in correspondence with Dr.

Philip Hughes. DML-J cherished a friendship with him from the time he had met him as a student. Hughes went to South Africa. On one occasion, confessing that his letters had been somewhat irregular, Lloyd-Jones assured his friend: 'Although I have been so poor as a correspondent I can say truthfully that never a day passes but that I pray for you and my longing to see you grows constantly.'[44]

He enjoined a group of students studying to enter the ministry to obey every impulse to pray. He added 'this I regard as most important'.[45] The prayer life of a preacher drastically affects both his preparatory work and sermon delivery in the pulpit. It is much easier to 'preach from a pulpit like this than to pray' he said as he warned against prayerlessness.

The promptings to pray come from the Holy Spirit. They illustrate Paul's injunction, 'work out your own salvation with fear and trembling. For it is God *which worketh in you* both to will and to do of his good pleasure' (Phil. 2:12-13 AV).

Responding to the Holy Spirit's stimuli may well lead the minister into some of the choicest experiences he ever has. This is especially the case when studying the Bible and wrestling with a text.

> You will experience an ease and a facility in understanding what you were reading, in thinking, in ordering matter for a sermon, in writing, in everything which is quite astonishing, so respond to it immediately, and thank God if it happens to you frequently.[46]

One of the reasons why Abraham is credited as being the friend and confidant of God was because he ordered his family life well (Gen. 18:17, 19 AV). Roger Weil places us in his debt by lifting the curtain a little on Lloyd-Jones's habit of family prayers. The Doctor had been discussing the worsening spiritual condition in his native land. Weil says:

> I will always remember the deep note of sadness in that part of his prayer when he interceded for Wales, that God who had so singularly blessed her in days gone by would revive His work there once more. It was that tone of sadness that stuck in my mind at the time—I did not realise how it grieved his heart. I suppose it was memorable, too, because while on our knees there together we were privileged to glimpse him on a more personal level than ever we could in the services at the chapel. It was not so much the words but something more like a *groan* in how he said what he did.[47]

Two great dangers confront the preacher in Lloyd-Jones's estimation. The first we have touched on—the danger of a natural eloquence. To rest on that alone is disastrous. The other is professionalism. It subdivides into two particular areas of temptation. These are in the realms of prayer and Bible study.

For a man to become a pray-er simply because of his office is a disaster. In other words, he prays because he has to. His professional life is detached from his person. A type of schizophrenia develops.

Similarly, in the study of the Scriptures, his calling might tempt him to abuse them. On several occasions, Lloyd-Jones let it be known that he felt Scripture examinations ran this risk. To probe the Bible and cram the head with knowledge in order to satisfy an examiner is a misuse of Scripture. To read the Bible with the sole purpose of teasing out a sermon dishonours it. Such wrong approaches stifle spirituality and run the danger of doing what he so often warned against, grieving the Holy Spirit.

> One of the most fatal habits a preacher can ever fall into is to read his Bible simply in order to find texts for sermons. This is a real danger; it must be recognised and fought and resisted with all your might. Do not read the Bible because you want to find texts for sermons, read it because it is the food that God has provided for your soul.[48]

Lloyd-Jones believed one should endeavour to read the Bible through every year. He actually used Murray McCheyne's Bible-reading scheme. The Bible should be read with humility and care. This especially applies to those who are called to preach. Once DML-J referred to a difficult passage of Scripture with the cautionary note that anyone who approaches this section without 'fear and trembling' is not really fit to expound Scripture at all.[49]

JOY AND SOLEMNITY

Does godliness exclude humour? No; those who knew Lloyd-Jones will testify to his great sense of fun.[50] But the Gospel is too serious and sensitive for the deliberate employment of humour in the pulpit.[51]

Some insight into his convictions on sobriety and happiness (which he would not have considered as mutually exclusive) is given in his careful treatment of the second beatitude; 'Blessed are they that mourn for they shall be comforted'. Some extended comment.[52] will not only furnish us with his views but it will also give yet another example of his preaching method and skills.

Dr. Lloyd-Jones reminds us that there is no description in the Gospels of our Lord's laughing. He agrees that the argument from silence is not conclusive. But he builds up a picture of 'the Man of Sorrows' who had such a heaviness when confronted with the sins of the world that the listener is ready to concede his point.

From this, he argues against levity, and a superficial jollity. There is almost a sense of relief when we come to his treatment of the second part of the Beatitude—'for they shall be comforted'.

'Comfort' he sees in terms of the consolations and joys which the Gospel brings. By the time he is through preaching this Scripture-studded sermon, he is able to employ such terminology as 'a serious joy'. He deepens our understanding of both happiness and joy. Read only half the sermon and you might be tempted to put it down in despair. But you will be doing Lloyd-Jones an injustice. He wants you to stay with him all the way.

His approach to preaching is as though he had a pair of scales in the pulpit. In one, he placed the 'negatives'.[53] He itemises issues that cause sorrow and, maybe, lead to depression. Just when you think there is no hope of ever being able to laugh and at the same time be spiritual he checks your premature conclusion. He attends to the other balance. He proceeds to do full justice to the Lord's teaching, the Scriptures and the development of a sanctified personality.

TESTIMONY

Embedded in the preaching of Lloyd-Jones is much that reveals his own heart and attitudes. Never quick to say anything impressive about himself, he does not show the same reticence when engaging in self-appraisal. On one occasion, he endeavoured to deal with the misguided approach to the person of our Lord in terms of his being our example. All we have to do is to copy him. Coupled to this, he linked another attitude which needed investigation, that one should make a determined effort to keep the Sermon on the Mount and all will be well. The flaw, common to both approaches, is the utter failure to grasp the uniqueness of the Gospel and the rottenness of the human psyche.

Lloyd-Jones narrows the criticism down and deals with the issue by taking it on board personally. In a choice, unanswerable and moving piece of argumentation he asserts:

Example of Jesus? I know of nothing that is so discouraging as the
example of Jesus! As I look at His moral stature, at His absolute perfection, as I see Him walking through this world without sin, I feel
that I am already condemned and hopeless. Imitation of Christ? It is
the greatest nonsense that has ever been uttered! Imitation of Christ?
I who cannot satisfy myself and my own demands, and other people
still less—am I to imitate Christ? The saints make me feel ashamed of
myself. I read of men like George Whitefield and others, and I feel that
I have not yet started. And yet, I am told to take this ethical teaching
of the Sermon on the Mount, this idealistic social teaching, and to put
this into practice! 'It is so marvellous,' they say, 'it will stimulate you';
look at Him and follow Him![54]

The only resolution to the problem of human weakness is the atoning
work of Christ. That, and the subsequent indwelling of the Holy Spirit,
positions the believer to strive after holiness.

HOLINESS

This, he taught, is not a feeling. Holiness is a life lived to the glory of
God and to his eternal praise.[55] Basic to his position on holiness was a
rejection of the old Keswick doctrine of a second experience. The maintenance of godliness involves the Christian in a fight which lasts
throughout the whole of life.

Lloyd-Jones opposed the teaching which suggests all the believer has
to do is to 'let go and let God'. There are no easy 'fixes'. Even the
Baptism of the Spirit, viewed as a critical experience, does not transport
the blessed person into an unblemished, holy life. The baptism empowers for service rather than positions for holiness.

James Packer is not using too extravagant language when he reckoned that, for Lloyd-Jones, maxims such as 'stop trying and start trusting' were scandalous. Even a cursory reading of the final two volumes
on Ephesians indicates the passion of DML-J's argument which negates
such unhelpful advice. 'In teaching holiness, the life of obedience to
Christ whereby one abides in Him, Dr. Lloyd-Jones saw quietest pas-
sivity as a kind of modern demon possessing evangelical minds and
needing explicit exorcism.'[56]

Packer continues that though Lloyd-Jones did not believe that
Romans 7 describes the war between the flesh and the spirit but rather
sets forth the condition of the believer in the period before his regeneration, he did pronounce on the reality of spiritual warfare and the life-

long struggle which Christians have against the world, the flesh and the devil.

SIN AND JUDGMENT

Holiness is a strong element in the ministry of DML-J. His teaching counterbalances another subject on which he also taught with strength and passion. We refer to sin and judgment. If sin is the disease, holiness is what should follow after the cure has been applied.

Lloyd-Jones believed that a man must discipline himself to hate sin. He must train himself to hold God in awe and be fearful of judgment. Observing this may well mean that he will be dubbed puritanical. So be it. The worthy Puritans were scorned as being 'specialists in sin'. Lloyd-Jones encourages us to analyse sin in order to get rid of it at all costs within ourselves.[57]

Few men in the twentieth century can have denounced sin so fiercely and warned of judgment to come more passionately than he did.[58] An excellent sermon of his, revealing not only what we dub his diagnostic approach to preaching but his presentation of the doctrine of sin, is found in his series on the Sermon on the Mount. He entitled it 'The Mortification of Sin'.[59] We try to adduce, though only partially, what might have been his preaching outline. Lloyd-Jones expounds our Lord's words: 'And if thy right hand offend thee, cut it off, and cast it from thee: for it is profitable for thee that one of thy members should perish, and not that thy whole body should be cast into hell' (Matt. 5:30 AV).

The Lord in a dramatic fashion demands discipline from members of the Kingdom which he has come to establish. Kingdom people live differently. DML-J explains the statement and in so doing reveals his approach in dealing with sin and, as a result, achieving godliness.

He raises and answers the question, 'How are we to cope with this problem of sin?' He starts his analysis by stating the obvious—it is not a case of external acts. The pollution is in the heart.

Typically he works out his propositions. To deal with sin we need to realise:

- Its nature and also its consequences.
- The importance of the soul and its destiny.
- Sin must be hated and everything must be done at all costs to attempt to destroy it.
- The ideal in this matter is to have a clean and pure heart.
- The goal is sin's mortification.

He picks up on the goal and, in typical fashion, makes his applications. In order to achieve this:

- The flesh must never be fed.
- The flesh must be restrained.
- The price that had to be paid to deliver us from sin must be appreciated.

All these resolves bring us to see our need of the Holy Spirit's enabling. DML-J appeals to Paul's injunction that we should attempt to mortify the deeds of the body. In striving thus, we align ourselves with the goal of the Lord. He died to deliver us from this present evil world. Faced with his love and his suffering, Isaac Watts's sentiments become our own, 'Love so amazing, so divine, demands my soul, my life, my all'. To achieve this surrender we need the infilling of the Spirit. It is through the Spirit that we are able to crucify the flesh. We work with him. He works with us.[60]

SPIRITUAL WARFARE

Basic to his concerns for personal and congregational godliness was also an experiential as well as theological approach to the hideous power of evil. We mean by this that, for Lloyd-Jones, evil was not an abstract quality—nor was it to be defined just as the absence of goodness. Evil is incarnated in Satan. The world, in which he has taken up residence, is infested with his emissaries. His malevolent activity is the only explanation for the story of Man and, at times, his obscene acts. What is more, the devil picks out the Church as an object of hate. Individual Christians are in the firing line. Satan's goal is to eliminate the glory of God, to undo the work the Lord achieved on the Cross. Christians should consider themselves as involved in mortal combat with the enemy of their souls.

During the period of Dr. Lloyd-Jones's ministry, some clerics within the Church of England went on record in a letter to *The Times* newspaper denying the existence of the devil.[61] DML-J protested. His was one of the few influential voices from within the Evangelical Church which gained any hearing. C. S. Lewis claimed that one of the great triumphs of the devil was his success in conning people into disbelieving his existence. In a manner reminiscent of Lewis and doubly interesting because it shows how Lloyd-Jones could skilfully use illustration, he warned:

Concealment is the whole art of angling. One of the first rules in fishing is to keep yourself out of sight, to camouflage yourself. Throw out your line and let it be a long one so that the fish does not see you sitting or standing by. Hide yourself! It is one of the first rules in angling; and the Devil is a past master at this.[62]

He went on to bemoan that the church is 'drugged and deluded, not aware that there is a conflict at all'.

He was even more anxious because he believed that modern thinking about evil influenced evangelical theology. There is a danger that the Evangelical Church is unclear on the nefarious activity and the powers of the devil in the present age. He believed there was a culpable failure to grasp the degree of malevolence and the extent of power that the devil has. He can invade the life of Christians. In some circumstances, this results not only in demon oppression but possession.[63] DML-J took to task one writer for affirming that demon possession had not taken place since the Apostolic era.[64]

For Lloyd-Jones, spiritual warfare was no phoney, imaginary war. The devil was real to him.[65] The stakes were high, the conflict bloody. Christians needed to defend themselves, 'to put on the whole armour of God'. He believed that sometimes the devil targeted one particular person, or church, or even a country in a malign fashion, doing his utmost to wreak destruction.[66] He preached probably the longest series on the wiles of the devil since the Puritan William Gurnall.[67] Surprisingly he did not deal with the issue of demon possession and exorcism even though he was examining the attacks of the devil on people.[68]

Why did DML-J preach so often on judgment and at length on the devil and his tactics? The answer is to do with his own personal concerns for godliness, coupled with the desire to urge the same on his listeners. In language almost reminiscent of his teaching technique, it can be argued that he enhanced the positive by warning about the negative. He confesses this in one of his sermons, 'thus far we have been almost entirely negative; but we have to be negative'.[69] The godly man knows even more about ungodliness. He is only too aware of it and thus he attempts to shun it. He preaches for godliness and preaches against ungodliness. This was Lloyd-Jones's practice. It is Pauline.

PURSUING RIGHTEOUSNESS

A favourite hymn of Lloyd-Jones was 'Take time to be holy'. Another has the line, 'the love of Jesus what it is none but his loved ones know'.

He asked his congregation if they did give the Lord time. Not to take the opportunity to pursue holiness results in a deficient knowledge of the Lord.

> . . . give Him opportunities of telling you. He will meet you in the Scriptures, and He will tell you. Give time, give place, give opportunity. Set other things aside, and say to other people, 'I cannot do what you ask me to do; I have another appointment, I know He is coming and I am waiting for Him'.[70]

He revealed his own practice as he further enjoined his hearers to look for the Lord and to expect him. He asked, 'do you allow Him, do you give Him opportunities to speak to you, and to let you know His love to you?'

When preaching through Ephesians, the Doctor confessed to his congregation that recently he had wanted to thank God in a certain matter. Apparently he had been short of time and his diary was full. He continued:

> I was on the point of offering up a hurried word of thanksgiving to God in order that I might turn to the urgent task; but realising what was happening, I suddenly said to myself: 'that is not the way to thank God. Do you realise whom you are about to thank?' Everything must be laid aside when you are turning to Him; everything, everyone, all things, however urgent. What are they compared with Him? Stop! Pause! Wait! Recollect! Realise what you are doing.[71]

OLD AGE

Early in his London ministry he challenged his congregation about this.[72] The sermon gives further insight into his own conviction concerning the ministry. It underlines the point made earlier that preaching should not be the sum total of the preacher's life. Expressed another way:

> That is why many a man dies suddenly after he has retired from business; and often a wise doctor will advise such a man not to give up altogether, but to go two or three times a week to his business . . . that applies in Christian work. A man may live on his own preaching instead of on Christ, just as a man can live on his business. But when old age has come he cannot do these things; his powers are failing him,

and he cannot appreciate the things of the world. And there he is left to himself! That is the test.[73]

Wesley is reputed to have said of the Methodists, 'our men die well'. The reason was that they spent their lives preparing for their departure. At another period in his ministry, DML-J challenged his congregation, asking if they were looking forward to heaven. He buttressed his comments by referring to Matthew Henry who said 'we are never told in the Scriptures that we should look forward to death: but we are told very frequently that we should look forward to heaven'.[74]

The concept that one can be so heavenly-minded as to be of no earthly use is absurd. Paradoxically, it is the heavenly-minded people who often get things done on earth. Lloyd-Jones would challenge his congregation from what were the bases of his own convictions and his own walk with the Lord:

How often do you think of heaven and rejoice when you think of it? Does it give you a sense of strangeness and of fear, a desire, as it were, to avoid it? If it does so to any degree, I fear we must plead guilty that we are living on too low a level. Thoughts of heaven ought to make us rejoice and be exceedingly glad. True Christian living is to be like Paul and to say 'to me to live is Christ, and to die is gain'. Why? Because it means, 'to be with Christ; which is far better,' to see Him and to be like Him.[75]

Lloyd-Jones deprecated Tennyson's idea in his poem 'Crossing the Bar':

Sunset and evening star,
And one clear call for me!
And may there be no moaning of the bar,
When I put out to sea.[76]

Elizabeth Catherwood remembered her father's response to her comment that it was beautiful: 'but it is wrong, it is wrong'.[77] Charles Wesley's imagery in his great hymn, 'Jesu Lover of my Soul', is to be preferred for it is biblical and therefore accurate:

Safe into the haven guide,
O receive my soul at last.

This is the Christian view of death.

It is going home, it is entering into harbour . . . not a setting out on to an uncharted ocean, not going vaguely into some dim, unchartered world. Not at all, but an entrance into the haven . . . therefore he faces death and says I am going home . . . So the fear of death is gone—he does not object to going because he knows exactly where he is going and to whom he is going. He thinks also of the abundant entrance.[78]

Lloyd-Jones would sometimes argue, when referring to men of great influence and opinion who had graced public life, that one should get hold of a good biography and read how they lived and died. How did they cope with the big issues? This would give a great insight into the value of their political or philosophical system. Did it work for them? Sadly, more often than not, the answer is no. In crisis situations and in the tremendous time of preparing for death, they were in trouble.[79]

By his own criteria, Lloyd-Jones should be judged. How did he die? The question is blunt. But if he raised it about others, it is right it should be directed to himself. Murray tells us that in those final weeks, he saw more smiles on Dr. Lloyd-Jones's face than he had ever known. This testimony becomes even more precious when one recalls that he had preached about the Lord making his presence very real to some saints at the point of departure. 'Many have testified to this immediately before their death—the greatest crisis of all. Suddenly he has appeared to them, and the people standing by the bedside have seen a smile upon their faces.' He went on to speak of an old friend who cried out that he had seen the Lord.[80]

Listen to him as he reminded his huge congregation in the 1960s of the help that the believer receives in 'that tremendous hour':

I fear that we neglect the ministry of angels; we do not think sufficiently about it. But whether we realise it or not, there are angels who are looking after us . . . We do not see the most important things; we only see the things that are visible. But we are surrounded by angels; and they are appointed to look after us and to minister to us— guardian angels. I do not pretend to understand it all; I know no more than the Bible tells me—but I do know this, that His servants, the angels, are my servants . . . they are looking after us . . . And I further know that when we come to die, they will carry us to our appointed place.[81]

Iain Murray, as we have seen, reached a peak of sensitivity when he recorded of Lloyd-Jones that his appearance in the last months combined the utmost gravity 'with more smiles than, it seemed to me, I ever remembered before; and his face often glistened especially when he prayed'.[82]

Days before he left for the land about which he had often spoken and to which, through the preaching of the Gospel, he had endeavoured to direct tens of thousands, he wrote to his wife (he was unable to communicate verbally) 'do not pray for healing. Do not hold me back from the glory'. Again, it is recorded that he was full of smiles for his family. What was happening? The Psalmist had touched on it long before the advent of modern biographies, 'they looked unto him and were lightened' (Ps. 34:5 AV).

When his physician wanted to prescribe more medication, he was reluctant. He pointed his hand heavenward. Not the moaning of the bar was heard, but the gentle, urgent call of his Lord brought by his messengers. DML-J practised what he preached. He did not live on his activity. He lived by faith. Preaching to others, he had first preached to himself; 'more and more I can see that ministers *must* preach to themselves' (his emphasis).

Before moving away from this subject in order to consider the earlier part of Dr. Lloyd-Jones's preaching career, we want to take our readers to one of the most striking passages he ever spoke on the subject of godliness. It is found in a message from his series on the Sermon on the Mount. Though he expresses himself in the second person, in effect, he lifts the veil and sets down what was his personal code of conduct and what his goals and attitudes were. The sermon is an exposition of the 'Narrow Way'. DML-J persuasively points out the route:

> To enter this way means to follow in the footsteps of the Lord Jesus Christ. It is an invitation to live as He lived, it is an invitation to become increasingly what He was. It is to be like Him, to live as He lived whose life we read of in these Gospels. That is what it means; and the more we think of it in that way, the greater will the inducement be. Do not think of what you have to leave; there is nothing in that. Do not think of the losses, do not think of the sacrifices and sufferings. These terms should not be used; you lose nothing, but you gain everything. Look at Him, follow Him, and realise that ultimately you are going to be with Him, and to look into His blessed face and enjoy Him to all eternity.[83]

7

The Earlier Years

*But what did you do about it when I warned you that
Sunday night in Aberavon? What effect have all my repeated
pleadings with you had upon you? Did you give up your sin?
Did you strive with all your might?*[1]

Ah! It is always madness that rejects Christ.[2]

Martyn Lloyd-Jones

Dr. Lloyd-Jones's ministry was thoroughly Evangelical. In the course
of one of his expositions, he quoted the reaction of a lady who complained about his ministry. The remark could well have been in the early
years. His critic was dismissive of him alleging, 'this man preaches to us
as though we were sinners!' Lloyd-Jones ruefully retorted 'Unthinkable!'
And he added that her assessment gave him both the greatest encouragement and pleasure.[3] Indeed, one of his first recorded comments on
preaching notes that the best sign a man can ever have that he is preaching the Gospel of Christ is that certain people take 'violent objection' to
what he is saying and feel a sense of 'grudge' and 'annoyance'.[4]

Lloyd-Jones protested against the use of the pulpit as what he called
'a coward's castle' into which a man might retreat to vent his spleen on
his enemies or simply as a place where he can express his own view. No,
this amounts to pulpit abuse. The legitimate use of the pulpit is when 'a
man is simply and honestly preaching the Gospel of Jesus Christ'. Such

an occupant may disturb his congregation and be judged 'an objectionable person' by some of them. Paradoxically, if this is the response, he
can take courage. This is precisely what happened to the Lord, 'almost
every time he preached there was a conference among certain people as
to how they could catch Him or destroy Him'.[5]

REVIEW

We have noted that 1949 was a critical year. Not only did DML-J have
an encounter with evil forces but in a very gracious way the Lord met
with him and filled him with the Holy Spirit.

R.T. Kendall is the second successor to Dr. Lloyd-Jones at
Westminster Chapel. He wrote an article reviewing three books of
Lloyd-Jones's sermons which had been preached at different times in his
pulpit career.[6] According to Kendall's evaluation, there is a discernible
difference in Lloyd-Jones's preaching prior and subsequent to the events
of 1949.

Kendall reasoned that in the earlier years, DML-J's preaching was
more intellectual and, in the later, more simple and biblical. Apparently,
Dr. Lloyd-Jones admitted as much to him in personal conversation. The
reviewer went on to comment that although certain aspects of Lloyd-
Jones's style remained constant, 'he obviously preached as he himself
was gripped more than when he employed the meticulous, balanced
exposition of each verse as he later came to do'.

The purpose of this chapter is to reflect on Dr. Lloyd-Jones's ministry before 1949 and to make some contrast with what was to follow.
After all, were it to be proved that his spiritual experience in 1949 was
not comparable to anything he had known previously and his preaching had effectively changed as a result, it would add personal testimony
to the argument that the baptism in the Spirit enhances the preaching
ministry in a notable fashion.[7] This is considered at the end of the
chapter.

It is appropriate here to quote in full Lloyd-Jones's comments on the
experience of Moody. The influence the American evangelist's testimony
had had on him was considered earlier.

> D.L. Moody, after his experience of thus having the Holy Ghost shed
> forth upon him, this baptism with the Spirit, said: 'I went on preach-
> ing the same, old sermons as I had been preaching before. But, he
> added, 'they were absolutely different'. And they were. And they were
> different in their results. The same sermons, and yet they were not the

same sermons. There was this demonstration of the Spirit and of power. It is the same with many others.[8]

Returning to Dr. Kendall's article, two comments are worth making. The idea of being gripped by the substance of the passage bespeaks unction more than intellectualism. Second, a careful investigation into the content of Lloyd-Jones's later sermons makes it debatable whether they are quite as meticulously balanced as is suggested by his reviewer. In other words, we are arguing that the differences pre- and post-1949 may not be quite so obvious or so significant.

EARLY MINISTRY

Our task now requires an examination of the extant sermons from the first period of ministry. Though far more material exists of Lloyd-Jones's preaching after 1949, there is still a good quantity of messages available to read which were delivered before this date.[9] We must stress the importance of this exercise. Any who wish to benefit from studying his structure and style of ministry would be well advised not to ignore the earlier period in favour of concentrating only on the later sermons contained in his published works.

No serious student of the ministry of Charles Spurgeon would bypass his New Park Street Pulpit.[10] There are to be found sermons from his early twenties which have a forceful, passionate, evangelistic style and are typically full of flashes of inspiration and quotable passages. In a remarkably similar fashion, this applies to Dr. Lloyd-Jones's messages. The comments of his publisher are apposite, '. . . it was given to him—in a manner reminiscent of some of the famous, younger preachers of other centuries—to proclaim the truth with unusual authority and with passion for the salvation of his hearers'.[11]

Elsewhere we have spoken of the outstanding blessing which attended the opening ministry when DML-J was preaching in his native Wales.[12] After coming to London, Dr. Lloyd-Jones's pulpit ministry became influential internationally. However, despite the blessing and the fruit which followed, revival was not to flow, even though he yearned for it. James Packer commented that 'it was a source of sadness to him that he never saw revival in England at Westminster Chapel as in a real measure he had seen in his South Wales pastorate in 1929-31'.[13] The fact that his early ministry was so singularly blessed, with much evidence of the working of the Holy Spirit, demands that we place special emphasis on this period in his preaching ministry.

EVANGELISTIC SERMONS AT ABERAVON

Particular attention should be given to this book. The sermons it contains are the first that DML-J delivered in his Welsh pastorate. Because they are hand-written, we adjudge them to represent and illustrate his earliest and considered views on homiletics and hermeneutics. Thus, our detailed consideration. The book is a sample from one hundred and twenty manuscripts which were apparently discovered in the attic of Dr. Lloyd-Jones's London home. They represent a great 'find', throwing light on his preaching style and philosophy. The publishers selected twenty-one of them for the book and reasonably claimed they represent an example of what gospel preaching should be.[14]

As is well known, Lloyd-Jones split his sermons into two categories: basically, instructional and evangelistic. Later, he spoke of a third this is illustrated in the material he used in his Westminster Friday evening Bible studies. Actually there is a great deal of overlap. Some of his most helpful, instructional addresses contain a good element of gospel and would stand on their own as gospel addresses. Conversely, some of his gospel sermons are excellent examples of instructional messages. He retained a fixed, commendable goal to ensure that each Sunday evening there would be a clear presentation of the essentials of the Gospel.

DML-J soon stopped his practice of writing out both Sunday sermons. Lack of time made this impossible. So he contented himself with a skeleton-draft of his morning message and writing out the evening sermon. He did this for ten years until, once more, lack of time caused him to discontinue the exercise, thus working at and preaching from sermon outlines at both services.

Preachers at the beginning of their careers would do well to copy Lloyd-Jones's early discipline in composing a full script. He then endeavoured to commit his script to memory. He felt that the latter practice was wrong because it became too mechanical. It became a recital and thus was not true preaching.[15] Nonetheless, writing the script out has value. The habit tunes the mind and helps the preacher to be more economical with words. Such is not always easy when preaching from a skeleton. A short outline can mean a needlessly long address. Word-economy can improve the effectiveness of the preacher and be appealing to the congregation!

DML-J illustrates the danger which confronts most preachers at the outset of their ministry (and some throughout the full course!) of cramming too much material into one address. In a very honest passage, he mentions his indebtedness to an older preacher with whom he shared a pulpit in the first twelve months of his pastorate in Wales. The elderly minister had not heard DML-J preach before.

> As we were being driven in a car together to have some tea at the house of the minister of the church, the old preacher, who was exactly sixty years older than I was, very kindly and with a desire to help and to encourage me gave me a very serious warning. 'The great defect of that sermon this afternoon was this', he said, 'that you were overtaxing your people, you were giving them too much . . . you are only stunning them and not helping them.' And then he said, 'You watch what I shall be doing tonight. I shall really be saying one thing, but I shall say it in three different ways.'[16]

Dr. Lloyd-Jones adds that he demonstrated his point very effectively.

Let us now concentrate on two of the recurrent themes found in the early sermons—many of which were to become constant in his later years.

JUDGMENT

One of the reasons Lloyd-Jones gave for leaving medicine was his increasing belief that he had a greater calling than endeavouring to cure those who were ill. He was to minister to those who were sick in soul and in danger of eternal judgment. Benefits received from the medical practitioner are short-lived. A patient has to move on into eternity to face God. How he fares then depends on his response to the Gospel. The cure of souls was of supreme importance. This conviction compelled him to say farewell to the medical profession.

Examples from his initial sermons illustrate how awesome he considered the judgment of God to be. There is no doubt that to warn people of this was one of the great stimuli which prompted the above course of action. His strong belief in the judgment of God was evident from the outset of the ministry. However unfashionable and unpalatable the doctrine might be, he preached it. He did not hesitate to warn of what Gilbert Tennent called 'the terrors'.[17]

> I am not afraid of being charged, as I frequently am, of trying to frighten you, for I am definitely trying to do so. If the wondrous love of God in Christ Jesus and the hope of glory is not sufficient to attract you, then, such is the value I attach to the worth of your soul, I will do my utmost to alarm you with a sight of the terrors of Hell.[18]

His conclusion is even more pressing as he endeavoured to draw in the net:

> Eternal remorse, eternal misery, eternal wretchedness, unchangeable torment, such is the lot of all who content themselves with just agreeing with and enjoying the Gospel, but who, for some reason or other, never forsake all else and embrace it with a whole heart. God save us all from it, as He is indeed waiting to do. For His Name's sake. Amen.[19]

The urgency of his presentation sprang from his conviction that only in the Gospel is there any way of escape, 'were it not for this we should all be damned'.[20] 'But if you reject God's offer, if you put anything else before it, if you begin to make excuses and insult God and to insist upon your own terms, then there is but one alternative—hell.'[21] 'If you feel that you have any right to demand pardon and forgiveness from God, I can assure you that you are damned and lost.'[22]

THE CROSS

Preaching on the wrath of God caused him to be even more earnest in spelling out the message of the Cross. This was done frequently. An observation was made that Lloyd-Jones did not place enough emphasis on the objective nature of the atonement in the first year of his preaching.[23] Apparently he was challenged about this in 1929.[24] In an interview with Carl Henry, he was asked if there was any ambiguity in his earlier preaching. He confessed, 'I preached regeneration as the great message but not justification (George Whitefield did the same, you know). I preached what I was sure of, but within about two years I came to see that was an incomplete message.'[25]

He took the corrective to heart. This is demonstrated by the powerful passages in his sermons which emphasise that the anchorage for our salvation is in the work of our Lord on the Cross. On one occasion, he employed gripping language invoking personal testimony to secure his point.

> I only know that my rags and tatters have really gone when I see them on the Person of Jesus Christ, the Son of God, who wore them in my stead and became a curse in my place. The Father commanded Him to take my filthy rags off me, and He has done so. He bore my iniquity, He clothed and covered Himself with my sin. He has taken it away and has drowned it in the sea of God's forgetfulness ... My only

consolation when I consider the past is that God has blotted it out. No other could do so. But He has done so. It is the first essential step in a new beginning. The past must be erased, and in Christ and His atoning death, it is![26]

Clearly, he was riveted by the Cross-work of the Lord. He applied its message to his hearers. He wanted them to 'admire' the life of Jesus Christ. But admiration and emotion are not sufficient. The congregation had to realise that the Cross had personal implications for them. He asserted that people would never feel their whole soul and entire being going out to God in gratitude, wonder and adoration until they were conscious of the fact that he died for them and experienced his life and power flooding their souls, cleansing and transforming them 'infusing power . . . turning your defeats into victories and liberating you from the power of sin'. He added, 'and that is offered to you tonight in the Gospel of Jesus Christ'.[27] On another occasion, he movingly declared:

> The sins of the whole world He had borne upon Himself, He had ful-filled the law, had silenced the jeers of all the devils, and had rendered satisfaction unto God. The sacrifice was completed.[28]

And again,

> 'If you really desire to honour and please me', says God in effect, 'hon-our my Son and please Him.' Accept Jesus Christ as the Son of God, trust to His death for your pardon, rely upon His merit and glorious Person for your justification and righteousness, and make it the busi-ness of your life to do all you can by His strength and help to please Him and obey His commands.[29]

NOTABLE COMMENTS

Possibly because the sermons we have available are in manuscript form, striking sentences stand out, making him, if anything, more quotable in his early ministry than in the later one. Here is a sample of some of his pronouncements:

On the Gospel:

> The narrowness of the gospel—I speak with reverence—is the nar-rowness that is in God Himself.[30]
> If you are not saved by it, you are of necessity condemned by it.[31]

On the futility of works:

They had constructed their ladders with rung after rung of good thoughts and noble actions, pious hopes and good deeds, but the highest rung was still infinitely short of the heavenly goal.[32]

On our Lord's preaching:

Christ never said anything accidentally. He had all the letters of the alphabet at his command.[33]

On the Church:

One of the most dangerous places to be is in the Church of the living God.[34]

On conversion:

The first move on the road to being a Christian is to cease to be a snob, whether social, intellectual or moral.[35]

On anaemic discipleship:

A spineless Christianity.[36]

On humility:

You will never be humble until you face yourself honestly.[37]

On death:

He will not only lead us to the river, He will be with us in the river and beyond it to all eternity. He is not only faithful in life but also in death. He will be with us to the end. To the end? Throughout the countless ages of eternity! For ever! What more do you need?[38]

STYLE

Certain features stand out in these early sermons. Dr. Lloyd-Jones's style is, by his own confession, deliberate.

The dramatic present[39]

This has the impact of enabling the hearer to witness a quoted event as though it is actually happening. In effect, it gives the congregation 'eyes'. An example occurs in an address entitled, 'The Straight Gate.'

Do you see the picture? There they all are near the gate, with one eye certainly on the gate, the other on the world and all it has to give. Suddenly, they realise the master of the house is shutting the gate, so they all make a mad rush and a wild dive for the door. But alas! the way is so narrow, the entry is so confined and they are such a crowd, that all they succeed in doing is to block up the road, hinder one another, create a state of panic and produce a stampede. The more frantic and violent they become, the more impossible do they make it for one another to get in! There they are struggling and cursing and fighting and groaning . . . do you now see the reason for striving while there is still time and before it is too late?[40]

Imagination[41]

Allied to this, but arguably deserving a separate category, is use of imagination. A sanctified imagination is a helpful tool, provided the preacher does not exploit it by engaging in flights of fancy! He is justified in suggesting what the larger framework in a narrative may have been. This intuitive approach needs spiritual sensitivity and should be employed cautiously, but it can help the hearer to 'see' facets of the narrative which might not immediately be obvious to them. Note, for instance, Lloyd-Jones's description of the Prodigal Son: 'Never has a more hopeless picture been drawn than that of this boy lost in the far country, amidst the husks and the swine, penniless and friendless, utterly hopeless and forlorn, utterly desolate and dejected.'[42]

In another sermon, the outline of which we endeavour to deduce later, he states: 'It needs little imagination *to read between the lines* the fact that Jairus had already tried many other means and methods and expedients to heal the child and save her life.'[43]

In later years, he spoke specifically about the use of imagination in sermons, realising its dangers but also advocating its advantages. 'Imagination has a real place in preaching the truth, because what it does is to make the truth lively and living.' A line, however, has to be drawn. This should be before the preacher is using imagination for its own sake, delighting in it and putting into a secondary place the only justifiable reason for using imagination—to make the truth clear.[44]

The applicatory principle[45]

On returning to the mining community in South Wales, Dr. Lloyd-Jones found that his medical education did not rob him of an ability to communicate to ordinary people and show them the pertinence of the Christian message to their own lives. He endeavoured to speak out to his contemporaries in a way that encouraged them to see that, though his ministry was rooted in history and was full of doctrine, it had life-changing significance for them.

He encouraged preachers to adopt this method. It was a constant in his own ministry. When engaged in his later, systematic expository ministry in London, he sometimes pointed out how remarkable it was that the verses he was expounding were applicable to the events which were capturing the newspaper headlines.[46]

The need to be relevant[47]

This is the other side of the same coin. The preacher who wishes to apply what he has to say will always want to be relevant. In a rare piece of autobiography, when preaching from the Ephesian Epistle, Lloyd-Jones reflected on his early days. He did this in a manner which we might expect from someone who was sensitive about speaking personally.

> I am going to be a fool, and say something about myself. I remember how, in the very first year when I began to preach, I was preaching in a service with an old preacher who was over eighty years of age. Having listened to my feeble effort, and having heard me for the first time, the old man made this comment which encouraged me very greatly. He said, 'Though you are a young man, you are preaching the old truths I have been trying to preach all my life.' He went on, 'You are preaching the old truths, but you have put a very modern suit on them.'[48]

One might have expected that this desire would have induced Lloyd-Jones to major on topical sermons. The fact is that only on very rare occasions did he attempt this in the course of his ministry. He would probably have assessed himself in the same way as he did his predecessor, Campbell Morgan—it was not his natural style and he could not do it effectively.[49]

It is possible for a preacher to be relevant and topical without resorting to topical sermons per se. In expository preaching, the text always controls the flow of the sermon. But its truth should be demonstrated topically. Contemporary subjects, material and incidents must be brought to bear as the exposition proceeds. In later times, Lloyd-Jones was accused of preaching what, in effect, were 'topical sermons'. Reference is made to this in a subsequent chapter. There were times when DML-J's preaching did not follow the classic expository style.[50]

Persuasiveness

Warning and pleadings are constants in Lloyd-Jones's early sermons. Often he resorted to short, staccato, exclamatory sentences. Do it! Make a break. Get to God and get right with God! Take your stand. Commit yourself! Venture on him! Trust him![51] At other times he employed probing interrogatives. This approach, as we shall see, became a constant feature in later messages. 'Allow me to ask a simple question, therefore. Do you know Him? Can you find Him when you need Him most of all? Is He ever with you and near you?[52]

Sometimes he allowed himself ten such consecutive challenges.[53] On one occasion, he even put up as a supplement to his volley of questions four exclamatory comments.[54]

Infrastructure

There are no standard three points with subsequent divisions of two or three subsidiaries. His structure will vary depending on the biblical passage that he is endeavouring to expound. He does not force his texts. There is flow, and cohesion. His introductions are designed to capture the imagination and interest and to involve the congregation. Sometimes, a couple of pages will be spent before he reveals what Jay Adams would call his 'purpose statement'.[55] Eventually, his goal becomes clear and the hearer appreciates that what preceded by way of introduction was logically leading to what was to follow. He preached with a view to presenting a systematic theology which combined warmth and an originality of thought.

From the early years, Lloyd-Jones did what, by God's grace, he was good at: making clear God's word from God's book. And there is more than a hint of the diagnostician as he probes the passage in hand.

HERMENEUTICS

Bernard Ramm asserts that hermeneutics is 'the science of the correct interpretation of the Bible'.[56] Concern for biblical accuracy is paramount for the preacher of integrity. He does not wish to fall foul of the charge of handling the Word of God deceitfully. Lloyd-Jones from the outset was committed to presenting an accurate explanation of the Scriptures. We have not found him manipulating its meaning in order to simplify the passage in hand or to squeeze it into a sermonic pattern or theological structure. From his earliest addresses, his high view of Scripture and commitment to expository preaching is clearly seen. We elicit the following principles from his first volume of sermons. Later, when we attempt an overall summary of his hermeneutical position it will be seen how consistent he was from his earliest days as a preacher.

Scripture contains no contradictions

Lloyd-Jones viewed Scripture as a whole; the expositor is thus to interpret it. As the Bible proceeds from the mind of God channelled through human agency, it is without discrepancy. Care should be taken in the interpretation of Scripture so that it does not appear as though one part is contradicting the other. There is no confusion in the Word of God.[57]

> What I do say is that there are no contradictions in Scripture and that to suggest that the teachings of Jesus Christ and Paul, or the teachings of Paul and the other Apostles, do not agree is subversive of the entire claim of the New Testament itself and of the claim of the church for it throughout the centuries, until the rise of the so-called higher-critical school some hundred years ago.[58]

Scripture is completely authoritative

He believed that the Bible is 'God's Word . . . a divine book which transcends all our categories and increasingly supplies our finite minds from its inexhaustible store of treasures.'[59] Thus, the Scriptures were his anchor point in a day when this was not a fashionable position.

Scripture yields its meaning as the Holy Spirit enlightens the reader

Because the Bible is no ordinary book, the reader is dependent upon the Holy Spirit to make its truth plain. In other words, there is a spiritual meaning to Scripture. This became a strong feature in Lloyd-Jones's ministry in later years.

CONTROLLING PRINCIPLES IN THE INTERPRETATION OF PARABLES

A good example of how Dr. Lloyd-Jones applied his hermeneutic is revealed in his approach to preaching on the parables. One Sunday evening, in what was ostensibly a gospel address, he taught his people how they should approach these stories which our Lord so skilfully related.

The parable to be expounded was the story of the Prodigal Son. By any standards, this is an outstanding address demonstrating how a well-worn passage of Scripture can still reveal fresh nuances of meaning and application when careful study, thought, and research is applied. It is laudable that in an address designed to make the Gospel message clear, the preacher determines also to show his congregation how to study the Scriptures. This further illustrates our point that the categorising of Lloyd-Jones's sermons from the beginning is not really possible. Instructional, devotional, evangelical—all merge, becoming identifiable facets of one sermon.

Guiding pointers to be absorbed in order to secure the correct meaning of the parables are:

They should not be interpreted in a way which causes confusion in our understanding of other parts of Scripture

The Bible as a whole is totally reliable and interpretation should therefore go in the direction of the general to the particular. Careful application of this hermeneutic helps the preacher avoid fanciful speculation. If a particular point vies with the general it should be re-examined. The interpretation is obviously flawed.

Negatively-deduced conclusions should be avoided

Lloyd-Jones was aware that the doctrine of the wrath of God is obnoxious to many people of liberal persuasion. They fail to contextualise the doctrine of the love of God within the whole compass of the Bible. The father in the parable of the Prodigal seems to fit in with their conception of the absolute loving nature of God. Thus the 'negatively-deduced conclusion' that wrath is not a quality which belongs to God at all. The same is argued about the doctrine of the atonement. It is not apparent in the parable. Such a deduction is felled by this hermeneutic as is the conclusion drawn by some that there is no need of a mediator between God and man for such is absent from the parable. This leads us to DML-J's third principle.

Each parable's purpose is to teach one great positive truth

This becomes clear in the story of the Prodigal Son. It is one of three parables. Our Lord employed this triplet to demonstrate the nature of his mission. He came looking for sinners even though this brought him the opprobrium of the Scribes and Pharisees. The parables of the Lost Sheep and the Lost Coin illustrate the character of his Father and the divine concern for sinful people. God is troubled for wayward people. He wishes them to be sought out and in repentance be reconciled to him. This was the divine charge given to his Son. The third parable describes the activity of the prodigal 'lest anyone should be so foolish as to think that we should all be automatically saved by God's love even as the lost sheep and coin were found'.[60] Divine sovereignty and human responsibility are marvellously married in this sample of our Lord's teaching.

The book, *Evangelistic Sermons*, is well entitled. Paramount in his convictions was the belief that he was called to preach the Gospel. Though later he would express convictions that the office of an evangelist was a foundational one in the Church and was not repeated, he was one of the best examples of a man with an evangelistic passion. We attempt to reduce one of his sermons to skeleton form to demonstrate how he took an incident in the Gospels and applied it evangelistically.

JAIRUS—COMPLETE SALVATION[61]

And, behold, there cometh one of the rulers of the synagogue, Jairus by name; and when he saw him, he fell at his feet . . . (Mark 5:22 AV).

Introduction:

- Extended comment on the Authorised Version's heading for the passage. (It concentrates on the miracle rather than the relationship between the Lord and Jairus).
- Argument for spiritual understanding of Scripture; what is important varies as the Spirit impresses truths upon us.
- Main thrust of the address—passage teaches believer how to face the future with all its difficulties, having encountered Jesus. 'Our Lord not only receives Jairus but they continue together.' Jesus—the Alpha and Omega, the beginning and the end of faith. To believe in the Lord Jesus means he will continue with you.

Application:

Have you had this experience? The narrative reveals how this blessing is obtained.

1 HOW IS JESUS TO BE APPROACHED?

Vital question; different ways in which people did this. Some were repelled by him; some were received with great kindness. Consider: 'whosoever cometh unto me I will in no wise cast out'. The difference in Jesus's response depended on the attitude of the enquirer.

With a deep consciousness of need:

● Jairus desperate because of his daughter's condition.
● Probably Jairus had tried other expedients.
● Jairus heard of the Lord and determined to come to him.

Application:

Have you approached him? Do you realise the urgency? Are you resting on your success? Are you satisfied with yourself? Realise the position you are in. Go to him.

With striking humility:

Jairus: man of importance, ruler of the synagogue. Jesus: peasant, nobody: yet Jairus prostrated himself before the Lord.

Application:

Those who fall at the feet of Jesus not out of curiosity but out of respect and deference are never disappointed. 'Not the righteous . . . Sinners Jesus came to save!'

With faith and obedience:

Jairus had confidence in Jesus' power; placed himself entirely in his hands. He did not complain when the Lord was delayed by the woman with the haemorrhage.

Application:

Our Lord does not expect us to understand but to trust him.

2 WHAT HAPPENS TO THOSE WHO DO APPROACH HIM?

They find:

● Jesus has to be known personally before he can be known properly. This requires submission to him.
● He is willing to receive them and deal with their immediate and subsequent problems. Jairus' household said the situation was hopeless. Remarks were directed at Jairus. Jesus intervened before the report spread and took control.

Application:

The devil will employ the same tactic. Our sins are too great. The situation is hopeless. We feel this is so. The Lord sovereignly intervenes and addresses the problem.

The Lord becomes the target of the opposition. Jesus took on the mourners who now pit themselves against him.

Application:

As he dealt with them so he will deal with those who would impede us. 'He that hath begun a good work will perform it until the day of Jesus Christ.' He is able 'to keep us from falling'.

Dr. Lloyd-Jones continued his ministry up to the outbreak of the Second World War. The first volume in his biography gives a compelling account of the blessing upon his ministry and the growth of the Church. It also chronicles his departure from Wales and the circumstances behind the invitation offered to him by the elderly Campbell Morgan who was in great need of help at Westminster Chapel. This was in the same year that Neville Chamberlain came back from Munich feeling he had appeased Hitler.

THE WAR YEARS

A largely unknown but powerful short series of studies exists which Dr. Lloyd Jones brought in the first years of his ministry in London and toward the close of the Second World War.[62] They illustrate how he attempted to deal with some of the questions, spiritual, theological, moral. and political, which were in the minds of his people.[63] There is, therefore, a blending of the expositional and topical, with the emphasis on the former.

The sermons are from the fourth and fifth chapters of Revelation and were preached in the latter part of 1944. They demonstrate a breadth of thought, theological insight and courage in interpreting the war effort in the light of Scripture. They remain a pattern of how preachers should teach the Bible when their country is passing through critical times without resorting to a patriotism which abuses Scripture in the misplaced interests of nationalism. Often in these situations, theological perception is blurred. This must be one of the great dangers confronting military chaplains. Such would find help in researching DML-J at this point.

Surfacing in this series is Lloyd-Jones's philosophy of history. An avid student of history himself, he often made reference to the subject in his preaching at Westminster. He taught that history can never be rightly comprehended unless the human story is viewed objectively and, therefore, biblically. In the passage he proceeded to expound, he reminds his congregation of the invitation issued to John. The Apostle was to step up to a higher vantage point and view the situation from a loftier plane (Rev. 4:1). Lloyd-Jones argued:

> If you would understand history, 'Come up hither'. Look into the heavens. Start with God. Get up on top of the great peaks and look down upon the earth. 'There's a divinity that shapes our ends, rough-hew them as we may.' Look at history and what you will find everywhere, and always, is not a story of the gradual ascent on the part of man, but this constant interfering with the story from above, this strange irruption of God into the human scene. Would you understand it? 'Come up hither'.[64]

He extrapolates from his passage three principles:

• The story of mankind, and of the world, must always be viewed as a whole.
• The story of mankind cannot be understood in terms of Man alone.
• The story of mankind cannot be understood by Man's own unaided efforts.

Having set the scene and marked out his parameters, he promises his congregation 'we are going to consider them [the propositions] further on subsequent Sunday mornings'. A week later, he picked up where he left off and redefined his purpose for going through this passage. It was, 'namely, to understand something of the meaning of the days through which we are passing . . . and . . . something of the meaning and purpose of history'.[65] He conceded that he had been dealing with the subject 'in a negative fashion'. Now, in a manner with which his congregation were to become increasingly familiar, he explained, 'I want to look at this matter in a more positive manner'.

Once more he affirmed the necessity of the Holy Spirit's illumination to enable the reader to understand the Scriptures, 'we must believe on the Lord Jesus Christ, and receive the gift of the Spirit; and then, and then only, can we begin to understand the meaning of history'.

So he sets out his positive principles reminding us that fundamental to John's revelation is his prior experience of the one on the throne. He argued:

- Man's relationship to God is more important than his relationship to history.
- Everything, history included, starts with God, is under God, and will end with God.
- John was given his vision of the eternal temple and the throne in the centre, and the one who is on the throne in order to enable him to bear the preview of history that was about to be revealed.

Lloyd-Jones held a pessimistic view of the future of Man. This is the only conclusion warranted by the biblical evidence. At the human level, the story is bleak. But John's vision, which is the backcloth of Revelation, enabled him and the reader to face the future with hope. DML-J typically analyses the passage and teaches that John is shown:

- Certain things about God himself: he is eternal; he is the Holy One; he is the Lord God Almighty.
- His relationship to the world: he is the Creator; he is also the King of the earth.
- God's relation to a world of sin: he is the righteous judge, he is the Saviour.

Lloyd-Jones concludes, 'as we think of today, as we think of the future, as we wonder what is going to happen, as we tremble on the brink of terrible things, let us with John turn aside, and turn away from it all for a moment and turn to God. Let us look to the Throne, and, with the elders and the beasts, prostrate ourselves before Him and cry out and say, "Holy, holy, holy, Lord God Almighty".'

In his third sermon,[66] he states, 'Biblical history is very definitely prejudiced'. It is written from God's standpoint and deals with Man's relationship to God. The scroll, which the One on the Throne has in his right hand secured by seven seals, is the account of the future history of mankind and of the world.

Lloyd-Jones sets down his definitive statement on his understanding of the biblical philosophy of history. There are two types. There is (i) the history which God permits and (ii) the history which God promotes.[67] The former is secular history; the latter is biblical. Sometimes, long periods seem to be dismissed in the Bible inasmuch as only a fleeting comment is employed. With some relish, Lloyd-Jones furnishes us with the example of Alexander the Great. The only reference to him is in symbolic form in the book of Daniel. He is called a he-goat! DML-J characteristically comments, 'great in secular history but from the standpoint of God a he-goat'. Alexander's Empire was permitted by God, it was not one of his promotions. These are illustrated by the breaking of the seals in the book of Revelation. Thus, his interventions. Lloyd-Jones describes such as, 'the grand history of God's redeeming purpose on this human plane'.

When history is perceived from the human angle, within the context of God's permissions, all is hopeless. Thus, John weeps. Lloyd-Jones dips into recent, tragic history to clinch the point, 'in 1914 all seemed to be going well, then came the crash'. He reminds his congregation as he comes to the end of his sermon, . . . this has not been a theoretical disquisition this morning . . . God knows what is going to happen . . . keep in mind the two types of history. See the significance of the fight between God and evil. Above all, remember that the ultimate outlook is glorious . . .'

His final message in the series[68] emphasised the main thrust of his teaching to his war-weary people. He had refrained from prophetic speculation which was so rife in Britain at that time. Various 'prophetic movements' held meetings often with capacity congregations. The speakers sought to identify the political situation with specific prophecies. Dr. Lloyd-Jones kept to the certainties. God is in control of the situation. The preacher encouraged his people to hope. Listen to him in this choice passage:

> Biblical history is essentially apocalyptic; it is essentially eschatological. You might not like those terms. But I defy you to give me better terms. History is in crisis . . . It is not a gradual climbing up to perfection. No! No! It is God coming in; it is God coming down. It is Christ intervening. It is God in Christ returning finally. It is Christ forming a new Kingdom.[69]

He rounded off the whole cycle of messages by asserting, 'My dear friends, the one question for you and me is this: Are we in the new Kingdom?' Typically the one question devolved into twelve! As he secured his main theme he turned the attention of his congregation once more to the Lamb on the Throne who not only died for our sins but is the superintendent of history.

REVIEW

Our lengthy discussion is necessary to give us the flavour of Lloyd-Jones's developing style in the early and difficult days at Westminster.

Here is no sensationalism. But there is passion, pathos, and honest exposition. Moreover, there is always recourse made to the sovereignty of God as he preached against the background of the dreadful conditions at Westminster, London, and the country as a whole.

Several points can be made about the sermons.

- They were biblical. He commenced from the Bible and reached out to the contemporary scene showing how the former related to the latter.
- He refrained from being partisan. The danger in a national calamity is to start with the situation and then to go hunting for solace-giving Scripture or on an eschatological paper-chase where the prizes go to the most ingenious in slotting a contemporary situation into the prophetic Scriptures.
- He enabled the congregation to relate what was happening to the overarching sovereignty of God. They learned that history is not a series of random events. God is still in control—the ultimate authority, the focal point of the final consummation. The congregation were thus lifted up higher to look down on the unfolding tragedy as John had done centuries earlier.

FURTHER SHORT SERIES

These sermons were followed by six consecutive studies on 'What is a Christian?', based on Romans 8:5-15 . Then came the expositions from 2 Peter, later to be put into book form. The publishers asserted that when Dr. Lloyd-Jones acceded to his London pulpit, it was his deliberate policy to prepare the congregation for an expository ministry. His sermons from 2 Peter are evidenced as a sort of stepping-stone for a preaching goal he was still to secure. In the Petrine addresses he did not deal with each verse. Longer sections are covered in one sermon than would be his custom in later years. Following this came his addresses, now published under the title *The Heart of the Gospel*, expositions from Matthew 12 and 13. It was these addresses which so influenced J. I. Packer. We quote his vivid description of being exposed to Lloyd-Jones's ministry.

> The preacher was a small man with a big head and evidently thinning hair, wearing a shapeless-looking black gown. His great domed forehead caught the eye at once. He walked briskly to the little pulpit desk in the centre of the balcony, said 'Let us pray' in a rather pinched, deep Welsh-inflected microphone-magnified voice, and at once began pleading with God to visit us during the service. The blend of rever-

ence and intimacy, adoration and dependence, fluency and simplicity in his praying was remarkable: he had a great gift in prayer . . . The sermon (as we say nowadays) blew me away. What was special about it? It was simple, clear, straightforward man-to-man stuff. It was expository, apologetic, and evangelistic on a grand scale. It was both the planned performance of a magnetic orator and the passionate, compassionate outflow of a man with a message from God that he knew his hearers needed. He worked up to a dramatic growling shout about God's sovereign grace a few minutes before the end; then from that he worked down to businesslike persuasion, calling on needy souls to come to Christ. It was the old, old story, but it had been made wonderfully new.[70]

As we have seen, Lloyd-Jones was no novice when he came to London. Nascent in some of his earlier addresses is the same proclivity to detailed exegesis which was to become the hallmark of his later ministry. In one of the first batches of sermons at Westminster, he devoted four addresses to expounding 1 Corinthians 14:13, 14.[71] In the series which so impressed Jim Packer, he devoted three sermons to the final verses.[72]

IN RETROSPECT

When I started researching DML-J's material, I expected to find that his preaching would reflect a marked change after 1949. I thought there would be an obvious difference in content, style, and fervour and imagined that the expository verse-by-verse exposition would be new and have little or nothing in the way of antecedents. The evidence hardly supports this notion.

These observations are the result of the sifting of this evidence.

• Basic to his addresses is an overriding aim to focus on one main point and then move from the centre to various aspects on the circumference. Interspersed is generous application. Hovering over the sermon as it unfolds is the obvious conclusion toward which the preacher is inexorably moving.

• In regard to his *Evangelistic Sermons*—his first addresses in his native Wales—the subject matter compels the sermons to range widely over the Bible. Though preachers mature and their views develop in the passing of time, it is remarkable how these sermons demonstrate what was to be a consistent, life-lasting hermeneutic. Indeed, the manner of preaching in which he seemed to revel and be so free when in his London pulpit can be traced back to the early preaching.

- Encouraging the congregation to reason matters out with him is a common denominator in his sermons irrespective of when they were preached. They reveal, furthermore, that from the beginning, his goal was to induce his largely working-class congregations to think through his argument as well as the Londoners. He treated both congregations with what we can only call the same loving respect.

- DML-J did sometimes preach several messages from one passage. He would develop this style and proceed at a much slower pace. What was to follow in terms of preaching method was incipient in earlier practices.

- He reveals a great ability to handle narrative passage from both Old and New Testament. Classic sermons worthy of study are 'The Shunamite Woman'[73] and 'The Mirage shall become a Pool'.[74]

- His pneumatology will be developed further though he was, throughout his preaching, committed to securing the spiritual understanding of the text as being a prime requirement for the expositor.

- The mind of the diagnostician is obvious.

- He claimed that 'a true and living interest in the Puritans and their works had gripped him since 1925 and his whole ministry had been affected by this'.[75]

- Built into his early style is his penchant for using the interrogative, moving from the general to the particular and always grappling with the mind before assaulting the will and appealing to the emotions.

- The heartbeat of an evangelist throbs through much of the material.

- He believed that special care should be given to the preparation of gospel sermons. He felt that this restored a balance to the ill-conceived idea that gospel preaching did not require so much time for prior thought and study.[76]

The pity is that these sermons were preached well before the days of tape recorders. We have to imagine the inflections, the pauses, the shouts, and, what one admiring theologian called in my hearing, the adenoidal 'growl' which probably became more pronounced over the years.

What then do we make of DML-J's conviction that Spirit baptism should affect preaching? It seems to us that this creates no problem in an evaluation of his own ministry. Elsewhere, we have formed the view that Lloyd-Jones's personal experience of the Holy Spirit's sealing should be placed just prior to the commencement of his ministry. What happened in 1949 was a further evidence of God's grace, another baptism in the Holy Ghost. It should be observed that this is fully consistent with

Lloyd-Jones's pneumatology which insists that the baptism in the Spirit, far from being a once-for-all experience, is repeatable.[77] It is quite possible that what had marked a man, say, at the outset of his ministry, can be experienced again.

Now we can look more closely into the mechanics of Dr. Lloyd-Jones's approach to preaching, concentrating particularly on his developed style and generally on the sermons which flowed from his London pulpit.

8

Diagnostic Preaching (I)

Starting from a clear view of what constituted theological and spiritual wholeness, he analysed everything and everyone systematically, as a matter of habit, to detect first of all what was disordered and then also what was lacking; for he recognised that what is not seen or not said, can be as significant a sign of spiritual or theological ill health as any actual sin or error. He was, in fact, a brilliant diagnostician both spiritually and theologically.

James I. Packer[1]

In the Bible, Lloyd-Jones was entirely at home, mentally at ease, aware that this book demanded his best thinking and would deepen his communion with God. The slightest intimation of God's presence, the subtle pressure of truth on the mind, the first discernible tremor of conscience should be given immediate and total attention; and then Bible study and prayer become the one act of communion.

James M. Gordon[2]

Our two quotations demand attention. Far from being randomly selected, they provide the springboard from which have developed this and the following chapter. In Lloyd-Jones was the combination of an acutely trained and tuned mind, and a deep spirituality. In the providence of God, these characteristics produced what we believe to be one of the finer demonstrations this century of a ministry that in type was truly apostolic. Listening to and watching Lloyd-Jones preach was like witnessing a person who at times was ignited, mixing passion and pathos with erudition and eloquence in a most unusual manner.[3] But it is our conviction that the combination should not be so rarely found. We are aware that we may appear to be casting a mould and suggesting that preachers should squeeze themselves into it. That is not our intention, though we are prepared to run the risk of being misunderstood.

There is a sense, as Lloyd-Jones would have affirmed, in which a man cannot be taught to preach. He is a preacher or he is not a preacher. But assuming that he is, his skills can be enhanced by a studied attempt at the two strengths which DML-J exhibited above all others: an enlightened mind and an impassioned heart. In this chapter, we again attempt to stay close to Lloyd-Jones the man in order to learn more of Lloyd-Jones the preacher.

'The words to which I would like to draw your attention this morning are to be found in . . .' Almost invariably, this was the way in which Dr. Lloyd-Jones would commence his preaching. For a less pretentious beginning to a sermon probably this has no rivals. But to those who heard him preach, they signalled that a curtain was about to be raised. Old truths with deeper clarity would be affirmed. What a congregation perhaps had never seen before would be revealed. For the next forty to sixty minutes, not only would a man expound Scripture, but a huge company of people would be involved in a compelling, often encouraging, sometimes painful interaction with the preacher.

The seemingly pedantic introduction would, for the thoughtful, be recognised as the establishing of a goal. 'The words' did demand the attention of the hearer. After all, they are no ordinary words. They had occupied the mind, thoughts, and prayers of the preacher in his preparation. He believed that they were the words of God for the gathered congregation. Nothing was more vital for him than to make the meaning clear to his hearers. Hopefully, this would result in bringing their lives more into harmony with God's will and living on earth with the sure knowledge that they would go on to live in heaven, the former being but a preparation for the latter.[4]

For Dr. Lloyd-Jones, preaching involved three elements: the sermon, which had been prepared and committed to notes; the congregation, with whom he would interact; and the Holy Spirit, who would influence the mental faculties, wills and emotions of both preacher and hearer. DML-J aimed for what might be called comprehensive interaction between himself and the assembled company. There is a cord of three strands which should not be broken. Without the endeavour of the preacher, the reaction of the congregation,[5] and the enabling of the Holy Spirit, whatever might result, preaching would not!

The point is important. It distinguishes between a Bible lecture and preaching. The former could be given without the inspirational element. In later years, Lloyd-Jones expressed what he felt to be the shortcomings of the lecturer. He chose a tour in the USA to do this. He referred to a celebrated speaker whose books were known both sides of the Atlantic. His method was one of biblical analysis where he would divide and subdivide the book into various categories. Because he was handling the text, he was reckoned to be essentially a biblical preacher—far more than most. But the theological system was not so obvious. It was not the speaker's intention to find such, lift it out, and apply it. He was content to illustrate and highlight the text. The method fell short of what DML-J considered preaching. It had limited value and did not go far enough: 'I say that Bible lecturing stops short of where true preaching begins.'[6]

HIS PULPIT

The pulpit at Westminster Chapel is quite unusual. It is semi-circular and spacious. It can be a lonely spot. The ceiling is high. Facing the preacher are not only the ground level of the huge sanctuary but also, rising up on either side, are two galleries. The architect, for some reason, did not connect the upper gallery. He left, as it seems from the pulpit, a huge gap filled by a large, ornate window. The preacher looks out into the abyss between the lower and upper gallery. DML-J recalled that the building intimidated one of his predecessors, Dr. J. H. Jowett.[7] But, threatening or not, for nearly thirty years the figure of Lloyd-Jones would be seen entering the pulpit area.

After the singing of the doxology and a hymn, he would open the pages of the huge Bible. Even casual visitors in the congregation would begin to appreciate that they were about to engage in what the preacher considered to be a holy act. They were to listen to the explanation of Scripture. Nothing is more holy nor more wonderful than the declaration of the Word of God through the exposition of a Bible passage.

DML-J's introduction was as deliberate as the use he made of the pulpit Bible. It was opened for the public reading of the Scripture passages. It remained open. Often, in the course of his exposition, he would turn its pages. The preacher, a man of medium build, cloaked in a Geneva gown, and with a serious disposition, made one thing quite clear: his sole authority was the Book.

Jowett, in his volume on preaching, referred to the way in which John Angell James used to open his pulpit Bible, and the equally subduing impressiveness in the manner in which he closed it.

These are not little tricks taught by elocutionists; they are the fruits of character. If they are learned as little tricks, they will only add to the artificiality of the service; if they are the 'fruits of the Spirit', they will tend to vitalise it.[8]

THE BIBLE

Dr. Lloyd-Jones's anchorage to Scripture was the reason why he gave such prominence to the Bible before he preached and in the act of preaching. He argued:

We are presenting the Bible and its message, that is why I am one of those who like to have a pulpit Bible. It should always be open, to emphasize the fact that the preacher is preaching out of it. I have known men who have just opened the Bible to read the text. They then shut the Bible and put it on one side and go on talking. I think that is wrong from the standpoint of true preaching. We are always to give the impression, and it may be more important than anything we say, that what we are saying comes out of the Bible, and always comes out of it.[9]

The turning of the Bible's pages backwards and forwards from the Old Testament and then into the New and back to the Old was a conscious act. By a combination of eye- and ear-gate the preacher was impressing his congregation that his sole argument depended on the esteem he had for this Book in which he seemed to live, move, and have his being.

There were times, in the course of his addresses, when he would engage in a biblical tour de force. Not for him to secure the point by an appeal to the main text, or to be satisfied with bringing up one other to buttress his conclusion. He would give a generous sample of related Scriptures. He would dip into many books, risking tedium, but always with the aim of impressing the listener that his argument was that of the Bible.

Preachers need care in adopting his technique. It demands great skill, not only in finding the variety of places but holding the attention of the hearers as the point is hammered home. DML-J nailed the issue because he wanted it to stay. He was a dogmatic theologian, and he did not apologise for it. Moreover, he wished his hearers to develop dogmatic convictions.

There is an example in his Romans series. Lloyd-Jones was expounding in the eighth chapter. He had warmed to his theme 'that the sufferings of this present time are not worthy to be compared with the glory which shall be revealed in us' (v. 18 *A.V.*). Even on the printed page, the 'thunder and the lightning' are apparent! Lloyd-Jones is obviously in his element. He had helpfully given the Christian view of time. The 'present time' is not the same as 'the time being'. It covers this whole age. But the Christian has his eye on the future. In one sense, this is 'beyond time' or 'when time shall be no more'. There, the glory of God will be revealed and experienced. We must constantly be thinking of this. It will be of practical help in coping with suffering in this present time. He goes on:

> This is such an important part of New Testament teaching, and such a vital essential part of the comfort and consolation that the Christian alone can know and experience and enjoy, that I must turn aside *for a moment* to show how constantly the Scriptures emphasise this very thing. Let us look at *some* examples.[10]

He then proceeded to take his hearers to no fewer than twenty-eight places in the New Testament where prospects of the glory are highlighted. And, in our calculation, we have not counted two or three references in the same chapter! The preacher has accepted what must have been a calculated risk—the danger of appearing tedious and straining the patience of his congregation. It is difficult to believe that Lloyd-Jones entered the pulpit with the intention of covering such a wide range of relevant Scriptures. Rather, elated by the sheer wonder of what he was emphasising and with the benefit of a remarkable memory and a mind which was soaked in Scripture he 'let himself go', a practice which as we have seen is actually traceable to the Apostle Paul.

The preacher had been overwhelmed by the sheer force of the teaching. To watch him doing this with zest was unforgettable. It convinced his hearers that his appeal was indeed to the Bible and to it alone. Examples of this are profuse throughout his books and taped sermons.[11]

We are reminded of the occasion when David Garrick, the actor, was on his way to hear Whitefield preach. He bumped into the philosopher, David Hume, and told him to where he was going. 'Why, you don't believe what Whitefield preaches', was the retort. 'No,' said Garrick, 'but he does'!

A preacher who is committed to the authority of Scripture will make his convictions known. Dr. Lloyd-Jones was horrified that any man might enter the pulpit and question the Bible:

> I tremble to think of the position of men who have been called to
> be stewards of the mysteries, men to whom God has entrusted His
> oracles, who themselves have attacked it, and undermined it, and
> shaken the faith of other people in it! There is nothing more than
> that.[12]

His dedication to expository preaching following the method of the Puritans was at a time when it had no well-known exponents in Britain. Popular opinion held that such an old-fashioned approach would not gain the attention of large numbers of people. After all, modernity was trailing films, television, glossy magazines, and comics. The visual was in. The verbal, in terms of the spoken word, was out. The twentieth century had tolled the death knell of preaching. Visual aids had reduced the attention span of the people . . . so the argument went.

The old preachers had their sand-filled hour-glasses in the pulpit. Some preachers were so enthusiastic in expounding their text that even when the sand had gone through the glass they would assert 'there is so much more in this passage—let's have another jar'! Involuntarily, they inverted the time-glass and continued. Lloyd-Jones would have approved! But those were days of antiquity, never likely to return, or so it was thought. It was largely left to him to disprove the point. He took up the thread of Bible exposition which had remained dangling since the days of Charles Spurgeon.

EXPERIENTIAL THEOLOGY

Theology means the word of God. Another not so well known but related term is *theophany*. This is a combination of two Greek words *theos* and *phaneo*. They are conjoined to give the meaning God-appearance. Theophany defines occasions in the Old Testament when the presence of God was manifested in an unusual way. An example is the incident when God revealed himself to Moses as he was hidden in the cleft of the rock (Exod. 33). One of the aims of biblical preaching is to transport a congregation into the presence of God.

We recall the words of Jacob when, after an extraordinary night, he left Bethel remarking, 'Surely the Lord is in this place; and I did not know it . . . How awesome is this place! This is none other than the house of God, and this is the gate of heaven' (Gen. 28:16, 17 *RSV*). Unwittingly, Jacob focuses the preacher's goal. In the New Testament, the disciples on the Emmaus Road had an encounter with the Lord Jesus. They testified to an emotional response as he conversed with them (Luke 24:32). Ideally, the Apostle Paul argued, when an outsider comes into the church, the ministry should be so relevant and pointed that he will fall down and worship. He will be humbled by a felt sense of the presence of God (1 Cor. 14:25).

DML-J believed that the faithful Bible preaching should lead to this. Accurate exposition is not the only goal. The Word of God leads to the God of the Word. It is arguable that theophany is the goal of theology. The preacher is not a scribe dealing alone with textual concerns. He desires the 'bush' to burn. He wants people to draw near to God. A successful 'preaching' leaves the worshipper with the echo of God's voice and with the recall of God's presence.

Dr. Lloyd-Jones's commitment to experiential theology, an emphasis which became more pronounced in his sermons from the 1950s, was one of the reasons why he was sympathetic to the ministry of A. W. Tozer. He was largely responsible for introducing Tozer's books to a British readership. On secondary issues, they were often poles apart. The common ground was their desire to encourage people to know God for themselves and not just about God. They desired a rebirth of preaching harnessed to the Word and fired by the Spirit. Such preaching impacts the mind, affects the conscience, tames the will and, in short, stimulates the work of sanctification. When Tozer argued that entry into the Christian faith should not rest solely on deductions made from a text and proceeded to argue that the preacher's first aim should be to turn a convert into a worshipper before a worker, DML-J found someone in step with his own convictions.[13]

There is a mysticism in some of Lloyd-Jones's preaching which caused many in earlier times to consider him to be halfway between a Calvinist and a Quaker[14] and, later, a Calvinist and a Charismatic! But he was firmly committed to the principle that experience and Scripture must be in alignment. If they are not, the experience should be contested and discarded. He believed the Quakers went astray because they failed to observe this principle. He referred to 'the tragedy of Quakerism', though he excluded George Fox from that assessment.[15] He claimed that 'the virtual departure of the people called Quakers from the Christian faith is (because) they put such emphasis on the 'inner light' that they ignore the Word'.[16]

DR. LLOYD-JONES'S SYSTEM

But what of Lloyd-Jones's system? Here, we must be careful. He eschewed methods and was curtly dismissive of homiletics. Before forty ministerial students, he unveiled his suspicions when he put up the rhetorical question—'What can be said for homiletics?' His revealing reply was, 'Not much'! On another occasion he was to refer to homiletics as 'almost an abomination'.[17]

We would be wide of the mark in concluding that Lloyd-Jones was bankrupt of a preaching method. His dependence on the Holy Spirit at the point of the delivery of the sermon in no way tempted him to be slovenly in preparation. He would not deal cavalierly with preaching. Even a casual reading of Murray's massive two-volume biography shows how far this was from his approach. His objection to homiletics needs to be seen against how it is taught in many seminaries and Bible colleges. A mechanical approach to Scripture, failure to depend on the inspiration of the Holy Spirit during preparation and delivery, a greater reliance on academic tools than seeking the enabling of the Spirit: against such things he reacted. But as his book on preaching reveals, he did have a method of study and a consistent hermeneutic. How did he come to Scripture?

To isolate this, we must remember the background from which he emerged. Consider Packer's description of his approach to preaching in our opening quotation to this chapter, especially the credit, 'He was, in fact, a brilliant diagnostician both spiritually and theologically.'

Careful listening to DML-J's tapes and perusing his sermons reveals the mind of a trained medical doctor diagnosing and applying spiritual truth. On several occasions, he argued that much could be learned about a minister and his methods from what he was before his conversion.

In issuing the call to preach, the Holy Spirit takes what a man was before he entered the ministry and harnesses it. Preachers often find that their previous occupation positions them well for what they are now attempting. The Holy Spirit employs differing personalities in the proclamation of the Gospel.[18] Old Testament preachers such as Isaiah and Amos had contrasting characters. One was a scholar, probably of princely stock, the other a rustic and a herdsman. Both brought their different gifts and personalities and were used by the Holy Spirit for the proclamation of God's word.

Lloyd-Jones had no formal training in theology. It has been argued that, despite his great natural abilities, foregoing this actually was a loss. A period of sustained theological study would have enhanced his natural gifting and helped him to tighten up in some areas where his theologising seems slack. This might also have tempered his comments on theological colleges.[19]

His medical knowledge often shows through in his expositions. Sometimes he employed it for illustrative purposes, at other times, to ensure accuracy in exegesis. On one occasion he took to task the 'saintly Bishop Moule'. He had reason to criticise Moule's grasp of what it means to be 'strengthened with might by his Spirit in the inner man' (Eph. 3:16 AV). Moule argued that a man without strength does not need strength to receive food, he just needs food! Respectfully, Lloyd-Jones disagreed. Citing illustrations from the Second World War and bringing his medical knowledge into play, he demonstrated quite clearly that to give a heavy meal to a hungry and weak man might well kill him. Such an individual first needs glucose injected into his veins. He requires a light diet. DML-J secured the point medically—strength is sometimes needed in order to receive strength. Then he clinches his exposition of the verse by typically taking his hearers to texts which show how the infant Christian is expected to move on from an intake of milk to a more substantial diet of meat: strengthened to receive strength!

Douglas Johnson encouraged a younger colleague to go and listen to him one Friday evening. He was informed that he would witness a demonstration of teaching similar to the old, Socratic style. This was the method which DML-J had learned from his former chief, Lord Thomas Horder, who had been King George V's physician. Horder would put up a number of possible diagnoses of a patient's puzzling condition. Having erected them like skittles, he would encourage his entourage of junior doctors to consider each one, whether it should be knocked down or allowed to stand. The one which remained would be the correct diagnosis. This process involved observation and logical deduction. It demanded deep thought.

Lloyd-Jones used this method in his study, in the pulpit, and when chairing ministerial fraternals. The majority of his sermons illustrate it. He wanted his congregation to think matters through. There is no virtue in ignorance. Every preacher should encourage his congregation to think along with him. Even when sitting under other ministries they should be taught to assess and check what is being said from the Scriptures. To see spiritual maturity developing in his congregation was balm to Dr. Lloyd-Jones's soul.[20] This is what was meant when earlier we summarised one of his goals as 'comprehensive interaction'. We sharpen the point further.

An excellent example occurs in his series on marriage, which is part of the lengthy treatment of the Epistle to the Ephesians. He feels that in the fifth chapter, toward the end, Paul's main purpose is to highlight the believer's relationship to the Lord.[21] The Apostle uses marriage as an appropriate illustration. In so doing, he presents a clear statement of the Christian doctrine of marriage. But this is basically by way of application, a spin-off from the main thrust. Thus, in order to understand the application—marriage—you must deal with the doctrine.[22]

DML-J proceeded to expound Paul's doctrine. The Lord bestows great blessings on the Church which are analogous to those of a groom's endowments. Lloyd-Jones urges the congregation to work out what the divine gifts are. 'What are the things he bestows on us?' He answers the question by putting up two headings from which stem several sub-divisions.

The headings are that the Lord gives us (i) his life and (ii) his privileges. As for his life, 'that is what happens is it not when a man gets married?' The husband gives himself to his wife. 'But let us look at it from the other aspect and realise that we are sharers in the life of the Lord Jesus Christ. It is a staggering thought about the Lord.'

'Let us go on to show this in its various manifestations'—he encourages the congregation to isolate several features about the Lord and how the believer benefits from what he is: his name, his dignity, his glory. In emphasising these he urges, 'think of the matter from the aspects of our dignity'. He continues, 'then attend to this'. Pressing the congregation further and introducing another sub-point he requests, 'Let me put it this way. Think of the Christian in relation to the angels.' The truth is affirmed that the Bride's destiny is greater than that of angelic beings!

The congregation is now poised to develop with him the second main heading; those who share the life of Christ also share his privileges. These include the Father's love. If that is not staggering enough, there is more. Everything is ours through Christ. Lloyd-Jones cites 1 Corinthians 3:21. But, so enraptured is he by the flow of the argument, and knowing he has the congregation with him, he puts in a revealing aside. . . . I am simply giving headings for you to think about and to meditate upon. We should spend much of our time with these points thinking about them . . . stop and think. Think even before you get on your knees.[23]

The pulpit may be ahead of the pew. But the distance should be measurable. The preacher believes the congregation to be close behind him, if not one with him in his thinking. So, he becomes somewhat confrontational 'I ask again, Am I not right when I say . . . ?' He coaxes the congregation into deeper thought and toward making further logical conclusions from the Scriptural premise that the Church is the Bride of Christ. Though once again we are running ahead of ourselves, we cannot leave off from this address without quoting DML-J's final paragraph with its outburst of passion, conviction, and—what surely must have been—unction.

> Having taken the church as His Bride, He bestows all that upon her. His prospects are ours, His glory is ours, all things are ours. The meek shall inherit the earth. We shall reign with Him over the whole universe, we shall judge angels. You and I! Such is the Christian! Such is the Christian church as the Bride of Christ![24]

DIAGNOSIS

DML-J looked back on his earlier years in the medical profession with gratitude. One of the favourite Puritan descriptions of the ministry was 'a physician of the soul'. This describes Lloyd-Jones. He believed the Lord led him to exchange his goal of assisting the healing of bodies in favour of the cure of souls.

Each of Lloyd-Jones's sermons opens with an introduction. This could be in the form of a reminder of what had gone before. (Some of this has been removed from the lightly edited sermons). The summary was especially for the benefit of those for whom the address would be a one-off and not part of a series. Each sermon had to be self-contained and able to stand on its own feet, even though it was part of a prolonged series.

After this, he would go on and challenge the intellect. This might take the form of diagnosing the text. He would break it open, consider several propositions which flowed from it, bring principles from parallel Scriptures in order to effect a comparison and enable deductions to be made. At the same time, as we have seen, the congregation would be encouraged to think.

APPEAL TO THE MIND

The preacher had always to aim for the minds of the members of his congregation. The address we recommended from the Acts of the Apostles is a very notable example. He severely criticised testimony which recounted a change in behaviour and attitude merely as the result of some experience. This leaves Christianity open to the butt of the psychologist who, with good reason, can cite other examples of the same things from the ranks of the cults. Christianity is based primarily on facts. These are to be clearly placarded before the congregation. The preacher is to reason with his people on the basis of the facts. Peter's sermon debut in the Acts of the Apostles is a glorious example. His main thrust is the fact of the Crucifixion and the Resurrection. Neither of these happened by chance, even though cruel and evil men were involved. Why did these things take place? And why was it important for the congregation to learn of these facts? Peter makes the issue very plain. This was to do with their salvation or condemnation. His audience was troubled by the facts being deliberately applied to their circumstances. Then they cried out, asking what they should do. The confrontation was at the level of the mind. This is a consistent note in Apostolic preaching. It is a repeated feature in that of Lloyd-Jones's ministry.

In another sermon on the Acts of the Apostles, he makes a similar point.[25] He puts the proposition that the Christian faith is based on objective happenings and events. He advises that this is the answer to any attack on Christianity launched at it from a psychological perspective. There are those who dismiss the faith historically and suggest, perhaps patronisingly, that though it does good, it is equivalent to the benefit that can also be acquired elsewhere. Many agencies can do people good: drugs, psychotherapy, auto-suggestion, and the like. Religion, too, can be good for some people. 'As long as it makes you better, carry on,' is basically the attitude. To proponents of this view, the point of dispute occurs when a believer dogmatically asserts, 'this is what happened to me, and it should happen to you too'. Lloyd-Jones's point is that this is never to be argued simply on the basis of experience. It has to argued on the foundation of solid facts. These events took place in history as a result of God's grace. About such facts you are to be aware and make a personal response.

New Testament preachers are not the only ones who made a consistent appeal to the facts. So did the Psalmists. 'When Psalmists are in trouble, they always recapitulate their history.' In general, the Old Testament writers appeal to the God of Abraham, Isaac, and Jacob. Their anchorage is not some mystical experience: rather it is with the Living God who has made himself known to them in our world of time and space.

Thus, to stimulate a congregation to think is part of the preacher's responsibility. Any study of a Lloyd-Jones sermon furnishes information on the way in which he went about achieving this goal.

THE CONGREGATION

Lloyd-Jones had an aversion to welcoming people into the church. It would go against the grain to bid good morning to the assembled crowd and add to it further words of greetings. The minister is not present to welcome people into the presence of God. He is one with them as they proceed to ask for the Lord to come among them.

DML-J could be misjudged in this. His disinclination for what might be called pulpit-banter did not mean he lacked warmth toward his people. His concept of worship and belief in the greatness of the God to whom praise was to be offered caused him to veer away from anything that might intrude. Nothing was to detract from directing glory to the Lord.

However, he often referred to his hearers as 'my dear friends'. At times, he seemed to take the congregation into his confidence. Many of them might have blushed inwardly when he quoted from some piece of history, assuming them to be as conversant as he was with the matter in hand.

Examples of his historical knowledge can be found in his addresses on the final chapter of Paul's letter to the Ephesians.[26] He familiarised himself with the military strategy of Alexander the Great as well as the generals of the First and Second World Wars. He felt able to contrast and criticise their style in order to draw supporting material illustrating his main concern—how the Christian soldier should cope in battle! Later in the series, he used his knowledge of the Roman shield, its composition and methods of use.

He would occasionally assume the congregation's knowledge of particular poets, dramatists, and hymn writers. 'You will remember . . .' was a typical introduction. This was not contrived, nor was it meant to be a form of flattery, as he quoted Shakespeare, Shelley, Byron, or Wordsworth. He wished to take the congregation with him. Bruise them; he will have to. Correct them; this is part of the preacher's task. Reveal their inadequacy; this too he will do. But he will also set them at ease in an all-out attempt to win them.

His successor, Glyn Owen, will help us here. At an Assembly of Free Church ministers in 1970 in Worthing, England, Owen likened the preacher in his evangelistic pursuit to a freshwater fisherman. Though he is out to catch the fish, adopts the right stance, casts his line with skill, and uses the appropriate hook with attractive bait, when he has a bite, he will damage the mouth of the fish as little as possible. With expertise and sensitivity, he lands the fish. Owen was not describing Lloyd-Jones's method, but the illustration fits well. For all the seeming sternness in his pulpit manner, there was a desire to coax as well as cajole. The wooing was not ingratiating. His view of Scripture and the high office of preaching would not allow for slapstick or bonhomie.

DML-J endeavoured to arrest his congregation at the point where they were, in order to show them where they might go within the grace of God. He assumed the members of the congregation were prepared to think. After all, would they be present before a pulpit, the occupant of which was known to preach at times for sixty minutes, if this were not the case?

Lloyd-Jones advised young preachers, 'Don't directly preach at the conscience or the will . . . no one likes personal confrontation and tends to switch off . . . we must take the conscience and will by stealth as it were, that is indirectly, from behind.'[27]

AN EXAMPLE

An early example which illustrates some of the factors highlighted is a sermon which, as far as I know, remains unpublished. Douglas Johnson recalled it. Lloyd-Jones was preaching from 2 Timothy 2. He began by explaining quietly that Timothy was young and inexperienced and worried by having the care of all the churches in his area. The Apostle Paul wrote to him not to be too concerned about the security and future of the churches—that was the Holy Spirit's task. Timothy should give his attention to what the Christians were like. This was what worried Paul; the lives of believers in a morally evil environment. Johnson goes on to describe how DML-J worked on the nature of Paul's call for Timothy to exercise his personal example and, by teaching, to change the lives of the Christians. This was all by way of background and introduction. Then Lloyd-Jones warmed to his subject more and really began to preach as he brought the hearer to his text! 'In a nutshell, the Apostle's advice was, "Nevertheless the foundation of God standeth sure, having this seal, the Lord knoweth them that are his. And, let everyone that nameth the Name of Christ depart from iniquity"' (v. 19).

The first part of the sermon was aimed directly at the intellect—'the foundation of God'. Lloyd-Jones amassed biblical information to prove the point over and again. No room for doubt remained. The individual Christian, indeed the Church as a whole, could rest assured. God's foundation was secure. The hearer's mind was rested by an exhortation to rely on the Lord's sovereignty.

'At this point' Johnson continued, 'the "jet-plane" began to move on the runway and soon it was lifted up and he was airborne.'

It will probably never be finally established who first used the aircraft analogy in describing his ministry. Its appropriateness has caught the imagination of several and it has become part of the folk-lore which surrounds him. But it is apposite. He would cruise down the runway sometimes two or three times. Each attempt would give further evidence of the assault on the mind. Then he would take off; 'he would let himself go'. This is what C. H. Spurgeon meant by his term 'the sacred anointing'. It is descriptive of the occasions when the Spirit is upon a preacher in an unusual manner.

Johnson described how the emotions of the congregation were arrested as Lloyd-Jones dealt with the expressions 'the Lord knows those who are his' and 'the secret of the Lord is with those who fear him'. 'One became quite excited about the Lord's hold and care for his children. The heart was at peace the more one thought about experiencing the Sovereign God's personal care.'

During this part of the address, he might become quite animated. In the earlier years, this was more pronounced. But even toward the end of his ministry, he could be demonstrative.

Dr. Lloyd-Jones believed preaching involved communication through personality. He remembered Demosthenes, whom he reckoned to be one of the great orators of all time. When the Greek was asked what was the first rule of great oratory, he gave a fulsome answer, 'the first great rule of oratory is action: and the second great rule of oratory is—action: and the third great rule of oratory is—action'.[28] DML-J went on to comment that an orator is not just a man who moves his lips and his tongue, his whole body is involved.[29]

At Westminster Chapel, the huge pulpit area became the backcloth against which the preacher would point to heaven and hell, to certainty and danger, God and Satan.

> If he shouts, it is not because his argument is weak, but because he is saying something about God that strikes at the moment of utterance as surpassingly strong. The most memorable of his sermons are those in which he is most completely caught up in his own declaration of the mighty works of God, and you see and hear this tremendously vital person saying these things in a way which shows him powerfully feeling them.[30]

Johnson remembered the third major development in the presentation of the address from 2 Timothy 2. Lloyd-Jones positioned himself for a frontal assault on the will and the conscience. (His colleague wryly worked on the aircraft analogy further, 'the Doctor was now at about 20,000 feet!')

'"And let everyone here depart from iniquity". Is there any place for sin and evil to exist within the believer?' DML-J showed the incongruity of the position. How can any Christian indwelt by the Spirit be comfortable with any form of compromise? He made an appeal for a holy life. Yet, the appeal was not based on emotion alone. It had gone deep into the mind. It pierced the conscience. And it opened the way for what Johnson called 'the grand slam'! What are we going to do in the light of all that we have heard? We must return with contrition and repentance.'

Nothing followed this. Nothing was necessary. A typical appeal as expected in evangelistic campaigns and which is part of the liturgy in some churches would have been as unnecessary as it would have been inappropriate. The appeal was basic. It was woven into the warp and woof of the total address. This is a consistent factor in Lloyd-Jones's preaching. Vital components were the pleadings and the application.

His addresses can be submitted to analysis. There is a form about them. There are identifiable stages. But these are not absolute. The application will flow like a stream and be found throughout. But, unlike the stream, the current can vary and often be surprisingly strong. It was as though he heard an echo from the crowd which listened to Peter on the Day of Pentecost. The people asked what they were to do. DML-J will tell them—always. Johnson was right. There would inevitably be a 'grand slam'. But there was a build up to it. He preached as an impassioned man, fired by the Holy Spirit, demanding and deserving a verdict.

Often at the conclusion of his message, there would be a hush among the congregation. Referring to the occasion above, Johnson remarked, 'Nobody left that building quite as they went in!'

The preacher can develop a diagnostic approach to preaching and delivery without it's, becoming dry and academic.

> How can a man be dull when he is handling such themes? I would say that a 'dull preacher' is a contradiction in terms; if he is dull he is not a preacher. He may stand in a pulpit and talk but he is certainly not a preacher. With the grand theme and message of the Bible, dullness is impossible.[31]

In the next chapter, we develop further the whole concept of preaching diagnostically. But we return again to Lloyd-Jones's invariable introduction, 'the words to which I wish to draw your attention are . . .'

The opening contains the goal, for him—and, one hopes, for any preacher who wishes to be biblical. These words are the words of God for the congregation at that particular point. As such, they are to be handled carefully, not thoughtlessly or lightly. They have demanded the preacher's prayerful study and preparation. He aims to have them preached in the power of the Spirit. The net result is that a contemporary word from an ever-living God will have accurately been brought before a people from whom a response is demanded.

In a passage dealing with the question of authority, Sidney Greidanus comments:

> The only proper authority for preaching is divine authority, the authority of God's heralds, his ambassadors, his agents . . . Accordingly, if preachers wish to speak with divine authority, they must proclaim the message of the inspired Scriptures, for the Scriptures alone are the word of God written; the Scriptures alone have divine authority. If preachers wish to preach with divine authority, they must submit themselves, their thoughts and opinions to the Scriptures and echo the word of God. Preachers are literally to be *ministers* of the word.[32]

It is this conviction that prompted DML-J's introductory formula. There was nothing mechanical about it. His opening actually announced a goal and expressed a felt conviction. He had an aim. This was to draw the congregation's attention to the passage, for in it was something they were not only to understand but to which they should respond. His belief was that the passage at hand was the Word from God which had to be preached on that occasion. His sentiments ran close to the Reformed Second Helvetic Confession of 1566 , that the preaching of the Word of God is the word of God.[33] Thus Lloyd-Jones's close alignment of preaching with prophesying;[34] without this goal and conviction a man should not preach.

9

Diagnostic Preaching (II)

My early training in medicine and surgery are always with me. I look at a text, diagnose the condition and decide where I am to make the first incision. I cut deep through the layers of the tissue until I reach the heart of the problem. I deal with it and then rebuild and sew it up.[1]

For forty-six years I have been trying to shed medical thinking but I am a complete failure, I still have to approach every problem, whether it is theological or anything else, in this medical fashion and I start with causes.[2]

Martyn Lloyd-Jones

In the description of what we have dubbed as diagnostic preaching, the element of certitude is one of its key features. Dr. Lloyd-Jones's certainty revolved around two convictions: (i) he was sure of the veracity of the message; (ii) he was equally sure of the plight of the hearers. The preacher is to analyse the sacred text and diagnose the state of the human condition. Then he is to apply the former to the latter.

The analogy of the doctor and preacher which we comment on from time to time can be pushed too far. It is appropriate here to insert a cautionary note. There are differences, beside common denominators, between a patient in the surgery and a person in the pew. Unlike a medical doctor, the preacher does not need to know the types of sinfulness represented by his congregation. He realises that sickness is a general condition. Its variants need not concern him.

> How does the physician deal with his patient? Well, the first thing he does is to ask the patient to give an account of his symptoms and his troubles . . . without this detailed, specific, special personal knowledge of the patient the physician cannot do his work; and it is at this point, I say, that there is such a striking contrast between the work of the physician and that of the preacher. The preacher does not need to know these personal facts concerning his congregations.[3]

We now move on to get a general perspective on how DML-J approached the week-by-week preaching schedule as he regularly ministered from his pulpit.

A NEW SERIES—THE OVERVIEW

Great care needs to be taken by anyone who contemplates following his practice. To begin preaching for several years on a book demands great conviction that this is the proper track to take.[4]

It is apparent that the last thing Dr. Lloyd-Jones did was just to plunge straight into the text. In one of his messages, he gave an unusual insight on why he opted to preach from the Sermon on the Mount.[5]

> Well, I do not know that it is a part of the business of a preacher to explain the processes of his own mind and his own heart, but clearly no man should preach unless he has felt that God has given him a message. It is the business of any man who tries to preach and expound the Scriptures to wait upon God for leading and guidance. I suppose fundamentally, therefore, my main reason for preaching the Sermon on the Mount was that I had felt this persuasion, this compulsion, this leading of the Spirit . . . [6]

It is of the utmost importance to wait on the Lord before embarking on such a venture.

After introducing a new series of sermons, he then prepared his congregation so that they were poised to get the greatest advantage from what was to follow. He gave an overview of what was in store. We will comment on this in more detail later when we enlarge upon one of his hermeneutical principles.[7]

Referring back to his series from the Sermon on the Mount, he strove to convince the congregation that what was to follow would be relevant to them. Not only would their understanding be widened but it would affect the way in which they lived their lives. Thus, he dedicated three addresses solely to his introduction. He proved that the Sermon on the Mount cannot be treated dispensationally. It is not to be understood merely as an extension of the Mosaic Law. Rather, our Lord laid down principles of conduct to be noted and incorporated into the lifestyle of believers. Such should govern their behaviour and conduct.

DML-J scorned the notion that the Sermon should be considered only as an ethical discourse—an adjunct to the social gospel: it applies for all time to believers but only to believers. Non-Christians cannot live by this code. They are not expected to. The Sermon presupposes a commitment to the Lord as Saviour. A work of grace is a prior necessity. With perception, he hammers the point in the third sermon. Note that he staked all this out before he actually touched the text!

Equally interesting is his approach to the Romans series. He encouraged people to read the Epistle through to ascertain what it contains in general. They should discover 'the big theme' and what 'the writer is setting out to do'.[8] Approaching a single chapter, the preacher should endeavour to help his audience get a 'bird's eye view'.[9]

He criticised those who try to subdivide the Epistle in an artificial fashion, using irony to make his point:

Are you content merely with an analysis of chapter one, or have you seen the message of that chapter? Are you content simply with having a kind of intellectual division of the Scriptures so that you can divide up the whole of the Epistle of the Romans in one night?[10]

He then proceeded to give an example of a man he heard endeavouring to do this:

It was so simple, you see. Chapter one, verses 1 to 15: General introduction. Verse 16: Statement of theme. Then right away to the end of chapter five: Justification by faith. Chapters six, seven and eight: Sanctification. Chapters nine, ten and eleven: The position of the Jews. Chapter twelve to the end: General application in a moral sense. Finished the Epistle to the Romans![11]

He disliked oversimplification, warning of anything which might distort the true meaning of Scripture by removing it from its context. For example, he had an intense dislike for the old promise boxes which used to be in vogue. The boxes contained Scripture verses rolled up side by side. A honeycomb appearance was the result. The user would blindly select one of the furled papers, open, and read it. That would be the verse for a particular occasion! But obviously such a lucky dip approach is contrary to every homiletical rule. Nonetheless, Lloyd-Jones felt that some preachers' approach to their text was comparable to this practice.[12]

His sermons from the Epistle to the Ephesians were to last for seven years. Once more, he encouraged his hearers to stand back and get the whole picture.

He invited them to imagine a scene from the National Gallery. Those who take their time are to be commended. They gaze at a picture for a long period, fixing their minds on what the artist is trying to convey. They benefit from the total masterpiece. This should characterise our approach to passages of Scripture: 'It is surely better to stand, if necessary, for hours before this chapter which has been given to us by God Himself through His Spirit, and to gaze upon it, and to try to discover its riches both in general and in detail.'[13]

A DETAILED CONSIDERATION

When the overall theme of the book has been mapped out, it is time to come to a detailed consideration. The telescope gives way to the microscope. But the former will not be discarded.

Lloyd-Jones's view of Scripture caused him not to hurry through the text. The preacher should not gallop through the text or treat Scripture as a Cook's tour![14] He will stay with a word, if necessary, in an attempt to fathom the depths of the text. He will come close up to it, handle it before the congregation. Gradually, as the text and the related Scriptures yield their meaning, other passages are placed alongside. Thus, when this method is consistently used over a long period, the Bible is brought into perspective though the exposition is centred on one book. Those who heard or read him on Romans found their total Bible knowledge increased enormously.

Expounding the whole through the particular is a legitimate, homiletical method, bearing in mind the Bible's own claims to inspiration.

Lloyd-Jones was wedded to the view of an inerrant Bible. As the Holy Spirit inspired the whole, it was right to expect a long view of Scripture to come into focus by considering one verse.

When criticised that he found more in a verse and a book than it contained—in other words, that he was guilty of *eisegesis* , reading into the text—he would defend his practice. The epistles contained but summaries of what Paul taught.[15]

ARRESTING THE CONGREGATION

To maintain a congregation's attention is a constant challenge for every preacher. Recall the argument that comprehensive interaction is a primary goal in Lloyd-Jones's approach to preaching. He deliberately attempted to keep the concentration of his congregations. Obviously, every preacher wants to do this. DML-J was more successful than most. So, we must ask, beside his natural giftings of intellect and speech, were there any features to be deduced generally from his sermon style of presentation which were of value in stimulating and maintaining interest? The enquiry is important. Most preachers need help in this area. How does one maintain a high interest-count? There are several traits in DML-J's sermons worthy of consideration, not unique to him, but his skillful use of them, plus his natural gifts within the grace of the Holy Spirit, enabled him to be an effective communicator.

The use of negatives

The employment of the negative is a helpful tool for the preacher endeavouring to secure a point in a particular statement. DML-J consistently applied this style of teaching. It is one of the most striking features in his sermons. Generally, his formula seemed to be: the more complex the text, the more effort is required in establishing what the text does not contain. 'To make positive statements is not enough; one has to be negative first so as to correct what one regards as false teaching.'[16]

Examples are strewn throughout his messages. This style is highly effective. Let me share a personal reflection. I remember hearing Lloyd-Jones when I was an undergraduate. I had invited my parents and an uncle to accompany me. It was their first exposure to this type of preaching. None of them was used to fifty-minute sermons. I worried how they would cope. The anxiety was needless. DML-J was in the middle of his Ephesians series. I can still see my uncle's head fixed in the preacher's direction as he strained forward and listened with rapt attention. It seemed as though my relative sprang mentally to life. Eventually, we left the church. Over lunch, the talk was of what the preacher had said. The satisfaction in my uncle's responses stays with me. He had been under the ministry of a preacher who had encouraged him to think his way clear through a passage. Dr. Lloyd-Jones's conclusions were definitely shared by one ardent listener! A judicious use of negatives brought clarity to him as the biblical passage was expounded.

When a building site is being cleared, the man in control issues instructions to his fellow workers to ensure that the demolition process is efficiently and successfully accomplished. Listening to DML-J conveyed the same impression. He directed the congregation in a convincing fashion. He showed what must go and what could not possibly be allowed to remain. It all sounded so obvious. The listener wondered why he did not realise it before!

Getting rid of what the text does not say is essential preparatory work. It clears the way to establish what it affirms, and what superstructure it can legitimately carry.

In diagnosing ailments, it is important to rule out what is not affecting the patient. This was Lord Horder's principle. It transfers well as a method of Bible exposition. The diagnostic approach to Scripture is an invaluable tool. This may sound too clinical and run the danger of producing the dull sermons Lloyd-Jones censures in some preachers. But adopting his method does not have to make a man pedantic and cold. As the preacher moves away from uncertainties, he warms toward his certainties. Conviction and passion enter in as he declares those truths about which he is sure.

Such certainty is not lost on the congregation. They have been involved in the construction of the argument and have been working with the expositor. Ideally, they will have a similar experience to that of the man whose eyesight the Lord restored, 'Once I was blind but now I see'.

To consider and then remove the negatives brings clarity and understanding. Here are two examples from Lloyd-Jones's sermons.

In his expositions on the Sermon on the Mount, at one point he engaged in establishing the meaning of the word 'meekness'.[17] He made a proposition which seems to be supported by Scripture generally. Meekness is not a natural quality. There is an element of 'givenness'. It is bestowed rather than developed. Thus the comment, 'No, it is not a matter of natural disposition; it is something that is produced by the Spirit of God.'

In order to get us closer to its actual meaning, he clears the ground more thoroughly. Meekness does not mean indolence; the idle man is far from meek. Nor does it mean flabbiness. It does not mean niceness. At this point, the congregation is deeply involved. They are encouraged to work through the options. In popular thought, niceness and meekness are quite close. There are nice dogs and nice cats and animals that are not so nice. But you would hardly use the word meekness to describe the former! His congregation observes the absurdity of the position. Niceness is ruled out as an equivalent. Relentlessly and logically he pursues the point. Weakness is rejected. So also is 'a spirit of compromise'— another misnomer accepted by shallow thinkers. 'Peace at any price' is not the attitude that the verse commends as being blessed.

Having done the ground work, he can deal with the matter positively. To leave it there would be quite unsatisfactory. The preacher clears the way in order to build. His audience must not be left without some definite conclusions. Lloyd-Jones goes on to the firm ground. In this case, he shows what the true nature of meekness is. He encourages them to seek after it.

He used the same approach in preaching on the Epistle to the Romans. He is in the middle of the second chapter of Romans and is dealing with the vexed question of the Jews' knowledge of the Law of Moses yet their failure to practise it. Compared with this is the manner in which some Gentiles, in responding to their consciences, actually become 'a law unto themselves'. Lloyd-Jones is particularly calling attention to verses thirteen to fifteen which are in brackets in the Authorised Version.

> We have spent some time in dealing with what this parenthesis does not say, and we have done that because so often people have tried to prove that it says a number of things which it simply does not say at all. We have seen that it does not teach justification by faith or the way of salvation. It does not say that anybody can keep, or is capable of keeping, or ever has kept the Law. It does not say that the Gentiles have the Law of God written on their hearts. And it does not say that if we live up to the light we have, we shall be saved.[18]

The quotation is actually his opening paragraph for a new sermon. Without apology, he reminds his congregation that he spent most of the time in his previous address using negatives. Lloyd-Jones was painstakingly thorough. He is convinced that now and only now are they in a position to realise what the text is really declaring. He is in no hurry. His high view of Scripture is his defence for proceeding slowly and carefully. It will not be so difficult to establish what the text is saying now that other options have been rejected.

> And so, having understood all that, we come now to what it does say, to its positive teaching, and this need not detain us very long, because

in dealing with the actual words, we were more or less giving a positive exposition.[19]

Those who are seriously concerned to improve their style of delivery by learning from Lloyd-Jones's method should read the ninth and tenth chapters in this series from Romans. Remember that the passage which he was expounding is far from easy. A preacher might well be disposed to gloss over the verses. Many do this, not because they are in difficulties themselves at an exegetical level; their problem is how to communicate effectively without wearying the congregation. How can they get the argument across without being wearisome? Lloyd-Jones had the gift of delving into Scripture, holding up obscure passages and by his 'diagnostic approach' involving the congregation in working through the text. We see shades of the operating theatre—a team of doctors under the leading consultant work together in examining the patient, exploring the problem, making the necessary cuts, and dealing thoroughly with the issue.

DML-J is not unique in employing this tool. This was the practice of Jonathan Edwards, from whom he drew so much inspiration. In the pursuit of his thesis on the nature of the affections, Edwards spent the central part of his book showing what they are not, then he proceeded to show what they are. Lloyd-Jones comments, 'that is typical Edwards—the negative and the positive'.[20]

This homiletical method does have Scriptural support. The classic example is found in the ministry of our Lord. There are several occasions when he led off with negatives. A reading of the Sermon on the Mount will furnish the enquirer with many instances—Matthew 5:17; 6:1-4.[21]

Sometimes our Lord will reverse the order, beginning with the positive and then moving on to the negative. Lloyd-Jones reminds us that he did this when giving his teaching on prayer.[22]

The employment of the interrogative

Another feature which stands out in Lloyd-Jones's preaching method and which he consistently employed was the use he made of questions. They are a helpful transitional tool in the hands of an expositor. They can take him and the congregation from one theme in an address to another. They also cause the congregation to think the answers through.

Questions arrest attention and are useful for applying the truth of what has been considered. Lloyd-Jones deliberately cultivated the method. In later ministry, he would sometimes fire off as many as sixteen consecutive questions. Frequently, he used between eight and four-teen. Here is an example of his grappling with the issue of Man's sinful nature. Once more he is immersed in a difficult passage of Scripture. The way in which he expounded Romans 7 has been the subject of debate and critique. But we are more concerned with the 'mechanics' of the exposition than its content.

To go through Romans 7 verse by verse and hold a thousand peo-ple's attention requires great skill. We observe him interacting with his congregation and, seemingly, interrogating his text. He refers to Paul's statement that sin within him is the cause of his evil bias.

> How does he arrive at this deduction? He seems to say, 'What I have just been saying raises a problem. Here am I, saying that what I do I do not want to do, I do not will to do. I do not approve of it, and I am in agreement with the Law which condemns it.' The question then immediately and obviously arises, how does sin happen at all? Why does this man sin at all? It is clear that it is not the Law that does it? Well then, what does? What is responsible? How does this come to pass?[23]

In his lectures on preaching, he highlighted the value of this method. He wished to help the student preacher improve his delivery and maintain the interest of his congregation by generously using the interrogative mood. Then he would be able both to apply and develop the message as he proceeded with the main thrust of the sermon. The approach stopped him from giving the impression that he was dealing with abstract, academic, or merely theoretical matters or that he conceived of the congregation in a passive fashion. The preacher was handling liv-ing truth. The congregants were not spectators. Ideally, they were to be involved. The use of questions helped to secure the goal.[24]

We cite another example, this comes from a sermon on Second Timothy:

> Are you relying on anything in yourself at this moment? If you are, you are not a Christian. Are you relying on the fact that you have been brought up in a Christian country? God have mercy upon you! If you still think this is a Christian country, I am afraid we are not speaking the same language. Are you relying upon the fact that you were chris-tened when you were a child, or that you were baptised when you were older—is that what you are relying on? Are you relying upon the fact that you are a member of a church and that your name is on a

roll—is that it? God have mercy upon you! Anyone can do that, especially today, when there is no longer strictness in these matters. Are
you relying upon the good you have done? Are you relying upon the
fact that you have never got drunk, that you have never committed
adultery, that you are not a murderer—are these the things on which
you are relying?[25]

Questions can affirm what has been covered and become a bridge to the
next section.

The method is also very effective at the end of the address. Some
books on homiletics emphasise that the application should come at the
conclusion. Lloyd-Jones consistently made his application throughout.
He intertwined it with the subject matter—especially in his Sunday
morning and evening ministry. However, Douglas Johnson is right in
detecting his flying at a higher altitude often, though not always, when
he drew to his conclusion. Then he sometimes opened the throttle to its
fullest limits and made a last attempt to sink convictions into the mind
in order to gain a response from the will of his listeners. There were also
times when he quietly, and pointedly, applied what had been said.
Occasionally a salvo of questions sealed the sermon:

My dear friends, I leave you with a question: have you been persuaded? Have you been persuaded about these things? As you are in
the midst of life, have you been persuaded of these things? Have you
been persuaded about him, who he is, what he has done? Are you sure
about these things? Have you trusted him, have you given yourself to
him, have you committed your whole eternal future to him? Is he mastering and dominating your life? Are you relying upon Him and the
power of His might? Is that your position? Have you been persuaded?
Listen to Him again: listen to Him as He says, 'I am come that they
might have life, and that they might have it more abundantly.'[26]

The use of illustration

Another characteristic of Lloyd-Jones's ministry which may surprise
some is his employment of illustration. A rapid reading of his books
might indicate that this was not a regular feature. Macleod passed comment on the infrequency of his illustrations and the 'even fewer personal
anecdotes'.[27]

On one occasion, DML-J recounted how he was confronted by an
individual who complained that in the sermon he had just heard there

was only one illustration whereas on a previous occasion there had been several![28]

Actually, he did make use of illustration though he exercised and advised caution in so doing. He was concerned to warn preachers not to confuse the valid quest of being simple with the vexed issue of being childish. To 'spoonfeed' a congregation is self-defeating. On the other hand, for the preacher to be unnecessarily academic, for him to cherish an ambition to be a 'pulpiteer' in the sense of some of the preachers of last century, is equally reprehensible. Fixing his point, he spoke of one woman who, having heard such a preacher, was asked if she enjoyed the sermon. Her memorable reply was, 'Far be it from me to presume to be able to follow and to understand the mind of such a great preacher'![29]

He justified and qualified the use of illustration in his book on preaching: 'The illustration is meant to illustrate truth, not to show itself, not to call attention to itself; it is a means of leading and helping people to see the truth that you are enunciating and proclaiming still more clearly.'[30]

One of the reasons why DML-J's use of illustration seems quite meagre is because he employed biblical incidents for this purpose. Indeed, this was his stated preference. In one sermon, he remarked that 'an illustration from everyday life might be helpful at this point. It is not to be compared with illustrations from the Scriptures'. He does, however, concede that certain people can be helped by employing the former aid.[31]

Sometimes he related a biblical illustration in a graphic way. An example of this occurs when he endeavours to impress upon the congregation the importance of coming before God and pleading for revival. Prior to finding evidence to support this from the New Testament, he went to the Old.

> In Genesis 32, we read that Jacob did something like that: 'I will not let thee go', he said.
> The man wrestled with him and said, 'It is the dawn, it is the breaking of day, let me go.'
> 'But I will not let thee go,' said Jacob. 'I'm not letting go until you give me my request'—wrestling Jacob. I have reminded you of how Moses did exactly the same thing. We have been considering it in Exodus 33 . Moses made a request,
> God said, 'Yes.'
> 'More,' said Moses.
> 'Right,' said God.
> 'More,' said Moses.

. . . And our Lord has taught us to pray like this. It is one of the most glorious and wonderful statements even he ever made about God and God's relationship to us. He said, 'You know, you must not just pray fitfully, you must become importunate. You must be like that man who suddenly is visited by a friend late at night. He has no food to give him, so he says, "Oh, my friend up the street will have some loaves." So he goes and hammers at the door.

'But the friend shouts and says, "I cannot come down, I am in bed and my children are with me."

'"No," says the man, "You must give me something. I know you have got bread and I've got a stranger here, I can't let him go without a meal." He goes on hammering.

'"I can't," says the man, "I'm in bed."

'But the suppliant goes on and on, until at last the man gets up and gives him the bread.'

The man in the bed, in our Lord's illustration, is none other than God himself.'[32]

Lloyd-Jones deliberately employed this dramatic style. It is quite proper for a preacher to do this. He has the example of our Lord[33] for justification. Remember how the Lord would envisage and cause his hearers to see the situation he so graphically described, especially in the parables, a method of teaching to which he was drawn: 'a sower went out to sow and *behold* . . .'

As we might expect, Lloyd-Jones appeals to the practice of his mentor, the Apostle Paul. DML-J refers to Paul's employment of analogy in Romans 6. He argues that Paul himself claimed to use his illustration in order to help his readers grasp the point. Lloyd-Jones adds, 'and that is the only reason for using illustrations or analogies'.[34]

They should never be used as an end in themselves. The sermon should not justify the illustration. Rather, the illustration will act as a window, creating interest, stimulating the imagination, holding the attention, and clarifying the truth.

DML-J further appealed to the manner in which the Puritans used this device. In citing their example, he warns against malpractice: 'These men used illustrations to illustrate and not merely to adorn the sermon. Nothing so prostitutes preaching as to use illustrations merely to draw attention to illustrations. We should abominate that.'[35]

It is arguable that Dr. Lloyd-Jones fell at least once at this hurdle of misusing illustration. In his famous series of sermons on revival, five were based on the verses in Genesis 26 verses 17-18, which refer to Isaac redigging the wells of his father Abraham. By any standards, the sermons are outstanding in putting across the burden he felt. And, in our judgment, they certainly represent the message and teaching of the Scriptures.

However, the Genesis passage has nothing to do with spiritual renewal whatsoever. To argue it does is to read into the incident far more than the text can stand. Of course, DML-J realised this. He was using the passage illustratively. But is this a legitimate or a flawed hermeneutic?

In the case of Lloyd-Jones, he was criticised for building so much on these verses.[36] He endeavoured to justify his treatment later. His argument was to draw a difference between spiritualising the Old Testament and using it illustratively. He claimed that he was adopting the latter method. And he cautioned preachers that in using the Scriptures in this fashion, they should make the congregation clearly understand what is happening. The preachers should offer an explanation, and he suggests this wording: 'as this particular thing happened in the realms of history so the same principle can or may be found in the spiritual realm'.

Speaking further about his own case, DML-J went on to contend:

Had I been spiritualising it, it would have meant that I was asserting that Isaac was doing something spiritual on that occasion, whereas I had gone out of my way to say that I was simply using this story as an illustration and pointing out that what Isaac did in the matter of water—ordinary water essential to life and the well-being of the body—provides us with a picture of a principle which is of value in the spiritual realm in connection with revival. I was not saying that he did anything spiritual, but showing that as he did not waste his time sending out prospectors to find a new supply of water but simply re-dug the old wells because he knew there was water there, it seemed to me to be the essence of wisdom in the spiritual realm and at a time of difficulty and spiritual drought, not to waste our time in seeking for a new 'gospel' but to go back to the book of Acts and every period of Revival in the history of the church. Now that is not spiritualising that old incident . . . because I was not saying that what Isaac did led to a revival.[37]

Using an incident from the Scripture to illustrate an aspect of exposition is legitimate. But to base the whole of a sermon and, in this case, several sermons, on a biblical event which at best can only illustrate is dangerous and should be avoided in case the method leads to abuse.

DML-J's mind was soaked in Scripture. The justification for the thrust of his messages lies deep in Scripture. The subject, handled by him, results in safe exposition which runs true to the whole sweep of the Bible. Lesser preachers, however, could easily go astray. The danger is that their ingenuity might work to adjust the controls of the particular verse and its immediate context. The safest hermeneutic is to ensure that Scripture's own parameters are maintained.[38]

Even the early Church had problems. One group particularly failed to allow Scripture to operate under its own controls as far as exposition was concerned. Allegorising became a way of life at the school of Alexandria and in the ministries of Clement and Origen. The prizes went to those who had the most fertile imaginations!

But we must return to our main point in this section. DML-J did use illustration effectively, especially when taken from the Old Testament. But he was perhaps over-cautious in warning preachers against the practice of collecting stories and writing them down in a book in the same way as a stamp collector catalogues his finds. Some might find this habit a useful one to cultivate. They would be in good company. The great Spurgeon did the same. Those with feebler memories than DML-J can thus surmount their handicap. A store of anecdotes is valuable and needs be no more artificial or an abuse than working on a skeleton address when travelling and presumably incorporating into it aspects which will help to illuminate the meaning of the passage.

An example of Lloyd-Jones's use of a story to illustrate a doctrinal point is that of the emancipation of the American slaves. He used this several times. The purpose of the illustration is to deal with the knotty problem of why, if believers are dead to sin and alive to God, they still do sin! Why are they so weak? What is wrong with them?

The answer is that Paul did not teach sinless perfection. What the Apostle affirms is that the Christian has moved out of the territory, out of the realm, out of the rule and the reign of sin. DML-J continues, 'There is all the difference in the world between being in a given position, and realising that you are in that position'. Lloyd-Jones introduces his illustration at this point,

Take the case of those poor slaves in the United States of America about a hundred years ago. There they were in a condition of slavery. Then the American Civil War came, and, as the result of that war, slavery was abolished in the United States. But what actually happened? All slaves, young and old, were given their freedom, but many of the older ones who had endured long years of servitude found it very difficult to understand their new status. They heard the announcement that slavery was abolished and that they were free: but hundreds, not to say thousands, of times in their after lives and experiences many of them did not realise it, and when they saw their old master coming near them, they began to quake and to tremble, and to wonder whether they were going to be sold. They were free, they were no longer slaves; the Law had been changed, and their status and their position were entirely different; but it took them a very long time to realise it. You can still be a slave experientally, even when you are no longer a slave legally. You can be a slave in your feelings when actually in respect of your position you have been emancipated completely. So it is with the Christian.[39]

The appropriateness of the illustration is obvious. When applied to the text, it causes a shaft of light to beam through. The point becomes clear. The goal of the anecdote is secured. The hearer has been helped to grasp the meaning of the passage.

Another example of DML-J's use of illustration to help his hearers grasp what seems a difficult concept occurs in a sermon on Paul's famous text, 'all things work together for good to them that love God, to them who are the called according to his purpose' (Rom. 8:28 *AV*).

It is a wonderful text. There are times when it seems utterly impossible to apply. The insensitive use of such a Scripture can cause a good deal of harm. Think of the faithful, loving wife who is suddenly and unexpectedly bereaved, or the father whose children are killed in a train crash. How can such events work together for good? Lloyd-Jones in his helpful exposition has recourse to a word picture from an elderly preacher of former years.

'How can you say that things which are working in opposite directions are for my good?' The old preacher answered by using the illustration of a watch. He said, 'Take your watch and open it. What do you see? You see that one wheel is turning in an anti-clockwise direction, but it is attached to another wheel that is working in a clockwise direction. You look at this machinery and you say, "This is mad, this is quite ridiculous; here are wheels turning in opposite directions; the man who made the watch must have been a madman". But he wasn't. He has so arranged this watch and put in a main-spring to govern all the wheels, that when it is wound up, though one wheel turns this way, and another that way, they are all working together to move the hands round the face of the watch. They appear to be in contradiction but they are all working together to the same end.'[40]

The story is excellent. It results in a visible picture being brought to the mind of the congregation. The simplest person can think the incident through. He can see the delicate workings of a watch. He knows that the wheels do go in opposite directions in the interest of maintaining a balance and producing a register of the time. He is now conditioned to move from the illustration of the watch to the explanation of the Scripture. The former makes the latter much easier. This illustrates the validity of illustration! Its legitimacy revolves around making the obscure and difficult passages plain and easier to comprehend.

A shorter, appropriate example of DML-J's use of this teaching aid occurs in a sermon when he is persuading his congregation to seek a fuller experience of God and greater spiritual maturity. What we have already may seem fulsome and significant. But we need to put it into context and consider how much more there is to be experienced.

A little child can paddle at the edge of the ocean, but out in the centre in the depths, the mightiest Atlantic liner is but like a cork or a bottle. It is illimitable. We enter into the Christian life as children, and begin to paddle; but we must go on and out into the depths.[41]

The use of imagination

It is said that on one occasion when George Whitefield was preaching in a room full of British aristocracy, he narrated a story of a blind man who had lost both his stick and dog, slowly moving toward a precipice. The account was so convincingly told and in such a gripping fashion that one of the hearers, Lord Chesterfield, stood up and shouted, 'By heaven's the beggar's gone!'[42]

A sanctified imagination is a great boon for a preacher and brings benefits to the congregation, enabling them to concentrate and be alert. One of the more significant preachers with this gift was Alexander Whyte of Scotland.[43]

On the subject, Lloyd-Jones remarked that there is not as much danger with it as there was at one time. He went on to allege that we have all become so scientific that there is but little room left for imagination. 'This to me is most regrettable because imagination in preaching is most important and most helpful.'[44]

DML-J spoke approvingly of employing this aid, though indicating that it carried dangers with it. As one would expect, it surfaces more in his narrative sermons and is also, as we have seen, a notable feature in his earliest preaching in South Wales.[45]

There is, however, a line that can be crossed which makes further use of the imagination illegitimate. DML-J thought it was a moot point in the illustration of the blind beggar whether or not Whitefield had breached it. If imagination takes us into the realm of the theatrical or fuels emotionalism, it is unhelpful. The pulpit is not the stage.

An early example of DML-J's restrained yet graphic use of the imagination centres on Herod,

> Ever and again Herod would go down to the prison to visit John. He knew that in doing so he was displeasing Herodias and most of the members of the court. Yet, he went and continued to go. There seemed to be a strange fascination for him in the prison with its remarkable prisoner and his extraordinary preaching. He felt himself drawn there.[46]

A later example of Lloyd-Jones employing his imaginative gifts occurs in one of his messages from the Sermon on the Mount. He is showing the stupidity of building on an inadequate foundation. He focuses on our Lord's teaching toward the end of the Lord's sermon. DML-J imagines someone coming along and arguing with the weak-minded builder:

> 'Look here, my friend, it is no use putting up a house like that on the sand. Don't you realise what may happen in this locality? You don't know what that river is capable of doing. I have seen it like a veritable cataract. I have known storms here that bring down the best-built houses. My friend, I suggest that you dig deep. Get down to the rock'—the foolish man would have dismissed it all and persisted in doing what he considered best for him. In a spiritual sense, he is not interested in learning from Church history; he is not interested in what the Bible has to say; he wants to do something, and he believes it can be done in his way, and away he goes and does it.[47]

Here DML-J is but widening a scriptural illustration. He adds colour but there is neither distortion of meaning nor purpose. The goal is to fix the picture firmly into his listeners' minds and make them more capable of fastening on to the truths embedded within the story.

Choice of words and sentence structure

Dr. Lloyd-Jones has been criticised for complex sentence structure and failure to define his terms. This is not without some justification.

Concerning vocabulary, not every one listening to him would have been over-familiar with the term 'oxymoron',[48] a word DML-J used as he tried to explain something of 'the surpassing knowledge of the love of Christ'. He confessed his frustration as he conceded, 'this is a point at which language fails us completely and the Apostle has to resort to this oxymoron in order to convey the idea that however much we have already, there is always very much more'. Nor would everyone be too sure what was meant when, in dealing with spiritual ill health, the good Doctor spoke about those 'hypochondriacal conditions, the valetudinarianism from which we all tend to suffer so much'![49] But he would explain technical terms, such as, 'aridities of the logomachy of theology', which means that you just become interested in words.[50]

An intriguing study was attempted some years ago on DML-J's choice of language and arrangement of sentences.[51] A sample was taken of his sermons to test comprehension. The results are worth considering.

The researcher, Argile Smith, cited an example of complicated sentence structure taken from a sermon in the Ephesians' series. (This message would have been reviewed by Lloyd-Jones before it went to press.) He was dealing with the end-time consummation of all things and continued: 'That brings us to consider what is meant by, and included in the "all things", for the dispensation, the plan, the purpose, which is being carried out at this present time and which began with the Incarnation, is that God might reconcile in Christ all things.'[52]

Smith follows his quotation of this awkward sentence by reasonably affirming that comprehension and sentence length are related. He refers to other authorities to substantiate the principle. Apparently, the easiest sentences to grasp are those with eleven to fourteen words; he contrasts this with DML-J's average of twenty-one per sentence.

Smith argues that, generally, sentences range from simple to complex to compound-complex. By this yardstick, he reckoned that Lloyd-Jones's hover between complex to compound-complex. Smith reviewed all the sentences in one sermon, finding eighteen per cent to be simple, forty-two per cent complex and forty per cent compound-complex.

With regard to syntax, he observed that Lloyd-Jones had a preference for active rather than passive verbs. This, the researcher reckoned, was advantageous for the listener in securing and maintaining attention. One quoted authority deemed that the active-voice verb is 'the engine power for the sentence'.

All this is fascinating stuff, which doubtless would have bemused Lloyd-Jones, who would possibly have been as chary of the linguistic analysis of messages as he was of the psycho-analysis of missionaries![53]

In one of his seminars at Westminster Theological Seminary, Professor Donald Macleod pointed out that few preachers actually speak in sentences. Our penultimate chapter gives evidence of Lloyd-Jones's unusual ability in this respect. The sermon was deliberately subjected to only a minimum of editing. Lloyd-Jones ranks alongside Spurgeon and the great orators in being able to speak in sentences—complex or otherwise. (Macleod is gifted in this area too.) This is the reason why DML-J was able, on retirement from Westminster, to release so many books. His transcripts were easily reducible to manuscript form.

In responding to and evaluating Argile Smith's findings, it must be remembered that Lloyd-Jones did not attempt a polished sermon style. Indeed, as we have seen, he was quite contemptuous of those who preached with the publisher in mind. Sermons should not be produced in the form of essays intended for publication. Though it is patently clear that Lloyd-Jones's messages are not as rough-hewn as those of most preachers, this was accidental rather than intentional. In the course of exposition he went with the flow of what he believed to be the Holy Spirit's prompting.

Lloyd-Jones did, however, have a trained and scholarly mind. Smith is correct and finds support from Macleod that DML-J was sometimes abstruse in his terminology and failed to explain the words he used.

It must be said that, in measure, Dr. Lloyd-Jones was conscious of this. Listen to him as he reasons the issue through:

> I have often had the experience of people who have been converted, and have then gone on and grown in the Church, coming to me some time later and telling me about what happened to them. What they have so often said is, 'When we first came to the Church, we really did not understand much of what you were talking about.' I then asked what made them continue coming, and have been told again and again that ' *there was something about the whole atmosphere that attracted us* and made us feel that it was right. This made us come, and we gradually began to find that we were absorbing truth unconsciously. It began to have more and more meaning for us.'[54]

As there is more to preaching than preaching, so there is more to listening than listening. A sense of God is what Lloyd-Jones wanted as he preached. He believed that a person could appreciate this even if all that was being said was not comprehensible. The felt presence of the Lord would then compel the individual to return again and again until the time dawned when his understanding was more on a par with his spiritual experience.

Such argument, it should by now be apparent, followed logically from Lloyd-Jones's theology of assurance. Intelligence is not the only faculty which is alerted and at play in receiving and responding to the Gospel message.

It is the Spirit who opens the heart and enlivens the understanding. Comprehension may well occur over a period: it is the nature of grace and knowledge to grow. Therefore, if immediate understanding is small but genuine, it can be expected to develop just as the Kingdom itself proverbially emerged from a grain of mustard seed to a plant over-arching the world.

Nonetheless, it should be emphasised that to be simple ought to be the goal of the preacher and that this was Lloyd-Jones's confessed target even when he missed it. Any unqualified criticism of DML-J in this area would have to come up with some explanation of why his books, if they are so complex, have sold in their tens of thousands and the foreign language editions have done well in some cultures very different from the one in which he preached.[55]

SERMON BASED ON NARRATIVE PASSAGES

DML-J is well known for preaching from the didactic passages of Scripture. He appeared to have the ability of taking a text and—as though wielding a hammer—giving it a sharp tap so it would crack open to reveal its kernel of truth and doctrine. This would usually be in the form of several propositions.

The logic contained in the 'kernel' seemed so obvious. Many preachers must have exclaimed, 'Why didn't I see that!' on reading Lloyd-Jones. Sometimes his expositions appear so exhaustive there appears to be nothing more to say, so the temptation is to give the congregation a modified version of what he preached! The way to avoid this is to approach the text with his methodology in mind. How would he have handled it?

Work it through, make the application plain as the skeleton emerges, and then read Lloyd-Jones. Such an approach relieves frustration and avoids, to some degree, plagiarism!

But, returning to the subject of narrative, it is not generally realised that Lloyd-Jones could handle this in a remarkable fashion and employ all his diagnostic skills in the process. He was never known as a narrative or character-study type of preacher. To some degree, this was because his published works flow mainly from his consistent expositions of Paul's epistles and the Sermon on the Mount. They are extracted from his Bible Study addresses and his Sunday morning ministry.

Much of his Gospel preaching on a Sunday night so far lies untapped by publishers as a source of instruction and example from which preachers might learn.

DML-J brought his analytical powers to bear in his use of narrative. There is an obvious relationship between this and the teaching styles we have just been considering. Sermons built on narrative are, of themselves, illustrative. A sensitive use of imagination is in order in the delivery of such sermons.

'A BLIND WORLD' ACTS 7:8-15 [56]

It will be helpful to take an example of one of Dr. Lloyd-Jones's unpublished narrative sermons, one of several which he preached from the Acts of the Apostles and specifically from the defence of Stephen before the Sanhedrin. This selection is influenced by the fact that, in an unusual manner, DML-J makes some asides which are very relevant to preachers, and the sermon demonstrates some of the aspects which, as we have noted, characterised his style.

The first Christian martyr stood in front of his accusers and effectively rehearsed Old Testament history. The account is found in the seventh chapter of the Acts of the Apostles. DML-J examined this passage. It became the basis for several sermons, each dealing with the contents of the chapter.

These sermons are classics by any standard. [57] In the summaries here, the main features of his presentation, as he moves between two narratives and engages in application, are in italics. This is not only to give a cameo of the address but to see how his diagnostic or analytical approach to preaching, far from being clinical and academic, can be contextualised in a lively, moving, and convicting sermon.

The first thing he did was to *demonstrate to the congregation how relevant the material is.* In this sermon, he was dealing with the story of Joseph's maltreatment by his brothers. Remember that Stephen is defending himself before the Jewish court.

In making the twin context meaningful to his hearers, Lloyd-Jones declares, '*The principles that confronted Joseph, that confronted*

Stephen in selecting his story from those of all the patriarchs, are exactly the same principles that confront you and me tonight.'

To learn from DML-J's style, observe beside *the use of negatives, questions, imagination,* and the like, his *speed in getting to application.* Some preachers leave this right to the end. This is wrong. As soon as possible, the preacher should justify why the congregation should listen to him. What personal significance has this message for them?

Lloyd-Jones supplied a little more of the narrative by telling the story in the same way as he related general illustrative material. Then he delved again into the circumstances of his hearers. This particular address was preached three weeks before Christmas. It afforded *opportunity to tie some application into the events suggested by the calendar.* Why did Christ come into the world? At first glance, it seems that this passage has little to do with the incarnation! He came, as did Joseph when he approached his brothers, to benefit mankind.

Dr. Lloyd-Jones proceeded to *draw a contrast* between Joseph's brothers and the way in which they treated him and the immediate biblical context of Stephen. This early Christian deacon used the Joseph story as he spoke to his detractors in his defence. He began to implant in their minds the idea that there was a parallel between him and Joseph, and them and the brothers.

DML-J broke in, at this point, and took Stephen's application further. This is quite fascinating. As the sermon unfolds, he asserts that Joseph is a type of Christ: 'there is no question of that at all'. Lloyd-Jones proceeded to demonstrate that *the way Joseph was treated is an incredibly accurate picture of the way in which the world has treated Jesus.* The verses in John's Gospel are a summary. 'He came unto his own, and his own received him not. But as many as received him to them gave he power to become the sons of God, even to them that believe on his name' (John 1:11-12 AV).

The world does not come to Christ for the same reason that the brothers did not cleave to Joseph. They were ignorant of their need of him. 'No man comes to Christ unless he is desperate.' The only way to show man how much he needs Christ is to expose his condition.

DML-J closes up on this vital point. He emphasises something that all preachers should appreciate: ' *You must preach the Law before you preach the Gospel.* You must preach the Old Testament before you preach the New.'

Significantly, Lloyd-Jones says *how much congregations can be helped by pictures, by stories, and by illustrations.* Stephen was aware of this. That is why Stephen alighted on the Joseph narrative. Somewhat unwillingly, DML-J concedes the problem that some people have in concentrating for more than ten minutes. He addresses and resolves it. How do you overcome the difficulty? *'Illustrations can help in maintaining attention.'*

As he unfolds the narrative further, he emphasises a point that he has advocated elsewhere. *The wise preacher should never directly confront the will of his hearers.*[58] He should take a circuitous route. He needs to get his congregation to think certain issues through at a historical level or just in principle. Then a ripe time will emerge for the preacher to hammer the points home, making them personal and confrontational.

This axiom is found in Stephen's address. The martyr had analysed the story of Joseph into its various components. This was to enable him to show the Sanhedrin that the errors of the brothers were likewise their mistakes. History has a way of repeating itself.

Lloyd-Jones freely lauds Stephen's technique and confesses, 'I am emulating his wonderful example this evening!' He picks on the rejection of Christ. Why was he tossed aside by the priests and clergy of the day? The answer is found within the New Testament context. Why is the Lord rejected today? The point is brought up-to-date.

Again, we pause and notice Dr. Lloyd-Jones's style. It is one of *relentless interrogation and application*. He darts in and out of two narratives—that of the Old and New Testaments—and projects himself to the present moment. He is alert and lives through the story. The congregation hear and feel it with him. Their minds are enlarged, their emotions are stirred. This surely is preaching as it should be!

Then he shows the reasons why the Lord is rejected today—by society in general and unbelievers in his congregation in particular. Actually, by this time they already know! It's there in the account of Joseph and Stephen's rejection. *By stealth DML-J has approached the will and exposed it.*

Having made his application moderately personal, he returns to the narrative. His next step is to put forward the specific reasons why Joseph's brothers rejected him. *He further reinforces what the congregation has already worked out.* The first cause was that the brothers did not like Joseph's claims. They dismissed the implication of his dreams.

It required no long sifting of the evidence to show that the same applied to the Lord. At the present time, the Lord Jesus is rejected from the pulpit not when he is presented as a politician or as a great preacher and teacher. Such suggestions will not warrant his dismissal. Exhibit him as a man among men and all is well. But press his claims, rehearse his

uniqueness—'I am from above, you are from below; I am from the
Father . . . he who has seen me has seen the Father'—and animosity will
be the product. Then, in that context, he is as unacceptable today as
Joseph was in history.

Again, referring to the calendar , DML-J links his argument to the
doctrine of the Virgin Birth. As Joseph's brothers effectively asked 'Who
are you to have men bowing down to your sheaf or to your star?', similarly people demand: 'Who is Jesus to have such doctrine claimed of
him? What is so extraordinary about him?'

Another cause of Joseph's rejection was envy. The narrative in
Genesis states, 'The patriarchs were moved with envy'. Lloyd-Jones
investigates the statement. Typically, he admitted, 'I want to give the
negative first.' It wasn't a matter of the intellect, or learning, or a lack
of knowledge or understanding which caused the brothers to reject
Joseph. This is paralleled throughout the ages. *Man's rejection of Christ
also has nothing to do with intellect* , learning, or understanding. So the
religious leaders of the day were both envious and frightened of the following the Lord gained. He was heard and esteemed for the authority
with which he spoke.

'Some of the greatest brains in history have been Christians', asserts
Lloyd-Jones. He refers to one of his predecessors at Westminster. John
Hutton sometimes quoted an example of a professor of his day who,
when confronted by skeptical, opinionated students listed a number of
thinkers who became believers. He started with Paul, went to Augustine,
then to Luther, Calvin, Whitefield, Wesley, Gladstone, and Pascal. By
way of application, he said, 'Gentlemen, I put it to you that the message
of the Gospel which proved satisfactory to such intellects is worthy of
your respect and consideration!'

What does cause rejection of Christ if it is not knowledge and intellect and science? Look at Joseph's brothers. They were hindered by
blindness. *Moral blindness leads to prejudice.* They never attempted to
think the matter through. 'Did you notice the statement in Genesis 37:11
(*AV*)? 'His brethren envied him; but his father observed the saying . . .'
Jacob had previously had dealings with God. He was not blinded by
prejudice but began to think.

Lloyd-Jones goes to Romans 7:24 in order to substantiate his case,
'O wretched man that I am'. At this juncture in the sermon, DML-J is
airborne! *He ranges over the Scriptures*, attacking worldly attitudes,
applying significant passages in the Bible which deal with the heart of
men. The preacher is now away from the actual narrative but *he is legit-*

*imately engaged in an extensive application of the general, biblical truth
that estranged man is accountable to God.*

'I have dealt with the cause of it, I have dealt with the explanation
of it, now I want to deal with the enormity of it. I come back again to
the brothers of Joseph'. Lloyd-Jones presses the *application further*.
With emotion and passion, he centres on the Person of Christ and the
rough treatment that the Lord endured at the hands of his accusers: the
ridicule, the mockery, the attempts to make him look foolish. DML-J
lifted this into the modern context and thought of the manner in which
people repeat the past in their religious broadcasts and debates. The
Lord is still the subject of ridicule.

Typically, Lloyd-Jones does a *diagnosis*, 'this is not intellect, this is
just the craven spirit of the brothers of Joseph of old . . . the enormity
of it all, trying to catch the Son of God with cynicism and mockery. The
brothers sold Joseph and they sold him to the Gentiles . . .' The preacher
returns to the main thrust of his text. Joseph in Egypt was sold as a
slave—'but God delivered him out of all his afflictions'.

In their blindness and prejudice, the brothers treated Joseph badly.
Yet, come a few years, and he will have them completely in his power.
They would come to him as beggars. How did he treat them? Did he tell
them to go and get their corn elsewhere? No, he freely forgave them and
saved them from destruction.

However, though this is a wonderful picture, *it is but a 'pale analogy' of what God in his Son has done.* Again, the preacher capitalises
on the time of the year when he is ministering. This is the message of
Christmas, 'For God so loved the world that he gave his only begotten
Son that whosoever believeth in him . . .' (John 3:16 AV).

He breaks off and applies the next part with passion to all types
and categories of people in his hearing. None deserves the gift! None
deserve the grace! *He introduces another Scripture to ram home the
point,* 'when we were God's enemies, we were reconciled to him through
the death of his Son' (Rom. 5:10). He asks, 'don't you see it in the old
story of Joseph and his brothers?' If men are not Christian it is because
they are in the same category as the brothers or the Sanhedrin. They are
blind to who he, the Lord Jesus, is.

At this point, DML-J is *gathering up all the logic that has preceded.*
He brings back earlier points and uses them as a salvo of gunfire. *He
now directly, and not indirectly, confronts the will. He does this almost
ruthlessly. He has earned the right to do so.* Relentless logic, historical
argument, contemporary facts, all have been marshalled in the preaching. Now he fires home, round after round. The blindness of men is the

consequence of an evil and sinful heart. All have such! There is nothing to be said for such people. There is nothing they can do! Hell faces them. But they can cast themselves on God's mercy. The Lord will receive sinners. This is why he sent his Son, to bring us what we need—life and hope, in this world and the one to come.

With fervency, pathos, passion, and prayer flowing from an evangelist's heart, he brings his address to a conclusion. He pleads with his hearers. And he implores the grace of the Lord, 'God open our eyes to the need of salvation.'

Our reason for dealing in some depth with this sermon example is not to attempt to reduce DML-J's method to a system. This really cannot be done. But in the preaching setting, method, and system are not necessarily synonyms. Remember how DML-J distinguishes between the message and the preaching. He does not appear to allow the prepared message to dictate the preaching style. At the point of proclamation, he really does have his sails set to the wind of the Holy Spirit. A discernible skeleton is there in his sermon—but often only just. He wants to be borne along by the Spirit.

Nevertheless, in the actual preaching, there are repetitive characteristics: the application, the pathos, the quiet voice, the shout, the calm beginning, the moments when he seems almost to dance on the text and then deliberately and passionately brings in the whole sweep of Scripture to give further depth and authority to what he is saying. And underneath all this is the desire to make what he has to say relevant. So he moves back and forth from the biblical scene to the contemporary world. The questions, the applications, the 'highs' and 'lows' in voice modulation are often used in a transitional fashion. They take the sermon from one aspect to another, ever unfurling the main theme, returning to it, and keeping central the maintenance of interest. He endeavours to demonstrate in the clearest possible fashion, using all the skills of a diagnostician, that 'the words to which I would draw your attention' are indeed the words of the Living God to a people who desperately need to hear them.

Having endeavoured to describe something of the manner of Lloyd-Jones's preaching, I now move on to a more technical consideration of his hermeneutics.

10

Checks

If anyone speaks, he should do it as one speaking the very words of God (1 Pet. 4:11).

I do not hesitate to assert that I am about to say things which are the most wonderful things that a human being can ever utter. I am about to tell you some of the most marvellous and mysterious things that a human being can ever hear.

Martyn Lloyd-Jones[1]

The task of the preacher is to make the message of the Bible plain. It has to be clear to him in order that it can be so for the hearer. As we have seen, Lloyd-Jones encouraged us to expect illumination even at the point of preaching. This is one of the blessings flowing from the unction of the Spirit resting on the preacher. New vistas of meaning and application can open up as the text is being expounded.

In his sermon preached at the opening of the London Theological Seminary,[2] DML-J identified several qualities to be looked for in a preacher. He especially highlighted inspiration. It is the preacher's supreme task to 'bring the Bible to life' and 'to thrill' his congregation. He repeated one of his major convictions: the preacher is in the pulpit not merely to give information and impart knowledge. He is there to move the congregation. He is to remember 'they have hearts as well as heads'. Thus, the 'first business of the preacher is to be inspirational'.

Sometimes the inspiration will occur when the preacher is least expecting it. He may enter the pulpit with a heavy heart even though he worked hard in his study. His sermon notes seem nothing more than a few dry bones or a handful of loaves and fishes. But the Holy Spirit comes and breathes upon the bones. As he is preaching, the sermon springs to a liveliness which moments before he would have considered impossible. The bread and the loaves multiply in the process of proclamation. All this is part of what DML-J called the romance of preaching. The preacher must always be willing for this to happen. Indeed, he must *will* it so! But it cannot be guaranteed.

The desire of the preacher to be borne along by the Spirit will in no way lessen his commitment to hard work in the study. He will copy the example of the leaders of the early Church. They were careful to delegate some duties to others who, in carrying them out, relieved the Apostles of responsibility, thus enabling them to give more time to the study of the Scriptures and doctrine (Acts 6:2).[3]

SKELETONS

A delightful, short essay provocatively entitled 'Skeletons in Dr. Martyn Lloyd-Jones' Cupboard'[4] recounts the lengths to which he went in preparing his addresses. The author supplements the information given in *Preaching and Preachers*. DML-J constantly worked at his skeleton outlines. In their original form, these would occupy several pages and then be reduced by whittling them down to a more manageable précis to take into the pulpit.

To look through his outlines is humbling. In the main, his final notes were written on the back of letters which had, more often than not, been sent to him by church secretaries hopeful that he might agree to speak at the anniversary of their churches. Earlier years of deprivation, during the Depression in South Wales, caused him never to be wasteful. The notes, in the well-nigh illegible handwriting that befits a medical doctor, were placed in orderly fashion in their respective category, the yearly batch being stored in a large envelope.

Working at skeletons should occupy a good deal of the preacher's time. But the benefits are enormous. DML-J concedes that he would never read his Bible without having pen and paper to hand, 'the moment something strikes me or arrests me I immediately pull out my pad. A preacher has to be like a squirrel and has to learn how to collect and store matter for the future days of winter.'[5]

REFERENCE POINTS

In trying to discover and learn from his method of sermon preparation, it becomes obvious that he acknowledged specific reference points. They would control his thought. They helped him sharpen his reasoning in order that he could arrive at positive conclusions and declare with conviction and passion what had been prepared.

Every preacher must have checks in order to safeguard the accuracy of his exposition. Dr. Lloyd-Jones recognised that handling and teaching Scripture is a serious business, 'To be a preacher, an expositor of God's Book, is one of the most dangerous things in the world.'[6] The Church in all ages has been harmed by those who have gone overboard into some forms of heresy. On the fringes of evangelicalism today, there are many who seem to have an orthodox platform for their views but actually distort the message, extracting verses with little reference to background and causing an imbalance.[7]

DML-J was compassionate in his attitude to heretics, although he had no sympathy with their heresies. They were generally good men who had gone astray because they failed to have points of reference. They entertained ideas which were unscriptural. They accepted them and built on them. Unwittingly, they moved away from the faith.

> The heretics were never dishonest men; they were mistaken men. They should not be thought of as men who were deliberately setting out to go wrong and to teach something that is wrong; they have been some of the most sincere men that the Church has ever known. What was the matter with them? Their trouble was this: they evolved a theory and they were rather pleased with it; then they went back with this theory to the Bible, and they seemed to find it everywhere.[8]

The preacher has a frightening responsibility. In teaching others, he must ensure the accuracy of what he proclaims. Lloyd-Jones had a high view of the Christian ministry. Preaching affects men's eternal destiny. God has ordained 'the foolishness of preaching' as a means of grace whereby men can enter into the blessings of salvation. Nothing is needed more in our world than ministers who grasp the message of Scripture and preach it with the unction of the Spirit. This is life-changing preaching.

Those called to the ministry must commit themselves to consistent hard work in ensuring the accuracy of what they are proclaiming. The ministry is no place for idle men.

Dr. Lloyd-Jones scorned what he reckoned to be the practice of upper-class families in England last century. The custom was to send a less able son into the Church! This revealed an utter failure to grasp the nature of the high calling. So awesome is the responsibility that, following C. H. Spurgeon, he advised men that if they could do anything else but enter the ministry they should do so!

He applied to himself these strictures about hard work. His sermon output was quite phenomenal, especially when the amount of reading behind it is considered. One reviewer said of his sermons that 'there is no sacrifice of scholarship'. Another, that professional theologians should take heed to what Lloyd-Jones was saying.[9] He did not fall back on his brilliance or his natural eloquence. He was never guilty of what R. C. Sproul would call 'winging it'![10] He worked at his skeletons in order to bring to his congregation a well-thought-out, accurate presentation of biblical truth.

His sermons are replete with examples of his own checking procedure.[11] A list of them is to be found half-way through his expositions of the *Sermon on the Mount*. This occurs when his immediate aim was to expound what is meant by the expression 'an eye for an eye and a tooth for a tooth' (Matt. 5:38-42). He explained how he approached the text.

We follow his reasoning around the verse in question. He claimed that our Lord's refinement of the pronouncement by Moses has often been misunderstood. The dominical assertion, 'I say unto you, that ye resist not evil' has been the subject of appeal by pacifists. They argue that their position is vindicated here. Of course, this is a highly important topic, especially when a country is facing war.

It is instructive to see how Lloyd-Jones approached the problem. Before addressing it head-on, he reminded his listeners of his controlling principles:

● The sermon is not to be viewed primarily as a code of ethics.

● It does not contain a 'rule of thumb'—to be mechanically applied.

● If our interpretation makes the teaching appear ridiculous it is wrong.

● If our understanding makes the position impossible it must be wrong.

● If our interpretation contradicts 'the plain and obvious teaching of Scripture at another point' it must be wrong.

● There is no contradiction in biblical teaching.[12]

These maxims he applied throughout his preaching career.

The word hermeneutics comes from the Greek *hermeneutikos*. This is the science of interpretation and particularly, according to the *Concise Oxford Dictionary*, the interpretation of the Scriptures. In this chapter, we are endeavouring to uncover Martyn Lloyd-Jones's hermeneutical method. This will help us to understand why he became such a faithful and esteemed expositor of the Scriptures. For convenience, we arrange his hermeneutical principles around three clusters.

THE SCRIPTURES

He was totally committed to their authority[13]

For Dr. Lloyd-Jones, approaching the Scriptures was akin to Moses' drawing near to the burning bush: they are a divine revelation. Handling them is a fearful privilege which should not be undertaken lightly. In opening one sermon, he actually likened himself to Moses. 'I seem to hear the voice that came of old to Moses . . . "put off thy shoes from off thy feet for the place whereon thou standest is holy ground" [Exod. 3:5]. We are in the presence of God and his glory; so we must tread carefully and humbly'.[14]

One of his earlier books to which reference has been made bears the title *Authority*.[15] The addresses he brought on the reliability and inspiration of Scripture were given at a time when Evangelical scholarship had not achieved its present respectability. In this slender volume, he set out his case for the primary authority of Scripture which he retained and to which he often referred his hearers throughout his ministry. Years after the publication of *Authority*, he queried:

> Do we realise, I wonder, what a privilege it is that we have these Scriptures, New Testament as well as Old? Do we realise the advantage of having an open Bible? Do we realise the advantage and the privilege of having the living oracles of God? Let me ask a further question: do we realise that our Bible is the Word of God? That is what the Scripture is saying.[16]

All revelation must be tested from this standard. In setting out a list of hermeneutical principles which controlled his expository style, Dr. Lloyd-Jones led off with the maxim that 'we must deal with Scripture alone.'[17] Those who are in breach of this principle, in effect, allow philosophy to intrude. For example, proponents of conditional immortality resort to their own preconceptions about the person of God. A God of love, they claim, would not consign people to endless punishment. 'But at that point they have ceased to argue from the Scripture only; they have sought refuge in philosophy.'[18]

The commitment is as much to the Old Testament as to the New

The whole Bible is to be acknowledged as the Word of God. He regretted that the New Testament was ever published on its own. Both the Old and the New Testaments should be studied.[19] Lloyd-Jones was concerned that some Christians so concentrate on the New Testament that they neglect the Old. He asks:

> Do you read your Old Testament every year regularly, as you do your New Testament? Do you go through your Old Testament at least once a year? You should. And how do you read your Old Testament? I find certain Christian people who only use their Old Testament, as they say, 'devotionally'; they read the Psalms, and perhaps the occasional prayer of a godly man, or a bit of history; they use it devotionally. You have no right to confine it to devotional use. God's truth is revealed there, and we need that revelation.[20]

The criticism might be levelled that Lloyd-Jones did not maintain this balance between the two testaments in his selection of passages for sermons. The greater part of his published works are from the New Testament.

It seems to me that there is substance in this charge. Nonetheless, two things should be noted. The vast majority of his published works are sermons which he directed to Christian believers and delivered on Friday evenings and Sunday mornings. Sunday evening's sermons were rarely published either in the Westminster Chapel's magazine or in book form. Reference to the tape-lists of his Sunday evening ministry reveals that he did preach from Old Testament passages. Indeed, he was quite masterly in handling Old Testament narrative. Remember also that it is part of Lloyd-Jones's method when expounding the New to return constantly to the Old by way of illustration and in order to highlight his argument.

The Bible is complete[21]

All the divine revelation is contained within one book. There is nothing further to be added. Thus, his problem with the Roman Catholic Church and the cults. Both are guilty of putting something alongside the Scriptures. Roman Catholics place their tradition and the authority of the Church. Generally the cultists, like the Mormons, have another book which effectively takes pre-eminence over the Bible and becomes the pivot on which their faith swings.

Lloyd-Jones's conviction on the entire sufficiency of Scripture affected his approach to claims about the restoration of the gift of prophecy. As we have seen, he consistently warns that, if a prophetic gift is used, one of the tests will be how it affirms and applies but does not add to the Scriptures. Neither should anything be subtracted from them. If the Church of Rome is guilty of the former, modernists are charged with the latter. Subtraction from and addition to Scripture cause the same problem; they effectively distort its message.

This method of expounding Scripture follows the pattern of the Lord

The criterion for Lloyd-Jones's preaching ministry was that our Lord constantly went to the Scriptures in order to substantiate the claims he made about himself. For him, the Scriptures were the final court of appeal. He recognised the inspiration of the smallest word. Far from abrogating any part of the Old Testament Scriptures, the Lord came to fulfil them. He appealed to them. DML-J argued our Lord was asserting, 'Check me and what I am saying. Check me by the Old Testament Scriptures. Go through them, search them. Pick them all out.'[22] If the Lord's ministry was set against the revelatory background and format of the Old Testament, so ought ours to be.

> It must be said, however, that the question of our attitude to the Old Testament inevitably raises the question of our attitude toward the Lord Jesus Christ. If we say that we do not believe in the account of the creation or in Abraham as a person . . . if we say that, we are, in fact, flatly contradicting everything our Lord and Saviour Jesus Christ said about Himself, the Law, and the prophets. Everything in the Old Testament, according to Him, is the Word of God.[23]

There are no contradictions in Scripture[24]

The Scriptures are entirely reliable. They are free from error. For a preacher to insinuate doubts about them into the minds of the congregation is a fearful responsibility. As we have seen, DML-J was horrified that any man might enter the pulpit and question the Bible. He dogmatically asserted:

> We are entirely confined to the Scriptures, and we can add nothing to them. We are in no position to pick and choose from them. We cannot say, I believe this and I reject that; I rather like the teaching of Jesus, but I do not believe in miracles . . . . The moment you begin to do that you are denying revelation.[25]

Leith Samuel recalled Dr. Lloyd-Jones's chairing of a debate in the late 1940s when James and David Torrance and James Barr 'waxed eloquent'. All of the men were later to become professors in some branch of divinity. They endeavoured to get Lloyd-Jones to shift his position on the authority of Scripture.[26] Was not the Bible like a regenerate man with an admixture of something from God and something far from perfect? DML-J's retort was that these men had selected the wrong model. The Bible is like Christ:

> As the human nature of Christ was without sin, so the human element in the Bible as originally written was without error, whether in geography, history, scientific allusion or any other aspect. In His providence, God has allowed some copyists to make an occasional and remarkably rare mistake, for example, in some numerals. But there are no textual mistakes that put any important truth at risk.[27]

There is a classic example of his applying the principle of the non-contradictory nature of the Scriptures in his Romans' series. He was dealing with chapter 8 verse 15 and therefore making comment on the way in which the believer has been freed from the spirit of bondage. A commendable feature of Lloyd-Jones's expositions is that he does not run away from difficulties. Though he did not need to introduce what he calls the 'terrifying minatory passages' in Hebrews 6 and 10 he does so, feeling that they throw light on the passage in Romans. From the Hebrews' verses, the conclusion might be drawn that the believer can fall from grace with no possibility of restoration. Such a view, however, contradicts other plain statements of Scripture. How then should the expositor proceed? DML-J would have him apply the maxim that Scripture cannot deny Scripture. The Bible is utterly consistent. 'With this fundamental postulate, we invariably approach this or any other problem in interpretation'.[28]

Lloyd-Jones then proceeded to tackle the issue thoroughly in the light of other relevant and clear passages giving a classic example of brave and logical reasoning.

VERSIONS

The reliability of the various versions of the Scriptures needs to be considered under the general theme of this chapter. After all, the greatest checks on the sermon are the Scriptures themselves. Thus, the version which the preacher chooses is of the utmost importance.

Dr. Lloyd-Jones always preached from the King James Version of the Scriptures. His predecessor at the Chapel had moved over to the Revised Version. DML-J generally had confidence in the Authorised, feeling that it was translated by godly scholars who were conservative in their convictions. What is more, when the translators added words in order to bring out the meaning of the text, he applauded the fact that they printed them in italics 'in contradiction to that of most modern translators'.[29] However, the cause of accurate exposition was paramount. DML-J was not slavishly committed to the Authorised Version. Where he felt it to be inadequate, he would say so.[30]

He went to astonishing lengths to discover the most accurate translation of a text. Few preachers would risk the tedium and the possibility of being thought pedantic by pursuing this so thoroughly. For Lloyd-Jones, the irresistible stimulus was his commitment to plenary inspiration. The Bible is no ordinary book, being directly inspired by the Holy Spirit. Our Lord valued it to the extent that he referred to the smallest letter and accent as having value. Should his preachers settle for less?

DML-J severely criticised versions which, without any textual grounds at all, leave out or interpolate even as much as a word, without indicating the liberty taken for the reader to note.[31]

Some modern versions, he treated almost with contempt. The advent of the New English Bible came at the same time as the launching of British Independent Television with its commercials. The New English Bible he considered as the ITV version![32] He was usually critical of the Schofield Bible,[33] feeling that its notes got in the way of the sacred text, but he thought the Amplified Version in general was 'excellent'. On one occasion, within a couple of paragraphs, he quoted seven different versions or offerings of translations by scholars in his pursuit of accuracy.[34] He referred to the Authorised Version, Revised Version, New English Bible and Revised Standard Version, and then went on to quote in favour of the rendering for which he has opted A. T. Robertson, J. N. Darby, and A. S. Way! Later, in the same series of sermons, he argued that one should always be suspicious of a translation which attempts to smooth out the styles of the writers of the various books.[35]

He was convinced that the biblical text, as originally given, was the oracle of God. It must be treated with the utmost respect, especially by the preacher. This is no ordinary book. It is worthy of intensive study. The preacher is to do all that he can to bring the pure Word of God so that all its potential and power might be released to affect the congregation.

INTERPRETING SCRIPTURE

Armed with an accurate version of the Bible the expositor now has the task of bringing home the truths the book contained as faithfully as possible. He will do this with several controlling factors exerting influence over his proclamation.

The Scriptures are to be interpreted contextually

Violence may be done if the text is removed from its setting and no consideration given to the place in which it is positioned. This requires the preacher to be fully informed about the background of the passage with which he is proposing to deal.

> The context is the greatest conceivable help to the exposition of any Scripture, because these men, enlightened and used as they were by the Holy Spirit, have themes, and they work out their themes; they are logical, and they reason, and they are clear.[36]

The Scriptures are to be handled with care. No meaning is to be read into them that they cannot fully sustain. In DML-J's preaching on the Sermon on the Mount, he had to deal with the subject of divorce. He underlined the importance of the whole Old Testament framework from which the Lord laid down his teaching and suggested a reference grid in order fully to grasp it.

> As we approach these verses, let us once more remind ourselves of their background or context. This statement is one of six statements made by our Lord in which He introduces the subject by the formula 'Ye have heard . . . but I say unto you' . . . The best way to approach the subject is to consider it under three headings. First of all, we must be clear in our minds as to what the law of Moses really did teach about this matter. Then we must be clear as to what the Pharisees and scribes taught. Lastly, we must consider what our Lord Himself teaches.[37]

People who go wrong in their interpretation of Scripture usually do so because they fail to pay attention to the context. Such a practice runs the risk of the text being manipulated to suit the presuppositions of the preacher.

> Now if that is true of individual verses, it is equally true of chapters; and it is particularly true of this eighth chapter of the Epistle to the

Romans. What is its context? The word 'therefore' puts us immediately on to the right track. It is a connecting link. The Apostle is drawing an inference, a deduction from something that has gone before, so we must first discover the exact reference of the term. 'There is therefore . . .' In the light of what has been spoken already by the Apostle, how are we to interpret the word?[38]

This hermeneutical principle can be narrowed down and presented in a slightly different form.

The New Testament is to control the Old, not the Old the New[39]

This is an important axiom, for revelation is progressive, and the final statement is in the New Testament. So the Old can, indeed, be poured through the New in an attempt to expound its meaning. As we have noted, his ministry appeared to have a New Testament bias, but a careful reading of his sermons reveals his using both. Although a lot of his illustrative material was taken from the Old Testament, it should be noted that he did not use it just as an anecdotal source book. That would have been to devalue it. The Old Testament is replete with doctrinal teaching. But the doctrine has to be refined and brought to its fullest expression as it is in the New. So it is important that this hermeneutic is clearly seen and employed by the preacher as he expounds the Scriptures. The New Testament will control the Old. He believed that adherents of reformed theology particularly ran the risk of reversing this order, especially in what he considered to be their over-regulated worship patterns. The Psalms of David lend themselves to their worship patterns more than the spiritual songs to which Paul makes reference![40]

Scripture should be interpreted with a movement from the general to the particular

As a medical doctor, DML-J was well aware of the need to treat the whole man. A sickness may be related to a general condition and can only be diagnosed and treated from that perspective. In interpreting Scripture, the possibility for faulty exegesis increases if the preacher plunges straight into a book without considering the whole sweep of its contents. The same applies to a chapter or part of a chapter. When he commenced a new series of studies, he consistently applied this principle. For example, he spent the best part of three years expounding the Sermon on the Mount. His opening sermons have as their purpose to get the hearers familiar with the overall teaching of the Lord. He acknowledged his method: 'First I want to look at this in general, because again I feel there are certain aspects of this truth which can only be grasped as we take it as a whole'.[41]

The monumental series on Romans lasted many more years than the one on the Sermon on the Mount. Nonetheless, he faithfully applied his basic principle and, indeed, suggested that all should follow his approach.

> I am going to give you a bird's eye view of it before we come back to look at it in detail. Now Bible students, let me commend to you the wisdom of doing that always. First of all, with any portion of Scripture, any paragraph, any longer portion, first of all take a bird's eye view of it—see the whole first, then come back and take it bit by bit and in detail. That, as I understand it, is the true way of approaching Scripture.[42]

He illustrated his principle again when he came to the seventh chapter of Romans. He advised that the 'secret' of expounding it is not to get lost in the details. He gives us more help.[43]

> First, let us look at the particular statements as if we held no view with respect to the whole section; let us try to discover what each statement says, and then, having arrived at what seems to be the meaning of each particular part, let us gather all together and try to arrive at a conclusion.[44]

In other words, he is following the inductive principle of reasoning. He goes so far as to assert that, unless the student adopts this strategy, it is impossible to grasp what Paul is teaching.[45]

However, his approach has pitfalls for the unwary. Care should be taken in implementing it. Seven years is a long time for a congregation to remember the opening sermons from the book of Ephesians. Added to this is the challenge of the rapid turnover, especially in down-town churches. Invariably, there will be people present at any given point who were not in the church at the beginning of the series.

Dr. Lloyd-Jones was aware that his method of exposition ran the risk of hearers getting lost in the wood. He tells us that there is always the danger that, when dealing with a great section of Scripture and looking at various details, one may lose the trend or the main argument of the section.[46]

The solution is to engage in frequent overviews. He occasionally summarises what has gone before, often in a lively fashion. It is a moot point whether he did this often enough. Certainly those wishing to follow his method of preaching and engage in verse by verse exposition would be well advised to stop frequently, revise, and fill in the preceding argument(s) for any newcomers in the congregation.

Once more he appealed to his experience in medicine. He criticised the drift in the medical profession to specialise too early. Symptoms and conditions that the patient exhibits needed to be seen with a view to the 'whole man'.[47] This diagnostic principle transfered perfectly into a safe hermeneutic for interpreting Scripture; thus his declared intention when he commenced his twentieth address from the Sermon on the Mount: 'It will be good for us, therefore, to remind ourselves again of the general outline of the Sermon so that every part will be seen in relationship to the whole.'[48]

Scripture must be interpreted by Scripture

We have commented on DML-J's use of illustration, but we recall that he would regularly interpret and illustrate Scripture by Scripture. In this, he seemed to be in his element. It is a consistent feature in his preaching. In doing so, he was being true to his own convictions about the nature of Scripture. This was the practice of Jonathan Edwards. Any random reading of DML-J's sermons throughout his preaching career will give ample evidence of the practice.

In his exposition on Romans, he preached seven sermons from Romans 8:16 (AV), 'The Spirit itself beareth witness with our spirit, that we are the children of God'. He reckoned that this is 'one of the most glorious statements concerning Christian experience found anywhere in the Bible from the beginning to the end.'[49] He continued to expound it in his second sermon on this 'series within a series' by remarking: 'We must follow a rule that should always be observed in interpreting Scripture, namely that we should interpret Scripture by Scripture. We should always look for parallel statements.'[50]

He then proceeded to line up several such Scriptures which he felt threw light on this great statement.

In Lloyd-Jones's style, anecdotes are relatively few, and contemporary illustration is moderate, but he habitually used Scriptural illustrations as a safeguard to ensure the correct interpretation of a passage. It also helps to demonstrate to the congregation what may be called the liveliness of the Scriptures and the way in which the Old and New Testaments are complementary. An excellent example is found when he deals with the Christian soldier and the devil's attacks. He illustrated his point from the account of David and Goliath and comments that these

Old Testament incidents, in addition to being history, are at the same time perfect parables of the great Scriptural truth taught in Ephesians 6, 'it is all there in that picture of David and Goliath'.[51]

A further acknowledgment of this hermeneutical principle is also found in his Ephesian studies. He was dealing with Paul's teaching on marriage. DML-J carefully examined his text and extracted several broad principles. Then he commented on the way in which he had wrestled with his subject.

> When I am confronted by a particular question I must not immediately apply my mind to it. I must first ask the questions, is there any principle, is there any doctrine in the Scripture that governs this kind of problem?[52]

Difficult passages should be placed alongside those that are more clear[53]

He advocated what in reformed theology is sometimes called the 'regulative principle'. This asserts that Scripture must be allowed to comment on Scripture. More specifically, passages which are clear should be placed alongside those that are difficult in order to grasp the true meaning. DML-J approvingly quoted the maxim of Lord Bacon which says that if we are wise, we will never let what we are uncertain about rob us of our certainties.

In the Sermon on the Mount, our Lord lays down teaching which is not always easy to grasp on first reading. It concerns Christian conduct. Care must be taken to bring other Scriptures to bear in order to ascertain what principles are to control Christian behaviour in certain circumstances.

For example, the Lord used his dominical authority and restated the Mosaic principle of an eye for an eye from a completely different perspective (Matt. 5:38, 39). A member of his Kingdom is not to resist an evil person but rather to turn the other cheek when struck. How does this align with instructions given later about Church discipline and the procedure of dealing with disputes if rights can never be asserted (Matt: 18:15-17)? What about our Lord's protest when he was struck by an officer in the presence of the High Priest (John 18:22-3)? Does this not contradict the instruction given in the Sermon on the Mount? Again, what do we make of Paul and Silas when they appealed on the grounds that they were Roman citizens and that the treatment doled out to them was illegal (Acts 16:37)?

A further example follows in sequence from the Sermon on the

Mount. We refer to the Lord's assertion that if a man has two cloaks he should give to the one who has none (Matt. 5:40-2).[54] At first reading, it seems somewhat unrealistic. One would be at the mercy of any professional beggar or drunkard. The principle behind the illustration must be secured in order to grasp what is expected of the Christian in this type of situation.

DML-J's hermeneutic suggests that our immediate understanding may indeed be correct, but if the literal interpretation contradicts what is stated elsewhere, it must be wrong. Scriptures balance each another. They do not cancel out. When Scripture is placed alongside Scripture, then we can expect the meaning to come into focus.

In dealing with apparent anomalies and contradictions in the Sermon on the Mount, he both warns and advises: 'Here we see most clearly the importance of taking Scripture with Scripture and never interpreting it at one point in such a way that it contradicts the teaching at another point.'[55]

He reminds us of certain things which are basic to the Sermon as our Lord taught it. There is an underlying principle that a Christian is to live differently when compared with a non-Christian. That is not because he is forcefully governed by a codified system of do's and don'ts. Rather, he has gone through a spiritual renewal which has so transformed him that he lives a life reflecting the character of his heavenly Father. As such, in the matter of personal rights, he will not assert his own. He is living at a completely different level and harbours a different outlook to that of the unbeliever. But, he is still a citizen in this world. He will be a member of a local community of Christians. He appreciates that in the world there is a civil law which, in many countries, controls relationships and patterns of acceptable behaviour, calling for punishment when such is breached.

Without such laws, there would be anarchy. When they are breached, they are to be challenged in the interests of society as a whole. Lloyd-Jones aimed to get his congregation to realise the two issues at stake: the maintenance of law, and the receiving of personal insults. A Christian has a duty to uphold the former and to challenge any breach of it. But he is not to be concerned about the latter. This also goes for church discipline. For the believer, this should be a reckoning force not for personal gratification but in the interests of the Kingdom.

As for the 'cloak', it serves to illustrate the materialistic spirit from which the believer has cut loose. Such had no hold on the Lord. No Christian should be so self-centred that he will not offer help to others and refuse to part with his possessions. Neither will he be so gullible and naive that he is at the mercy of the trickster or professional beggar.

Lloyd-Jones, in elucidating the teaching, takes us to John's assertion that any man who is genuinely in need should be helped by the believer. Refusal to do so negates his claim to be a Christian! (1 John 3:17, 18). But, to ward off gullibility and avoid giving to a man who might take what is offered and use it for alcohol, or who is just plain lazy, Lloyd-Jones makes us consider Paul's statement, 'if any would not work, neither should he eat'. Thus, we have a perfect example of DML-J's hermeneutic!

A preacher who wishes to be a true expositor should commit himself to all the above maxims which are demonstrably present in the sermons preached by Dr. Lloyd-Jones. These checks cannot be ignored, but just having them all in place does not necessarily guarantee accuracy or relevancy in the subsequent preaching. The Bible is not an ordinary book. It was born in the minds of men over many centuries. The author was the Holy Spirit and his role is not concluded. So let us consider another important aspect of Dr. Lloyd-Jones's checking procedure.

THE SPIRITUAL INTERPRETATION OF THE SCRIPTURES

As we have seen, Dr. Lloyd-Jones's pneumatology is the key to the understanding of his philosophy of preaching. One would therefore expect a strong link between the two in his convictions about preparing for preaching. We have noted elsewhere that he believed that there is generally an inseparable link between the Word and the Spirit. Applying this principle to preaching, he taught that the preacher needs the illumination of the Holy Spirit in order to interpret the Word accurately.

DML-J argues for this strongly, though he would have distanced himself from schools which allegorise the Scriptures or interpret them in a mystical fashion. His position rests not only on the claims of the Bible itself but the application of logic. If the Holy Spirit inspired the Scriptures, it is reasonable to assume that his help will be required in growing into an understanding of them and in applying them to the immediate, contemporary situation. Remember Lloyd-Jones's usual introduction to his sermons—'the words to which I want to draw your attention . . . '—DML-J was referring to words inspired by the Spirit. Properly expounded and applied, they are, indeed, the words from the Lord for a preacher's congregation. This reflects the Puritan maxim concerning preaching[56] that preaching the word of God is the word of God. This, Lloyd-Jones believed. Certain conclusions can be drawn from this conviction.

The Holy Spirit alone is the interpreter of Scripture.

Our Lord promised that when the Holy Spirit came, he would lead the disciples into all truth (John 16:13). We have already examined in some detail DML-J's understanding of the anointing mentioned in John's epistle. This anointing is necessary in order to expound Scripture. Sheer intellectual gifting in itself is insufficient. Lloyd-Jones claimed that every bit of intelligence we possess is needed in order to read the Scriptures. But, even though 'all our faculties and propensities must be employed', more is required. 'Even that is not enough. We must pray for the illumination and inspiration of the Holy Spirit.'[57]

Spiritual truth must be spiritually discerned. Without the Spirit's tuition the preacher and the hearer are at a loss. DML-J expressed this conviction in the strongest terms possible, arguing that the Bible is only for the children of God. The unbeliever cannot understand it.

In a message in which he referred to the Sermon on the Mount, he applied the Saviour's words about casting pearls before swine and warned about the indiscriminate placarding of Scripture before people.[58] Unless the Bible is read 'in the Spirit' the total impact registered may well be just poetic and aesthetic.

George Thomas, who was elevated to the House of Lords and is now known as Viscount Tonypandy, is a fellow countryman of Lloyd-Jones. He was the Speaker of the British House of Commons for many years. He unwittingly furnished evidence of Scripture having an impact for the wrong reason. He was honoured to be asked to read an appropriate passage from the Bible for the wedding of Prince Charles and Lady Diana Spencer. He selected 1 Corinthians 13. He mentioned on a BBC interview about his life some years after the marriage how, as a result of the reading, he received a sheaf of mail. People were impressed by it. Where was it to be found? The sad thing was that the interest aroused had to do with the beauty of the language enhanced by the musical intonation of the Welsh accent. The Scriptures had not been heard in the Spirit.[59] They were appreciated for the wrong reason. The illustration helps us to sharpen in our minds what were Lloyd-Jones's convictions about the spiritual understanding of Scripture. We emphasise that it has nothing to do with mysticism, it has everything to do with truth. The point is singular and of great significance.

In his series from the Ephesian Epistle, DML-J had, in the systematic fashion in which he went through the verses, to cover the expression where Paul prays for his readers that 'the eyes of their understanding might be enlightened'. This he perceives to be the work of the Spirit. If the Spirit does not open eyes, then preaching 'would be quite useless and void'.[60]

Spiritual illumination and mental exertion are compatible

Though Lloyd-Jones believed in the inspirational element in preaching, he would not condone the abuse of the text that if we open our mouth the Lord will fill it (Ps. 81:10). He said that 'people have held some very strange, odd views with regard to preaching' from mishandling this verse and a similar one in the Gospels which affirms, 'take no thought how or what ye shall speak; for it shall be given you in that same hour what ye shall speak' (Matt. 10:19 *AV*).[61] Though insights and flashes of knowledge may be granted in the course of preaching as a man is in the pulpit, the preacher must not skimp on his preparation. We have noted his stressing the need for hard work; it is a recurrent theme in Lloyd-Jones's convictions. He parallels the need with Oliver Cromwell's dictum, 'Trust in God but keep your powder dry': believe God for blessing but study as hard as you can and show that you deserve it.

The final appeal for the true meaning of the text, however, is not to scholarship. There are scholars who, with all their academic prowess, still differ in their interpretations of a text. 'He may be a genius or a great scholar but it will not help him here. Truth is spiritually discerned. And nothing and no-one can enable us to do that apart from the Spirit of God Himself.'[62]

In one of his earliest sermons preached at Westminster Chapel, he tackled the question of why Bible study is dull for some people. In answering it, he made an interesting observation which ties in with what we have found him claiming in an earlier chapter. The reason why Bible study may be uninteresting for some is that they have accustomed their minds to unwholesome literature. The solution is within the sovereignty of the Spirit. He tells us:

Here, then, comes the gracious promise and comfort of the Holy Spirit, 'Ye have an unction from the Holy One,' says John, 'and ye know all things.' By the illumination of the Holy Spirit I am enabled to see and appropriate and to comprehend something of this precious truth.[63]

Thus, the Spirit's role is to enlighten the speaker as he studies the Word of God, wanting to enter into its truths. DML-J takes this up when dealing with the 'great mystery' of the relationship of the Lord to the Church. He reasoned that 'apart from the anointing and unction which the Holy Spirit alone can give, we shall not be able to understand it at all'. Of course, the unbeliever cannot grasp the truth of what the believer finds difficult to comprehend. But a 'mystery' in the New Testament, though inaccessible to the unaided human mind, can still be understood with the Spirit's aid. Lloyd-Jones becomes very pointed. He argues that the greatest brain in the world is but a tyro, less than a babe when it comes to these things. He is spiritually dead and has no understanding whatsoever. Of the union of Christ with the Church the fact is, 'This is spiritual truth and it is to be understood in a spiritual manner.'[64]

The Holy Spirit wishes to aid us in coming to an understanding of the truth of his word

Jung has a most useful expression to convey the thinking of Lloyd-Jones in this area. He speaks of the 'congeniality of the Spirit'. By this, he is referring to the willingness of the Spirit to help the sincere student of Scripture.[65] Dr. Lloyd-Jones preached sermons in which he warned against grieving the Spirit.[66] His positive corrective is that we should live in a manner which pleases the Holy Spirit. The Holy Spirit is a person. Therefore, he registers embarrassment. As a consequence, he can withdraw his presence. His inspiration can be quenched and his flame can be extinguished. On the other hand, such is the congeniality of the Spirit that he wants to draw alongside the believer. Of all people, preachers should determine to keep in step with the Spirit. By so doing, they will be well positioned to benefit from the Spirit's promptings and enablings. Jung puts the point over well as he speaks of the indwelling Spirit and the Bible: 'As the still surface of the water can beautifully reflect the heaven above, so a hearing heart, given by the Holy Spirit, can correctly grasp the mind of God who wrote it.'[67]

Cultivation of spiritual disciplines brings the preacher into a mind set in which he can mirror in his preaching what he has seen of the Lord, his truth, and his purposes. Such a conviction as this provides a needed corrective to the bias in many modern books on homiletics which overlook the pneumatic in favour of the pedestrian. The marrow of New Testament preaching must not be exchanged for the mechanics of homiletic theorising. Such transactions vie with the folly of Esau when he surrendered his birthright for a bowl of soup! A scholastic attitude needs to be wedded to a spiritual aptitude.

This congeniality of the Spirit affects the preacher at the point of proclamation and the hearer at the point of reception.[68] It is not argument, nor logic, nor eloquence that eventually wins the day. It is the work of the Spirit within the heart of the man who hears the Word. No man truly believes and submits to the authority of Scripture without the inner witness. The Spirit confirms within the man the authority of what he hears. Lloyd-Jones appeals to Paul's argument, 'the natural man receiveth not the things of the Spirit of God: for they are foolishness unto him: neither can he know them, because they are spiritually discerned' (1 Cor. 2:14 *AV*).

Scripture contains what Lloyd-Jones calls the family secret. 'It is a secret that is only enjoyed by the Lord's people.'[69] He takes us to the Book of Revelation and to the reference concerning 'the hidden manna' and 'the new name' which 'no man knoweth saving he that receiveth it' (2:17 *AV*). Lloyd-Jones exclaims, 'the "hidden manna"! The white stone with a name written on it which nobody can understand save the recipient'. He explains that this is a secret love between two persons which they have kept between themselves. This is the love of which the Apostles are speaking. The world knows nothing of it. This is shared only by those who are part of the Redeemed Community. Bernard of Clairvaux makes the point clear when referring to the quality of Christ's affection for his own and encourages us to sing:

> The love of Jesus what it is
> None but his loved ones know.

To interpret the Scriptures the expositor must have a right heart and a disciplined mind. He will use all his academic skills to plumb its depths and make its teaching clear and relevant. Thus DML-J advises:

> Above all we must apply the Scriptures. We have the Spirit in us, our mind is enlightened . . . We must put these things together. Nothing is more dangerous than to put a wedge between the Word and the Spirit, to emphasise one over against the other. It is the Spirit and the Word, the Spirit upon the Word and the Spirit in us as we read the Word.[70]

He has secured his point; the Spirit's help is necessary for the preacher's success.

We bring our chapter to a conclusion. It is vitally important for preachers to have safeguards in their ministries. Dr. Lloyd-Jones fully appreciated this himself. When a preacher is committed to the full authority of the Word of God, he wants to proclaim it accurately. No mortal man alone can expound what Thomas Carlyle, in a favourite quotation of DML-J's, called 'the immensities and infinities' of the Bible.[71]

Every available help is needed. There are more which we will introduce in our next chapter.

11

Balances

My main advice here is to read your Bible systematically. The danger is to read at random, and that means that one tends to be reading only one's favourite passages. In other words one fails to read the whole Bible. One of the most fatal habits a preacher can ever fall into is to read his Bible simply in order to find texts for sermons. This is a real danger; it must be recognised and fought and resisted with all your might.[1]

Martyn Lloyd-Jones

His preaching was the expression of his singularly well endowed personality, the fusing together of all the aptitudes, opportunities, discipline, experience and learning that God had given him. Add to these his exemplary diligence in direct pulpit preparation—especially his painstaking attention to exegesis and to orderly arrangement—and we see something of the secret of the extraordinary quality of his preaching . . .[2]

Donald Macleod

Alongside what we might call the 'internal checks' of Scripture—an attempt to keep tryst with the Bible's own claims—there are others which Lloyd-Jones recognised. Obviously, the Scriptures' own claims took priority for him and must do for us. But there are other safeguards which are worthy of consideration. Speaking generally, they can be conceived as external disciplines to be applied in the whole process of preaching and preparation. If what occupied us in the previous chapter are 'the Checks' here are 'the Balances'.

The preacher is called to proclaim the whole counsel of God. To major on one theme alone is to risk distortion. DML-J could be very critical of organisations which existed for the promotion of one truth[3] be they holiness or second-coming movements. Scripture in its entirety is to be studied and preached. We consider, therefore, four other controls which the expositor might embrace and work at in order to ensure he presents a balanced proclamation of the Word of God in a comprehensive and accurate fashion; two have to do with theology—as a system and in its historical context. Another deals with biblical language and what facility a preacher should develop in this area. The last concerns the types of sermon which a full-orbed ministry should seek to present to congregations.

SYSTEMATIC THEOLOGY

The Bible is a body of divinity within which are many strands. These inter-relate and interweave so that one links into another. One strand is dependent on the other. They merge to form one tapestry. Expressed another way, it can be argued that, although the various books were given over a period of centuries and through many people, the result was a complete Bible. This is the Holy Spirit's gift to the Church. He is the author. In the Bible, there is an underlying unity of exposition without a rigid uniformity of expression.

The interlocking teachings form a corpus. This is what Puritans like Thomas Watson called 'A Body of Divinity'. Shifting the metaphor a little, it is as the shell or the infrastructure of the building. Systematic theology is an attempt to lift this out and use it as a basis for study and exposition. The possession and comprehension of such is a boon to those who are called to expound and explain Scripture to others. DML-J recognised the value of this.

The advantages are obvious and they become apparent as his sermons are carefully studied. His argument can be expressed thus:

A systematic theology provides a safeguard for interpretation

The Bible lecturer may be able to proceed without a doctrinal infrastructure. But this is not the case with the expositor. He needs reference points to which he can go as he endeavours to focus his grasp on what the Scriptures say. Lloyd-Jones emphasises the need,

To me, there is nothing more important in a preacher than that he should have a systematic theology, that he should know it and be well grounded in it. This systematic theology, this body of truth which is derived from the Scripture, should always be present as a background and as *a controlling influence in his preaching.*[4]

A systematic theology helps the preacher to see one truth in the light of another. Thus, it assists him in understanding the particular passage or text on which he is going to preach. It helps him to develop a tidy mind and thought pattern. As the truths within the passage become clear to him, he can hold them in tension with other biblical doctrines.

DML-J held such a procedure to be in line with the phrase 'comparing Scripture with Scripture'. Truth is not fragmented, it is part of a whole.

An example of this being practised in the ministry of DML-J is his millennialism. Though he believed in the restoration of Israel, he was committed to the A-millennial scheme. In other words, he saw no future one-thousand-year reign on earth by the Lord Jesus when he returns in power and glory. The Second Advent will usher in the Eternal Age.[5]

He claimed that the Lord reigns now in his Church. Lloyd-Jones was consistent in his eschatology throughout his ministry. He presents a powerful defence of the A-millennial position.[6] Nonetheless, he warned against slavish adherence to systems.

Systematic theologies have their dangers![7]

Theopneustos is the Greek term which, in the Authorised Version, is translated 'inspired'. The reference is to the manner in which the Scriptures were given. They are God-breathed. The claim hardly applies to systematic theologies! Helpful though they are, they have their weaknesses. The preacher is not to be enslaved to such. They are grids. They are reference points. They are not infallible guides:

> . . . is it not a terrible danger that some of us, sometimes, tend to read the Scriptures, not so much to be enlightened and to be taught, as to confirm our own theologies, our own ideas, and our own prejudices? We are all guilty of it. For instance, it is the danger of the Calvinist, who looks for one thing only and ignores difficulties. It is equally the danger of the Arminian . . . In the name of God, I say, let us be careful that we do not go to the Scripture with such a prejudice that we pick out only what agrees with our theory and ignore and forget the rest![8]

Some have pointed out inconsistency in the way in which Lloyd-Jones handled Scripture and the charge is levelled that he was not always a precise theologian. However, Professor I.H. Marshall favourably comments, 'To be sure, there are places where he admits that we cannot entirely understand the ways of God as presented by Paul, but such humility is needed in a theologian.'[9] Certain aspects of the biblical revelation are beyond human ability to grasp fully. Therefore, we cannot expect all of Scripture to slot into our little systems. The human mind will never totally comprehend or systematise the revelation of God. The preacher will be unable to regulate all details of exposition and place them into what DML-J calls 'some intellectual order'.

Any attempts to expound the mind of God are going to be fraught with difficulty. Part of the task of the expositor is to wrestle with such issues and to recognise his limitations and the shortcoming of all theologies. Thus, the warning of Dr. Lloyd-Jones , as he brought his hearers to a difficult point of exposition:

> But my dear friends, we are talking about God and we are but human beings! We are looking into the Eternal, the character of God, and our business is to accept our Scripture not to try to evade a problem . . .[10]

LANGUAGES AND SYNTAX

Undue time should not be spent on mastering the biblical languages. A danger facing theological colleges and seminaries is the tendency to put so much emphasis on academics—including a disproportionate time for grasping the Hebrew and Greek languages—that they miss the most essential element, the spiritual development of the students helping them to develop their preaching gift. Lloyd-Jones felt it was significant that two of the greatest English preachers at the end of the last century, Joseph Parker and C.H. Spurgeon, did not have a formal, academic education.

The preacher is not called to gain the competency which befits a Greek or Hebrew specialist. Skills at that level are really not required. This does not mean that DML-J was against the study of languages in themselves. A man should learn enough to be able to handle the commentaries, thereby having the best scholarship available for reference. Few preachers have the linguistic abilities of scholars who have given their lives in the pursuit of these disciplines. But the dedicated preacher, in his preparation, will ensure that he has consulted the authorities and is clear about the textual nature of the passage he is expounding. The rudiments of the language are all that need to be mastered. DML-J gave a clear presentation of his views in the inaugural address of the London Theological Seminary.[11]

The ability which the preacher has had to track down the root meaning of the Scriptures should be carefully and cautiously used in the course of exposition

On numerous occasions, Lloyd-Jones shared the fruit of his research in this area. He did this especially when dealing with a difficult passage which may have baffled his congregation and where expositors have differed in their interpretations.

In his sermons on Romans, at times he seemed to lift out a word from the text for concentration. Then he quoted the dictionaries so that, together with his audience, he could determine the meaning of the word in the context of the verse. Thus his treatment of part of Romans 1:28, 'And even as they did not like to retain God in their knowledge' (*AV*). The quotation refers to the fashion in which Gentiles rejected the revelation of God. DML-J was not too happy with the rendering of the King James Version. He thought the Revised Standard Version 'is much too weak'. He gave his preference, 'they did not approve of God' and then supplied his reasoning. Paul, he argued, used a term generally associated with testing and especially the testing of metals. Gold is a good example: an expert can detect whether a particular metal is gold or not by applying certain tests. As a result, he may keep or throw away the sample. Incredibly, mankind has largely adopted such an approach to the person of God! 'Having "tested" Him [they] decided to reject Him!'[12] The excursion into the root meaning of the word in the original language enabled DML-J forcefully to bring out man's culpability.

Note that this was not just the use of scholarly ability. Such a practice is only to be shunned by the preacher if he is employing it to impress his hearers. Lloyd-Jones's aim was to give his congregation 'eyes' to see the enormity of man's folly. He taught that scholarship should never be sacrificed in the pulpit, nor should it be paraded in a proud way which serves to enhance the reputation of the speaker. 'Refer to Greek and Hebrew dictionaries, quote the languages if they are essential to a clear presentation of the text,' seemed to be Dr. Lloyd-Jones's maxim.

Tracking down the root meaning of a word and providing a congregation with a simple explanation is a time-honoured method of exegesis. DML-J sometimes laboured it to the extent that one critic reckoned his sermons were of the stock of which lectures are made! Our conclusion is more sympathetic and, possibly, more accurate. He

did this when the text was particularly difficult or powerful.
Furthermore, he went to such lengths because it was his conviction
that each word of Scripture is of great importance. 'Lay hold on every
word here; do not yield anything, not a single letter of any word'.[13] It
is worth slowing the pace of exposition in order to treat the text accurately and to be clear in the presentation of truth. He knew that he
might be trying the patience of his hearers. He admitted as much when
dealing with the person of Christ in a further sermon in the Roman
series. 'Is anyone still disappointed because I am going so slowly?
Would you have preferred me to have rushed over these verses in order
that I could take you to chapters six, seven, and eight? If so I despair
of you.'[14]

The measure of the despair would have been the failure of the congregation to have grasped the importance of what was being attempted.
They, too, must be taught to appreciate that the ground on which they
are standing is holy; one does not rush toward the 'Bush' that speaks,
but should approach it cautiously, humbly, and thoughtfully.

In an astonishingly powerful address on Psalm 1, in which he
experienced great unction, the clock had obviously gone round more
quickly than Dr. Lloyd-Jones had realised! In view of this, and for the
convenience of the congregation, he decided to shorten the remaining
part of the sermon. He opted simply to list his headings. Suddenly and
dramatically, or so it must have seemed to his hearers, he paused. Then
he publicly sought the forgiveness of God. It was an incredible
moment. He pleaded with the Lord to absolve him from what he
believed to be the sin of speeding up and shortening a message simply
because of the time factor. What did time matter when he was dis-
closing God's word to the congregation?. He was addressing them on
the most important thing in the world: the way of salvation and
renewal; how a man is blessed by 'being planted by the rivers of
water'. He then went on slowly in his exposition, but with a remarkable passion as he pleaded with men and women to ensure they were
in a right relationship with God.[15]

As for caution, DML-J was concerned that the practice could cause
the preacher to take leave of the immediate context. He speaks about a
snare in Bible study, 'You just become a student of words, and you turn
up your lexicon, and that is valuable because it is essential to know the
meaning of a word. But you must pay attention to the context also. Let
the context speak to you as well as the particular meaning, otherwise
you can be easily side-tracked and you can become a heretic without
realising it'.[16]

Enquiry into the grammar and the etymology of words can be of great value to the preacher and the congregation in the exposition of the Scriptures

Lloyd-Jones took pains to discover the specific and related uses of a word in order to bring out its true meaning. In his sermon on 'The Stimulus of the Spirit'[17] in Ephesians 5:18, he led an investigation into the nuances of the word 'excess'. The context is Paul's contrast between a group of inebriated people and another group filled with the Holy Spirit.

The lexicon reveals that the term 'excess' is found earlier in the New Testament. It describes the profligacy of the Prodigal Son when, in the far country, he squandered his father's resources. DML-J noted the Authorised Version's description. The lad 'wasted his substance in riotous living' (Luke 15:13). 'Riotous' translates the same word as 'excess' in Ephesians. Lloyd-Jones proceeded to illustrate the meaning further and spent a lengthy paragraph in so doing. The result was that, in a gripping fashion, he clearly communicated the depths of meaning within the term. It enabled him to conclude that the parable is the best exposition of the word 'excess'—'the most perfect commentary on the verse'! In answer to the question 'What is a Christian?' he responded 'I cannot think of a better way of describing him than this: he is the exact opposite of the Prodigal Son.'

Later, in the same series he strove to find the significance of the word 'therefore' within the context of Paul's teaching on marriage (Eph. 5:23). He felt troubled because he had occasion to disagree with Charles Hodge. The issue was why Paul referred to the Lord as 'The Saviour of the Body' just after acknowledging him as the Head of the Church and then followed on with the conjunction 'therefore'. Hodge felt Paul's reference to the Lord as Saviour had little to do with the immediate argument; rather, it should be viewed as an expression of praise, an ejaculation that Paul could not help.

With customary diligence, Lloyd-Jones sifted the context and then shared the fruit of his consultations with a couple of lexicons.

> But what of the word which is translated 'Therefore' at the beginning of verse 24? Now, this is really interesting. I have gone to the trouble of consulting some of the best Lexicons on the point. It is a Greek word, *Alla*, and I find that it need not be translated always as a kind of antithesis to something which is an opposite and a contrast. Take, for instance, the *Greek/English Lexicon of the New Testament* [edn 1952, by W. F. Arndt and F. W. Gingrich [CUP, 1957], one of the best

and most authoritative. 'They actually say this: that what it really means is 'Now' or 'Then'. I quote them, they say, 'It is used to strengthen the command', not to imply a contrast or a difference . . . And they actually pick out Ephesians 5:24 as an illustration.[18]

Dr. Lloyd-Jones proceeded to show how the word 'Saviour' does not always refer to the way in which the Lord gave his life and shed his blood for the Church—though that is 'the common meaning'. It can also mean preserver. He directed his hearers to 1 Timothy 4:10 where our Lord is called 'the Saviour of all men'. He preserves all men, causing his sun to rise on the just and the unjust and giving food to all. So the husband is called to be the preserver of his wife. DML-J has come full circle! He has demonstrated by the use of the historico-grammatical process not only the reason why Paul described the Lord as the Saviour of the body at that point in his argument, but also why he proceeded with a 'therefore'. Far from the former being merely an ascription of praise, it is, as the conjunction implies, part of the Apostle's sustained argument.

A further example of this, showing how the act of preaching can be improved by recourse to the historico-grammatical checking procedure of a passage or word, is found in an address from the Romans' series. Lloyd-Jones is pursuing the meaning of 'Abba' and 'Cry' in the text we 'have received the Spirit of adoption whereby we cry, Abba, Father' (Rom. 8:15). Abba is an intimate term. DML-J said it might be translated as 'Dad' or 'Papa'. 'Cry' is a strong word. 'Some of the authorities tell us that it originates in the screeching of a certain kind of bird and that it is a "cry of vociferation".'[19]

By the time he is finished with his analysis, he has implanted a very powerful word picture indeed into the minds of his congregation. The power and liveliness of the text has been made grippingly clear. All this has been achieved in the interests of accurate and full exposition. The method is highly commendable.

HISTORICAL THEOLOGY

History was an important discipline for Dr. Lloyd-Jones. We have, in our earlier studies, seen how he divides it into two sections—the history which God promotes and that which God permits. As far as he was concerned, there are only two philosophies of history worth considering—that of Hegel and that within the Bible and, especially, as refined in the New Testament.[20] There is an unseen history at the back of history; it is a spiritual history which underlies the secular and in the light of which the latter becomes unimportant.[21]

The preacher must be literate historically. It is from this perspective that he will be able to trace the hand of God and thus have greater competence in interpreting the Scripture in its contemporary setting. In this respect, the uninformed preacher handicaps his own ministry.

> I would like to lay it down as a principle that there is great value in the reading of Church history and a study of the past, and nothing surely is more important for us at this present time than to read the history of the past and to discover its message . . . It is very foolish to ignore the past. The man who does ignore it and assumes that our problems are quite new, and that therefore the past has nothing at all to teach us, is a man who is not only grossly ignorant of the Scriptures, he is equally ignorant of some of the greatest lessons even in secular history.[22]

Familiarity with the history of the Church and the writings of great preachers of the past will help in the development and maintenance of one's own ministry. Dr. Lloyd-Jones's scattered references to this warrant the conclusion:

There is personal value in reading historical theology

DML-J had a very high view of the sovereignty of God. Even a cursory study of his sermons reveals that he immersed himself in Puritan theology. This had not always been the case in his life. His interest in the eighteenth century was heightened when he 'discovered' Jonathan Edwards as a result of conversing with one of his contemporaries who was studying divinity at Oxford. A book he subsequently obtained from the list of his friend's recommendations had a chapter on Edwards. He wanted further information but was unable to procure such. Two years elapsed and he found a couple of volumes of the preaching of Jonathan Edwards in a second-hand bookshop. He bought them for five shillings. He tells us 'I was like the man in our Lord's parable who found the pearl of great price. Their influence upon me I cannot put into words'.[23]

Edwards was not the only man from whom Lloyd-Jones found help, but no one made a greater impact on him. Listen to him contrasting Edwards with other worthies:

> I am afraid, and I say it with much regret, that I have to put him ahead even of Daniel Rowland and George Whitefield. Indeed I am tempted,

perhaps foolishly, to compare the Puritans to the Alps, Luther and
Calvin to the Himalayas, and Jonathan Edwards to Mount Everest!
He has always seemed to me to be the man most like the Apostle
Paul.[24]

He was also indebted to Thomas Goodwin, especially, as we have seen,
his doctrine of the Holy Spirit. Richard Sibbes, too, was an inspiration,
never failing to do him good when he felt a bit depressed. He was at
home with John Owen and Charles Hodge. He commended younger
men to develop his habit.[25]

A knowledge of the works of these outstanding men has the effect
of 'a cordial to the soul' to use a phrase from the *Homilies* of the
Church of England. It helps a man to develop his spirituality and
coaxes him into attempting to aim higher in his own ministry.
Remember Lloyd-Jones's remark that if a man felt he had done particularly well in preaching one Sunday, he should take from his library a
copy of Whitefield's sermons, read some, and then realise how far short
he had fallen and how much more territory he had to cross before he
had really arrived as a preacher! But there are other benefits besides
personal ones in having an ever deepening knowledge of the preaching
and theologies of earlier men.

A knowledge of historical theology acts as a stimulus and a
checking point, helping a preacher to safeguard the accuracy of
his own exposition

Certainly this was the position Dr. Lloyd-Jones adopted. He was interested to read what recognised expositors had to say and would examine how they handled a difficult passage of Scripture. He would be
particularly concerned to test himself as to how Jonathan Edwards
might have handled the passage on which he had to preach.

It is legitimate for a preacher in his preparation to ask how Calvin
or Whitefield might approach a text. Undiscriminating people may dismiss the theologians and great preachers of Church history as yesterday's men, but such a cavalier approach serves only to underline the
critic's immaturity. To fail to learn from the pulpit of the past is to
impoverish that of the present. Incredibly, as we have noted, some have
reckoned that these giants of yesteryear had no experience of the Holy
Spirit's power. They are conceived to have been dry academics. Nothing
is further from the truth. Some, in the full sense of the term, were
divines. Their ministries and their lives seemed impregnated with the
power of God. To read their works, far from raking over the bones of

the dead, is more akin to touching the grave of Elisha. Our perusal should be accompanied by a sincere prayer that the power which touched their ministries might impregnate our own!

As one might expect, judging from this trait in Lloyd-Jones's preaching, it was not only the theologies of the men which influenced and inspired him. The point is secured in our next deduction:

A knowledge of historical theology and the experiences of previous generations of preachers helps the expositor to avoid interpreting some passages merely from the ethos of his own day

Dr. Lloyd-Jones makes the point succinctly in one of his sermons. He was preaching on the verse 'The Spirit . . . beareth witness with our spirit that we are the children of God' (Rom. 8:16 AV.)

> If we bring all Scripture down to the level of our own experience and understanding today we shall often rob it of some of its greatest glories. But if we look at the long history of the Christian Church, and pay attention to certain things that are to be seen in individuals and in groups of Churches and perhaps in a whole country, at times, we shall be given an insight into what we have in this verse . . . read the lives of the saints, read the story of certain unusual people who have adorned the Church of God, and listen to what they have to say.[26]

For DML-J, a crime occurs when a preacher succumbs to the temptation to water down the promises of Scripture simply because he and his generation have not entered into the full blessings of which they speak. Against such treatment, he raises a strong protest. To be a careful expositor demands that the preacher should be familiar with happenings in past generations when God granted revival. This will help him to realise the potential for the present day. He will be inspired to preach with knowledge and passion. Encouraged by the certainty of what God has done in the past and is able to do in the present, he will encourage his congregation to seek the good Lord for similar blessing. This is the reason why Dr. Lloyd-Jones preached his revival sermons on the centenary of the revival in America, Ireland, Wales, and parts of England.

Not every generation has experienced this phenomenon. But the Church in every generation has a right to know what God has done and what he can still do. To interpret Scripture in the light of contemporary Christian experience may not do it justice and could lead to dilution or, worse, distortion of its message.

*A knowledge of historical theology, however, still requires the
preacher to bring his tentative conclusions to the bar of
Scripture*

As with systematic theologies, so with the study of historical theology,
there are definite limitations. No systematic theology is perfect, neither
is any one preacher even if he did live in the sixteenth or eighteenth century! The wise student of historical theology will learn from others, but
he will consider none as infallible.

Sometimes Lloyd-Jones showed his disagreement with John Calvin,
though generally he referred to the reformer as 'the great' or 'the
mighty' when he did so![27] DML-J did not slavishly follow Benjamin
Warfield.[28] He would respectfully question Hodge and Haldane. When
he considered them to be wrong, he would say so. But he would not do
this without considerable thought. Listen to him as he took issue with
the former. He studies, inspects, and questions Hodge's handling of a
verse in Romans. But he warned: 'No one should do that lightly. But we
are reminded that no man is infallible: we do not believe in popes. We
are entitled to examine the exposition of any man, however great and
learned he may have been?'[29]

Almost in the same breath, he felt compelled to take Robert
Haldane to task. He ventured a humorous aside, quoting King David in
a completely different context, 'Let me be yet more vile!' And then he
added that it is no small thing to disagree with two giants at the same
time!

The study of historical theology and the works of the preachers and
preaching methods of the past is invaluable. However, Scripture alone
prevails as the ultimate authority. Lloyd-Jones gives wise advice about
the value of research and reading, but warns that 'the function of reading is to stimulate us in general, to stimulate us to think, to think for
ourselves'. He urged the preacher to 'take all you read and masticate it
thoroughly. Do not just repeat it as you have received it; deliver it in your
own way, let it emerge as a part of yourself with your stamp upon it'.[30]

The preacher is to be a craftsman. He needs to be constantly working at his task. He is called to make the Word of God clear to those who
come within the hearing of his ministry.

CATEGORIES OF SERMON

There remains another area for us to investigate. It can be legitimately
placed in this chapter on Balances because it deals with types of sermon.

We refer to classes of message which the preacher is to deliver. Sometimes these will be influenced by the needs of the congregation.

DML-J has fixed and interesting views about congregations. Good preaching and good listening are as cause and effect.[31] Preachers derive something from the congregation.[32] On the other hand, a preacher who is dependent on a congregation is not fit to enter the pulpit.[33] He was dogmatic that the congregation should not control the basic ministry. The pulpit and not the pew exerts authority.[34] None of this means the preacher is to be insensitive to the particular requirements of his charge. He should endeavour to assess the condition of people who gather to hear him 'and to bear that in mind in the preparation and delivery of his message'.

As might be expected, Lloyd-Jones appealed to Paul for justification. Consider how the Apostle tailored his teaching material and style to the needs of immature Christians: 'I gave you milk, not solid food, for you were not ready for it. Indeed you are still not ready (1 Cor. 3:2).

The Corinthians were not dictating to Paul, but his assessment of them influenced the fare that he placed before them.

Our Lord, when addressing individuals, did not handle any two people in exactly the same way. DML-J cites the instances of his conversation with Nicodemus and Nathanael and the Woman of Samaria. He thinks that one of the best examples of this is the manner in which Jesus handled the cross-questioning by Pilate and Herod. To the former he made a response, but he had nothing to say to Herod, who should have known better and who just had a morbid unhealthy curiosity (Luke 23:3, 9). The conclusion is that:

> Our Lord, when dealing with people in terms of the same truth, dealt with them in different ways and accommodated His way of teaching to the person. He did not vary the truth, but he varied the particular method of presentation.'[35]

Lloyd-Jones demonstrated in his own teaching method the principle which he believed all preachers should adopt:

> The first thing a teacher in any realm has to do is to assess the capacity of his hearers, his pupils, his students, whatever they are. This fundamental rule should be constantly in the mind of the preacher, and we need to be reminded of it constantly, and particularly when we are young. The chief fault of the young preacher is to preach to the people as we would like them to be, instead of as they are.[36]

DML-J concedes that this factor will also act as a balance to the amount of time given to a particular sermon. In the mid-years of Puritanism, he felt that people were trained to listen to lengthy sermons. This is not the case now. For a young preacher not to appreciate this means that he will empty his church.

What is more, when an assessment is made of a congregation, the preacher needs to get it right. DML-J cites himself as an example of one who was considered to be a believer for many years before he actually became one, 'so anybody assuming, as most preachers did, that I was a Christian was making a false assumption . . . what I needed was preaching that would convict me of sin and make me see my need and bring me to true repentance and tell me something about regeneration'.[37] At the human level, the reason for his late entry into the Christian fold was because of a wrong appraisal by preachers of the congregations.

So now we must face the issue of the classification of Lloyd-Jones's sermons. Generally speaking, they were all expository.[38] His aim was to 'exposit'—make plain—the text. Sometimes, as we have noted, he would deal more with the broad sweep of biblical teaching than the specifics of the passage which he was considering. And he would take more liberties than are found in what we might call 'classic exposition'. Indeed, his tendency might cause some to think that a number of his sermons ran close to being a hybrid between expositional and topical.[39]

Lloyd-Jones consciously subdivided his sermons. In form, they are what is technically called kerygmatic or didactic.[40] Kerygma concerns the salvation of man. It describes the announcement of the Gospel. In the New Testament, it refers to both the proclaimer and the act of proclamation. DML-J explains, 'that is what has to determine evangelistic preaching'.

Didache means teaching. Didactic preaching contrasts with kerygmatic preaching inasmuch as the former 'expresses the revelation of Christ conceptually and logically in doctrines'. Lloyd-Jones defines didactic preaching as 'that which builds up those who have already believed—the edification of the saints'.[41]

THE GOSPEL SERMON

It is powerful, kerygmatic preaching which brings the Church into being. Lloyd-Jones finds 'a perfect example' of it in the Epistle to the Thessalonians. In the opening chapter, the effects of the preaching of the Gospel are described. The listeners turned from their paganism to serve the living and true God (1 Thess. 1:9-10). The preaching of the kerygma centres on the being of God—'Him declare I unto you'. It moves on to a proclamation of the law. God's relationship to the world is described. Man is responsible. It is the business of the preacher to emphasise his culpability. 'The trouble with people who are not seeking for a Saviour and for salvation, is that they do not understand the true nature of sin.' It is the 'peculiar function of the law' to affect the conscience of men. The Puritans and Whitefield saw this. It is embedded in Paul's theologising, 'Nay I had not known sin, but by the law (Rom. 7:7 AV). DML-J picks up on the Puritans:

> In their preaching of the Gospel, they generally started with a presentation of the Law. They knew that man would not understand salvation unless he understood the nature of sin. So they expounded the Law of God, showing its relevance, and by means of it, they brought men and women to an understanding of what sin really means in the sight of God.[42]

Within this is set forth man's responsibility to the God whose Law he has willfully broken. Conviction of sin occurs in the case of the sensitive sinner who longs for salvation.

Once a week there should be a Gospel address.[43] Lloyd-Jones made this a life-time practice. Though he eschewed the idea of an altar call, he was passionate in applying the Gospel persuasively. Some of the most emotional moments in his preaching were when he was pleading for the sinner to respond to the offer of salvation in a fashion resembling Charles Simeon of Cambridge, one of his predecessors of the last century whose pneumatology Lloyd-Jones also favoured.

Remarkable examples of DML-J's preaching in this fashion are to be found throughout his ministry.[44] Why was he so determined to preach evangelistically? In an unusual biographical note, he informs us that he was one of the second generation of Christians in South Wales since the revival of 1859. He believed that one of the less helpful consequences of the move of the Holy Spirit in his native land was the tendency of ministers to assume that all the members of their congregation were saved. Thus, there was a trend away from Gospel preaching. He comments as a result:

> I discovered later that I had never really heard a truly convicting evangelistic sermon. I was received into the Church because I could give the right answers to various set questions; but I was never questioned or examined in an experimental sense. I cannot reprobate too strongly

this tendency to assume that because people come to church that they therefore must be Christian, or that the children of Christians are of necessity Christians . . . I am urging that all the people who attend a church need to be brought under the power of the Gospel.

In a moving account of his testimony, he lamented that his own father probably died without ever hearing the Gospel. Thus, a combination of personal circumstances plus the convictions that he held from reading the Scriptures compelled him not only to preach the Gospel passionately but to encourage other ministers so to do.

EXPERIMENTAL SERMONS

However, though the preacher is to fulfil the role of an evangelist in the general sense of the term, that is not his only responsibility. There is 'the other side'. By this, he is referring to the need to encourage Christian maturity, 'the building up of the saints'. He believes that to secure this a teaching ministry must be practised. He enlarges on his point, 'I would subdivide (it) into two sections: that which is more primarily experimental, and that which is instructional.'

Experimental or experiential preaching—Lloyd-Jones uses the terms as synonyms—was an outstanding feature of his ministry. He sought to bring a corrective from a barren intellectualism on one hand and an easy believism on the other. The latter he recognised as 'that grievous Sandemanian heresy', a teaching which reckons feelings are unimportant.[45] Eaton points out that the crusade-style of evangelism which was on the rise in the 1950s seemed to play down 'conviction of sin'.[46] A simple formula became the key held by counsellors as they dealt with their converts. Plain belief was all that was required. 'Do you accept that Jesus is Lord and that he died for your sins?' An assent to the question meant the enquirer was told he was now a Christian.

This was contrary to all that DML-J affirmed. Again, we quote from Eaton, 'it must suffice to say that Lloyd-Jones saw Sandeman's view of faith as disastrously opposed to experimental religion'.[47]

He also, as we have seen, felt that many in the Church had fallen short of full assurance because that doctrine was inadequately preached. There was nothing to look forward to on earth after conversion. One had received all that there was to receive at that point. He argued against this position and, possibly, never more strongly than when preaching on the 'Quenching of the Spirit'. In a powerful address from his Ephesian series, he declaimed against the concept that the Baptism of the Spirit and regeneration were identical. This is tantamount to quenching the Spirit: 'it has been the popular view for many years'. He works out the consequences on the part of the convert who is inclined to believe that as he was baptised with the Spirit at conversion 'there is nothing for me to seek, I have got it all'. Lloyd-Jones passionately denounces this in words which have often been quoted:

> Got it all? Well, if you have 'got it all', I simply ask in the Name of God, why are you as you are? If you have 'got it all' why are you so unlike the Apostles, why are you so unlike the New Testament Christians?[48]

Lloyd-Jones's commitment to experiential sermons is, again, a reflection of the influence that Paul the Apostle had on him. He credited Paul as a great theologian. But by no means was he an academic theologian—all mind and no heart. Paul's experience of God throbs through his epistles and, as we have seen, is one of the reasons he frequently breaks away from his main theme in order to praise and extol the Lord.

We have already noted the similarity in emphasis here between DML-J and A.W. Tozer. Both men urged their respective congregations to seek God for themselves. Both were pragmatic in their approach to theology. If the doctrine was correctly understood and the hearers knew that depth of experiences of the grace of God were possible this side of eternity, the latter would be persuaded to seek the Lord even as a despairing, thirsty deer seeks for the water-brooks.

EXPOSITIONAL SERMONS

This was the type of address that Dr. Lloyd-Jones delivered on a Friday night. Examples of this kind of message abound because of the successful release of the Romans' series, all of which were preached on Friday evenings.

Here he deliberately taught the Bible to people whom he presumed to be Christians. He engaged in verse-by-verse exposition which involved close and detailed reasoning. We are not saying that such addresses were devoid of Gospel content. Some of the Romans' sermons are first-class Gospel messages and could quite easily have fitted his confessed objectives for Sunday evening ministry. On the other hand, some were experiential addresses. The nature of the text dictated this. Take, for example, his messages on spiritual experience from Romans 8:16.[49]

It is difficult to draw any major, consistent differences between his

Romans' and Ephesians' series in terms of type, even though the latter were preached on Sunday mornings, the occasion he dedicated to preaching experientially.

Lloyd-Jones wanted his congregation to be theologically literate: thus his concern to preach expositional sermons and his unqualified advice for younger preachers to attempt the same. Some of Lloyd-Jones's instructional sermons are very powerful.[50]

The preaching content in his sermons does not fit too snugly into the categories he defined, but this does not invalidate his basic advice.[51] We must remember, too, his counsel that preachers should be applicatory as they deliver their messages. Also, recall his warning about diluting the experiential passages of Scripture. Promised blessings are redeemable by the grace of God's Spirit in any era of Church History. As such, the Scriptures are not to be 'dispensationalised'. Holding this advice in tension and working it into regular pulpit practices does mean that at times the kerygmatic will merge with the didactic and the expositional will become experimental. But Lloyd-Jones appreciated this and he did warn that his divisions should not be considered watertight.

REVIEW

Though the subject matter of the last four chapters is of the highest importance, we must not let it cause us to be adrift from Dr. Lloyd-Jones's moorings. All the 'technicalities' can receive attention and be implemented, yet, the sermon might not burn. We return to Lloyd-Jones's basic premises: there is more to preaching than preaching and there is more to preaching than preparation. Basic to good preaching is a desire to be enlivened by the power of the Holy Spirit.

Leigh Powell wrote three highly instructive articles about Lloyd-Jones's ministry.[52] He coined the expression 'quicksilver exchange' by which he endeavoured to describe what happens between the Holy Spirit, the preacher, and the listener, bringing power to one and enlightenment to the others. It is right for the preacher to have his checks and his balances. But he still needs to seek God for this 'exchange'. This is another way of saying that he awaits the ignition of his sermon. Donald Macleod seals the point as he describes Lloyd-Jones's ministry:

> He acted all his life on the principle that the heart can be reached only through the head. Yet, his sermons never became lectures. The truth quickly ignited his soul; and he, as quickly, communicated the fire to the audience.[53]

It is appropriate that most of the next chapter is devoted to an address preached by Dr. Lloyd-Jones in which, in expounding Scripture, he makes a significant statement about preaching per se.

12

Not in word only

This sermon was preached by Dr. Lloyd-Jones in Canada. The editing has been very slight. I include it in this book not only because it is a message worthy to stand on its own and be read as it conveys the burden of the preacher, but also because it is a good example of his preaching style, his approach to his text, his desire to be relevant. It shows quite clearly the high value that he placed on the Holy Spirit for his empowering in order to make the message burn. The Tape reference is S628.

The words to which I want to draw your attention are found in the first chapter of Paul's first Epistle to the Thessalonians. I want to emphasise in particular the fifth verse which reads like this: 'For our gospel came not unto you in word only, but also in power, and in the Holy Ghost, and in much assurance' (AV).

But why am I saying that I want to emphasise that in particular? I do not propose to confine myself to it only because, as you must have noticed from the reading, there is one theme really in the chapter and it is the whole theme of the presentation of the Gospel. Now, I say that there is no more important subject than this. The whole state of the Church and the whole state of the world demands that we should pay very earnest attention to this matter of the presentation of the Gospel. We believe that it is the Word of God. We believe it is the only hope for the world tonight.

We know here is God's answer to our every need and the problem is how are we to get this message over to the masses of the people in all the countries of the world. Well, this is the problem which is being recognised and acknowledged by every branch of the Christian Church. There is no section of the Church that I am aware of that is not urgently concerned about this very matter at the present time. They have got a new term for it. They call it today, 'The problem of communication'. We are rather fond, as you know, of inventing slogans and of using new terms and this is the term for today, of all terms, that is being bandied around in the Christian Church and in our various conferences and councils—the problem of communication.

How are we to communicate this message to the masses of the people who are outside the Church and who are not Christians? It is a problem in the homeland, in every homeland. It is the problem on the mission field. Now we are being told today that this is a new problem for this reason. So many changes have taken place in the world. We are being reminded almost ad nauseam that we are the mid-twentieth-century people. We are the people of the atomic age. We are the post-war people. We are, some say, the post-Christian people. We are told that, owing to the advance of knowledge, and particularly science, we are confronted by a situation such as never confronted the Christian Church before in her whole great and long history. The problem is of communicating this message to men and women who no longer are familiar with our terminology. That, we are told, is the great problem. People today do not know what is meant by justification and sanctification and all these other terms that we use. They have lost their knowledge of these terms and therefore this problem of communication is something which is quite new. Thus, great attention is being paid to it.

Some say that what is needed is a new translation of the Bible. That was the great argument for the so-called *New English Bible*. We must have a Bible, they say, that Tom, Dick, and Harry can understand. They do not understand the archaisms of this King James Version. We must get a translation in the language of the people so that everybody will be able to understand it, and therefore, the suggestion seems to be that as long as they can understand the words, they will understand the meaning and are likely to become Christians. There are all sorts and kinds of proposals put before us. We must perfect our methods, we are told. We must learn the methods of big business advertising. We are told that we must modernise everything: in order that we may get this message right over to the masses of the people who are outside the Christian Church.

Now, you are all familiar, I am sure, with this argument and with this position. All I want to try to do is to show you this, that there is nothing new at all in the situation which confronts us and that the sooner we realise it the better. The problem confronting us is precisely the problem that has always confronted the Christian Church.

You know the world never varies. The world is always the same. The world is always godless; the world is always Christless; the world is always opposed to God. And it hates God. Oh, I know that it wears different clothing. I know that it uses different terminology from age to age and century to century, but that is only on the surface. The world and its mind and its crooked heart, never varies at all. Unfortunately, the only variation is in the state and the condition of the Church. The world remains a constant in its position and therefore I argue that there is no need for us to feel that our problem is new or novel or unique. I want to try to show you from this one chapter of only ten verses that the problem that confronts us is precisely the problem that confronted the early Christian Church, the problem that confronted the Apostles, the original preachers of the Gospel.

Now, the Apostle puts it before us here in a most interesting manner. It is said by the authorities that this is the first letter that he ever wrote. That makes it interesting in and of itself, but what is still more interesting is this, that in this one chapter he reminds the members of the Church of Thessalonica of how it was the Gospel came to them. 'Our Gospel,' he said, 'came unto you not in word only', but he is reminding them of how it came and that is the thing to which I want to call your attention.

Now what was the position confronting the Apostle? Well, I want to show you that it was precisely the position that is confronting us today. Here was this great Apostle with just a handful of companions with him probably, travelling round from city to city. What were the conditions? Well, it was a pagan society. He was here in Macedonia, a part of modern Greece, and these people were pagans, they knew nothing about Hebrew literature. They knew nothing about biblical terminology and they were living a life of vice and sin and degradation: amazingly like the modern world. The Apostle begins to preach his Gospel in this utterly pagan, godless society.

I suggest to you that is perfectly analogous to the situation confronting us in Canada, the United States, Great Britain, or any other country under the sun at this present moment. But here the Apostle tells us how he faced that situation and how, as the result of his facing it in that way, a Church came into being in Thessalonica which bore a very wonderful testimony.

My dear friends, there is no need to look for anything new, there is only one thing for the Church to do today. There is only one thing for the individual missionary to do, and that is to go back to the New Testament and discover the Apostolic method and the Apostolic manner. The tragedy of the situation is that we think we need something new, whereas what we really need is this old, old Gospel preached in the old method and after the old, Apostolic manner.

Here, the Apostle puts it in very simple and plain terms before us. He tells us that there were two main factors in the spread of the Gospel in the ancient world. The first was the preaching of the Apostles. That was essential; they were the people to whom the message was given. The Lord commissioned them. He called them. He sent them out. He gave them the message. Apostolic preaching, obviously that comes first.

But you notice here that he tells us that was not the only factor. There was a second factor in the spread of the Gospel in that ancient world. What was that? Well, it was the life and the witness and the testimony of the people who believed the Gospel. The Apostle pays great attention to that. Let me show it to you. Let us read from verse 6 onwards. He says:

> And ye became followers of us, and of the Lord, having received the word in much affliction, with joy of the Holy Ghost. So that ye were ensamples to all that believe in Macedonia and Achaia. For, from you sounded out the word of the Lord not only in Macedonia and Achaia, but also in every place your faith to God-ward is spread abroad; so that we need not to speak any thing. For they themselves shew of us what manner of entering in we had unto you, and how ye turned to God from idols to serve the living and true God (*AV*).

Now, that being interpreted means this. 'You know,' says the Apostle, 'you good people, members of the Church of Thessalonica, have made my task of preaching very much easier. What I find now', said the Apostle, 'is this. Since I preached to you, since you believed the Gospel and became members of the Church, what I find is this. When I go to a place, I begin to speak and they interrupt me and they say, yes, we know all about you, we know who you are, we have heard about those people down in Thessalonica. We have heard of what happened to them as the result of your preaching. You know, the noise has spread abroad throughout all the world and you are opening the doors for me. Everybody is talking about you. They say, have you heard of what has happened in Thessalonica as the result of the preaching of Paul? The whole world, he says, is talking about it. So that as I visit a place, I find they are ready to listen. They are curious to hear. They want to know about this message that has wrought such a transformation in your lives and in your whole way of living.'

Very well, this is the second factor, and I want to emphasise the two factors this evening.

What can we do to bring this glorious message, the glorious Gospel of the blessed God, to the masses of the people? Well, the first thing I say is this: the pulpit must do its work. We must know what to preach and how to preach it, but that alone is not enough. Our preaching must be verified in the lives of you good Christian people who are called to work in an office, in a factory, in some profession. You are to be the living proofs of the truth of the message. That is how it happened in the first century. This preaching was demonstrated to be true by the lives and living of the people of Thessalonica and everybody was talking about them. And so, the door of opportunity was opened widely for this great and glorious message of the Apostle.

Very well, let's look at these two things together because the Apostle tells us that there are two things that are common to the two factors.

The first thing is the message that was preached. 'Our Gospel came unto you not in word only,' that is the message. But there was this other factor, 'not in word only, but also in power, and in the Holy Ghost, and in much assurance'. Now there are the two things: the message and the power of the Spirit upon it! That is to be seen in the Apostles. It is to be seen equally in the people who believed the message and became members of the Christian Church.

Let me hold these two things before you this evening. Unless we return to these two things, my dear friends, we might as well give up. This is how Christianity began. This is how Christianity has continued. Look at all the great revivals and reformations of history. What are they? They are nothing but a return to the Book of the Acts of the Apostles. It is when the Church comes back to this, to the message and the power of the Spirit upon it that you get revival and re-awakening and men and women turning to God to serve him with all their being.

Very well, let us look at these two things. Let's look at the message for a moment. What is it we are to preach? What is Christianity? Is it not an appalling thing that we need to ask that question? But we do need to ask it. There are all sorts and kinds of things passing as Christianity today that I, at any rate for one, cannot recognise as Christianity at all. What is the Christian message? Well, the Apostle tells us.

The first essential characteristic of our message is that it is the proclamation of the greatest good news that mankind has ever heard. And, if there is no Gospel in our message, it is not the Christian message. Yet, you know there are many in the world today who claim to be preaching the Christian message but the message to them is nothing but a constant talking about, and protesting about, atomic or hydrogen bombs and war and this, and that, and the other.

If you take your impression of what Christianity is from the newspapers and so much of the television and the radio, well you would think it was nothing, I say, but a protest against war and armaments and about the colour question and various other political and social matters. Now, I am not here to say that Christianity has nothing to say about these matters. What I am here to say is this: that is not good news. The thing that makes the Christian message a Gospel is that it is a proclamation of good news.

It is not just topical comments on the latest scandal in the newspapers or the latest bit of news. It is not that we spend our time in telling kings and princes and presidents and prime ministers how they ought to be running their countries and how they ought to be solving the international problem. We are not qualified to do so.

I have not come here tonight to tell you what the Queen of England and her Government or the President of the United States, or anybody else ought to be doing. I am not familiar with the facts. I have not got all the data before me. It would be presumption on my part to tell them or give them advice as to what they are to do. That is not my calling.

The business of the Christian preacher is to announce—proclaim, the good news: the Gospel, the greatest good news that the world has ever heard!

And then the Apostle goes on to define it further. This good news, this Gospel, is something that is stated and proclaimed 'in word'—'in words'. Now, you notice that the Apostle puts it in a very interesting manner. He says, our Gospel came not unto you 'in word only'. But when he says that it did not come 'in word *only* ', he is saying that it *did* come 'in word'. If I say that something does not only happen, I mean it does happen like that but there is something in addition. And that is what he is saying. He said, 'our Gospel did come to you in word, it came in words: but it did not come only in words. It came also in power, and in the Holy Ghost, and in much assurance.

Why am I troubling to emphasise this point? Well, I am doing so, unfortunately, because again it has become necessary to do so. We are living in an age, my dear friends, when men and women dislike doctrine. They dislike theology. They dislike definitions. We are living in a weak

and a flabby age that dislikes precision. We are living in an age when
people tell us that Christianity is something that is so wonderful that it
can't be defined at all.

What makes a man a Christian? Well, they say, you know you can't
tell. But it is a wonderful spirit that a man has within him. It is a wonderful feeling. What is Christianity? Well, Christianity is doing good.
There are men who are being praised as the greatest Christians of this
century who deny all the essential tenets of the Christian faith, but they
are regarded as great Christians. Why? Because they have made sacrifices and because they are doing good.

What is it that makes a man a Christian? What is Christianity? Can
it be defined or can it not be defined? We are living in terrible days—in
days of confusion, in days of muddle, in days of uncertainty. We are living in days, I say, when there is a positive objection to definitions of the
Christian faith. They dislike what they call propositional revelation.
There was a slogan a few years ago that put it like this. It said,
'Christianity is caught, not taught.' It's a wonderful Spirit that gets you.
You do not know what it is, you can't describe it, you can't define it,
but you feel it is wonderful. 'It is caught not taught.' And there is this
great objection today to propositional revelation or propositional truth.
They say not only can you not define the Christian faith, you must not
even attempt to do so; it is a foolish thing to do. It is like trying to dissect the aroma of a flower. It is a wonderful thing, but it is a mystical
thing. You can't reduce it to terms and to definitions.

Let me give you one example of what I am trying to say. I remember reading a book about five years ago which had a very wonderful
title. It was called *Ultimate Questions*. It was about this whole question
of the Christian faith. But this is what the man said in the book. He said,
'You know Christianity is something like this. It is as if a man were told
by somebody that if he only climbed to the top of a certain great mountain he would have a wonderful view when he got there. If you only get
to the top of that mountain, you would see a great panorama stretching out before you such as you have never seen in your life.' The man is
told this. And he begins to feel a desire to see it. So one day he gets up
early and he travels in his car. He has to leave it. He begins to walk along
lanes. He even leaves them. He begins to cross fields and tracks and at
last he is at the foot of the mountain and then he begins to climb up and
to scale the heights. The sun is shining in the heavens. It doesn't matter,
he wants to see this view. On and on he goes, eventually on hands and
knees, holding on to tufts of grass, scaling the sides of rocks, cutting his
hands and his knees. It doesn't matter. On he goes and, at last, he arrives

at the summit and there stretching out before him is this glorious panorama. What does he do about it? Well, says the man in the book, he does not go home and try to define it, try to say it is 'like this' and it isn't 'like that' and reduce it to some propositions. 'Why,' says the man, 'the thing is ridiculous. What the man does is this: he just stands there on that mountain top with his eyes and his mouth wide open, lost in surprise and amazement and wonder.' 'No, no,' he says, 'he does not define it and describe it and dissect it. I can image him singing,' he says, 'but what I cannot image him doing is to try to reduce it to a number of propositions.' That is the popular teaching.

We are being told today with this ecumenical spirit that seems to be taking everybody up and which will eventually take Protestantism back into Rome if we are not careful, we are being told that it is just this wonderful spirit you have and that if you are against Communism you are a Christian of necessity, whatever you may believe, and so on. It is something that eludes definition.

My dear friends, this is a most important question. I do not know of any more urgent question tonight than just this one question. Can Christianity be defined or not? According to the Apostle Paul it can. 'Our Gospel', he said, 'came unto you in word', and this is what the Church has said throughout the centuries.

Were it not so tragic, this would be very amusing. I know many people who hold this modern view that Christianity can't be described, can't be defined, can't be stated in propositions and yet the very self-same people go to their Church Sunday by Sunday, and at a given point in the service they get up and they recite together the Apostles' Creed! What is that? It is a series of definitions. It is a series of propositions. And later they recite the Athanasian Creed and the Nicene Creed. What are these? Still more elaborate definitions and descriptions of the truth.

Why was it that the Church ever had these creeds? There is only one answer. The Church produced the creeds because she had to do so to defend the faith. Even in the New Testament we see false teaching beginning to creep in and the Apostles have to deal with it. They have to denounce it. They contend for the Faith. It became worse after the days of the Apostles, and there were all sorts of false gospels and false creeds and false ideas and the Church was in terrible danger. So, the Fathers of the Church, under the leading and the guidance of the Holy Spirit, met together in their great Councils. What for? Well, in order to draw up definitions of the faith. They said 'it is this', but 'it is not that'. They defined and described heresy, and they denounced it. They did it in order to guide and in order to protect the people.

You see, the early Church councils, the early ecumenical councils, met together in order to define the faith. Modern ecumenical councils meet in order to say that the faith cannot be defined. That is how far we have travelled from the days of the early Church ,and this not only happened in the first century.

Do you remember what happened after the great Protestant Reformation? Well, this is what happened: almost immediately after that great outburst, that great outpouring of the Spirit, the leaders of the Church found it was absolutely essential to define and to describe their faith. So they drew up their great confessions of faith. You have your Augsburg Confession. You have your Heidelberg Catechism. You have the Thirty-nine Articles of the Church of England. You have the great Westminster Confession that is supposed to be believed by the Presbyterian Churches of the world. What are these great confessions? They are nothing but definitions of the faith. They are nothing but descriptions of what is true, and what is not true, in terms of exposition of Scripture.

So you see, the Church, in all her great periods, has always been very concerned to show that the Christian Faith is something that can be defined, described, stated in propositions. Yet, the majority of men and women in the Christian Church today are denouncing this whole idea. I want to show you that they are not only departing from the almost unbroken tradition of the Christian Church throughout the centuries, they are denying the teaching of the Apostles themselves at the same time.

Let me show it you from this one chapter. 'Our Gospel came not unto you in word only', but it *did* come in word. What was that word? In a very remarkable manner the Apostle tells us. Have you ever noticed that in verses 9 and 10 of this little chapter you have a perfect synopsis of Christian doctrine?

For they themselves shew us of what manner of entering in we had unto you, and how ye turned to God from idols to serve the living and true God. And to wait for his Son from heaven, whom he raised from the dead, even Jesus, which delivered us from the wrath to come.

What was it that the Apostle preached about? Did the Apostle preach politics to these people? Did he say to them that it is about time you banded yourselves together and raised an army to rid yourself of the yoke of the Roman Empire? Did he object to the taxation? Did he protest against the various things that were happening? That was not his message at all.

What was the content of the preaching of the Apostle Paul? He tells us. Where did it start? What was its beginning? What was its first point? He answers, '*God!*' Apostolic preaching starts with the Being of God! Oh, I do want to emphasise this. Christian preaching, you know, does not start with man. There are too many of us starting with men today. We are all so subjective. We start with ourselves, our needs, and then we always want something to satisfy us. Christianity never starts with man. It always starts with God.

Let me say this, even at the risk of being misunderstood, the Christian proclamation does not even start with the Lord Jesus Christ. It starts with God the Father, God the Creator.

I believe this is much of our trouble at the present time that we start with the Lord Jesus Christ. We say to people, come to Jesus and you will get this, that, and the other. That is not Christian preaching. Christian preaching starts with God. This is how the Apostle preached. He saw these people, he saw they were worshipping idols, he saw that they were making gods for themselves. They sometimes made them out of wood or stone or precious metals. They made their gods. They built temples to them and then they served them. They worshipped them; they offered sacrifices to them. They were worshipping idols. The Apostle started there, and what he said to them was this, 'You know, you are worshipping nothing. These idols, they have no existence, you've made them, they have no life, they have no power, they can't do anything. They are liars, they are emptiness, they are a vacuity, there is nothing there.' He exposed to them the utter folly of idolatry, how these men were bowing down to nothing—to a lie, to a supposition, to a projection of a man's mind, to a creation of man's own idea. Nothing there—idols, vanities!

But he went on to tell them that was not the serious thing. The serious thing was this: while they were worshipping these dumb idols, these vanities, this emptiness, they were not worshipping the only true and living God. So he began to tell them about him. He began to tell them about the God who had created the whole universe.

Here is the true God, here is a living God: those idols—they can do nothing. You have to carry them about. They can do nothing at all. They have no power, they have no life. 'But there is,' he says, 'a living God.' And so he began to tell them about the God who created everything out of nothing at the beginning. The God who said, 'Let there be light, and there was light'; the God who created everything that is, and man as the crowning glory of it all, was made in his own image and likeness. He made him lord of creation. Paul told them about God, the God of the Hebrews, the only God, the only true and living God. He began there.

And then he went on to tell them the vital importance of all this, for God had created man for himself. He had created man in order that through man he might govern the universe, he had created man in order that man might be his companion, in order that man might live to his glory. As the first question and answer in the shorter catechism of that Westminster Confession puts it, 'What is the chief end of man?' The answer is, 'The chief end of man is to glorify God and to enjoy him for ever'. The Apostle preached that to them. He said, 'You know, man is not just an animal. Man does not do just what he likes and pleases, he has been made in the image of God. God has given him a law, he was meant to live according to it.'

Why is this important? It is important because man is a responsible being. And his life in this world is a life under God and when it comes to an end it is not the end. Man goes on and then he stands before God in the judgment. Did you notice the last words 'and to wait for his Son from heaven, even Jesus, which delivered us from the wrath to come'.

Now here was Apostolic preaching. The Apostle looked at these people and he said, 'Look here. You have been worshipping these vanities and you have not been worshipping and serving the only true and living God and yet you will have to stand before him because you are human beings. You are men and women, and he puts up possibilities in you and he will examine you in the light of them. You have got a soul in you and you have got to give an account of it to God. Can you do so? Have you lived to his glory? If you have not, you will be under the wrath of God, you are even under it now'.

'Repent', he said, 'turn to God, for your whole eternal future depends upon your relationship to God'. He said that God has revealed through the people, the Jews, throughout the running centuries that he is a holy God, and a righteous God and a just God, a God who hates sin, a God who is of such a pure countenance that he cannot even look upon sin. He said you, all of you, are moving toward him, and you will stand before Him in a final judgement.'

That is how the Apostle preached. That is the Apostolic message. Not the political conditions of the Roman Empire, not certain injustices of this or that, but man, in the profanity of his being, under God and under the wrath of God!

'Hear me', says somebody, 'I thought you took some time just now to tell us that the message of this Christian Church is Gospel, is good news. It does not sound very much like good news to me at the moment.'

All right, my friend, I quite agree with you. This is only the introduction to the sermon. You know I am beginning to think that half the trouble in the Christian Church is this, that we have forgotten the introduction. We are in such a hurry, we say, come to Jesus and the people do not come to Jesus. Do you know why? I can tell you. They have never seen any need of Jesus. They have never realised the truth about themselves. They come to Jesus if they are miserable and unhappy, if they want physical healing, if they want guidance, if they want all their problems solved. That is not the way to come to Jesus. It is no use simply telling people, 'Come to Jesus'. They have got to see their need of him.

You know, before you come to the Gospel, you need the Law. Before you begin to talk about salvation, you preach about God. The world today is as it is because it has forgotten God. Man is the centre of the universe. Man's needs come first and last. God, the Almighty, the Everlasting, the Eternal God, who is over all, and still reigns, is forgotten!

But, thank God, the message did not stop at that point. Having thus shown them their need and their desperate plight and state, the Apostle went on to tell them about the Gospel, and here it is. The whole of it is in verse ten: 'And to wait for his Son from heaven whom he raised from the dead, even Jesus.'

He began to tell them about Jesus: who he is—Jesus of Nazareth, the Carpenter, son of Mary and of Joseph. He began to tell them about this young Galilean that suddenly appeared upon the scene at the age of thirty and began to preach the Gospel; he was once a boy of twelve and he could confute and confound the doctors of the Law in the temple. He told them about this amazing person and his astounding teaching, his miracles, his marvellous deeds. Jesus! Who is he? He tells them that this was none other than the Son of God, his Son from heaven, even Jesus.

What is Christian preaching? Here it is: the doctrine of the incarnation. My friends, you can't do without doctrine, if you try to, you shall soon have no Gospel and you will be preaching nothing but some kind of glorified humanism which is not Christianity. Christianity is doctrinal. It is a matter of definitions, it is words, it is theology and here it is: the incarnation: Jesus, Son of God, Jesus of Nazareth, born of a Virgin, born miraculously! That is doctrine, essential doctrine in the Christian faith, the doctrine of his person, two natures in one person. You do not understand? Neither do I! Did you ever think you could? This is the doctrine. Jesus, Son of God—two natures, one person.

Here he is, the Son of God come from heaven to earth. The whole doctrine of the incarnation of the virgin birth—you cannot be Christian without believing these truths in particular, these propositions. These are the essentials of the Christian faith. There is no Christianity apart from them.

If he is just a man to you, a good man, a political agitator or the pale Galilean, that is not Christianity. Christianity is the doctrine of the incarnation.

When the fulness of the time was come, God sent forth his Son, made of a woman, made under the law, To redeem them that were under the law' (Gal. 4:4-5).

That is what Paul preached. Then he went on to tell them this astounding thing about his death upon a cross which delivered us from the wrath to come. He told them about the death of this amazing person, Jesus of Nazareth, the Son of God. And you notice that what Paul preached to them was that 'he delivered us from the wrath to come'. In other words, he did not merely tell us how to deliver ourselves. He did not come just to teach us how to live and to give us an example and a pattern and a fillip to our endeavour. He did not come merely to tell us to sacrifice ourselves. No, no. He came to do something for us. He has delivered us. So, he expounded to them the doctrine of the atonement. And you have no Christianity without that.

He showed them how, by dying on the cross, he was bearing our sins and our punishment. As he puts it in writing to the Corinthians:

God was in Christ, reconciling the world unto himself, not imputing their trespasses unto them; and hath committed unto us the word of reconciliation (2 Cor. 5:19 AV).

Or as the Apostle Peter puts it:

Who his own self bare our sins in his own body on the tree, that we, being dead to sins, should live unto righteousness: by whose stripes ye were healed (1 Pet. 2:24 AV).

The message of the cross! We must be clear about this. What is the message of the cross? What is the message concerning the death of Christ? Is it that there he is just proclaiming that though you are doing this to my Son, I still love you? No, no, that is not enough! There is substitution here. There is punishment here. He is the Lamb of God that taketh away the sin of the world. God hath laid on him the iniquity of us all, by his stripes we are healed. We behold him stricken, smitten of God.

The great transaction—when God takes your sins and mine and puts them on His Son and smites him, punishes him for us, and thereby offers to us a free forgiveness and salvation which delivered us. He has done it. It is all in Him. He has not come to tell us what to do. He has done it for us. He took our place. He died our death. He bore the punishment of our sins. That was Apostolic preaching. And it is preaching that comes in words. It is a particular doctrine, it is specific, it can be defined. But then you notice he goes on to remind them also to wait for his Son from heaven, whom he raised from the dead.

The Resurrection! And how important it is! I find there are so many today who no longer believe in the literal, physical resurrection. 'No, no, they say, what matters is that Jesus still lives and influences us. We don't believe that he literally rose in the body out of the grave. They say it doesn't matter. Doesn't matter! Would Paul ever have written 1 Corinthians 15 if it didn't matter? What he says is that if Christ be not risen from the dead, our preaching is in vain and your faith is in vain. You are yet in your sins. If in this life only we have hope in Christ, we are of all men most miserable. Now here is Jesus Christ risen from the dead. The doctrine of the Resurrection!

My dear friends, how appalling it is that men say that the Gospel does not come in words, that definitions don't count, that it does not matter what you believe as long as you are a good and a nice man and as long as you want to call yourself a Christian. No, no! Without the literal, physical resurrection, there is no Gospel. There never would have been. 'Delivered for our offences' says Paul in Romans 4:25 (AV), and 'raised again for our justification, declared to be the Son of God with power according to the spirit of holiness by the resurrection from among the dead'.

Here, in this mighty event, God is proclaiming his Son and proclaiming that his work was sufficient. The reconciliation has been accomplished. You can't be a Christian without believing these particular doctrines, and to wait for his son from heaven. Yes, He ascended into heaven and He took his seat at the right hand of God and there He is waiting until His enemies shall be made His footstool.

Don't be dejected, Christian people. He is on the throne. 'All power is given unto to him in heaven and in earth.' He sits, he reigns, he waits, until his enemies shall be made his footstool and he will come again, not as the babe of Bethlehem, but as the Lord of Lords, King of Kings riding upon the clouds of heaven surrounded by his holy angels, and he will come to judge the world in righteousness. He will destroy all evil and sin. The devil and Satan and hell and all shall be cast to the lake of perdition and Jesus shall reign where ere the sun does his successive journeys run, his kingdom stretch from shore to shore till moon shall wax and wane no more. His people are waiting for it, waiting, for the great day. The adoption with the redemption of our body and the ushering in of this kingdom that never was on land or sea, the new heavens and the new earth wherein dwelleth righteousness.

That was Apostolic preaching! And may I say this in passing, you can't preach that in twenty minutes!! I want to say this in the name of God. You Christian people have a great responsibility. You are in too much of a hurry to get home to your televisions. Give your preachers time. If they preach the Gospel, give them time. These mighty truths can't be declared in a few minutes. Let's look at them, let's glory in them, let them speak to us. This is the Apostolic message and if you do not want to go on hearing about this, I tell you, in the name of God, you are not a Christian. You have never been one. These are the things that will occupy the saints throughout the countless ages of eternity. This is the message. This is the Gospel. Here it is, in words, in definitions, in propositions, in theology, in doctrine. Do you believe it? Have you received it?

But wait a minute, the Apostle said that it came not in word only, but also in power, and in the Holy Ghost, and in much assurance.

I want to emphasise this as much as the other. I am not going to keep you. But I do want to emphasise it. Orthodoxy is absolutely essential. I do not care if you have a world Church; if it doesn't proclaim this truth, it will be useless, it will be a travesty. Orthodoxy is absolutely essential. But orthodoxy alone is not enough. A church can be perfectly orthodox and at the same time perfectly dead and perfectly useless. The Apostolic message was orthodox but there was something else. Our Gospel came not unto you in word only but also in power, and in the Holy Ghost, and in much assurance.

What is he talking about? He is talking primarily about himself as he preached to them. He says, 'You know when I preached to you, I knew that it was not merely I, Paul, that was speaking. I knew that the Spirit was using me. I knew that I had got the power of the Holy Ghost. I knew that he had clothed himself upon me. I knew that I was nothing but the vehicle, the channel, the instrument. I knew that I was being used. I was preaching with much assurance. I knew something was happening, I *knew* that he was working in you.'

You see, the Apostle always relied on the power of the Holy Spirit.

It is not enough that we be certain of our message. We must be equally careful about our methods, and the Apostle's method was—trusting the Holy Spirit. Listen to the way he puts it in the second chapter negatively. I begin at verse three:

> For our exhortation was not of deceit, nor of uncleanness, nor in guile; But as we were allowed of God to be put in trust with the Gospel, even so we speak; not as pleasing men, but God, which trieth our hearts. For neither at any time used we flattering words, as ye know, nor a cloak of covetousness; God is witness: Nor of men sought we glory, neither of you, nor yet of others, when we might have been burdensome, as the apostles of Christ (1 Thess. 2:3).

What does he mean by all that? What he says is this: 'You know when I preached to you I was not concerned about pleasing men. My only concern was to please God'. The Apostle never tried to ingratiate himself with his congregation.

I cannot imagine the Apostle Paul bouncing up on to a platform, cracking a few jokes to put the congregation at ease, and then entertaining them with flippancies in order just to play upon their feelings. The thing is unthinkable. No, no! This blessed message is in power, in the Holy Ghost, in much assurance.

Listen to the way he puts it in writing to those Corinthians. He went among them, he says, 'in weakness and in fear and in much trembling'. There was no self-confidence in this man. This man was not a great master of ceremonies commanding a great crowd. No! 'in weakness, fear, much trembling'. Fear that he would stand between the people and this blessed message. 'Our speech and our preaching', he says, 'was not with enticing words of man's wisdom, but in demonstration of the Spirit and the power'.

Nobody talked about him. Indeed, the Corinthians criticised him. They said 'his presence is weak'. The Apostle was nothing to look at. Let's never forget that. He was not a handsome fellow. He was a short man, according to tradition, bald headed, bent nose, with inflamed eyes, almost repulsive and offensive. His presence was weak and his speech, they said, offensive. It didn't matter. The speech was in demonstration of the Spirit and of power.

My dear friends, our methods are as important as our message and we must not use the methods of the world. We must not be so concerned about results that we resort to devious doubtful methods. We must not play with men and try to entice them and ingratiate ourselves. No, no!

The proclamation of this blessed word is to be in the demonstration of the Spirit and of power. 'I knew', said Paul, 'I preached with much assurance'.

That was Apostolic preaching. It was also the preaching of Martin Luther; it was the preaching of John Calvin; it was the preaching of John Knox who could make Mary, Queen Mary of Scots, tremble in her seat and make her more afraid of his prayers than of the army of England.

Beloved people, where have we gone to? What has happened to us? When shall we come back to this? This is the need, this is the way, this is God's way in all revivals and reformations: the preaching of the word in demonstration of the Spirit and of power! That's how Christianity spread at the beginning. That's how it has always truly spread throughout the running centuries.

Just a word on the other side before I close. That was the truth about the Apostles. It was equally true about the people. What he says about them is this, 'the word of God which ye heard of us, ye received it not as the word of men, but as it is in truth, the word of God, which effectually worketh also in you that believe (1 Thess 2:13 AV).

You see what is happening to them? Here was this little Apostle preaching in the mighty power of the Holy Ghost, and with this assurance. These pagan, unenlightened, ignorant people living a life of vice and evil and sin, as they listened to him said, 'These are not the words of a man, there is something more here'. They realised that they were the words of God. What made them realise that? Oh, the working of the same Spirit that was working in the Apostle in them.

It is the Holy Spirit alone that can convict of sin. It is he alone that can enlighten the darkened human mind. It is he alone that can give a man life anew. And, as Paul was preaching in the power of the Spirit, the Spirit was working powerfully in them and they received the Word.

They were totally ignorant. They knew nothing about God or about the Lord Jesus Christ or the Holy Spirit. These ignoramuses: they believed! The power of the Spirit enlightened them. That's how missionary work is done. That's how the Gospel can alone be preached in any country, whatever the background, whatever the conditions. He worked in them, and they believed, and they received it. 'And ye became followers of us,' he said, 'and of the Lord having received the word in much affliction with joy of the Holy Ghost.' This was their story.

They believed the Gospel and they followed the Apostles and they joined the Church. It led to great affliction, they were persecuted by their relatives and friends, they became the outcasts of society. It did not make any difference. Though they were in much affliction they were filled with the joy of the Holy Ghost. Having seen this truth they were ready to die for it if necessary. And many of them did die for it. They saw that nothing matters but a man's relationship to God and his eternal destiny. Nothing else matters though they were dealt with so cruelly. They smiled in the face of it all and some of them, as they were later cast to the lions in the arena, just thanked God that at last they had been accounted worthy to suffer for his Name's sake. And the result of this was, you see, that everybody talked about them. It was a genuine work. I know it was genuine. I can prove it to you. They turned to God from idols, 'to serve the living and the true God'.

It was not just a question of coming forward at the end of a meeting and signing a card and then forgetting about it the next day or a week or a fortnight. No, no! These men were born again. The Spirit had done his work and they turned to God from idols, they left the idols, they left the world, they left their sin. They entered into the life of Christ and took their place in the Christian Church and everybody saw it and everybody talked about it. And you know, they not only began but they went on with it. This is the great thing in verse three: 'Remembering without ceasing your work of faith, and [your] labour of love and [your] patience of hope in our Lord Jesus Christ, in the sight of God and our Father' (1 Thess 1:3 *AV*).

They went on with it. It was not a flash in the pan. It was not an emotional excitement. The work had been done; they were new men and women in Christ Jesus and they went on, come what may. And what was the result? The result was that everybody was talking about them. 'from you sounded out the word of the Lord not only in Macedonia and Achaia, but also in every place your faith to God-ward is spread abroad; so that we need not to speak anything' (v.8). This is what happened, you see.

Men and women living in Thessalonica would stand on their street corners and they would suddenly see a man going along to a meeting and they would say, 'Do you see that man? Do you remember what that man used to be like? He was a drunkard; he was an adulterer; he was a wife beater; he was a scandal; he was a shame. But look at him now! His face is different; he dresses differently; everything is different. His wife is different; his children are different; his home is different. What is it?' 'Ah, well', said one of the others, 'I can tell you. He has been like this ever since that man Paul came to preach. Ever since he heard that man Paul, he has been a different man.' The greatest need of the hour, as I see it, is a mighty outpouring of the Spirit of God to authenticate, to prove, the truth of this one and only message. Let us go on preaching the truth, but let us at the same time pray unto God to open the windows of heaven and to baptise us anew and afresh with the power of the Holy Ghost. Amen.

13

Retrospect

Pray also for me, that whenever I open my mouth, words may be given me so that I will fearlessly make known the mystery of the Gospel, for which I am an ambassador in chains. Pray that I may declare it fearlessly, as I should.[1]

The Apostle Paul

It is time now for us to look back across the course which we have pursued in our endeavour to chart Dr. Lloyd-Jones's philosophy of preaching. Our intentions are to engage in a final summary highlighting afresh some of the major convictions which he held about preaching and how these might help the ordinary preacher.

We also need to apply them to Third World countries. In some of these, the Church is growing at a phenomenal rate. If preaching by definition should be expository, then to what degree is Lloyd-Jones's preaching method helpful in this large section of the Church in the twentieth century? Failure to assess the needs of pastors in these countries is not only shortsighted, it is tantamount to ignoring a large slice of Christendom: so this is brought into perspective in our final chapter.

PROPHETIC PREACHING

I have deliberately spent four chapters on DML-J's preaching grid—dealing with his diagnostic approach to the text and inquiring into his reference points in sermon preparation. In doing this, though I have occasionally referred to the need for dependence on the Holy Spirit, I have run the risk of distancing ourselves from what was DML-J's basic conviction about preaching, namely, the need to experience the sacred anointing and thus know the smile of God. This is one of the features which will always be associated with Martyn Lloyd-Jones in the history of preaching.

I am not suggesting that he was the only preacher to have high-lighted the need to rely on the Holy Spirit. But his was the most influ-ential voice to sound forth a warning in the twentieth century about the danger of preaching degenerating into some art or craft form, con-centrating on technicalities, system, and planning but neglecting the primary need of spiritual dynamics in the ministry. Gordon Fee warns:[2]

> The danger always lies in letting the form and content get in the way of what should be the single concern: the Gospel proclaimed through human weakness but accompanied by the powerful work of the Spirit so that lives are changed through a divine-human encounter. *That is hard to teach in a course on homiletics, but it still stands as a true need in genuine Christian preaching.*

Lloyd-Jones, anticipating Fee, supplied his corrective in his approach to preaching. Listen again to what he had to say on the subject. It is found in an address where he deals in general with expository preaching. 'Oh, there is preaching and preaching! What is the test of preaching? I will tell you; it is power! . . . And that was the sort of preaching you had from the Protestant reformers.'

Then, in a most revealing comment, he makes an evaluation about the ministry of the reformers: 'It was *prophetic* preaching, not *priestly* preaching. What we have today is what I would call priestly. Very nice, very quiet, very ornate, sentences turned beautifully, prepared carefully. That is not prophetic preaching!'[3]

'Priestly preaching', as he construed it, is essentially intellectual but devoid of the Holy Spirit's power. Such may be doctrinally correct but still arid. It can empty churches and repress evangelistic appetite and enthusiasm. It breeds a fatalism, causing the minister to think all he needs to do is to prepare a theological discourse each week and leave it at that. This for Lloyd-Jones is the unacceptable face of Calvinism: unwarranted, unattractive, and unbiblical. He sternly warns against it. Surely he was right to do this almost throughout the long period of his ministry especially when he felt responsible, in some measure, for the resurgence of interest in the Reformers and their works.[4]

However, to write Lloyd-Jones off as affirming that unction is all that is vital to preaching is absurd for, as we have seen, he says a great deal more than this. But he does repeatedly argue that the afflatus of the Spirit is the prime requisite. I reiterate that one cannot separate Lloyd-Jones's pneumatology from his homiletics. Without doubt, he was correct when he laid down the maxim 'there is one thing that gives a preacher authority, and that is that he be "filled with the Holy Spirit"'.[5] And the preacher must come before the Lord on every occasion he enters the pulpit in order to seek for this divine enabling.

If, toward the end of a successful preaching and church-planting ministry, the Apostle Paul still needed to ask his own converts, the Ephesians, to pray that he might be given power to open his mouth and boldly proclaim the Word of God, how much more do we need to remember that 'fire in the mouth' is linked to 'prayer on the knees'. And that, however successful a ministry may have been and however much experience a preacher may have, he still requires a fresh anointing each time he enters his pulpit.

DML-J teaches us that a man is never more vulnerable, never more exposed, never more lonely, and never more in need of the Lord's presence than when he preaches. He has every right to copy Moses' example when, in a slightly different context, the Hebrew leader displayed a reluctance to take on additional duties for the Israelite community without first obtaining from God a guarantee that the Lord would be with him (Exod. 33:12-17) for the assignment. Moses' serious approach to his responsibilities pleased the Lord. We are right to assume the same principles apply for the preaching ministry. An ever-deepening knowledge of God and sense of his presence are the preacher's priorities.

DML-J is surely also correct when he appeals to Paul's declaration—that he delivered to the Corinthians what he had first received from the Lord—as illustrating what should be the source and stimulus of preaching (1 Cor. 11:23). The transaction between the preacher and the congregation has, as a vital prelude, a prior exchange between the preacher and the Lord. This can come when he is in the study. It can also happen at the point of preaching as he delivers what he is receiving. Or, it can be a combination of both. Preaching and prophesying become so close that the one is subsumed into the other. A preacher who believes this and prayerfully looks forward to it can expect enhancement in his ministry.

CRISIS THEOLOGY

It is inaccurate to make a simplistic tie-in between Lloyd-Jones's theology of the Holy Spirit and modern day Pentecostalism. DML-J had great respect for some Pentecostal preachers and applauded their evangelistic concerns. But he did not rubber-stamp all that went under this banner. Nor can he be accused of being responsible for opening the floodgates to the various charismatic groups in the Church. Had he lived longer, doubtless he would have treated the Charismatic Movement in some of its more recent developments with the same degree of caution and concern shown to Pentecostalism. There would not have been a wholesale dismissal or embrace but an endeavour to assess what was of the Holy Spirit and what was purely psychological—the result of failing to interpret the Scriptures accurately.

Certainly he would have criticised the trend which confuses ultimate glory with immediate grace. There is to be a marvellous consummation for which nature groans and to which we should look forward. And though there may be divine in-breakings, and glimpses of what is yet to come, this should never cause the projections of the life of the disciple as painted by the Lord and his apostles to become blurred. Here we have no abiding city, no guarantees of prosperity, no absolute claims for a clean bill of health. Here we toil in 'this uncertain earthly life and pilgrimage'. Our task is to daily take up the Cross. Assuredly DML-J would have dispensed with extravagant claims while remaining open to reports of 'seasons of refreshing'.

It was Lloyd-Jones's purpose to demonstrate that a crisis theology of the Spirit which brings beneficial results for the preaching ministry is a position the roots of which go back well before the birth of modern movements, be they Holiness, Pentecostal, or Charismatic, to the Reformation and beyond. Accuse him of lending weight to charismatic extremes and you are also pointing a finger at other worthies who stand alongside and historically in front of him. To claim he represented the Puritans and Reformers totally is to assert too much. To deny that he has a lineage traceable back to Puritanism is to fly in the face of historical facts.

Moreover, such a crisis theology of the Spirit which he espoused can be defended from the New Testament particularly from the Acts of the Apostles. The formulation of this theology was crucial to Dr. Lloyd-Jones's pneumatology for he felt that to a large degree the experience it promises affects a man's ministry. It can grace it with a freedom and a flow which are the concomitants of unction, the products of the sacred anointing. Freedom and flow, however, are not to be identified necessarily with spontaneity. He had disagreeable things to say about cavalier approaches to preaching.

In his book, *Spiritual Depression*, he warns against a preacher dropping down on his knees beseeching the Lord for power. 'I think that may be quite wrong. It certainly is if it is the only thing the preacher does. The way to have power is to prepare your message carefully. Study the Word of God, think it out, analyse it, put it in order, do your utmost.'[6]

He endeavoured to strike a balance. If preparation forces the preacher into a straight-jacket from which he cannot break free, then it robs the ministry of the necessary pneumatic element. Surely this warning is admissible.

We have already conceded that one does not have wholeheartedly to embrace his pneumatology to benefit from DML-J's corrective about unction as the supreme necessity for preaching powerfully (though, I find his position biblically satisfying and historically justifiable).

As DML-J differed from and contradicted his predecessor Campbell Morgan,[7] so it is arguable that Evangelicals will never formulate a doctrine of the experience of the Spirit that all will embrace.

Few preachers, however, will deny the need to come before God for an empowering, like that experienced by Jonathan Edwards and D. L. Moody, which will have the effect of giving their ministry greater authority and influence. Whether such experiences are called crisis experiences, the fullness of the Spirit or the baptisms in the Spirit is not so important. To seek God for such is.

HOT COALS OR WARM ASHES?

Neither, as we have seen, does DML-J confuse this freedom with what we might call 'Welshness'. Many Welsh people seem to possess a natural eloquence. (Lloyd-Jones occasionally contrasted the Welsh temperament with the English, and the latter did not always fare too well!) The Welsh are more passionate and more demonstrative as a race. Their accent is melodious and pleasing to the ear. As DML-J's tapes illustrate, the sermons he preached varied in the pace at which he presented them. He increased or reduced his speed of preaching and modulated his voice with great effect. This was not theatrical. What conditioned him was the feeling he had for the truth that he was expressing, and this controlled the pace and the volume. Sometimes there were shouts, sometimes the pregnant pause, often the imploring, pleading tone, sometimes the solemn, fearful warning, and sometimes, it must be added, he engaged in a low monotone. This was usually at the beginning of the sermon before he 'took off'!

It is no accident that the Principality of Wales has produced some of the finest orators—politicians like David Lloyd-George, Aneurin Bevan, and George Thomas, as well as great preachers such as Daniel Rowland, Howell Harris, and Christmas Evans (the last rated by some to be more gifted than Charles Spurgeon).

However, it is not the talents of the orator, as in extempory fashion he woos his audience, which Lloyd-Jones envisages as he urges freedom in the pulpit. Far from it. He wants preachers to introduce their carefully prepared theme as they begin 'to open up the Word' (a choice expression of the Puritans). But, at all times, they should follow the impulse of the Spirit. *He* must have supreme control for he is there behind and within and around the preacher, stimulating the sermon, directing its communication, shaping the preaching, animating the speaker, and adjusting the flow of words. All this is indicative of the smile of God upon the preacher. True preaching *is* the transmission of a message from God. Surely DML-J is not asserting too much in claiming this as the ideal for which the preacher should crave.

Light is shed on the 'mechanics' of preaching by considering the fashion in which the Scriptures were given, for though Scripture is uniquely inspired, the preacher longs to be activated in a similar vein albeit at a much lesser level of inspiration.

The Apostle Peter informs us that 'prophecy never had its origin in the will of man, but men spoke from God as they were carried along by the Holy Spirit' (2 Pet. 1:21). The picture is of a ship with sails unfurled, driven by the power of the wind. Though Lloyd-Jones does not, as far as I know, employ the analogy, there is ample evidence to indicate that this illustrates his position. To be imprisoned by a prepared sermon form is unbiblical. The Apostles were not so fettered. If a preacher is over-committed to structure, he runs the danger of placing more reliance on his systems and presentation than on the immediacy of the Spirit and his prompting. Undue dependence on such form works both to the preacher's and to the congregation's disadvantage. Instead of the hot coals of prophetic preaching, both are left with the barely warm ashes of priestly ministry which is sad for the preacher and bad for the congregation.

PREACHING AND 'THE AFFECTIONS'

It is no secret that Jonathan Edwards influenced Lloyd-Jones, for DML-J regularly confesses this. It is also well known that Edwards, in a worthy endeavour to assess the movement of the Spirit at a time in America known as the Great Awakening, analysed and interpreted its several facets. His scholarly and biblically based research is classic. His method was that of the spiritual diagnostician: shades of what was to come in Lloyd-Jones's approach. Edwards's investigation of the phenomena inspired one of his greatest works[8]. He used the term 'affections' as a synonym for the emotions.

I have on several occasions referred to DML-J's concern that modern preaching runs the danger of being cerebral, issuing from the head rather than the heart. He gave repeated warnings, for he believed biblical preaching should have both as its human source. Thus, any work purporting to be on Lloyd-Jones's preaching method would remain incomplete without enquiring into the religious affections and the preacher. We can conveniently narrow our enquiry to a consideration of two items. Dr. Lloyd-Jones considered passion and pathos to be essential components in ministry.

It must be evident by now, even to those who never heard him, that there was a great deal of passion in his preaching. Such, he believed, must issue from within the preacher at the point of delivering his burden. Moreover, this ought to occur naturally and not result from planning. Passion occurs because the preacher can scarcely contain himself. He is consumed by his subject. When the volcano erupts, the smoke belches out and lava flows. Thus it is with preaching: when the fire burns the effects are manifest.

DML-J lamented that often in our pulpits are men who do not capture the burden of his ministry in the same way as their forebears. He cited the case of his hero, George Whitefield, who 'it seems, almost invariably as he was preaching would have tears streaming down his face'. Lloyd-Jones continued:

> I feel we are all under condemnation here and need to be rebuked. I confess freely that I need to be rebuked myself . . . Why are not modern preachers moved and carried away as the great preachers of the past so often were? The Truth has not changed. Do we believe it? Have we been gripped and humbled by it, and then exalted until we are 'lost in wonder, love and praise'?[9]

A passionless pulpit leads to a lethargic laity. DML-J felt it to be terrible that the Church should 'merely consist of a collection of very nice and respectable people who have no concern for the world, people who pass it by, drawing their skirts in their horror at the bestiality, and the foulness, and the ugliness of it all'.[10]

Generally fire and fervour within the church spread out from the
pulpit. But the occupant must be discriminating for 'there is nothing of
which a preacher needs to be more sure than that the zeal and fervency
in his preaching is not produced by his natural temperament or his sermon, but by real belief in Christ'.[11]

Artificiality is to be shunned. Lloyd-Jones was quite contemptuous
of what he called the 'professional preacher' who was out to make an
impact. Speaking from the sixth chapter of Ephesians which describes
the Christian as a soldier, he makes a forceful contrast, 'There is nothing that I know of that is so utterly opposed to what the Apostle is teaching here as the professional preacher, the man who adopts a manner and
a voice, the so-called parsonic voice, and all the other characteristics of
"the cloth".' The professional in a pulpit is a great curse. He is a man
who is really fighting for the enemy. He is a quisling in the army of the
living God!'[12]

Linked to passion is pathos. Both are to do with feelings. Pathos too
is well illustrated in George Whitefield's preaching. DML-J is harsh on
himself when he said of pathos that this was 'the one thing more than
any other . . . lacking in my own ministry'.[13]

Pathos like passion is not basically stimulated by intellectual appre-
hension, though that plays a part. It stems from a felt realisation of the
dilemma of men, a great desire for their salvation and equally a love for
the Lord. Man should fear the 'terror of the Lord' and so should the
preacher. Equally the preacher should be constrained by 'the love of
Christ'. Bunyan speaks well for every pulpit occupant who, having dis-
charged his message with both passion and pathos, reminisces without
apology, 'I did preach what I did feel, what I did smartingly feel'. This
summarises Lloyd-Jones's conviction and practice.

As we have seen, he believed that the 'heresy of Sandemanism'[14] was
a reason why the pulpit sometimes was lacking in emotion. He cited the
experience of his earlier compatriot, Christmas Evans,[15] who for some
five years embraced Sandeman's teaching and lost his fire as a result. He
was 'weary, weary of a cold heart toward Christ and His sacrifice and
the work of His Spirit'. But Evans gave himself to a period of earnest
prayer and recalled 'on a day ever to be remembered . . . and having
begun in the Name of Jesus I soon felt as it were the fetters loosening
and the old hardness of heart softening, and, as I thought, mountains of
frost and snow melting within me'. He went on to intercede for three
hours for the churches in Anglesey under his charge. His testimony was,
'From that time I was made to expect the goodness of God to the

churches and to myself. Thus the Lord delivered me, and the people of Anglesey, from being carried away by the flood of Sandemanism.'[16]

Readers will remember earlier references to Lloyd-Jones's description of the Apostle Paul that 'he let himself go'. For preachers not to risk that is to run the opposite danger of curbing all affections, stifling freedom, stopping the flow, and thus quenching the Spirit. The priestly remains but the prophetic never bursts into life, with the consequence that no sacred anointing is detectable.

Though modern preachers may know little of Robert Sandeman or, alas, Christmas Evans, they would do well to wait before the Lord as the Welshman did and ask for a rekindling of any fires which have burnt low or for a greater Pentecostal ignition to bring passion and pathos into their ministries.

SIMPLY PREACHING?

It is perhaps appropriate under this heading also to take a side-step and make some comment on Dr. Lloyd-Jones's practice in respect of children and church services. No provision was made at Westminster Chapel in his time for activities within or parallel to the main service. No part was designated for boys and girls. The 'Family Service' concept did not feature. There was a Sunday school, but this was small compared with the size of the congregation and it met in the afternoon. Children who remained in the sanctuary were expected to be well behaved.

Westminster Chapel had a large preponderance of students and professional people—much more than the average congregation. The issue of children was probably not a big one. Although there is some housing half a mile or so away from Westminster Chapel, the building is flanked by office blocks, hotels, and apartments for business people.

A delightful (but possibly apocryphal) story is told of two stewards who were graced with the names of Gilbert and Sullivan. They considered it to be their responsibility to keep errant youngsters in check. One day, Lloyd-Jones was confronted by an annoyed teenager who told him that the one thing wrong with Westminster Chapel was that there was too much of Gilbert and Sullivan about it! Alas, the sequel has been lost. Whatever the truth, the fact is that children were expected to be quiet and, it was hoped, copy the astonishing example of a twelve-year-old girl.

The young lady was a devoted listener of DML-J. He referred to her once when arguing that those who concentrated on what he was endeavouring to say would be able to follow him. He had been unwell, necessitating the invitation of a number of supply speakers to the pulpit. Consequent, on Dr. Lloyd-Jones's return, he was delighted to receive a note from his young friend acknowledging how pleased she and her brother were to have their regular minister back in the pulpit as he was the only one that they could follow! Understandably, DML-J said the letter was one that he treasured. Would to God we had more twelve-year-olds of this calibre in our congregations!

Lloyd-Jones once told me, with great joy, of a meeting he addressed at the Free Trade Hall in Manchester. This was at a time when Edwardian clothes had made a come-back among some sections of Britain's young people with the emergence of the so-called Teddy Boy. A group of these formed part of his congregation. At the end of the meeting, they went to DML-J and told him they had appreciated what he had to say because they could follow him as opposed to other preachers.[17]

Several times, Dr. Lloyd-Jones asserted that preachers should be uncomplicated.[18] He referred to Martin Luther who, on one occasion, reviewed his own approach to preaching by admitting:

> I regard neither doctors nor magistrates, of whom I have above forty in the congregation. I have all my eyes on the servant maids and the children. And if the learned men are not well pleased with what they hear, well the door is always open.[19]

Lloyd-Jones significantly adds, 'that surely is the right attitude'. In other words, he agreed with Luther in defining that a minister's goal should be rudimentary preaching coupled with a conscious striving to avoid all unnecessary embellishments. DML-J further stated that it was generally true in any profession or calling that the real expert or genius reduces complexity to simplicity:

> Think of the difference between a great teacher and a pupil, or a great professional and an amateur in any sport, or in music. This is seen supremely, of course, in the preaching of our blessed Lord and Saviour. Though He handled such profundities, His essential pattern was always a very simple one. How often has this been forgotten in life and in the Christian church herself![20]

The woman who did not expect to understand a celebrated preacher rightly earned DML-J's censure.[21]

Perhaps the name of Lloyd-Jones does not naturally spring to mind when thinking of simple preaching. But the fact remains that he was sought out by some who were biblically illiterate and who grew in knowledge under his ministry. Increasing book sales are further evidence of his popularity as a teacher. Moreover, the average preacher does not hold all his congregation all the time. But there are moments—periods—when the ministry is more direct, easier to grasp, and heightened by the power of the Spirit. Children often take in more than is generally credited to them, especially when an atmosphere becomes 'electric' and there is a felt sense of the presence of God.

THE ROLE MODEL?

Macleod, who rates Lloyd-Jones as one of the outstanding preachers of all times, warns:

> There is a tendency in some quarters to regard the Doctor's method of preaching as the only valid one. Bound to the idea that to be an expository preacher can only mean engaging in a microscopic analysis of the Pauline epistles, many a young man has begun his ministry with Ephesians 1 verse 1 and lost most of his congregation by the time he got to verse 14.[22]

This book would not have been attempted were it not for my belief that Lloyd-Jones's preaching method, with qualifications and modifications, is an invaluable model for preachers. We defer to Macleod's view, however, and state our main reasons.

There must be other approaches to preaching even on the sole basis that DML-J's expository style cannot be transferred to preaching through parts of the Old Testament. Applying Dr. Lloyd-Jones's method to, say, the prophecies of Isaiah and Ezekiel, would take a life-time for complete exposition!

DML-J could handle texts in a detailed way superbly. But, as we had occasion to note, this could lead him into delivering what, in effect, were topical addresses where the text served more as a convenient launching pad to cover subjects 'writ large' in the whole sweep of biblical teaching rather than in the immediate context.

This is not to suggest that this method is invalid; some of the most helpful and relevant messages Dr. Lloyd-Jones preached are published in his book, *Christian Warfare*—exceptional for quality and originality of thought by any standards, but hardly an example of expository preaching in the classical sense.

One of his predecessors' method of preaching should not be too quickly dismissed. Again, we refer to Campbell Morgan. He did not build up his international reputation without a substantial gifting. Systematic theology apart, it is interesting that Morgan and Lloyd-Jones impressed one another and worked in tandem for some while. DML-J regarded Morgan as the most intelligent man he had ever met. Morgan preached from a large biblical canvas. His aim was to give an overall sweep of a book. Sometimes he took a study on one book at a time. Often the result was superb. Read, for example, his perceptive sermon from the beautiful, short book of Ruth[23] or consider his messages from the prophecy of Hosea.[24]

As far as I am aware, Lloyd-Jones never attempted the 'broad sweep', on a regular basis. In a sense, it was a great pity for had he brought his gifts to this wider approach to exposition, the results would have been impressive.

To present a bird's eye view of a book within the compass of a sermon can be of great value to a congregation. Lloyd-Jones agreed with this. A series of addresses on consecutive books can assist the hearers to get into perspective the total message of the Bible. The unfortunate man who endeavoured to preach on the whole of Romans in one evening when Dr. Lloyd-Jones was present might possibly have given a broad outline of its contents, notwithstanding the alliteration and over-simplification. Maybe he would have claimed that this actually was his aim rather than a futile attempt at the impossible—an exposition of Romans in one night. Had one of this preacher's congregation found himself the following Friday in Westminster Chapel, he would have benefited from a first-rate study of a small portion of Paul's letter, but unless he had been present at one of the infrequent occasions when Dr. Lloyd-Jones himself attempted an overview, he would have gone away with but a fragment of understanding of the actual contents of the epistle.

Our conclusion is that DML-J's method is a valid one, right for him and for what the Lord was doing through him in London during nearly three decades and in certain circumstances right for us. But there are other approaches, as he would be the first to concede. Also, as he reminds us, a preacher needs always to be familiar with the abilities and the needs of the constituency that he is serving and direct his preaching to that constituency.

SINGLE TEXTS?

This logically leads us to reflect on whether preaching should be on sole texts. Lloyd-Jones raised and answered the question. He was thinking in terms of random texts which do not belong to a series, 'You take a particular verse or paragraph here and another there, so that there is no sequence or connection between the sermons from Sunday to Sunday.' In his mind was the approach of Charles Spurgeon who strongly advised against the style which Lloyd-Jones eventually adopted.

DML-J regarded Spurgeon as possibly the greatest preacher in the nineteenth century but remarked, 'he (Spurgeon) did not believe in preaching a series of sermons; indeed he opposed doing so very strongly. He said that there was a sense in which it is impertinent for a man to decide to preach a series of sermons.' Lloyd-Jones revealing adds, 'I myself was brought up in that tradition. We never heard a series of sermons based on a book, or part of a book of the Bible or a theme.'

What caused DML-J to differ and adopt a method which contrasted with that to which he was accustomed? He does not tell us, but we are probably right in assuming it was again the influence exerted on him across the centuries via Jonathan Edwards whose method resembled the Puritans. Thus, DML-J's preaching style was closer to them that was that of Spurgeon.

It should be remembered that though series of sermons charac-terised Lloyd-Jones's preaching career, he was not so committed that he would never consider another approach. We have noticed that he broke away from his Ephesians' discourses, putting them aside for the best part of a year in order to preach his addresses on Revival. Mention, too, has been made of his widely circulated book *Spiritual Depression*. All stu-dents of DML-J's ministry should absorb its contents and study the homiletical structure of the messages.

The sermons stem from a range of texts and incidents in the Bible. They are expounded in such a fashion that the link is obviously the sub-ject rather than sequential verses. The topics covered deal with spiritual struggles, testings, and hardship. The paper-back book was well received. Later in its publishing life, the book was recommended on one occasion by George Verwer on board MV *Doulos* when Operation Mobilization's ship was in the Port of London. DML-J was to preach to an audience which was packed in from stern to bow. Some eight hun-dred (mainly) young men were present. At the sight of them, DML-J was in high spirits and narrated something of the story behind the book after he had courteously thanked Verwer for his personal and warm introduction.[25]

Dr. Lloyd-Jones proceeded to give the background to *Spiritual Depression*, relating how, years before, impressions had been placed on his mind of certain seemingly random subjects which he then jotted down. These were to become the basis of a preaching agenda. He told the story again in *Preaching and Preachers*:

> . . . one morning while dressing, quite suddenly and in an over-whelming manner, it seemed to me that the Spirit of God was urging me to preach a series of sermons on 'spiritual depression'. Quite literally while I was dressing, the series took order in my mind, and all I had to do was rush as quickly as possible to put down on paper the various texts, and the order in which they had come to me, in that way. I had never thought about preaching a series of sermons on spiritual depression; it had never occurred to me to do so; but it came just like that.[26]

He went on to assert, 'I am quite confident that the preaching of that series of sermons was dictated to me by the Spirit Himself.'

There are times when a whole series of sermons should be devoted to giving the sweep of biblical revelation—themes, doctrines, should and can be helpfully taken. There are occasions when a particular verse will strike the preacher during the course of his own devotions and studies. It seems to glow and an urge to preach on it grows. Care should be taken; this could well be the Holy Spirit impressing upon the mind what is to be the fare for his charge the next time the pulpit is entered or on some occasion in the near future.

A MODEL FOR THIRD WORLD PREACHERS?

As I have observed in introducing this chapter, the Church is burgeoning in Asia and Africa and South America more than in so-called First World countries. If Lloyd-Jones's ministry is a gift of God to the Church as a whole, it is reasonable to assume that his style of preaching has value for Third World pastors.

Lloyd-Jones's journeys though intensive within Britain and embracing the United States and Canada (as recorded in the biographies), did not take him into the Third World. Even his trip to South Africa found him basically addressing European ministers and churches. Though he travelled thousands of miles, he did not have experience of preaching anywhere but in Western societies. This was unfortunate for it deprived him of first-hand experience of what life is like for tens of thousands of pastors and church leaders who minister in environments where the Church is not so established and access to books and colleges not so easy, if at all possible. Doubtless, in the light of exposure Dr. Lloyd-Jones would have modified his radical views on, for example, lay preaching. Many pastors have to be employed in other work as there is no way in which they could be supported by their congregation.

In the expanding church of (say) Zaïre, without itinerant preachers, local congregations would not be supplied. I recall one pastor in that country pleading with me for help as he could not cope with the demands of *eighty* churches over which he had oversight. His library consisted of one well-thumbed Bible, and a couple of light-weight books carefully standing on an up-turned orange box which served as a desk in his mud hut. He is typical of many church leaders.

Had Dr. Lloyd-Jones been able to visit China—virtually an impossibility from 1950 to the end of his ministry—he would have discovered an extraordinary situation which, again, might have caused him to make some modification of his views of ministry which he basically formulated in and applied to a Western society. What would he have made of reports of thirteen-year-old girls, in some areas, teaching congregations!

Expository verse-by-verse ministry is difficult when perhaps only one member of a congregation, numbered in hundreds, actually has the Bible. Similar problems loom in Bangladesh, India, and Pakistan. Sometimes congregations are hardly literate. Often the Scriptures are only partially available, if at all, in the language or dialect of the people. Here the notion of opening and deliberately turning the pages of a large, pulpit Bible and preaching in an almost controlled noise-free atmosphere is impossible.

Nonetheless, the fact remains that there is a desperate need for the style of ministry represented by Dr. Lloyd-Jones. He is quite right when he declares that all ministry, including Gospel addresses, should be expository. Many Third World pastors require training in the rudiments of expository ministry. They must be weaned away from the story-telling, anecdotal approach to preaching where a series of incidents are hung around a text and little attention is paid to the context. For thousands of preachers and congregations, this is the general fare Sunday by Sunday.[27]

My experience is that narrative preaching is by far the best method to adopt in many countries where access to Bible or reading ability is limited. A Bible incident can 'live' in the minds of the congregation. But sermons based on narrative can, as Lloyd-Jones demonstrates,[28] be truly expositional. In preaching thus, the preacher should be asking why this incident was recorded in the Bible. What is its purpose? What truths are concealed within it? What are the best ways in which to lift these teachings out of the passage and apply them to the culture in which he is ministering? DML-J did this effectively; his ministry from narratives being among the most powerful of his sermons.

This chapter was written in the aftermath of an experiment when some thirty or so potential young preachers, the majority of whom did not have English as a first language, were invited to several consecutive seminars on the preaching method of Lloyd-Jones. This happened aboard MV *Doulos*, May 1993 , when she was berthed in Capetown. Some knew of his ministry, but hardly any had ever heard him preach. Part of the course involved listening to one of his sermons randomly selected. It is interesting to note their critique.

They found it to be (i) totally lacking in humour, (ii) sparsely studded with illustration, (iii) saturated in Scripture references, (iv) increasingly gripping and (v) it left them with a sense of the greatness of God, a desire to hear more preaching like this, and to cultivate such a style for themselves.

The case is especially interesting as it is indicative of a general desire in the mushrooming churches of Asia and Africa for preaching that is thoroughly biblical. The vast majority of Church leaders and mission workers in Third World countries declare that their churches desperately need simple, practical, expository preaching.

BUT GOD!

Not only is this heading the title of one of Lloyd-Jones's most famous and frequently preached sermons,[29] it also prompts the preacher to realise that, despite his weakness, when God is at work in his sermon, powerful results will follow. It further serves to remind him that at the end of all worthy preaching, the congregation is left with a concept of the greatness of God, who alone can cure their sin and bring sanity to this confused world.

The preacher's goal—remember our illustration from the ministries of Samuel Rutherford and our quotations from A. W. Tozer—is to leave the congregation with a sense of God. Theophany should feature more prominently, if not in the vocabulary of the preacher, certainly as the hope in his heart as he preaches.

It was this desire, coupled with his pneumatology and his convictions about unction, which rightfully earned Dr. Lloyd-Jones a place as one of the greatest preachers of this century.

In an earlier chapter, I referred to Robert Murray McCheyne because of the impact the Scottish preacher made on DML-J. In a lecture given in 1961 at the Puritan Conference, he again referred to him, asserting that there was a 'radiance about him'. There was also a presence about DML-J, especially when he came into the pulpit, to which hundreds testified. His bearing and dignity gave the impression of a man who, to quote a favourite hymn, had taken time to be holy. Richard Baxter advised ministers:

> In the name of God, brethren, labour to awaken your own hearts, before you go to the pulpit that you may be fit to awaken the hearts of sinners ... O, brethren, watch therefore over your own hearts; keep out lusts and passions, and worldly inclinations; keep up the life of faith and love, and zeal; be much at home, and much with God ... a minister must take some special pains with his heart, before he is to go to the congregation: if it be then cold, how is he likely to warm the hearts of his hearers? Therefore, go then specially to God for life.[30]

The preacher who has 'gone to God for life' will often give evidence of this long before the sermon in his demeanour and in his pulpit praying. In addition to our earlier references to DML-J's manner of intercession and to regular phraseology, we cite part of the prayer which he spontaneously offered in one of his Puritan lectures:

> O Lord our God, we come into thy holy presence and we come O Lord to worship Thee; we come to praise Thy name. Great God of wonders, all thy ways are Godlike, matchless and divine ... O Lord, we come in the Name of Thy dear Son. We recognise that we have nothing else to plead, we have nothing which we can present before Thee. We are all, by nature, the children of wrath, even as others and we have sinned against Thee deliberately and spurned the Voice Divine so often, followed our own wills, been proud of ourselves, of what we are, not even recognizing that what we are is the result of Thy gracious gifts to us.
>
> O God, we see how poor, sinful and vile we have become as a result of man's original disobedience and sin and fall, and our own misdeeds and transgressions. So we come and we plead only the Name and the blood of Thy dear Son, and we do thank Thee that in Him we know that we have this access. Lord, make us all sure of it. Forgive us if we ever come into Thy presence in His Name yet uncertainly. Grant us all the full assurance of faith that we may know our acceptance, that we may rejoice in Thy presence and praise Thy Name.
>
> We thank Thee together for the energies of thy blessed Spirit. We

thank Thee that He does work within us both to will and to do of Thy good pleasure ... We thank Thee that He brings us back to Thee, that suddenly He visits us and causes us to read Thy Word and to turn unto thee in prayer. O Lord, we have never seen and known so clearly that, were not this salvation Thine from beginning to end, we would still be undone.

We know it is Thy work and that Thou art continuing it within us, and we humbly thank Thee for His disturbing us, for His convictions, for His drawings, for all His movements with us. O God, we thank Thee for this and our prayer is that we may know this in a greater, a mightier manner. O Lord enable us to pray in the Spirit ...

Revive Thy work, O Lord, in the midst of these evil days. Hear us in our prayer, and lead us on now by Thy Spirit that we may pray truly unto Thee. We ask it in Christ Jesus' Name. Amen.[31]

The prayer reads well but one had to hear the intonation—the groans and the urgency which were part of it to appreciate fully the sense of the greatness of God and the unworthiness of men which were fundamental to Lloyd-Jones's convictions and made such an impact on the congregation.

THE LAST OF THE PURITANS?

J. I. Packer does a fascinating diagnosis of Puritan preaching.[32] He presents it in cause and effect style showing what Puritan preachers believed and the consequence this had upon their ministry.

He claimed the Puritans clung to (i) the primacy of the intellect, (ii) the supreme importance of preaching, (iii) the life-giving power of the Holy Scriptures, and (iv) the sovereignty of the Holy Spirit.

If the above are considered to be the cause, several consequences follow: such preaching was (i) expository in method, (ii) doctrinal in content, (iii) orderly in arrangement, (iv) popular in style, (v) Christ-centred in orientation, (vi) experimental in interests, (vii) piercing in application, and (viii) powerful in manner.

It should be apparent from what has preceded in this book that, had we not disclosed that Packer was analysing the Puritans, it might reasonably have been construed that he was dissecting Lloyd-Jones's ministry!

Dominant in DML-J's sermons is an appeal to reason.[33] Equally obvious is the fashion in which propositions are justified by a relentless appeal to the Scriptures which he recognises as supremely authoritative.

It may seem unnecessary to state that he believed in preaching. Though this was his conviction, readers may be surprised to hear a concession which he made after forty years in the ministry. He stated that he did not understand preaching. It puzzled him—'. . . I do not think I am any nearer a solution than I was at the beginning'![34]

What he meant was that preaching has a mysterious element in it. He returns to express a cherished notion which sprang from personal experience: 'A man is sometimes lifted out of himself in the act of preaching. It is as though he is taken over. He is in the realm of the Spirit. He is being inspired; he has an authority which convicts and convinces people . . .' This is the drum-beat of Puritanism with its conviction in the supremacy and wonder of preaching.

DML-J was so close to them it may seem reasonable to call him the last of their stock. Whether or not this will prove to be accurate remains to be seen. Puritan preaching is desperately needed as we approach the twenty-first century.

Moreover, we should always hesitate to dub anyone with the title 'the last of . . .' How, in this case, can we tell who was or will be the last of the Puritans? Their preaching has had a bad press recently.[35] But the Church desperately needs men of the stock of Lloyd-Jones, experimental Calvinists equipped with a theology and borne along by the Spirit which enables them to proclaim the glorious Gospel of the blessed God.

How can a man know that he can so minister? What qualifications must he have? What sort of man must he be? In our attempt to study Martyn Lloyd-Jones, his teaching on the sacred annointing, and his approach to homiletics, it is right to let him have the last word.

These are the things that make the preacher. If he has the love of God in his heart, and if he has a love for God; if he has a love for the souls of men, and a concern about them; if he knows the truth of the Scriptures; and has the Spirit of God within him, that man will preach.[36]

APPENDIX

I have taken the liberty of frequently referring to Dr. Lloyd-Jones by his initials DML-J. He invariably preached from the Authorised Version of the Bible. Scripture references in the general text of this book, however, are mainly from the New International Version.

Dr. Lloyd-Jones's volumes on Romans and Ephesians are numbered in succession but do not necessarily relate to chapter number. His sermons on Romans 8, for instance, are actually spread over volumes 6, 7, and 8. To help my readers: in quoting any of the books on these Epistles, I have added the volume number in brackets thus:

EPISTLE TO THE ROMANS

(R1) *The Gospel of God*: Chapter 1 (1985)
(R2) *The Righteous Judgment of God*: Chapters 2:1-3:20 (1989)
(R3) *Atonement and Justification*: Chapters 3:20-4:25 (1970)
(R4) *Assurance*: Chapter 5 (1971)
(R5) *The New Man*: Chapter 6 (1972)
(R6) *The Law: Its Function and Limits*: Chapters 7:1-8:4 (1973)
(R7) *The Sons of God*: Chapter 8:5-17
(R8) *The Final Perseverance of the Saints*: Chapter 8:17-39
(R9) *God's Sovereign Purpose*: Chapter 9 (1970).
(Published by Banner of Truth Trust, Edinburgh, and Zondervan, US).

EPISTLE TO THE EPHESIANS

(E1) *God's Ultimate Purpose*: Chapter 1 (1978)
(E2) *God's Way of Reconciliation*: Chapter 2 (1972)
(E3) *Unsearchable Riches of Christ*: Chapter 3 (1979)

(E4) *Christian Unity*: Chapter 4:1-16 (1980)

(E5) *Darkness and Light*: Chapters 4:17-5:17 (1982)

(E6) *Life in the Spirit in Marriage, Home and Work*: Chapters 5:18-6:9 (abbr. *Life in the Spirit*) (1974)

(E7) *Christian Warfare*: Chapter 6:10-13 (1976)

(E8) *The Christian Soldier*: Chapter 6:10-20 (1977).

(E6)(Banner of Truth and Zondervan).

OTHER MAIN VOLUMES FROM WHICH REFERENCES
HAVE BEEN EXTRACTED

Authority (Inter-Varsity Press, Leicester, 1958)

The Doctor Himself and the Human Condition (CMF, 1982)

Evangelistic Sermons at Aberavon (Banner of Truth, (1983)

Expository Sermons on 2 Peter (Banner of Truth, 1983)

Faith on Trial (Inter-Varsity Fellowship, 1965; Eerdmans, US)

The Heart of the Gospel (Crossway Books, Eastbourne, 1991)

Healing and the Scriptures (Oliver Nelson, 1987), the US title of *Healing and Medicine* (Kingsway, Eastbourne, 1987)

I Am Not Ashamed: *Advice to Timothy* (Hodder & Stoughton, London; Baker Book House, US, 1986)

Knowing the Times (Banner of Truth, 1989)

The Life of Joy (Hodder & Stoughton, 1989)

The Plight of Man and the Power of God (Hodder & Stoughton, 1942)

Preaching and Preachers (Hodder & Stoughton, 1971; Zondervan, 1972)

Prove All Things (Kingsway, 1985; Harold Shaw, US, 1985)

The Puritans: *Their Origins and Successors* (Banner of Truth, 1987)

Revival (Crossway Books, 1987)

Sanctified through the Truth (Crossway Books, 1989)

Studies in the Sermon on the Mount, 2 vols (Inter-Varsity Fellowship, 1960; William B. Eerdmans Publishing Co, US, 1959, 1960)

Spiritual Depression: *Its Causes and Cure* (Pickering & Inglis, 1965; Eerdmans, 1965)

Truth Unchanged, Unchanging (Crossway Books, 1993)

Why Does God Allow Suffering? (Crossway Books, 1994)

The two biographies by Iain H. Murray on which I have drawn are:

Martyn Lloyd-Jones: *The First Forty Years 1899-1939*, and

Martyn Lloyd-Jones: *The Fight of Faith 1939-1981*.

Both are published by Banner of Truth, and the latter contains a full list of Dr. Lloyd-Jones's publications.

DETAILS OF THE TAPE MINISTRY

Tape catalogues of the sermons of Dr. Martyn Lloyd-Jones are available from:

England
 The Martyn Lloyd-Jones Recording Trust, 25 High Street, Ashford Kent TN24 8TH
Australia
 Koorong Books Pty Ltd, 17-19 Ryedale Road, West Ryde, NSW 2114
United States of America
 Sound Word Associates, PO Box 2035, Mall Station, Michigan City, Indiana 46360
Singapore
 Martyn Lloyd-Jones Tapes, 413 Tagor Avenue, Singapore 2678.

NOTES

These are numbered and are placed at the end. To facilitate tracking down a note they have been grouped into chapters. Some notes are lengthy; I resisted editing them down feeling they might be of particular interest to preachers. Nor could I resist including several anecdotes which, though not germane to the main thesis, add colour and, hopefully, a little relief to the text!

THE 'PILGRIMAGE' OF DR. MARTYN LLOYD-JONES

1899 Born December 20 in Cardiff, Wales
1921 Graduated as a medical doctor
1925 Member of the Royal College of Physicians
1926 Determines to be a Minister of the Gospel
1927 Marries Dr. Bethan Phillips
1927 Ordained to the ministry
1927 Commences his pastorate at 'Sandfields', Bethlehem
1927 Presbyterian Church, Aberavon
1939 Joins Dr. Campbell Morgan as co-pastor at Westminster Chapel
1949 Passes through the 'Dark Night of the Soul' and subsequently experiences an outpouring of the Spirit
1959 Publishes *Revival* and *The Sermon on the Mount*
1966 Calls on evangelical Christians in the United Kingdom to leave doctrinally mixed denominations. (This address can be found in *Knowing the Times* pp. 246 ff.)
1968 Resigns the pastorate at Westminster

NOTES

TITLE PAGE

1. *Lectures to My Students*, in 3 vols (1st series, Passmore & Alabaster, 1881, Zondervan, 1980), p. 96; also quoted by Iain H. Murray, *The Fight of Faith*, p. 264.

INTRODUCTION

1. *Preaching and Preachers* (Hodder & Stoughton, London, 1971).
2. Arnold A. Dallimore, *George Whitefield, The Life and Times of the great evangelist of the 18th century revival*, (Banner of Truth, London, 1970).
3. *Preaching and Preachers*, p. 18.

CHAPTER ONE: *The Smile of God*

1. *Revival*, p. 295.
2. *Preaching and Preachers*, p. 99.
3. Ibid.
4. Iain Murray, *The Fight of Faith*, p. 130.
5. *Knowing the Times*, p. 263.
6. *The Puritans*, p. 45.
7. *New Dictionary of Theology* (IVP, 1988) eds S. B. Ferguson, D. F. Wright. Article 'Lloyd-Jones D. M.' by I. H. Murray. R. T. Kendall supplied the background: apparently Professor Brunner attended Westminster Chapel for a morning service. On its conclusion he introduced himself to Lloyd-Jones in his vestry and remarked that he had just listened to the finest sermon he had ever heard from a minister of the Reformed Faith (personal communication).
8. Lawrence O. Richards, *Expository Dictionary of Bible Words* (Zondervan, 1985).
9. Cf. Lev. 8:12 ; cf. Num. 6:8 (JB); cf. Ps. 133.
10. Ps. 105:15 , where anointing and the prophetic office are linked.
11. *Dictionary of New Testament Theology*, ed. Colin Brown (Paternoster Press, 1975) vol. 1, p. 119.
12. Op. cit., p. 55.

13. pp. 75 ff.
14. *Revival*, pp. 148-237 ; *Joy Unspeakable*, sermons by DML-J, ed. Christopher Catherwood (Kingsway Publications Eastbourne), p. 122.
15. Cf. pp. 22, 50.
16. *Revival*, p. 182.
17. For information on such a period in the life of Dr. Lloyd-Jones , cf. p. 46 and *The Fight of Faith*, pp. 207 ff.
18. *Joy Unspeakable*, p. 122.
19. *God's Ultimate Purpose* (E1), p. 395.
20. *Christian Unity* (E4), p. 172.
21. *Preaching and Preachers*, p. 106.
22. *Life in the Spirit* (E6), p. 172; *Christian Unity* (E4), p. 173 where DML-J informs us that his conviction of a definite call to the preaching ministry caused him to put on one side a strong letter from the secretary of a Missionary Society urging him to use his skills as a doctor in India where the Society had a great need.
23. *Christian Unity* (E4), p. 172.
24. *God's Way of Reconciliation* (E2), p. 459.
25. *Christian Unity* (E4), p. 172.
26. Ibid., p. 173 ff; for a further and longer statement of Lloyd-Jones's view on the call to the ministry, *Preaching and Preachers*, pp. 103-7.
27. *Christian Unity* (E4), p. 175.
28. *Preaching and Preachers*, pp. 197, 108; but note his comment with regard to his predecessor, G. Campbell Morgan, who was turned down by the Methodist Church when he applied for ordination, 'but that is the exception which proves the rule; and you do not legislate for exceptions and hard cases'.
29. *The Unsearchable Riches of Christ* (E3), pp. 55, 56.
30. *Christian Unity* (E4), p. 200.
31. Lloyd-Jones's mother did not consider him to be the most gifted of her sons in this area. 'Martyn, an orator! You should have heard our Mervyn!' Harold Lloyd-Jones, referred to always as Mervyn by his mother, was a parliamentary candidate for the Carmarthen constituency but caught a cold at an election meeting and died of pneumonia. DML-J's other brother, Vincent, was a former president of the Oxford University Union when C. S. Lewis was in residence. He entered the legal profession. A devastating barrister, he became a judge of the High Court and was knighted for his services. (Douglas Johnson—personal correspondence.)
32. Personal correspondence. DML-J makes reference in one of his sermons to the possibility of his having gone into politics. The context of his remark was the grace of God which had redeemed him and brought him into the ministry, a calling that he rated more highly than any other profession because of the eternal consequences of the message of salvation; *The God of Miracles* (Tape 2082), Acts 7:30-3. The sermon is a classic illustration of the way in which DML-J clung tenaciously to his argument, relentlessly building up his case and in the process of exposition mapping out the Old Testament narrative which is the basis of Stephen's address; cf., pp. 217 ff.
33. pp. 111 ff.
34. *Preaching and Preachers*, p. 98.
35. I credit this phrase to Professor Donald Macleod, a cessationist himself, who nonetheless argued most eloquently in the course of some memorable lectures delivered at Westminster Theological Seminary (California) in January 1990 that true preaching is essentially charismatic.
36. Cf. pp. 191-2.

37. *Knowing the Times*, pp. 276, 277.
38. *The Fight of Faith*, p. 338.
39. Ibid., p. 517.
40. Personal conversation with Edmund Clowney.
41. *The Fight of Faith*, p. 568 (letter to members, Westminster Chapel May 30th, 1968.)
42. *Chosen by God*, ed. Christopher Catherwood (Highland Books, Crowborough, 1986) p. 87.
43. pp. 73 ff.
44. pp. 50 f: cf. *Joy Unspeakable*, p. 122.
45. *The Gospel of God* (R1), p. 209.
46. J. Oswald Sanders, *Men from God's School* (Marshall, Morgan and Scott), p. 174.
47. Cf. his extended comment on both Goodwin and William Perkins, *The Puritans*, pp. 384, 385.
48. J. I. Packer, *A Quest for Godliness* (Crossway Books, 1990), p. 313.
49. *The Puritans*, pp. 101-28, 282-302.
50. Ibid., p. 122.
51. *Revival*, p. 306; cf. *The Puritans*, p. 126: 'we must seek the power of the Spirit which was given to George Whitefield. . .'
52. *The Puritans*, p. 124.
53. Ibid., p. 122.
54. Ibid., p. 125; it is interesting to compare the descriptions we have from Whitefield and Harris with Lloyd-Jones's own experience. He believed that in the very course of preaching a sense of authority comes. He argues the case in his sermon 'A Gospel of Power', (Tape 5628). One of the most remarkable examples of this afflatus befalling Lloyd-Jones occurs in another sermon in which he sets out to demonstrate that Paul's teaching constitutes divine revelation and is utterly authentic, 'The Authority of the Gospel', (2 Cor. 4:1-6) (Tape 5548).
55. Ibid., p. 294.
56. For further information on Harris's approach to preaching and his dependence on the Holy Spirit cf. Richard Bennett, *Howell Harris and the Dawn of Revival* (1909; repr. Evangelical Press of Wales, 1987). The introduction by Dr. Lloyd-Jones indicates the measure in which he was inspired by his fellow-Welshman.
57. *Authority*, p. 86.
58. *The Puritans*, p. 293.
59. Michael A. Eaton, *Baptism with the Spirit—The teaching of Martyn Lloyd-Jones* (IVP, 1989), p. 10.
60. Cf. p. 287; it must be added, however, as the reading of any volume in either the Romans' and Ephesians' series demonstrates, his sermons were almost without exception the same length unless this is a quirk of the editing procedure!
61. *The Gospel of God* (R1), p. 1.
62. *Preaching and Preachers*, p. 248.
63. *The Preacher and Preaching, Reviving the Art in the Twentieth Century*, ed. Samuel T. Logan Jr. (Presbyterian & Reformed, Phillipsburg, 1986), p. 125.
64. *The Puritans*, p. 121: comment on Whitefield and Lloyd-Jones's criticism of ministry devoid of feeling.
65. The story is told in *Authority*, p. 88 and retold in *A First Book of Daily Readings from the Works of Martyn Lloyd-Jones*, ed. Frank Cumbers (Epworth Press), p. 251. DML-J related a similar incident concerning John Livingstone of Scotland, *Joy Unspeakable*, p. 126.

CHAPTER TWO: *Background*

1. Cf. Christopher Catherwood, *Five Evangelical Leaders* (Hodder & Stoughton, London, 1984), p. 174.
2. Cf. D. Cartwright, *The Lives of Stephen and George Jeffreys* (Marshall Pickering, London, 1986); the Elim Church differs in its doctrinal statement from the rest of British Pentecostal Denominations. It does not assert that glossolalia (speaking in tongues) is the 'initial evidence' of the baptism in the Spirit.
3. Peter Hocken, *Streams of Renewal* (Paternoster Press, 1986), p. 87; cf. Dr. Hocken's additional comment on DML-J's reservations about the Charismatic Movement, p. 228, n. 43.
4. *Joy Unspeakable*, cf. introduction by Christopher Catherwood, p. 11.
5. Observe the unusually strong language he used to denounce the trend toward a cerebral, non-experiential evangelicalism which he perceived to have its origins in the 1850s, 'I know of no people who have such a responsibility at the bar of eternal judgement as the people from roughly 1850 until today . . .' ibid, p. 121.
6. Later published (cf. Introduction, p. xviii).
7. *Chosen by God*, p. 91.
8. In *Joy Unspeakable* he gives some account of twenty-six people who knew what he believed to be the sealing or Baptism of the Spirit. He refers, in passing, to as many again without giving so much detail.
9. *God's Ultimate Purpose* (E1), pp. 243-89.
10. Cf. p. 39.
11. *Joy Unspeakable*, p. 112.
12. Further reference to Tauler, *The Puritans*, p. 374.
13. *Joy Unspeakable*, p. 125.
14. Ibid., p. 25.
15. Ibid., pp. 106, 107.
16. Dr. Peter Masters wrote two critiques of Lloyd-Jones. The first he entitled, 'Opening the Doors to Charismatic Teaching (analysing the latter-day abandonment by Dr. Martyn Lloyd-Jones of orthodox Holy Spirit theology)' and the second, 'Why did Dr. Lloyd-Jones Yield to Quasi-Pentecostal Ideas?', *Sword and Trowel* (Metropolitan Tabernacle, London, 1988), No. 2. We subsequently refer to them as Masters (i) and (ii): this reference (ii), p. 32.
17. Banner of Truth edn, 1969 , pp. 108-9; *The Sons of God* (R7), p. 342.
18. Ibid., p. 342; for his understanding of Sibbes's distinction between conversion and the sealing, cf. *God's Ultimate Purpose* (E1), p. 284.
19. *The Works of Thomas Goodwin* (James Nichols, Edinburgh), vol. 1, pp. 233, 236, 237; *The Sons of God* (R7), p. 344.
20. *Great Biblical Doctrines*; *Baptism of the Holy Spirit* (Tape DML-J 28, No. 2.)
21. *The Works of Jonathan Edwards*, vol. 1, p. xvii; cf. pp. 299 ff.
22. Jonathan Edwards, *The Religious Affections* (1st pub., 1746; Banner of Truth edn, 1961).
23. Dr. Michael Eaton warns that a critic of Lloyd-Jones's could easily protest at some of the illustrations he gives of the Baptism with the Spirit. Jonathan Edwards's experience of the Son of God as mediator was never interpreted by Edwards as a Baptism of the Spirit and he explicitly denies the interpretation of Romans 8:16 taught by Lloyd-Jones. Eaton goes on to ask (and responds positively) whether such experiences should be so categorised. He claims that, unless they are, it leaves them to be explained as 'theologically *random* experiences' (his italics) corresponding to no particular pattern of interpretation and thus become 'interesting stories but there is no reason why anything like these experiences

should happen to anyone else' *Baptism with the Spirit—The Teaching of Martyn Lloyd-Jones* (IVP, Leicester, 1989), p. 238; cf. pp. 77 -80; cf. Eroll Hulse, ' . . . Dr. Martyn Lloyd-Jones, in his zeal for revival and his desire to preserve the doctrine of power for preachers, which is commendable, tended to put the label of Baptism of the Spirit on experiences which were really wonderful discoveries of the power, beauty and glory of God', *Crisis Experiences* (Carey Publications, Haywards Heath, 1984); cf. J. I. Packer on Lloyd-Jones's historical 'generalisations', *Chosen by God*, p. 39; also Packer's endorsement of Lloyd-Jones's claims that some of the Puritans' pneumatology, especially their interpretation of Romans 8 verse 16 and Ephesians 1 verse 13 (the sealing of the Spirit) was in accord with Lloyd-Jones's position, p. 54. Packer supplies the qualifying corrective to Masters's almost totally dismissive comment of DML-J's use of historical illustration, essay (ii).

24. *The Sons of God* (R7), pp. 321, 322. *Joy Unspeakable*, p. 63.
25. *What Baptism did you receive?* (Tape 1080).
26. *Metropolitan Tabernacle Pulpit*, vol. XXVIII (1882), pp. 310, 311; *The Sons of God* (R7), p. 396; cf. pp. 242, 243.
27. p. 63.
28. Tape 1080 , op. cit.
29. *Revival*, pp. 207, 208. He makes a similar statement in the early years of his London ministry, *Baptism of the Spirit* (Tape DML-J 2, No. 2).
30. *The Sons of God* (R7), p. 235.
31. Ibid., p. 356.
32. *Preaching and Preachers*, p. 101.
33. That a persons may be born again and have not received the Holy Ghost is perfectly certain according to the Scriptures. *Collected Writings of J. N. Darby* (Stow Hill Bible and Tract Depot, 1965), Doctrinal No. 9, vol. 31, p. 263 (reference supplied by me). But cf. J. Peters's qualification on Darby's shifting views in this area, *Martin Lloyd-Jones—Preacher* (The Paternoster Press, Exeter, 1986), pp. 145-7.
34. Mackintosh said, 'We consider Acts 19 verses 1-7 does most clearly show that persons may be disciples and believers and yet not be sealed with the Holy Ghost' in *Things Old and New*, vol. x, p. 198; *The Sons of God* (R7), p. 357.
35. *Joy Unspeakable*, pp. 45, 46.
36. *The Sons of God* (R7), p. 356.
37. Ibid., p. 338.
38. Eaton, op, cit., p. 119. Eaton considered that Lloyd-Jones went beyond all his theological forebears and likened what he calls DML-J's 'mysticism' to that of George Fox.
39. *The Fight of Faith*, p. 209.
40. Ibid., p. 220.
41. *The First Forty Years*, p. 99.
42. Conversation with Carl Henry, *Chosen by God*, Ch. 5, p. 96.
43. *The First Forty Years*, p. 101, (my italics). Decades later his grandson, Christopher Catherwood, edited DML-J's sermons from the opening chapter of John's Gospel. They were largely on the sealing of the Spirit. His choice of title, *Joy Unspeakable* (Kingsway, Eastbourne, 1984; Harold Shaw, Wheaton, Ill., 1985), would have won his grandfather's approval; cf. Richard Sibbes for a similar exposition, *Works of Richard Sibbes* (Banner of Truth, Edinburgh vol. 2, p. 440.
44. Ibid., p. 121.

45. Bethan Lloyd-Jones, *Memories of Sandfields 1927 -1938* (Banner of Truth Trust, Edinburgh, 1983).
46. *The First Forty Years*, pp. 203 ff.
47. Ibid., p. 146.
48. *Evangelistic Sermons* (Banner of Truth, 1983).
49. Personal conversation with DML-J.
50. Op. cit.
51. *The Heart of the Gospel*, (Crossway Books, 1991).
52. Ibid., p. 27.
53. *The Heart of the Gospel*, Introduction, p. 8
54. *Preaching and Preachers*, p. 58; DML-J refers to Whitefield's famous comment in response to an approach by a printer to publish his sermons. Lloyd-Jones clearly understands 'lightning and thunder' as referring to aspects of unction which 'come(s) into the act of preaching and cannot be conveyed by cold print. Indeed, it almost baffles the descriptive powers of the best reporters.'
55. In his highly pastoral book, *Faith on Trial*, p. 32, he speaks of his own experience. Lloyd-Jones was initially referring to the Psalmist's anguish of mind. Though unable to go forward, 'he knows enough to prevent him going down, but his problem is as acute as it was before'. DML-J challenges his hearers: 'Do you know that spiritual position? Have you ever been there?' And then significantly he confesses, ' *I have been there many a time.*' The phrase 'dark night of the soul' is actually traceable to St John of the Cross. It is the English title of a book he wrote, first published in Spanish.
56. *Preaching and Preachers*, p. 309.
57. Cf. *God's Ultimate Purpose* (E1), pp. 255, 256.

CHAPTER THREE: *Unction*

1. *Preaching and Preachers*, p. 325.
2. 'Obituary Martyn Lloyd-Jones', *The Monthly Record* (Free Church of Scotland, April 1981), p. 84.
3. Eaton, op. cit.
4. *Joy Unspeakable*, p. 120.
5. For a statement of Dr. Lloyd-Jones's position, cf. *Preaching and Preachers*, pp. 304-14; *Knowing the Times*, p. 275.
6. *Revival*, p. 114; *Joy Unspeakable*, p. 129.
7. *Spiritual Depression; Its Causes and Cure* (Pickering and Inglis, pp. 299, 300.
8. He used similar terminology to describe his understanding of the 'prayer of faith' (James 5:15) and to explain how the disciples were able to perform miracles. On each occasion the 'faith' is given; *The Doctor Himself and the Human Condition* (Christian Medical Fellowship, London, 1982), p. 88. The gift is not a permanent possession. So, with unction, when it occurs it is as a result of the dynamism of the Spirit working through the preaching ministry at any one point.
9. *Chosen by God*, p. 87.
10. Cf. p. 87.
11. *Preaching and Preachers*, pp. 115 ff.
12. *Knowing the Times*, p. 274.
13. *The Christian Soldier* (E8), p. 135.
14. *The Puritans*, p. 124.
15. DML-J may well be quoting James Thornwell, whose ministry had so impressed him. He believed him to be one of America's finest preachers. Dr. J. W. Alexander, in recalling Thornwell's ministry described one of his sermons, 'burning hot

argument, logic in ignition, and glowing more and more unto the end: it was *a memoriter* (from memory), and with a terrific *contentio laterum* (developing his argument by means of an antithesis)' quoted in Douglas Kelly *Preaching with Power: Four Stalwarts of the South*, Banner of Trust, Edinburgh, 1992), p. 73.

16. *Preaching and Preachers*, p. 88, where he gives a negative example of a preacher who was not ignited by his subject, and p. 97, for his positive statement.
17. Sanders, op. cit., p. 180.
18. *Preachers and Preaching*, p. 314.
19. Ibid, p. 43.
20. *Revival*, p. 124.
21. Ibid, p. 192.
22. *Preaching and Preachers*, p. 96.
23. Ibid. pp. 84 , 85.
24. Masters (ii).
25. Contrast *Authority*, p. 72; *Joy Unspeakable*, p. 48.
26. *God's Ultimate Purpose* (E1), p. 275 , also p. 279 where he states that terminology such as 'baptism' and 'sealing' is not the crucial thing, the experience is.
27. Ibid., pp. 246-9; cf. *Joy Unspeakable*, pp. 46-8.
28. *Joy Unspeakable*, p. 156; cf. B. F. Westcott, *St John*, introduction Adam Fox (James Clarke & Co, 1958), p. 100.
29. *Joy Unspeakable*, p. 48; *Sons of God* (R7), p. 326 for an extended treatment of his position.
30. *The Unsearchable Riches of Christ* (E3), p. 258.
31. Thomas Goodwin, *An Exposition of Ephesians*, (Sovereign Grace Book Club, 1958), p. 244.
32. *Goodwin's Works* (James Nichols, Edinburgh), vol. 16, p. 12.
33. *The Monthly Record*, (Free Church of Scotland, November 1981), p. 227.
34. *Joy Unspeakable*, pp. 47, 48 (my italics).
35. *Authority* p. 72; cf. 'Under the Power of the Spirit' Sermon on 2 Corinthians 4:1-7 (Tape 5553) where he repeats his argument that our Lord needed the empowering of the Spirit to enable him to commence his ministry but he does not apply this in his usual manner of pressing believers to seek for a further experience of the Spirit themselves.
36. Ibid., p. 74.
37. *Metropolitan Tabernacle Pulpit* (Banner of Truth Trust, Edinburgh, 1971), vol. 28, p. 304. Note Spurgeon's earlier comment in the same sermon—his text was John 7:8, 9—'Let us not be satisfied with the sip that saves, but let us *go on* to the baptism that buries the flesh and raises us in the likeness of the risen Lord; even that baptism into the Holy Ghost and into fire which set us all on flame with zeal for the glory of God. . .', p. 303 (my italics).
38. *Preaching and Preachers*, pp. 307, 308.
39. *What Baptism did you receive?* John 1:26 -33; (Tape 1080) should be heard for those wanting to hear Lloyd-Jones arguing his case. Though the address is from his lengthy series on John 1 it is actually based on the account of Apollos receiving ministry from Priscilla and Aquila (Acts 18: 24-6).
40. e.g. *Preaching and Preachers*, p. 314 'In any case how do you decide what was meant for them only, or what is for us also? On what grounds do you do that; what are your canons of judgment? I suggest that there is none save prejudice'.
41. *Christian Warfare* (E7), p. 274; quoted by Dr. John Stott, *The Message of Acts* (The Bible Speaks Today Series, IVP, 1990), p. 9.

42. *The Gospel of God* (R1), pp. 223, 224.
43. *Christian Unity* (E4), p. 71; cf. *Revival*, p. 50; *Joy Unspeakable*, p. 36.
44. Cf. his comment in *The Sons of God* (R7), p. 298, where he refers to the general experience of New Testament Christians, '(they) had a spiritual experience, and insight and understanding which distinguishes them in a very striking manner from the vast majority of Christians at this present time'.
45. *Revival*, p. 162.
46. Masters (i), p. 24.
47. Ibid., (ii), p. 34. 'In criticising what is referred to as DML-J's teaching on "a mystical baptism experience" as a cure-all policy for the ills of the church in general, and preachers in particular, the essay goes on, "that was the thesis which Dr. Lloyd-Jones presented as a sincere yet (I believe) panicked response to the lack of blessing which he perceived to be in the reformed churches".'
48. Ibid (i), pp. 26 , 27; also his comment that *Joy Unspeakable* and *Prove All Things* are 'major tragedies' which have done 'incalculable harm', the latter of which hits 'rock bottom' in its treatment of speaking in tongues.
49. *Christian Unity* (E4), p. 183 ff; (R1), p. 148; *Authority*, p. 59.
50. *Christian Unity* (E4), p 189: where he takes a cessationist line on prophets and prophecy. 'Surely it [the prophet's office] was temporary, and for this good reason, that in those early days of the Church there were no New Testament Scriptures. . . But once these New Testament documents were written the office of a prophet was no longer necessary.' He finds significance in the complete lack of reference to such an office in the later, pastoral epistles.
51. Ibid., p. 192.
52. *Spiritual Gifts* (i) sermon on Romans 12:6 (Tape 3312) for an extended comment and critique of modern attempts to help people to speak in tongues. He warns that this is often purely psychological and could run the danger of being satanic; cf. *The Spiritual Experience* sermon on John 4: 17-30 (Tape 1178) where he makes an observation he repeated on several occasions, that if a person could speak in tongues at will he doubted the authenticity of their experience.
53. Cf. p. 83.
54. Cf. pp. 80 ff.
55. *The Doctor Himself*, p. 88. (In conversation in the early 1970s he told me that he had never had personal evidence of a healing miracle. Most claims that he encountered were capable of other explanations.)
56. Masters (ii), p. 32. Lloyd-Jones is reckoned to have embraced what is curiously called a 'romantic notion' of preaching. But DML-J is in good company: the Westminster and Banner of Truth Conferences follow suit, p. 33.
57. *Christianity Today* (February 8th, 1980) vol. 24, No. 3, p. 16 (164). The editorial goes on, inaccurately, to state that Lloyd-Jones was in process of preparing his spiritual autobiography.
58. *The Fight of Faith*, pp. 706, 707. Murray records his reactions to accounts from two men who had been trained in James Kennedy's methods. I was present and recall the occasion well. A clear presentation was made of the procedure espoused by Evangelism Explosion. Emphasis was placed on Kennedy's Calvinistic presuppositions. With cutting conviction, DML-J criticised what he had heard. His biographer took notes. Lloyd-Jones asked for scriptural justification for such techniques, 'it is certainly not in Acts 8:4. . . we all agree that people are not acting as witnesses as they should but instead of asking, "Why are things as they are", we are being given a patent, cut-and-dried remedy which says we must train the people'. Murray also drew on DML-J's reminiscences from his Sandfields' days,

'I never trained a single convert how to approach others but they did so. . . if our people cannot explain the way of salvation to unconverted men we are deplorably bad preachers'. Possibly the heart of his convictions is exposed in the comment of a couple of young preachers who were told by Ebenezer Morris, 'if you two live long enough you will see a time when no one will come to the Society meeting. At such a time do not try to drag unconverted people into the church but wait on the Lord and seek him. . .'

59. The Rev. Herbert Carson resigned his position as an Anglican vicar, sharing Lloyd-Jones's views about the compromised position of the Anglican Church. He was for some time assistant to DML-J. Carson is a gifted, sought-after expositor. Some were of the opinion that he might well have been Lloyd-Jones's successor. He eventually accepted a call to the Knighton Evangelical Free Church, Leicester. He wrote *Farewell to Anglicanism* (Henry E. Walter, Worthing, 1969).

60. Masters (ii), p. 34. It is inaccurate to assert that Lloyd-Jones inherited a large congregation or to attribute its further growth to the famous name of Westminster Chapel and to reaffirm that 'he *began* with numbers on his side' (italics in original). Arguably, even more famous is the Metropolitan Tabernacle. The fame of a building does not guarantee a congregation, which rose and fluctuated between one and two thousand people over three decades.

CHAPTER FOUR: *'Suing God'*

1. Goodwin, ibid. pp. 247, 248.
2. *Revival*, p. 295.
3. *Christian Unity* (E3), p. 298.
4. *Revival* p. 236.
5. Cf. p. 5.
6. Cf. The excellent and detailed survey of *chrisma*, its possible meaning and application in the present context, in Raymond E. Brown, *The Epistles of John, A New Translation with Introduction and Commentary*, (Geoffrey Chapman, London., pp. 341-9, 359-61; Brown also cites Jeremiah 31:34, 1982 , and generally comments, 'once again then the author seems to be invoking the memories of the conversion/initiation/baptismal experience of his readers'.
7. *Authority*, pp. 76, 77 'There are three main ways in which assurance comes to us. . . the first is that which is obtained by applying ourselves to the bare Word of the Scripture as the authoritative word of God. . . It can become a kind of 'believism'. . . We need something further which is the second ground of assurance'. He sees this described in 1 John in the tests the Apostle lays down to demonstrate whether or not a person is truly a believer (3:11-4:21). 'That is a much safer form of assurance than the first, which was entirely objective. . .' The third is that defined by Paul in Romans 8:16, 'The Spirit itself beareth with our spirit, that we are the children of God.' DML-J comments, 'this is not a form of assurance that I may deduce from the Scriptures, or from evidence which I find within myself. Here is a direct witness of the Spirit. . . It is possible for us to have the first two grounds of assurance without having this third'. This should be compared with his comments in *Joy Unspeakable*, pp. 91 ff. (the former quotation comes from addresses he gave in 1953, the latter twelve years later).
8. *God's Ultimate Purpose* (E1), p. 261; cf. *The Sons of God* (R7), where he asserts 'He (the Holy spirit) enables us to undersand these things. The "anointing", the "unction of the Holy One" the Holy Spirit dispenses truth' and links this with Paul's prayer on behalf of the Ephesians that they may have enlightenment (1:17, 18), p. 178.

9. *Authority*, p. 39 (my italics).
10. Ibid., p. 79.
11. Eaton, op. cit., p. 55 , 'If [in Calvin's view] the Baptism of the Spirit was not a self-conscious experience it certainly led to hope and joyfulness of which one could not but be immediately aware'; cf. *John Calvin's Sermon on Ephesians* (Banner of Truth Trust, 1973), p. 77, where Calvin argues that, as a result of the sealing of the Spirit, 'being once assured that God takes us for his children. . . we do not cease to be always and infallibly persuaded that he is our Father to lead us to the glory of heaven'.
12. Ibid, p. 103; In a useful chapter on John Owen, Eaton shows DML-J's development of thought and refers to the mutual influence of Owen and Thomas Goodwin (DML-J's views are in direct lineage with Goodwin). 'In neither Owen's nor Goodwin's teaching was the gift of the Spirit precisely identified with regeneration; it was to be sought by every Christian. Whereas Goodwin tolerated the idea of a time-gap between conversion and sealing, Owen evidently thought of this blessing being given to the Christian soon after his coming to faith.' DML-J was perfectly aware, of course, that Calvin (and Luther) differed from him on assurance, cf. *The Sons of God* (R7), p. 246, also his comment on the Westminster Confession (chap. XVIII) in which the Divines drew a distinction between being saved and knowing that you are saved, p. 247.
13. *The Divine Conquest* (STL Books Edition, 1979): the extended quote is, 'For he cannot love a God who is no more than a deduction from a text. He will crave to know God with a vital awareness that goes beyond words and to live in the intimacy of personal communion', p. 25.
14. *Preaching and Preachers*, p. 314. He had argued this earlier in *Revival*, p. 185.
15. Cf. p. 53.
16. *The Gospel of God* (R1), pp. 223, 224.
17. *Revival*, p. 185 (my italics).
18. *Preaching and Preachers*, p. 16.
19. *The Fight of Faith*, p. 604.
20. In reviewing *The Sons of God* (R8), Robert Strong was quite right when he criticised the book's being issued under the description of a commentary; 'it is not so to be classified. There are very few footnotes, no index, no bibliography, a minimum of documentation. Yet a comprehensive scholarship is discerned', *Westminster Theological Journal*, p. 409.
21. *The Gospel of God* (R1), pp. 223, 224.
22. *Joy Unspeakable*, p. 90.
23. Wayne A. Grudem, *The Gift of Prophecy in 1 Corinthians* (University Press of America, Washington, D.C., 1982), revised and republished as *The Gift of Prophecy in the New Testament Today* (Kingsway Publications Ltd, Eastbourne, 1988); Roy Clements, *Word and Spirit, The Bible and the Gift of Prophecy Today*, (UCCF Booklets, Leicester, 1986) (a popular summary of Grudem); Clifford Hill, *Prophecy Past and Present* (Highland Books, Crowborough, 1989); Victor Bugden, *The Charismatics and the Word of God* (Evangelical Press, Welwyn, 1985), pp. 25-44
24. Cf. Eaton, op. cit., p. 186, 'Lloyd-Jones firmly believed in the possible continuation in the church of gifts of the Spirit'.
25. *The Puritans*, p. 382; cf. his comment on Queen Elizabeth I's downgrading of 'prophesying', ibid, p. 375. The use of this word by Perkins and the monarch does not imply prophecy in the present, charismatic sense.

26. Lloyd-Jones expressed his view on local church worship in four very significant tapes in the Ephesians series *Worship in the Spirit* (4156); *True Melody* (4157); *Singing to the Lord* (4158); *Giving thanks always unto God* (4159) (sermons on Eph. 5:19, 20). Unfortunately these stimulating sermons were, for some reason, not included in the relevant volume on the Epistle; cf. also in the Romans' series *Worship Ancient and Modern* (3318), *Worship, the Old the New* (3319) (sermons on Rom. 12:6-8).

27. The danger of DML-J being 'claimed' by groups wishing to profit by his undoubted influence was anticipated and decried by Donald Macleod in ' *The Lloyd*-Jones' Legacy', *The Monthly Record*, (Free Church of Scotland, October 1983), p. 209; also by R. M. Horn (*Evangelical Times*, 1982): Horn comments that a cynic might think that 'several Doctors had once lived, one Doctor who is claimed as charismatic, one Doctor who supports a "one man ministry" and another Doctor who supports participation. . .'

28. *Westminster Record* (1945), Campbell Morgan Memorial edn, p. 61, 'those wonderful campaigns. . . There had been great visitations of the Spirit. Men and women had been converted by the thousand. . . The evangelists (Moody and Sankey) had done their work; it was a time for the teacher and God sent him (Campbell Morgan).

29. Iain Murray, *The Puritan Hope* (Banner of Truth, London, 1971), p. 188; the assessment is that of Thomas de Quincey.

30. Arnold Dallimore, *The Life of Edward Irving—The Forerunner of the Charismatic Movement* (Banner of Truth, Edinburgh, 1983).

31. Murray, op. cit., pp. 197-202.

32. Ibid., p. 200.

33. Dallimore, op. cit., p 77 ff. Irving believed that Christ inherited the fallen nature of Adam. Thus he was subject to the same temptations as other men. His life was a constant battle against sin. He was always victorious but it was possible for him to have fallen. So Irving denied the doctrine of the impeccability of Christ; his position has been embraced by other ministers today without paying 'the great cost' which he did. Karl Barth espoused this doctrinal position; cf. Thomas A. Smail, *Reflected Glory—The Spirit in Christ and Christians* (Hodder & Stoughton, London, 1975), p. 68 , also chapter 7.

34. *The Fight of Faith*, pp. 72, 73; for a further, extended comment on Irving by Lloyd-Jones at a much later time in DML-J's ministry, cf. ' *Spiritual Gifts* (iii), sermon on Romans 12:6 (Tape 3314).

35. Cf. Dallimore's evaluation, op. cit., p. 176. For a more sympathetic treatment of Irving, cf. Gordon Strachan, *The Pentecostal Theology of Edward Irving* (Hendrickson Publishers Inc., 1973, repr. 1988).

36. *Christian Unity* (E4), p. 189.

37. Ibid., p. 191.

38. Ibid., p. 188.

39. 'The Baptism of the Spirit', *Great Christian Doctrines* (Tape DML-J 28 Nos 1-4).

40. *Knowing the Times*, p. 276 (my italics).

41. *Spiritual Gifts* ' (ii), sermon on Romans 12:6. (Tape 3313). In this address he asks again 'if any gifts have been in evidence (in the history of the Church) why not all of them?' He proceeds to warn of the danger of interpreting Scripture in the light of experience instead of our experience in the light of Scripture. He made the same point a week earlier when referring to 1 Corinthians 13 and Paul's comment about knowledge, tongues and prophecies, 'we cannot go along with the argument that the latter two are rendered void with the completion of this canon without

applying that to the former. . . that is not interpretation it is prejudice', *Spiritual Gifts* (i) (Tape 3312).

42. *Preaching and Preachers*, pp. 73 ff.; *The Influence of Greek Ideas and Usages Upon the Christian Church*, ed. A.M. Fairburn (Williams & Norgate, London 1890, The Hibbert Lectures, 1890), cf. Eaton, op. cit., p. 216.
43. *Preaching and Preachers*, p. 74.
44. *Life in the Spirit* (E6), p. 161.
45. *Knowing the Times*, p. 276.
46. *The Puritans*, pp. 282 ff.
47. Ibid., pp.21 ff.
48. *Knowing the Times*, p. 276.
49. *Puritans*, p. 295 (my italics). He repeats his opinion in *The Gospel of God* (R1), p. 2.
50. Personal correspondence; cf. Calvin's *Commentaries on Micah*, verse 8 (and the following prayer); cf. Calvin on Luke 4 verse 18, 1 John 4 verse 1. Schuringa remarks 'there is a tendency among many to see the Baptism of the Spirit as a post-Reformation development. I am increasingly convinced, however, that it was already present in Calvin though in seed form due to the battles he was already fighting with Rome.'
51. *The Puritans* pp. 386, 387.
52. Ibid., p. 387.
53. *The Fight of Faith*, p. 373.
54. *The Puritans*, p. 120.
55. *Healing and the Scriptures*, p. 28, cf. fn. 391; Wood Row Society Portfolio, ed. Rev. Thomas McCrie (from manuscripts in the library of the Faculty of Advocates, Edinburgh, 1842).
56. *Revival*, p. 135.
57. In regard to the so-called Kansas City prophets (for an uncritical account, cf. David Pytches, *Some said it Thundered* (Hodder & Stoughton, London, 1988); for a critique of the book and the prophets, cf. Clifford Hill, *Prophecy Today* (1990) vol. 6, Nos 4, 5 , and recent trends in some quarters for personal revelation to be part of the worship service; there can be no doubt as to DML-J's position. Though he did not deny that God can give unusual insights and indicate future happenings, for this to become almost 'centre-stage' and incorporated into an order of expected events would have left him entirely unimpressed and, one imagines, extremely critical.
58. Donald Gee was the only theologian of note among early Pentecostal Church leaders in Britain. He was principal of the Assemblies of God Bible College for many years. Author of several books and editor of the internationally circulated magazine, *Pentecost* (the editorials of which were sometimes outstanding), he was a respected Bible teacher. His interests at a more ecumenical level surfaced after his death, cf. Hocken, op. cit., pp. 195-7.
59. *Spiritual Gifts* (iv) (Tape 3315, my italics).
60. *Spiritual Gifts* (ii) (Tape 3313).
61. *Spiritual Gifts* (iii) (Tape 3314).
62. *Knowing the Times*, p. 276.
63. Bethan Lloyd-Jones, *Memories of Sandfields*.
64. *Studies in the Sermon on the Mount*, vol. 1, ch. 27, p. 280.
65. *Christian Unity* (E4), p. 191.
66. *Spiritual Depression*, p. 298.
67. *The Christian Soldier* (E8), p. 135.

68. *Joy Unspeakable*, p. 225.
69. *God's Ultimate Purpose* (E1), p. 298.
70. *Preaching and Preachers*, p. 85.
71. *The Christian Soldier* (E8), p. 116 (my italics).
72. *The Select Works of Jonathan Edwards* (repr. edn, Banner of Truth, Edinburgh 1974), vol. 1 , p. 54. '. . . Edwards wrote and read the greater part of his sermons; his left elbow rested on the cushion or the Bible, and his right hand was rarely raised but to turn the leaves of his fine, almost illegible notes. We find in these things no explanation of the fact that he was one of the most successful preachers since the days of the Apostles. He defies interpretation in any natural or worldly terms.' Cf. John Piper, *The Supremacy of God in Preaching* (IVP, 1990), p. 49, 'He had no studied varieties of the voice, and no strong emphasis. He scarcely gestured, or even moved, and he made no attempt by the elegance of his style, or the beauty of his pictures, to gratify the taste and fascinate the imagination (but he preached). . . so that the solemn attention of the whole audience is riveted from the beginning to the close, and impressions are left that cannot be effaced . . .' (quoting Serono Dwight, (ed.) *The Works of Jonathan Edwards* (1834 edn; repr. edn, Banner of Truth, Edinburgh; 1974), vol. 1 , p.: xxi).
73. p. 123; *Spiritual Gifts* (Tape 3313).
74. p. 51.
75. Tape 1080. This sermon should also be listened to because it gives a classic example of DML-J's preaching style. He 'pours' the narrative dealing with Apollos, Priscilla and Aquila (Acts 18:24-19:7) through his key text John 1:26, 33. This is a marked feature in his ministry. It also furnishes an illustration of his retelling a biblical incident in a compelling and meticulously accurate way. He defends spending time with the event on the basis that historical narratives in Scripture are of the utmost importance. They reveal the Holy Spirit's selection. Thousands of incidents might have been recorded. The chosen ones therefore are of great significance. Twenty years or so had passed since the death of John and the resurrection of Jesus. And yet twice in this narrative Lloyd-Jones finds the distinction being made between the baptism of John and the baptism of Jesus. He uses the grammatico-historical approach in order to clarify the meaning of certain words and concepts. Within the sermon are indications of how he arrived at propositions, worked them through and buttressed them biblically, made excursions into church history and laced the whole message from start to finish with generous amounts of practical application and exhortation.
76. DML-J did not think the 's' should be capitalised.
77. *God's Ultimate Purpose* (E1), p. 300 (my italics).
78. *Preaching and Preachers*, p. 325.

CHAPTER FIVE: *Pauline Influence*

1. *Joy Unspeakable*, p. 123.
2. *The Gospel of God* (R1), p. 236.
3. *God's Sovereign Purpose* (R9), p. 128.
4. Ibid., p. 117.
5. *Christian Unity* (E4), p. 251.
6. *I am not Ashamed—Advice to Timothy* (Hodder & Stoughton, London, 1986), p. 39.
7. *Under the Power of the Spirit*, (Tape 5553).
8. *Expository Preaching*, (IVP, 1986), p. iv.
9. *God's Sovereign Purpose* (R9), p. 128.

10. W. Barclay, *The Epistle to the Romans* (St Andrew's Press, Edinburgh, 1955), pp. 137-41.
11. C. H. Dodd, *Commentary on the Epistle to the Romans* (Moffatt Series).
12. *God's Sovereign Purpose* (R9), p. 171.
13. Ibid., p. 283; cf. *Christian Warfare* (E6), p. 175.
14. *Chosen by God*, p. 147.
15. *Assurance* (R4), p. 283.
16. pp. 1 ff.
17. *The Fight of Faith*, p. 68.
18. *Authority*, p. 80; cf. comment on that Apostle's physical appearance in Philip E. Hughes, *The Second Epistle to the Corinthians*, from the series *The New International Commentary on the New Testament* (Wm B. Eerdmans Pub. Co., Grand Rapids, 1962; 6 th edn, 1977), p. 1.
19. *The Gospel of God* (R1), p. 205.
20. *I am not Ashamed*, p. 42 (my italics).
21. He did not, of course, prevent this from happening. Donald Macleod criticised his failure and went so far as to warn about 'the emergence of a Doctor-cult' in 'The Lloyd-Jones Legacy', *The Record* (Free Church of Scotland, October 1983), pp. 207-9. J. I. Packer reckoned, in effect, his chairmanship of the Westminster Fellowship made DML-J bishop 'to literally hundreds of clergy in all demoninations', *Chosen by God* p. 43. Nonetheless, our point is valid, he did not consciously or deliberately promote a following. These were men who were drawn to him because of the confidence they had in him.
22. *The Gospel of God* (R1), p. 211. This would be asking too much of a medical doctor. There are generous references to DML-J using his professional knowledge scattered throughout his sermons; *I am not Ashamed*, pp. 54, 55; *Christian Unity* (E4), pp. 262, 273.
23. *Christian Warfare* (E7), p. 211.
24. Ibid., pp. 212, 213.
25. Ibid., p. 213.
26. Cf p. 106.
27. *Christian Warfare* (E7), p. 230.
28. *Sermon on the Mount*, vol. 1, p. 289.
29. One of the rare occurrences is found in *The New Man* (R5), p. 79. He was referring to baptism, 'it is a very wrong procedure to bury someone who is only in a state of dying!' When preaching on Psalm 1 , he referred to a man who was lost and asked an Irishman how to get to Belfast. The response was 'If I was lost and wanted to get to Belfast I would not start from here'!
30. *God's Way of Reconciliation* (E2), p. 307; *Sermon on the Mount*, vol. 2, p. 96.
31. *God's Sovereign Purpose* (R9), pp. 250, 251.
232.Ibid., p. 92.
33. *The Gospel of God* (R1), p. 199.
34. *Preaching and Preachers*, p. 119: the quotation continues ' . . . but if a man is a born preacher you can help him a little—but not much. He can perhaps be improved a little here and there'; cf. *Training for the Ministry* (Tape 5715).
35. *The Gospel of God* (R1), p. 188.
36. Ibid., p. 227.
37. Ibid., p. 227.
38. Ibid., p. 226 (my italics).
39. Ibid., p. 186.

40. *God's Ultimate Purpose* (E1), p. 210. *The Sons of God* (R7), p. 166 , cf. p. 225); cf. [Paul] was not a pedant, thank God. He often breaks the rules of grammar; and here he has actually left out the verb, which must be supplied in order to get at his meaning!'
41. *Christian Warfare* (E7), p. 202.
42. *The Gospel of God* (R1), pp. 186, 187.
43. Ibid., p. 188.
44. p. 20.
45. *Chosen by God*, p. 51.
46. *God's Sovereign Purpose* (R9), p. 248.
47. Ibid., p. 7; cf. *Christian Unity* (E4), p. 51; *Preachers and Preaching*, pp. 72, 79; *Sermon on the Mount*, vol. 2, p. 112.
48. *God's Sovereign Purpose* (R9), pp. 117, 118.
49. *Studies in the Sermon on the Mount*, vol. 2, pp. 129, 130.
50. *Faith on Trial* (Paternoster Press, London), p. 75.
51. *Training for the Ministry* (Tape 5175).
52. *The Sons of God* (R7), p. 213. *The Law: Its Functions and Limits* (R6), p. 213.
53. *Sermon on the Mount*, vol. 2, p. 86.
54. *God's Sovereign Purpose* (R9), p. 117.
55. Ibid., p. 96.
56. Cf. Sir Fred Catherwood's example of this style of approach, *Chosen by God*, ch. 7, pp. 125 ff.
57. pp. 199ff.
58. *The Law: Its Functions and Limits* (R6), p. 225.
59. *The Gospel of God* (R1), p. 30 (my italics).
60. *The Law: Its Function and Limits* (R6), p. 225.
61. *The Gospel of God* (R1), p. 188.
62. Consider Romans 8: 37-9 , 10: 33-6; Ephesians 3: 20, 21.
63. *Preaching and Preachers*, p. 240.
64. *The Gospel of God* (R1), p. 33.
65. *God's Ultimate Purpose* (E1), p. 288.

CHAPTER SIX: *Godliness*

1. *I am not Ashamed*, pp. 106, 107.
2. Cf. J. I. Packer, *Knowing God* (Hodder & Stoughton, London, 1973), p. 14, for a similar example of remarkable oratory of this quality from the ministry of the young C. H. Spurgeon.
3. *Preaching and Preachers*, pp. 109, 166.
4. *Lectures to my Students*, pp. 12, 13. Also quoted in John Stott, *I believe in Preaching* (Hodder & Stoughton, 1982), p. 264.
5. *Healing and the Scriptures*, p. 14.
6. Cf, *Letters of Samuel Rutherford* with an introduction to his life by Andrew Bonar.
7. *The Fight of Faith*, p. 738.
8. *Sermon on the Mount*, vol. 2, p. 278.
9. James M. Gordon, *Evangelical Spirituality* (SPCK, London, 1991), p. 294.
10. *Sermon on the Mount*, vol. 2, p. 266.
11. Andrew Bonar, *Robert Murray M'Cheyne* (Banner of Truth Trust, 1960).
12. John Macpherson, *Duncan Matheson, The Scottish Evangelist* (Morgan and Scott).
13. *Revival*, p. 57; cf. *Preaching and Preachers*, p. 86.

14. Sidney Greidanus; *The Modern Preacher and the Ancient Text* (Wm B. Eerdmans Publishing Co, Grand Rapids, 1988; also IVF, Leicester).
15. Haddon W. Robinson, *Expository Preaching, Principles and Practice* (IVP, Leicester, 1986), p. 24.
16. John Peters, *Martyn Lloyd-Jones Preacher*, (The Paternoster Press, Exeter, 1986).
17. *The Fight of Faith*, p. 743.
18. *Knowing the Times*, p. 276.
19. Robinson, *Expository Preaching, Principals and Practice*, from the introduction by J. A. Motyer, p. vii.
20. *The Fight of Faith*, p. 108.
21. *True Melody* (Tape 4157).
22. *Joy Unspeakable*, pp. 211, 212.
23. Eaton, op. cit., p. 134; commenting on DML-J's 184 sermons on the first four chapters of John's Gospel, he says, 'the majority of these sermons are strongly experiential in flavour, the mystical element in Lloyd-Jones' thinking reached its peak in this series. Even visual experiences of Jesus are not excluded. . . these sermons contain what surely must be the richest exposition of the Baptism with the Spirit from a Puritan viewpoint since the days of Thomas Goodwin's sermons on Ephesians 1 verse 13.'
24. Cf. p. 46.
25. *The Fight of Faith*, p. 220.
26.. *God's Ultimate Purpose* (E1), p. 344.
27. *Joy Unspeakable*, pp. 73, 74 , quoting Thomas Goodwin: '"this is the next thing we get in this world to heaven; you can have no more: you can have no more until you come there. . . It is faith added and raised above the ordinary rate."'
28. *God's Ultimate Purpose* (E1), p. 347.
29. Brother Lawrence (Nicholas Herman of Lorraine), *The Practice of the Presence of God* (Heart and Life Booklets, London; H. R. Allenson Ltd, 1906 edn).
30. *God's Ultimate Purpose* (E1), p. 348.
31. Cf. *The Unsearchable Riches of Christ* (E3), chaps. 13-24.
32. Cf. *The Heart of the Gospel* (Crossway Books, Eastbourne, 1991), foreword by J. I. Packer, pp. 7-9.
33. *Prayers of Martyn Lloyd-Jones* (Tape 5075).
34. *Preaching and Preachers*, p. 303.
35. *The Gospel of God* (R1), p. 386.
36. *Sermon on the Mount*, vol. 2, p. 29.
37. Ibid., vol. 2, p. 29.
38. *The Righteous Judgment of God* (R2), p. 218; *The Sons of God* (R7), p. 224.
39. *God's Ultimate Purpose* (E1), p. 16.
40. Tape DML-J 15 contains a sample of his prayers (some of the taped sermons also have the concluding prayer retained).
41. *The Preacher, His Life and Work* (Hodder & Stoughton, London, undated), p. 155.
42. *Sermon on the Mount*, vol. 2, p. 46.
43. *God's Ultimate Purpose* (E1), p. 352.
44. *The Fight of Faith*, p. 130.
45. *Preaching and Preachers*, p. 170.
46. Ibid., p. 171.
47. *The Fight of Faith*, p. 202 (italics in original).
48. *Preaching and Preachers*, p. 172.
49. *The Law: its Function and Limits* (R6), p. 177.

50. Dr. Packer describes him as 'a supremely cheerful, affable, humorous man' in *Chosen by God*, p. 35; cf. his remarks in an interview with Dr. Carl Henry, founding editor of *Christianity Today*, ibid., p. 104.
51. *Preaching and Preachers*, p. 241, 'the place of humour is that it is only allowable if it is natural. The man who tries to be humorous is an abomination and should never be allowed to enter a pulpit.'
52. *Sermon on the Mount*, vol. 1, p. 53.
53. Cf. pp. 199 ff.
54. *Christian Warfare* (E7), p. 33.
55. *The Law: Its Function and Limits* (R6), p. 66.
56. *Chosen by God*, p. 53.
57. *Sermon on the Mount*, vol. 1 , p. 247.
58. *The Authority of the Gospel* (Tape 5548). In the process of applying his message DML-J preached on wrath and hell in a fashion I have heard none other do. For any serious student of his preaching this sermon is essential listening. However, warnings of judgment are scattered throughout the whole of his ministry. In the light of the prevailing debate on annihilationism, in some quarters of the Evangelical Church, it should be stated that he rejected it completely. He never soft-pedalled the fearful nature of the judgment of God against sin even when addressing colleagues from his previous profession, cf. the lectures and sermons he gave at the Christian Medical Fellowship's conferences. *The Doctor and the Human Condition* (Christian Medical Fellowship, 1982), chap. 1; cf. fn. 391.
59. *Sermon on the Mount*, vol. 1, p. 242.
60. Ibid., p. 251.
61. *Christian Warfare* (E7), p. 5.
62. Ibid., p. 106.
63. Cf his lecture to the Christian Medical Fellowship, where not only does he claim that Christians can be possessed but goes on to give an example of exorcism and deliverance, *Healing and the Scriptures* (Oliver Nelson, Nashville, Tenn.) p. 166. The book was originally published in 1982 by the Christian Medical Fellowship, London, and called *The Doctor and the Human Condition* (chaps 1-8). With additional addresses it was published in Britain by Kingsway with the title, *Healing and Medicine*, in 1987. Commenting on the latter edition, Murray remarks that the lecture 'The Supernatural in Medicine' is abridged, a third of it being missing including his more detailed analysis of Kathryn Kuhlman's claims and teaching. Murray notes that the Kingsway title is misleading. 'The book in fact contains little on healing and the addresses. . . are limited in their value by the context in which they were originally given to fellow medics who were already versed in the Scriptures. . .' He reasonably offers the opinion that 'if DML-J had been preparing addresses for a world readership there would probably have been some considerable difference in emphases', *The Fight of Faith*, p. 787.
64. Ibid., p. 159. He was referring to Jay Adams, of whose many books *Competent to Counsel* is the most well known. Note Peter Masters's riposte, Essay (i), p. 30, where Masters quotes from another of Dr. Adams's books, *The Big Umbrella*, and claims that Lloyd-Jones 'woefully misread the chapter. Adams does not say that demon possession cannot now take place. In fact, he says the exact opposite.' But then Masters has to quote Adams's words when speaking of the Western World and noting what he calls 'the rare incidence, *if not the entire absence* of demonic possession in modern times' (my italics). Whatever the merits of either opinion, the charge is hardly sustained that Lloyd-Jones does 'a grave injustice by distorting the view'.

65. *The Fight of Faith*, p. 208.
66. *The Christian Soldier* (E8), p. 302.
67. Cf. William Gurnall, *The Christian in Complete Armour* (Blackie and Son, Glasgow, 1864; rep. 1964 , Banner of Truth Trust, Edinburgh).
68. The resultant books are entitled *Christian Warfare* (E7), twenty-six sermons on three verses: Ephesians 6: 10-13; and *The Christian Soldier* (E8), Ephesians 6: 1 -20; cf. my fn. 690 , p. 264.
69. *The Christian Soldier* (E8), p. 52.
70. *The Sons of God* (R7), p. 62.
71. *God's Ultimate Purpose* (E1), p. 330.
72. *Expository Sermons on 2 Peter*, p. 50.
73. Ibid.
74. *Faith on Trial*, p. 111
75. *Sermon on the Mount*, vol. 1 , pp. 147 , 148.
76. *The Oxford Book of English Verse 1250-1918 (Oxford University Press) p. 857.
77. *Chosen by God, p. 143.*
78. Expository Sermons *on 2 Peter, pp. 51, 52.*
79. *Cf.* Faith on Trial, which is an exposition of Psalm 73. The series of sermons not only contains excellent examples of 'diagnostic preaching' but the fourth shows how Lloyd-Jones preached about the end of life. There he encouraged a study to be made of the way in which influential men coped. He cited, among others, Charles Darwin and H.G. Wells, pp. 51, 52. He concluded with a further reference to the Wesleys' claim that 'our men die well'.
80. The Christian Soldier *(E8), p. 123.*
81. Life in the Spirit *(E6), pp. 205, 206.*
82. The Fight of Faith, *pp. 744, 747.*
83. Sermon on the Mount, *vol. 2, p. 236.*

CHAPTER SEVEN: *The Earlier Years*

1. *Evangelistic Sermons*, p. 36.
2. *Ibid.*, p. 112.
3. *Revival*, p. 71.
4. *Evangelistic Sermons*, p. 52.
5. *Ibid.*, pp. 53, 54.
6. *Church of England Newspaper* (August 25th, 1989); 'Vintage Stuff from Dr. Lloyd-Jones', review of *The Life of Joy* (Hodder & Stoughton), *Sanctified through the Truth* (Kingsway), and *The Righteous Judgment of God* (R2) (Banner of Truth).
7. It should be noted that Dr. Lloyd-Jones did not hold that the benefits of this experience applied only to preaching. He also believed that it was perceivable in the way in which people pray in public. They are given a greater power and facility with words. It empowers for evangelism and the work of the Lord generally (cf. p. 73—third quotation).
8. Cf. n. 96, p. 37.
9. An exhaustive bibliography is included in *The Fight of Faith*, pp. 799-809. The following is some of the most significant material. *Evangelistic Sermons preached at Aberavon*; *Why does God allow War ?*; *The Plight of Man and the Power of God*; *The Life of Joy* (eighteen sermons); *Truth Unchanged, Unchanging* (addresses delivered to the Alumni Association of Wheaton College); *Expository Sermons on 2 Peter* (first published in the *Westminster Record* 1948-50) these twenty-five sermons were preached between October 1946 and March 1947; *The*

Heart of the Gospel (who Jesus is and why he came), preached through the winter months of 1948-9 , *Knowing the Times* contains four addresses pre-1949. Other pre-1949 sermons are to be found in various copies of *The Westminster Record*, Westminster Chapel Bookroom, Buckingham Gate, London, SW1 6 BS. Copies are kept at the Evangelical Library, Chiltern Street, London W1 M 2 HB (established in part as a result of Dr. Lloyd-Jones's prompting, it contains a unique collection of Puritan material and virtually all his books and pamphlets). See also, 'Author's Notes pp. *xvii—xix*.

10. Sermons preached by C. H. Spurgeon between 1855 and 1860 (repub. Banner of Truth, 1963).

11. *Evangelistic Sermons*, p. x (my italics).

12. Cf. p. 41.

13. *Chosen by God*, p. 55.

14. *Evangelistic Sermons*, p. x.

15. *Knowing the Times*, p. 275.

16. *Preachers and Preaching*, p. 257; also quoted in John MacArthur Jr, *Rediscovering Expository Preaching* (Word Inc, 1992), p. 325.

17. Milton J. Coalter Jr, *Gilbert Tennent, Son of Thunder* (Greenwood Press, 1986), p. 46. Coalter quotes from Tennent's book, *A Solemn Warning*, in which he claims that 'terrors first, comforts second' coincided with God's own treatment of the soul. The Holy Spirit converted the human heart by convicting it of its sins before supplying the Gospel balsam to sin's deep wound.

18. *Evangelistic Sermons*, p. 161; cf. *The First Forty Years*, p. 216.

19. *Evangelistic Sermons*, p. 161.

20. Ibid., p. 131.

21. Ibid., p. 146.

22. Ibid., p. 235.

23. Eaton, op. cit., p. 125.

24. Ibid., p. 126; cf. *The First Forty Years*, pp. 190-1.

25. *Chosen by God*, p. 107; *The Gospel of God* (R1), p. 62.

26. *Evangelistic Sermons*, p. 238.

27. Ibid., p. 201.

28. Ibid., p. 88.

29. Ibid., p. 50.

30. Ibid., p. 275.

31. Ibid., p. 55.

32. Ibid., p. 197.

33. Ibid., p. 271.

34. Ibid., p. 259.

35. Ibid., p. 16.

36. Ibid., p. 177.

37. Ibid., p. 48.

38. Ibid., p. 257.

39. *The Law: its Functions and Limits* (R6), p. 184.

40. Ibid., p. 35.

41. *Preaching and Preachers*, pp. 224 ff.

42. *Evangelistic Sermons*, p. 228.

43. Ibid., p. 247 (my italics).

44. *Preaching and Preachers*, p. 239.

45. Ibid., p. 77.

46. *The Kingdom of God* (Crossway Books, 1992), cf. publisher's note and chap. 8.

47. *The First Forty Years*, p. 147.
48. *The Christian Soldier* (E8), p. 291; presumably this was the same minister who advised him about the content of his addresses, cf. p. 153.
49. He broke his rule at least once at Westminster when Campbell Morgan pressed him to speak at a national youth meeting held at the Chapel. He agreed provided Morgan would not be present. The previous day Lloyd-Jones had listened to a Welsh international rugby match. He used the game as the launching pad for his address. He was disturbed to find his colleague sitting in one of the front pews, but had no option but to proceed. At the close Morgan went into the vestry, put his arm round him and said, 'Damn you Lloyd-Jones, would you have had me miss that'! (Personal conversation.)
50. Cf, p. 264 , n.690
51. *Evangelistic Sermons*, p. 236.
52. Ibid., p. 170.
53. Ibid., p. 289.
54. Ibid., p. 233.
55. *Preaching with Purpose, The Urgent Task of Homiletics*, (Zondervan Publishing House, Michigan, 1982) pp 27 ff.
56. Bernard Ramm, *Protestant Biblical Interpretation*, 3 rd rev. edn (Baker, Grand Rapids, 1970), p. 11; also quoted in MacArthur, op. cit., p. 28.
57. *Evangelistic Sermons*, p. 223.
58. Ibid., p.224.
59. Ibid., p. 243.
60. Ibid., p. 227.
61. Ibid., pp. 241 ff (preached Aberavon, June 2nd, 1935). It should be noted that this is my deduction of what constitutes the skeleton of the address.
62. Entitled 'A Preview of History', *Westminster Record* (Feb-May, 1947), vol. 21 , Nos. 2-5.
63. Further examples are found in *Why does God allow War?* (5 sermons).
64. 'A Preview of History', *Westminster Record*, vol. 21, No. 2, p. 10.
65. Ibid., vol. 21, No. 3.
66. Ibid., vol. 21, No. 4.
67. Ibid., p. 28.
68. Ibid., vol. 21, no. 5.
69. Ibid., p. 38.
70. *The Heart of the Gospel*, Foreword by J. I. Packer, pp. 7, 8.
71. 'Paul's Order of the Day', *Westminster Record* (1942), vol. 16, Nos. 9-12.
72. Ibid., pp. 154-92.
73. 'The Shunamite Woman', *Westminster Record* (January 1939), vol. 13.
74. *The Mirage shall become a Pool* (Westminster Bookroom, Westminster Chapel, London 1947).
75. *The Puritans*, p. 237.
76. Cf. p. 151 , and *Preachers and Preaching*, p. 216.
77. p. 46 f.

CHAPTER EIGHT: *Diagnostic Preaching (I)*

1. *Chosen by God*, p. 40.
2. Op. cit., p. 293.
3. There are many examples of what we are trying to define in the huge tape library. I suggest that a student of his ministry would do well to hear his sermon entitled *The Great Fact of Prophecy* (Tape 2003). It demonstrates how in a series of

expository addresses (he was preaching through the Acts of the Apostles and had come to chapter 2 verses 14-36) the preacher can also be topical. This message was delivered on the occasion of the death of Winston Churchill. Skills of eloquence, erudition, scholarship, but above all blazing passion, combine to make this an extraordinary sermon by any reckoning.

4. Cf. *Sermon on the Mount*, vol. 1, p. 89.
5. 'The preacher whilst speaking should in a sense be deriving something from his congregation. There are those present in the congregation who are spiritually-minded people . . . they make their contribution to the occasion.'—*Preaching and Preachers*, p. 84; cf. *Knowing the Times*, p. 273.
6. *Knowing the Times*, p. 268. His comment should be considered in full. He was doubtless referring to his predecessor at Westminster Chapel, G. Campbell Morgan, who was a famed Bible lecturer. He published the *Campbell Morgan Bible* which incorporated his analysis, in chart form, of each book. DML-J esteemed Morgan as a great Bible illustrator. When he preached at Dr. Morgan's memorial service he called him 'the most intelligent man that I ever knew'. One author has said that 'the singular glory of Dr. Morgan's work is its non-theological nature in the systematic sense'- Leith Powell, *The Gospel Witness* (Canada), vol. 60. No. 2 , April 1981. Amazingly, the memorial sermon indicates that he and Lloyd-Jones rarely discussed their theological differences. If it seems inappropriate for DML J to have made such a stinging criticism of his late predecessor, it has to be said that Lloyd-Jones could be sharply critical of those with whom he disagreed; cf. Packer's testimony in describing how Lloyd-Jones strongly expressed his differences with him over ecclesiology in *Chosen by God*, p. 44; but also note Packer's balancing remark, *The Fight of Faith*, p. 232.
7. 'The very building seems to be possessed with a subtle kind of antagonism, and the people in the gallery seem to belong to another planet' was Jowett's assessment. The Chapel was built in 1865 for the ministry of the Rev. Samuel Martin, a popular preacher in Spurgeon's day, and cost £18,000. J. H. Jowett's biographer seems to share his subject's views calling it 'incredibly ugly'! Arthur Porritt, *J. H. Jowett* (Hodder & Stoughton, London, 1924).
8. J. H. Jowett, *The Preacher, His Life and Work*, Yale Lectures, 2nd edn. (Hodder & Stoughton, London) p. 163.
9. *Preaching and Preachers*, p. 75. *The Puritans*: the practice of having a large Bible in the pulpit, p. 378; further warning against closing the Bible after reading and proceeding with the preaching, p. 382.
10. *The Final Perseverance of the Saints* (R8), pp. 31, 32 (my italics).
11. Cf. his treatment of the word 'hope' in *The Christian Soldier* (E7), p. 315. He is expounding what Paul means by the helmet of salvation. DML-J found himself disagreeing with 'the great Charles Hodge' who reckoned it meant the present enjoyment of salvation. Lloyd-Jones believed it included this but it meant much more. Hodge had missed 'the real thrust'. DML-J proceeded to cite a generous number of New Testament Scriptures which bear out his claim that Paul had a future realisation in mind.
12. *The Righteous Judgement of God* (R2), p. 172.
13. Cf. DMJ's warning about simply giving 'the convert something to do', *Christian Unity* (E4), p. 223 and his declaration that our coming together in public worship should be a foretaste of heaven, *God's Ultimate Purpose* (E1), p. 308.
14. Douglas Johnson tells how in 1929 when Lloyd-Jones was preaching in Cardiff a minister of his denomination leaned over to him and said, 'I can't make you out Martyn, are you a hyper-Calvinist or a Quaker?' Lloyd-Jones asked what his

problem was. His enquirer continued, 'Well, you talk about God's sovereignty like a hyper-Calvinist and spiritual experience like a Quaker'! (Personal correspondence: also quoted in *The First Forty Years*, p. 191, where the comment is added 'but the Cross and the Work of Christ have little place in your preaching'.)

15. *God's Way of Reconciliation* (E2), p. 328.
16. *Life in the Spirit* (E6), p. 161.
17. *Preaching and Preachers*, p. 118.
18. *The New Man* (R5), p. 256 , Lloyd-Jones's extended comment; cf. n. 182.
19. Cf. Macleod, *The Lloyd-Jones Legacy*. It is interesting, in this respect, when he preached the inaugural sermon on the opening of the London Theological Seminary, he recognised that his presence there might be thought curious to some for whom the 'poacher had turned out to be the gamekeeper!' *Knowing the Times*, p. 356.
20. *The Gospel of God* (R1), p. 240. Speaking of his congregation he admits, 'They have delved into the doctrines; they are taking hold of something. To watch this happening is a great privilege . . . there is nothing I know of that is comparable to watching the Holy Spirit dealing with people, searching them, examining them, revealing truth to them, while you watch their growth and their development.'
21. *Life in the Spirit* (E5), p. 195.
22. He was criticised in a review of *Life in the Spirit*. The writer, with some justification, reasoned that his method of exposition was to 'lift an idea or concept from the passage and then deal with it topically relating it to other passages of Scripture'. This can side-track the preacher on to peripheral matters. 'A good illustration of this can be found in the second section of the book dealing with marriage, where we find eight sermons devoted to Christ and his bride the Church. . . and only three sermons dealing with the duties of husbands and wives. Not only does this reverse the Pauline order where the Christ-Church relationship illumines the husband-wife relationship rather than vice-versa, but also draws unwarranted assumptions from the text. One of the reasons for this is surely the fact that it is difficult to preach twenty-six sermons on such a section without treating it topically', John Bolt, *Calvin Theological Journal* (Nov. 1976), volume 11, No. 2. Not quite so pointed is another review of the same book where the comment is made about his expository style, 'the texts serve as platforms for wider concerns. To some this might be objectionable, but we all use a framework of some sort in interpretation and Dr. Lloyd-Jones's masterly use of the 'analogy of Scripture' generally does not distort the distinctiveness of the passage', *Westminster Theological Journal* (Fall 1976), vol. 39, No. 1.
23. Ibid., p. 202.
24. Ibid., p. 207.
25. *Father, Son and Holy Spirit*; (Tape 2033).
26. *The Christian Soldier* (E8), cf. pp. 271, 272, 283, 284, etc.
27. Personal communication, Douglas Johnson.
28. *Preaching and Preachers*, p. 82, where he also mentions the way one of his predecessors Dr. J.A. Hutton 'believed that a preacher should preach with the whole of his body'; cf. *The Puritans*, p. 117, where he quotes Demosthenes and comments on the preaching style of Whitefield.
29. *The Puritans*, p. 117, Here Lloyd-Jones is endorsing the preaching style of George Whitefield.
30. *Twenty Centuries of Great Preaching: An encyclopedia of Preaching*, ed. Maier Sangster, vol. 11, p. 268, quoting J.I. Packer. An unpublished, doctoral thesis,

quoting R.T. Kendall, states that Lloyd-Jones barely moved in the pulpit but stood centrally to it. The statement is inaccurate though he was less animated in later years, Argile A. Smith Jr , *David Martyn Lloyd-Jones—A Critical Examination of his Preaching* (University Microfilms Information Service, Michigan, 1977), p. 148.

31. *Preaching and Preachers*, p. 87.
32. *The Modern Preacher*, pp. 12, 13.
33. *Praedicatio verbi Dei est verbum Dei.*
34. pp. 80 ff.

CHAPTER NINE: *Diagnostic Preaching (II)*

1. Peters, *Martyn Lloyd-Jones—Preacher*, p. 64.
2. Welsh Oration to the British Medical Association, 1973 , quoted in *The Fight of Faith*, p. 760.
3. *Preaching and Preachers*, p. 133.
4. Cf. pp. 289 ff.
5. Cf. p. 306.
6. *Sermon on the Mount*, vol. 1, p. 9.
7. pp. 220 ff.
8. *The Righteous Judgment of God* (R2), p. 1.
9. Ibid., p. 7.
10. Ibid., p. 13.
11. Ibid., p. 13, cf. our comment on this incident, p. 305.
12. Cf. his comment about displaying texts around the home and the use of books grouping together a selection of texts with no reference to the context, *Christian Unity* (E4), p. 14; also *The Righteous Judgment of God*, (R2), p. 8.
13. *God's Ultimate Purpose* (E1), p. 171.
14. *The Gospel of God* (R1), p. 228.
15. Cf. p. 108.
16. *God's Ultimate Purpose* (E1), p. 260.
17. *Sermon on the Mount*, vol. 1 , pp. 67f.
18. *The Righteous Judgment of God* (R2), p. 128.
19. Ibid., p. 128.
20. *The Puritans*, p. 363.
21. Cf. *Sermon on the Mount*, vol. 1, pp. 130-3, where he employs eight negatives before moving on to positives; p. 170, where he refers to our Lord's method; p. 182, similarly Also *The New Man* (R5), p. 93, where Dr. Lloyd-Jones illustrates this teaching method in working through the benefits for the believer of our Lord's death and resurrection (Rom. 6:5-8); cf. William Hendriksen's illustration and comment on the Lord's use of this method, *New Testament Commentary, Matthew* (Banner of Truth, Edinburgh, 1973), pp. 688, 689.
22. Ibid., vol. 2 , p. 45.
23. *The Law: Its Function and Limits* (R6), p. 203.
24. *Preaching and Preachers*, p. 77. In his Ephesians series he advocates this for general Bible study, 'One of the secrets of enjoying the study of the Bible is to discover the art of asking questions . . .' Cf. *Christian Unity* (E4), p. 82.
25. *I am not Ashamed*, p. 137.
26. Ibid., pp. 221, 222; cf. *God's Ultimate Purpose* (E1), p. 446, where in his final chapter, and by way of application of the whole series of messages, he brings his address to a powerful conclusion by firing twelve questions at his congregation. The sensitive fashion in which this was done is further emphasised by linking the

questions with several staccato-style sentences in the imperative mood: 'Are these things real to you? Feeble, defeated saint, do you know all this power of God is in you? It is there because you are "in Christ" and His life is flowing into you. *Realise it. Believe it. Trust to it. Act upon it*' (my italics).

27. *The Lloyd-Jones' Legacy*, p. 207; cf. *The Doctor Himself and the Human Condition*, introduction by Douglas Johnson, p. 5. Note Johnson's reasoning, 'his teaching ability was such that illustrations were few . . .'
28. *The New Man* (R5), p. 242.
29. Ibid., p. 243.
30. *Preaching and Preachers*, p. 233.
31. *The Sons of God* (R7), p. 268.
32. *Revival*, pp. 261, 262.
33. *Sermon on the Mount*, vol. 1, p. 216.
34. *The New Man* (R5), p. 243.
35. *The Puritans*, p. 386.
36. Donald Macleod, 'The Primacy of Preaching', (*The Monthly Record*, Free Church of Scotland, 1980), pp. 63-5.
37. *Preaching and Preachers*, p. 231; also quoted by K. D. Jung, 'An evaluation of the Principles and Methods of the Preaching of D. M. Lloyd-Jones ' (ThD thesis, Potchefstroom University, June 1986) p. 152; cf. *The First Forty Years*, p. 252.
38. It is interesting to compare DML-J's defence of his use of the analogy drawn from Isaac redigging the wells of Abraham with the cautionary note he sounded in respect to William Gurnall's 'great book', *The Christian in Complete Armour*. 'His tendency is to over-elaborate the details. It was, perhaps, the common temptation that confronted the Puritans—the tendency to allegorise overmuch, or to turn a parable into an allegory', *The Christian Soldier* (E8), p. 182.
39. *The New Man* (R5), pp. 25, 26, 130; *The Sons of God* (R7), p. 104.
40. *The Final Perseverance of the Saints* (R8), p. 169.
41. *The Unsearchable Riches of Christ* (E3), p. 154.
42. Lloyd-Jones relates the story in *Preaching and Preachers*, p. 237.
43. Alexander Whyte, *Bible Characters* (Marshall, Morgan & Scott, London, 1952, 2 vols).
44. *Preaching and Preachers*, p. 235.
45. Ibid., p. 158.
46. *Evangelistic Sermons*, p. 155.
47. *The Sermon on the Mount*, vol. 2, p. 299.
48. *The Unsearchable Riches of Christ* (E3), p. 236.
49. *The Christian Soldier* (E8), p. 99.
50. *The Life of Joy*, p. 51.
51. Argile Smith, op. cit.
52. *God's Ultimate Purpose* (E1), p. 201; Argile Smith, op. cit., p. 137.
53. Cf. *Healing and the Scriptures*, p. 146, for his views on the use of the service of psychologists by mission organisations.
54. *Preaching and Preachers*, p. 128 (my italics).
55. Some of his books have been translated into Dutch, Japanese, Portuguese, German, Spanish, Danish, Hebrew, Korean, Thai, Slovak, Finnish, Welsh, and Chinese; cf. *The Fight of Faith*, Appendix 6, pp. 799 ff.; cf. pp. 302 ff.
56. Tape 2071.
57. Tapes 2001-110 , covering Acts 1-8. The Recording Trust gives a brief outline of the main thrust of each sermon.
58. *Christian Unity* (E4), p. 252.

CHAPTER TEN: *Checks*

1. *The Law: its Function and Limits* (R6), p. 51.
2. *Training for the Ministry* (Tape 5715).
3. *The Christian Soldier* (E8), p. 135.
4. Iain Murray, *Banner of Truth Magazine* (May 1990), No. 320, p. 8.
5. *Preaching and Preachers*, p. 173.
6. *Christian Warfare* (E7), p. 180.
7. For examples of this see Michael Horton et al, *The Agony of Deceit—What Some TV Preachers are Really Teaching* (Moody Press, Chicago, 1990), an evaluation of the claims of several preachers whose ministry seems orthodox to thousands of people but is an amalgam of Scriptural teaching and speculative thinking. A common fault of the preachers cited is an inadequate hermeneutic which has led them to the borders of heresy.
8. *Sermon on the Mount*, vol. 1, p. 11; cf *Christian Unity* (E4), p. 190.
9. *Expository Times*, June 1972, p. 282. The article is an evaluation of Lloyd-Jones's book *Assurance* (R4); the reviewer, Professor I. Howard Marshall of the University of Aberdeen commented, 'a preacher may gain insights into the biblical text that escape the scholar in his study. This preacher is also a scholar in his own right . . .'
10. *The Preacher and Preaching—Reviving the Art in the Twentieth Century*, p. 119.
11. A detailed study of these has been done by K.D. Jung to whom I am indebted, cf. n. 559.
12. *Sermon on the Mount*, vol. 1, pp. 273 ff.
13. *Authority of the Word*, sermon on Acts 6:1-7 (Tape 2058). This sermon is of great value. It not only includes a very powerful argument against a liberal approach to the Scriptures but is an excellent example of his preaching manner of starting 'low' and finishing 'high' as with great passion he reasons with his congregation and secures his various propositions.
14. *God's Ultimate Purpose* (E1), pp. 13, 14.
15. *Authority*, three addresses in Canada, 1957, (IVF, US edn, IVP, 1958; Banner of Truth, 1984).
16. *The Righteous Judgment of God* (R2), p. 171.
17. *The Final Perseverance of the Saints* (R8), p. 277.
18. Ibid., p. 277.
19. *Sermon on the Mount*, vol. 1, p. 191.
20. *The Gospel of God* (R1), p. 92.
21. Ibid., p. 91.
22. *Authority*, p. 52.
23. *Sermon on the Mount*, vol. 1, p. 187.
24. *The Final Perseverance of the Saints* (R8), p. 277.
25. *The Unsearchable Riches of Christ* (E3), p. 37; cf. n. 500, p. 180.
26. James Barr wrote two books highly critical of the view Lloyd-Jones espoused, cf. *Fundamentalism*, 2nd edn (SCM Press, 1982); *Escaping from Fundamentalism* (SCM Press, 1984).
27. *Chosen by God*, p. 191.
28. *The Sons of God* (R7) p. 223.
29. *The Perseverance of the Saints* (R8), p. 371.
30. Cf. *The Gospel of God* (R1), p. 331 where DML-J takes issue with the Authorised Version over its use of the word 'vengeance' in reference to God's judicial action, preferring both the Revised Version and the Revised Standard Version.

31. *God's Ultimate Purpose* (E1), p. 200, where he criticises the Revised Version and Revised Standard Version compared with the Authorised Version for the omission of a word.
32. *God's Sovereign Purpose* (R9), p. 75, where he is trenchantly dismissive of the New English Bible, contrasting it with the Authorised Version, the Revised Version and Weymouth.
33. *Sermon on the Mount*, vol. 1, p. 14; *The Final Perseverance of the Saints* (R8), p. 209.
34. *The Final Perseverance of the Saints* (R8), pp. 125 , 126.
35. Ibid., p. 159.
36. *The Righteous Judgment of God* (R2), p. 92.
37. *Sermon on the Mount*, vol. 1 , p. 253.
38. *The Law: Its Function and Limits* (R6), p. 259.
39. *Joy Unspeakable*, p. 264.
40. *Worship, the Old and the New* (Tape 3319).
41. *Sermon on the Mount*, vol. 1, p. 32.
42. *The Gospel of God* (R1), p. 318.
43. *The Law: Its Function and Limits* (R6), p. 168.
44. Ibid., p. 179.
45. *The Final Perseverance of the Saints* (R8), p. 95.
46. *God's Way of Reconciliation* (E2), p. 351.
47. *Training for the Ministry* (Tape 5715).
48. *Sermon on the Mount*, vol. 1, p. 210.
49. *The Sons of God* (R7), p. 285.
50. Ibid., p. 296.
51. *The Christian Soldier* (E8), p. 107.
52. *Life in the Spirit* (E6), p. 93.
53. *The Final Perseverance of the Saints* (R8), p. 280.
54. *The Sermon on the Mount*, vol. 1, p. 280 ff.
55. Ibid, vol. 1, p. 284.
56. Cf. n.521, p. 194.
57. *The Unsearchable Riches of Christ* (E3), p. 266.
58. *The Final Perseverance of the Saints* (R8), p. 202.
59. There is a passing comment in *Mr Speaker—The Memoirs of Viscount Tonypandy* (Century Publishing, London, 1985), p. 16; cf. *Evangelical Sermons*, where in an early sermon DML-J warns against reading the Bible in a general poetic and aesthetic fashion, p. 91.
60. *The Unsearchable Riches of Christ* (E3), p. 110.
61. *The Christian Soldier* (E8), p. 134.
62. Ibid., p. 328.
63. *Expository Sermons on 2 Peter*, p. 19.
64. *Life in the Spirit* (E6), p. 184.
65. Jung, op. cit., p. 90.
66. *Christian Warfare* (E7), pp. 263-88
67. Jung, op. cit., p. 92.
68. *Authority*, p. 39.
69. *The Unsearchable Riches of Christ*, (E3), pp. 210, 211.
70. *Prove All Things*, p. 79.
71. *Authority*, p. 48; *God's Way of Reconciliation* (E2), p. 161.

CHAPTER ELEVEN: *Balances*

1. *Preaching and Preachers*, pp. 171, 172.
2. Obituary, Martyn Lloyd-Jones, *The Monthly Record* (Free Church of Scotland, April 1981), p. 84.
3. *Christian Warfare* (E7), p. 184.
4. *Preaching and Preachers*, p. 66 (my italics).
5. 'Nowhere in the Bible are believers encouraged to look for a coming millennium. Christians are exhorted everywhere to look forward to the coming of the Lord and the glory which shall be revealed . . .' *The Final Perseverance of the Saints* (R8), p. 84, on the Eternal State, cf. p. 89.
6. Ibid., cf. chap 7 for a clear statement of his millennialism. For his position on the Jewish nation in prophecy, cf. Tapes 3285-92 (from his series on Romans 10) especially *The Future of the Jews* (3291), and *Conversion of the Jews* (3292).
7. *Training for the Ministry* (Tape, 5517).
8. *The Righteous Judgment of God* (R2), p. 9; *Christian Unity* (E4), p. 251, where he mentions a 'good friend' who took him to task because in his expositions on Ephesians 1 he never mentioned the word Calvinist!
9. *Expository Times*, June 1972.
10. *The Righteous Judgment of God* (R2), p. 58; cf. *Sermon on the Mount*, vol. 1 , p. 174; cf. *The Gospel of God* (R1), p. 387, 'My friends, we are not meant to understand all we read in the Scriptures. It is beyond us. Our minds are too small . . .'
11. *Knowing the Times*, p. 368.
12. *The Gospel of God* (R1), p. 383.
13. *The Final Perseverance of the Saints* (R8), p. 388. Here DML-J is expounding the text, 'He that spared not his own Son, but delivered him up for us all, how shall he not with him also freely give us all things?' (Rom. 8: 32). He prefaced the quote in our main text, 'I repeat that every single word is of inestimable importance, charged with the glorious doctrines of the Christian Faith.'
14. *The Gospel of God* (R1), p. 127.
15. *As a Tree Planted* (Studies in Psalm 1) (Tape 41 , No. 2).
16. *God's Sovereign Purpose* (R9), p. 46.
17. *Life in the Spirit* (E6), p. 14.
18. Ibid, p. 122; cf. in the same vol, p. 47—his analysis of the word 'full' in dealing with the believer's experience of the Holy Spirit; also his appeal to C. W. Wuest's *The Untranslatable Riches from the New Testament Greek* (Eerdmans, Grand Rapids, 1956) in order to establish the meaning of the verb 'to baptise'; also, *Joy Unspeakable*, pp. 175-6.
19. *The Sons of God* (R7), p. 241 ff.
20. *Evangelical Sermons*, p. 282.
21. *God's Way of Reconciliation*, p. 13.
22. *Revival*, p. 24.
23. *The Puritans*, p. 352.
24. Ibid., p. 355.
25. *Revival*, p. 197.
26. *The Sons of God* (R7), pp. 298, 299. Chap. 27 of this vol. is given wholly to the narrating of the experiences of seventeenth, eighteenth and nineteenth century men although Lloyd-Jones is still attempting to expound Rom. 8: 16; cf. pp. 31 ff.
27. *The New Man* (R5) p. 151; *The Sons of God* (R7), p. 80; *The Final Perseverance of the Saints* (R8), p. 188.

28. He questioned particularly Warfield's dismissive treatment of miraculous phenomena, 'Tertullian and Augustine both made use of the argument that miracles were happening in their time and age in defence of, and as a part of their apologetic for, the Christian Faith; and I have never been satisfied with Warfield's answer to that', *Healing and the Scriptures*, p. 28.
29. *The New Man* (R5), pp. 17, 18, cf. p. 96 where he strongly dismisses a comment of 'great scholars like Sanday and Headlam', also cf. p. 151 'even the great John Calvin went astray at that point', cf. p. 372.
30. *Preaching and Preachers*, p. 181.
31. Ibid., p. 155.
32. Ibid, p. 84.
33. *The Gospel of God* (R1), p. 253.
34. *Preaching and Preachers*, p. 143.
35. *Sermon on the Mount*, vol. 2. p. 186.
36. *Preaching and Preachers*, p. 144; note the incident which he records at the beginning of his ministry, of an older preacher telling him to remember that in the average congregation only one in twelve is intelligent, p. 257.
37. Ibid., p. 146.
38. Ibid., p. 72.
39. Argile Smith comments, 'treating the text as a source of an implied subject allowed Lloyd-Jones to use the same text for a number of sermons. For example, he selected Ephesians 6:10-13 as the text for twenty-six consecutive sermons. Seventeen of these sermon subjects were implied but not explicitly stated in the passage', op. cit. p. 119. His remarks are based on *Christian Warfare* (E6), pp. 108-373, nineteen sermons which expound 'the wiles of the Devil' covering such subjects as The Enemy, The Enemy Described, The Origin of Evil, Heresies, Cults, Attacks on Assurance, etc.: perceptive sermons drawn from the general teaching of Scripture but not expository in the classical sense of working out and being confined to the immediate parameters of the passage.
40. *Preaching and Preachers*, p. 62.
41. Ibid.
42. *The Law: Its Function and Limits* (R6), p. 114.
43. *Preaching and Preachers*, p. 148.
44. See his series on the Acts of the Apostles preached between 1965-8 (Tapes Nos. 2001-110).
45. Robert Sandeman lived in the eighteenth century and wrote *Letters of Theron and Aspasio* (4th edn, J. Turnball, Edinburgh, 1803) in order to review the Methodist, James Hervey's *Theron and Aspasio: or a series of Dialogues and Letters upon the Most Important and Interesting Subjects* (2 vols, London, 1813). In Sandeman's book, Aspasio is the potential convert. Theron (Hervey) affirms that feeling is involved in faith. Sandeman wrote his work to correct this 'error'. For him faith was simply believing in Jesus. DML-J illustrated the approach of those who followed Sandeman; 'they used to take that verse out of Romans Chapter ten: "that if thou shalt confess with thy mouth the Lord Jesus thou shalt be saved", and teach that the way to be saved, therefore, was to confess with the mouth the Lord Jesus. "Do not worry about your feelings", they said. "Don't worry about anything. The Scripture says that if you say that, you are saved. So if you do say it, then you are saved"', *The Righteous Judgment of God* (R2), p. 95; cf. *Atonement and Justification* (R3), p. 213. For an extended treatment of DML-J on Sandemanianism, cf. *The Puritans*, pp. 170-90.
46. Eaton, op. cit., p. 212.

47. Ibid., p. 212. Note Eaton's critique of what he believes to be DML-J's failure fully to grasp Sandeman, pp. 214, 215.
48. *Christian Warfare* (E6), p. 280; cf. *Westminster Record*, Sept. 1964, vol. 39, No. 9; also David Watson, *One in the Spirit* (Hodder & Stoughton, London, 1973), 4th imp, 1974.
49. Tapes 3160-7.
50. We particularly recommend the sermons contained in *The Final Perseverance of the Saints* (R8) (Tapes 3168-206).
51. *Preaching and Preachers*, p. 63.
52. *The Gospel Witness*, vol. 6, Nos 2-4, April 1981.
53. 'Lloyd-Jones' Legacy', *The Monthly Record* (Free Church of Scotland, April 1981), p. 84.

CHAPTER THIRTEEN: *Retrospect*

1. Eph. 6:19-20.
2. *The First Epistle to the Corinthians* (Eerdmans Publishing Company, Grand Rapids, 1987), p. 96 (my italics).
3. *Knowing the Times*, p. 102 (my italics).
4. Cf. *The Puritans* and *Knowing the Times*; these contrast with other books inasmuch as they give a sample of DML-J's ministry on a variety of subjects over three decades. The steadfastness of his convictions in respect to preaching, unction and the doctrine of the Spirit is especially noteworthy.
5. *Knowing the Times*, p. 160.
6. *Spiritual Depression*, p. 298.
7. C. Campbell Morgan, *Acts of the Apostles* (Pickering & Inglis, London, 1968), p. 39.
8. *The Religious Affections* (1746; Banner of Truth, Edinburgh, 1961).
9. *Preaching and Preachers*, p. 90.
10. *Revival*, p. 195.
11. *Sermon on the Mount*, vol. 2, p. 266.
12. *The Christian Soldier* (E8), p. 286.
13. *Preaching and Preachers*, pp. 93, 94.
14. Cf. n. 696, p. 266.
15. *The Puritans*, p. 190.
16. R. A. Ramsbottom, *Christmas Evans* (undated private publication, Flair Press Ltd, Northampton), p. 53.
17. Cf. *The Fight of Faith*, p. 374 , for a further example of youngsters responding favourably to DML-J's ministry.
18. Cf. pp. 214 ff.
19. *Preaching and Preachers*, p. 128.
20. *The Unsearchable Riches of Christ* (E3), p. 82, cf. the *Westminster Confession of Faith*, (Free Presbyterian Publications, Glasgow; Banner of Truth, Edinburgh), pp. 379 ff, the section on 'Of the Preaching of the Word' especially where the preacher is enjoined to preach to fulfil a seven-fold criteria; painfully, plainly—abstaining also from an unprofitable use of unknown tongues, strange phrases, and cadences of sound and words; sparingly citing sentences of ecclesiastical or other human writers, ancient or modern, be they ever so elegant—faithfully, wisely, gravely, with loving affection and as taught by God.
21. *Preaching and Preachers*, p. 122; cf. n. 551, p. 206.
22. ' *The Lloyd-Jones' Legacy*', *The Monthly Record*, p. 209.

23. *Living Messages of the Books of the Bible* (Fleming H. Revell, New York, 1912), p. 113.
24. *Hosea, the Heart and Holiness of God* (Marshall, Morgan and Scott, London).
25. Operation Mobilization and its literature arm, Send the Light (now called OM Books), have been responsible for distributing many thousands of copies of DML-J's books in various parts of the world. (OM Books now publish *Spiritual Depression*.)
26. Op. cit., p. 190.
27. One of the admirable goals of Westminster Theological Seminary, Escondido (California) post-graduate department is to encourage the production of handbooks and helps, audio as well as visual, for such Third World pastors. The Proclamation Trust, St Peter's Church, Cornhill, London EC3 V 3 PD has as one of its aims the holding of preachers' conferences in the Third World as well as in the United Kingdom in a worthy attempt to inspire expository preaching. Invariably the Ship Ministries of Operation Mobilisation stock books of help to ministers and hold pastors' conferences at the ports where they dock. The Martyn Lloyd-Jones Recording Studio is also sympathetic to requests for tapes from English-speaking pastors in developing countries.
28. Cf. pp. 319 ff.
29. Tape 4041.
30. Richard Baxter, *The Reformed Pastor* (Banner of Truth, London, 1974, pp. 174, 61). I owe the quotation to J. I. Packer, *A Quest for Godliness*, p. 179.
31. For the full prayer, cf. *The Puritans*, p. 52.
32. Packer, op. cit., p. 281 ff.
33. Lloyd-Jones was no follower of Thomas Aquinas or Aristotle, however. Though he emphasised the importance of reason he did not believe that reason alone could produce faith. When the bridge has been crossed and a man has his eyes opened to accept the fundamentals of the faith—the Being of God, the revelation of God through Christ, then reason comes into its own: thus the necessity for expository preaching and building Christians up in the Faith; cf. *Heart of the Gospel*, p. 19, *The Christian Soldier* (E8), p. 202, *Sermon on the Mount*, vol. 2, p. 130.
34. *Knowing the Times*, p. 258 (the lecture was given at Westminster Theological Seminary in 1967, two years before he gave his series of lectures on preaching, which were subsequently published).
35. Packer, op. cit., p. 280.
36. *Preaching and Preachers*, p. 120.

GENERAL INDEX

Logan, Samuel T., Jr., 305 (n. 63)
Logic, Paul and DML-J, 117-8
Logos and *Rhema*, ix
Luther, Martin, 43, 47, 92, 214, 275, 288

MacArthur John, Jr, 321 (n. 16)
McCheyne (M'Cheyne), Robert Murray, 128-9, 130, 136, 138, 294
McCrie, Thomas, 314 (n. 55)
Mackintosh, C.H., 49, 307 (n. 34)
Macleod, Donald, 57, 67, 200, 209, 239, 256, 289
Macpherson, John, 317 (n. 12)
Man, pessimistic view of, 166
Marriage, DML-J's sermons on, 181-3
Marshall, I.H., 242, 327 (n. 10)
Martin, Samuel, 323 (n. 7)
Masters, Peter, 74, 76, 306 (n. 16), 319 (n. 64)
Matheson, Duncan, 128-9, 317 (n. 12)
Meekness, 196
Menuhin, Yehudi, 121
'Message', 84-5
Millenialism, 241
Moody, D.L., 48, 87, 150-1, 283
Moravians, 48
Morgan, G. Campbell, 94, 158, 164, 283, 289, 304 (n. 28), 313 (n. 28), 322 (n. 49), 323 (n. 6)
Morgan, David, 58-9, 99
Mormon Church, 222
Morris, Ebenezer, 311 (n. 58)
Motyer, J.A., 318 (n. 19)
Moule, C.E.D., 181
Murray, Iain H., 30, 50, 51, 53-4, 87, 146-7, 180, 327 (n. 4)
Musical analogies in sermons, 116
Mystics and mysticism, 43, 179

Narrative, sermons based on, 210-6
Negative statements in preaching, 195-8
New English Bible, 225,
New Testament, relations with Old Testament, 227

Old age, 144-7
Old Testament, relations with New Testament, 227
Operation Mobilization, 291, 332 (n. 25)

Oratory, Welsh, 283-4
Origen, 204
Owen, Glyn, 185
Owen, John, 41, 44, 45, 46, 83, 248, 312 (n. 12)

Pacifism, 220
Packer, J. I., 39, 55, 115, 132-3, 151, 168-9, 173, 180, 296, 319 (n. 50), 322 (n. 70)
Parables, treatment, 160-4
Parker, Joseph, 242
Pascal, Blaise, 43, 214
Passion in sermons, 285-7
Paul, St
  Christ-centred, 121-2
  and Holy Spirit, 120-1
  humour, 109-10
  influence on DML-J, 103-23, 255
  personality, 106
  sensitivity, 110
  submission, 108
  teaching method, 110-9
Pedan, Alexander, 92
Pentecost, Day of, 58, 69
Pentecostalism, 40-2
Perkins, William, 86, 305 (n. 47)
Persuasiveness in sermons, 159
Pessimism, 166
Peter, Apostle, 52
Peters, John, 307 (n. 33), 318 (n. 16)
Philpott, J.C., 47
Piper, John, 315 (n. 72)
Pneuma, 39
Pneumatology, 39, 42-3, 47, 49, 58, 84, 171, 232, 281, see also Holy Spirit
Porritt, Arthur, 323 (n. 7)
Powell, Leigh, 59, 256
Prayer, 133-4, 135
  personal, 136-8
Preachers
  authority, 250
  requirements, 297
  spiritual exercises, 96-7
  and unction, 96
Preaching
  clarity in, 287-9
  diagnostic, 173-89, 191-216
  doubts on, 17-9
  fire in, 284-7
  DML-J's style, 174-5

Syntax of the Bible, 245-6
Systematic theology, 240-2

'Tape ministries', xiii
Tauler, John, 43, 306 (n. 12)
Tennent, Gilbert, 61, 153, 321 (n. 17)
Tennyson, Alfred, Lord, 145
Tertullian, 330 (n. 28)
Theology
 crisis, 282-3
 experiential, 132, 178-9
 historical, 246-50
 systematic, 240-2
Theophany, 178, 294
Theopneustos, 241
'Therefore', meaning, 245-6
Third World, 279
 and DML-J's style, 292-4
Thomas, Geoffrey, 130
Thomas, George, Viscount Tonypandy, 233
Thornwell, James, 17, 106, 308 (n. 15)
Time, 177
Torrance, David and James, 224
Tozer, A.W., 84, 123, 179, 255, 294

Unction, xii, 20, 31-2, 35, 50, 54, 55, 80, 100, 283
 absence, 98
 and congregation, 63-4
 in 1 John 2:20, 27; 81-4
 and Paul, 120-1
 power, 62
 reception, 95-101
 see also Anointing

Verwer, George, xv, 291

Wales, DML-J's ministry, 52-4, 152-3
War, and DML-J, 164-7
Warfield, Benjamin, 250
Watson, David, 331 (n. 48)
Watson, Thomas, 240
Watts, Isaac, 142
Way, A.S., 225
Weil, Roger, 137
Wells, H.G., 320 (n. 79)
Welsh eloquence, 283-4
Welsh Calvinistic Methodist Church, 43
Welsh revivals, 58, 91, 253
Wesley, Charles, 97, 145, 214, 236
Wesley, John, 47-8
Westcott, B.F., 66, 309 (n. 28)
Westminster Chapel, 77, 287-8
 and children, 288-9
 DML-J at, 287-9
 pulpit, 175-6, 187
Westminster Fraternal, 36
Whitefield, George, xii, xiii, 18, 19, 33-4, 38, 41, 46, 61, 91, 97, 115, 140, 154, 177, 207, 214, 247, 248, 253, 285, 286
Whyte, Alexander, 206
Williams, William, 131
Witness, 85-6
Women, and preaching ministry, 93
Wood Row Society, 92
Word, the, 89
Words and sentences, DML-J's usage, 208-210
Wordsworth, William, 185
Works, DML-J on, 156
Wuest, C.W., 329 (n. 18)

Zaïre, (293)

SCRIPTURE INDEX